The Muridiyya on the Move

NEW AFRICAN HISTORIES

SERIES EDITORS: JEAN ALLMAN, ALLEN ISAACMAN, AND DEREK R. PETERSON

David William Cohen and E. S. Atieno Odhiambo, *The Risks of Knowledge*

Belinda Bozzoli, *Theatres of Struggle and the End of Apartheid*

Gary Kynoch, *We Are Fighting the World*

Stephanie Newell, *The Forger's Tale*

Jacob A. Tropp, *Natures of Colonial Change*

Jan Bender Shetler, *Imagining Serengeti*

Cheikh Anta Babou, *Fighting the Greater Jihad*

Marc Epprecht, *Heterosexual Africa?*

Marissa J. Moorman, *Intonations*

Karen E. Flint, *Healing Traditions*

Derek R. Peterson and Giacomo Macola, editors, *Recasting the Past*

Moses E. Ochonu, *Colonial Meltdown*

Emily S. Burrill, Richard L. Roberts, and Elizabeth Thornberry, editors, *Domestic Violence and the Law in Colonial and Postcolonial Africa*

Daniel R. Magaziner, *The Law and the Prophets*

Emily Lynn Osborn, *Our New Husbands Are Here*

Robert Trent Vinson, *The Americans Are Coming!*

James R. Brennan, *Taifa*

Benjamin N. Lawrance and Richard L. Roberts, editors, *Trafficking in Slavery's Wake*

David M. Gordon, *Invisible Agents*

Allen F. Isaacman and Barbara S. Isaacman, *Dams, Displacement, and the Delusion of Development*

Stephanie Newell, *The Power to Name*

Gibril R. Cole, *The Krio of West Africa*

Matthew M. Heaton, *Black Skin, White Coats*

Meredith Terretta, *Nation of Outlaws, State of Violence*

Paolo Israel, *In Step with the Times*

Michelle R. Moyd, *Violent Intermediaries*

Abosede A. George, *Making Modern Girls*

Alicia C. Decker, *In Idi Amin's Shadow*

Rachel Jean-Baptiste, *Conjugal Rights*

Shobana Shankar, *Who Shall Enter Paradise?*

Emily S. Burrill, *States of Marriage*

Todd Cleveland, *Diamonds in the Rough*

Carina E. Ray, *Crossing the Color Line*

Sarah Van Beurden, *Authentically African*

Giacomo Macola, *The Gun in Central Africa*

Lynn Schler, *Nation on Board*

Julie MacArthur, *Cartography and the Political Imagination*

Abou B. Bamba, *African Miracle, African Mirage*

Daniel Magaziner, *The Art of Life in South Africa*

Paul Ocobock, *An Uncertain Age*

Keren Weitzberg, *We Do Not Have Borders*

Nuno Domingos, *Football and Colonialism*

Jeffrey S. Ahlman, *Living with Nkrumahism*

Bianca Murillo, *Market Encounters*

Laura Fair, *Reel Pleasures*

Thomas F. McDow, *Buying Time*

Jon Soske, *Internal Frontiers*

Elizabeth W. Giorgis, *Modernist Art in Ethiopia*

Matthew V. Bender, *Water Brings No Harm*

David Morton, *Age of Concrete*

Marissa J. Moorman, *Powerful Frequencies*

Ndubeze Mbah, *Emergent Masculinities*

Patricia Hayes and Gary Minkley, editors, *Ambivalent*

Mari K. Webel, *The Politics of Disease Control*

Kara Moskowitz, *Seeing Like a Citizen*

Jacob S. T. Dlamini, *Safari Nation*

Cheikh Anta Babou, *The Muridiyya on the Move*

Alice Wiemers, *Village Work*

Judith A. Byfield, *The Great Upheaval*

Laura Ann Twagira, *Embodied Engineering*

The Muridiyya on the Move

Islam, Migration, and Place Making

⁓

Cheikh Anta Babou

OHIO UNIVERSITY PRESS ⁓ ATHENS, OHIO

Ohio University Press, Athens, Ohio 45701
ohioswallow.com
© 2021 by Ohio University Press
All rights reserved

First paperback edition printed 2021 by Ohio University Press
Paperback ISBN: 978-0-8214-2467-4

Printed in the United States of America
Ohio University Press books are printed on acid-free paper ⊗ ™

31 30 29 28 27 26 25 24 23 22 21 5 4 3 2 1

Library of Congress Cataloging-in-Publication Data
Names: Babou, Cheikh Anta, 1958– author.
Title: The Muridiyya on the move : Islam, migration, and place making / Cheikh
Anta Babou.
Description: Athens : Ohio University Press, 2021. | Series: New African histories |
Includes bibliographical references and index.
Identifiers: LCCN 2020052831 | ISBN 9780821424377 (hardcover)
Subjects: LCSH: Muridiyyah. | Islamic sects.
Classification: LCC BP195.M66 B33 2021 | DDC 297.4/8—dc23
LC record available at https://lccn.loc.gov/2020052831

For Bamba

Contents

Illustrations

Acknowledgments

Writing this book has been a labor of love, largely because the stories I tell here are stories of family members, friends, and acquaintances. In some ways, these are my own stories, too. For over two decades I have been doing research among Senegalese and Murid immigrants across Africa, Europe, and the United States. I have been intrigued by their trials, tribulations, and resourcefulness in trying to make a living abroad in difficult conditions while preserving enduring connections with home. I could not have written this book without their generosity in sharing their life stories and archives, facilitating contacts with important sources of information, and welcoming me into their houses. I am eternally grateful to all of them.

I wish to acknowledge the support of many institutions, archivists, mentors, colleagues, and friends. Several grants from the School of Arts and Sciences at the University of Pennsylvania supported the research for this book. Funding from the Center for Africana Studies helped launch this research. A grant from the University Research Fund and a Research Opportunity Grant provided resources for research in France, Italy, and Senegal. The "Success Project" led by Bill Easterly at the Development Research Institute at New York University funded fieldwork in Gabon, Côte d'Ivoire, and Senegal. A visiting professorship at the Ecole des Hautes Études en Sciences Sociales in Paris gave me the opportunity to conduct archival and library research in France. A yearlong residential fellowship at the Wissenschaftskolleg zu (Institute for Advanced Studies of Berlin), allowed additional library research and the drafting of the first chapters of the book.

I have also benefited from the support of the West African Research Center in Dakar, which graciously offered office and computer facilities during my fieldwork there. I am most grateful to Abdoulaye Niang, Professor Ousmane Sène, director of the West African Research Center, and to the center's wonderful staff. Parts of chapter 1 are drawn from my article "Urbanizing Mystical Islam: Making Murid Space in the Cities of Senegal," *International Journal of African Historical Studies* 40, no. 2 (2007): 197–223.

Portions of chapter 4 appeared in *African Diaspora Journal* 4 (2011): 27–49, as "A West African Sufi Master on the Global Stage: Sheikh Abdoulaye Dièye and the Khidmatul Khadim International Sufi School in France and the United States." I thank both journals for the permission to reprint the texts here. I would like to thank the Senegalese National Archives, the Service Régional des Archives in Saint Louis and Dakar, the French National Archives of Pierrefitte, the Archives Diplomatiques of Nantes, and the Archives d'Outremer in Aix-en-Provence. I am grateful to Samba Camara for facilitating contacts with archivists in Dakar. I remain indebted to the incredible librarians of the Wissenschaftskolleg zu.

Several colleagues have read and commented on the entire text. I would like to give special recognition to my friend and mentor, David Robinson, whose unwavering support and encouragement have been a constant source of inspiration. I have benefited greatly from the close reading and suggestions of Jean Copans, Ellen Foley, Allen Roberts, and Eric Ross. Eric generously helped design and draw the maps. I thank the graduate students in my spring seminar for reading the manuscript and sharing feedback. Many colleagues have read and commented on drafts of chapters. I thank Muhammad Abdu al-Rahman, Barbara Cooper, Christine Dang, Jeremy Dell, Victoria Ebin, Steve Feierman, Marie Miran Gouyon, Katie Hickerson, Ousmane Kane, Kenda Mutongi, Kathy Peiss, Sophia Rosenfeld, Lynn Thomas, and Jean Louis Triaud. These colleagues' observations and suggestions have greatly enhanced the quality of my work.

I must also express my thanks to the two anonymous readers and to Jean Allman, Allen Isaacman, and Derek Peterson, the editors of the New African Histories series for their insightful suggestions. I am grateful to Gill Berchowitz and Stephanie Williams at Ohio University Press for their guidance in preparing and submitting the manuscript. The recommendations of Tyler Balli and Michael Sandlin, my project editor and copyeditor, are greatly appreciated.

I have benefited from the support of numerous Murid shaykhs and disciples in Senegal and in the diaspora who opened their private libraries and archives to me and graciously took time to respond to my questions. Omitting the names of some of them here does not diminish my gratitude to them. In Senegal, I particularly wish to thank Sëriñ Baabu, Akhma Faal, Amar Faal, Mustafa Jaañ, the late Elhaaj Bamba Jaw, Bamba Jeey, Elhaaj Njaga Gey, Fadel Gey, Sëriñ Lo, Sëriñ Mustafa Mbakke Gaynde Faatma, Sëriñ Maam Moor Mbakke, Sëriñ Xaasim Mbakke, and Aafia Ñaŋ. In Abidjan, I have benefited from the help of Njaay Gaucher, Elhaaj Bamba Gey, Mustafa Maar, and Cerno Sulay Sall. In Libreville, I thank Amadu

Basum, Imam Paap Jaañ, Babakar Jeŋ, and Asan Murtalla Jóob. In France, I owe a great debt of gratitude to Amadou Dramé, Aale Faal, Góora Jóob, Ibra Jóob, Sulaymaan Jaxate, Sulaymaan Juuf, Abdulaay Ley, Saer Njaay, Imam Mamadou N'Sangou, and Aly Sidibé. In Italy, I thank Imam Fallu Mbakke and Saam Jóob. I have been doing research in the US Senegalese and Murid communities since 1999, and over the years I have greatly benefited from their generosity. I wish to thank Chuck Abraham, Cheikh Amar, Muhammad Abdu al-Rahman, Daam Baabu (NYC), Daam Baabu (Cin), the late Maamur Baabu, the late Balozi Harvey, Móodu Buso, Abdulaay Caam, Sylviane Diouf, Pape Dramé, Shilo Lamp Faal, Michelle Fara Kimball, Elhaaj Shaykh Mbuub, Aisha McCord, Sultana A. Muhammad, Elhaaj Ndaw, Murtada Njaay, Ami Jaxumpa, Pape Ibrahima Sow, and Ahmed Sugu.

My warmest gratitude goes to my wife, Faatim Jóob, to Jaara, and to my son and occasional assistant, Bamba. I am eternally indebted to them for their love and support.

Cheikh Anta Babou
Philadelphia, April 2020

Abbreviations

ADN	Archives Diplomatiques de Nantes
ANF	Archives Nationales de France (Pierrefitte)
ANS	Archives Nationales du Sénégal
AOF	Afrique Occidentale Française
BIFAN	*Bulletin de l'Institut Fondamental d'Afrique Noire*
CHEAM	Centre des Hautes Études d'Administration Musulmane (After 1958, Centre des Hautes Études administratives sur l'Afrique et l'Asie Modernes.)
DEA	Diplôme d'Étude Approfondie
JAH	*Journal of African History*
IFAN	Institut Fondamental d'Afrique Noire
INSEE	Institut National de la Statique et des Etudes Economiques
KST	Kër Sëriñ Tuubaa
MICA	Murid Islamic Community in America
NOI	Nation of Islam
ORSTOM	Organisation pour la Recherche Scientifique et Technique Outre-Mer, now Institut pour la Recherche et le Développement (IRD)
SOCOBA	Société de Construction et Bâtiment
SRDAD	Service Régional des Archives de Dakar

Note on Orthography

This book makes extensive references to written documents and oral testimonies in several languages, most notably Wolof, French, and Arabic. I have opted for a simplified orthography in transcribing foreign languages into English. I use the official Senegalese spelling system to write Wolof words but use the double vowel to express the elongated Arabic sounds. I maintain "kh," as in *khidma*, and "q," as in *qadi*. All plural nouns are marked by adding "s" to the singular. I have kept Wolofized Arab words in their Wolof spellings, unless found in titles of Arabic books or in Arab names. Proper names of African actors and places, except for authors of published works, are spelled according the rule explained above. I have kept some French and Arabic words and expressions in italics throughout, while I have put most others appearing recurrently throughout the text in italics only for the first citation.

Introduction

"THEY COME by trainloads, cars, trucks, horse- and donkey-drawn carts, and some by foot. They are all headed to Tuubaa."[1] This is how, in 1949, French administrator Paul Merle Des Isles described the Great Màggal (annual pilgrimage) of Tuubaa held annually on the forty-seventh day of the Muslim calendar.[2] The same scene can be witnessed today, but pilgrims now come from the four corners of the earth (some by chartered flights), and over the years their numbers have soared. When Des Isles submitted his report, there were a hundred thousand visitors that year; now the Màggal attracts four million people on average to this annual pilgrimage.[3] The story told in this book is about these pilgrims: a story about the dispersal of a Muslim immigrant community across Africa, Europe, and the United States. It is also a story about the connections that members of this wayward community still have to one another.

The Muridiyya on the Move contributes to emerging scholarship on transnational Muslim migration by exploring the religious life of Murids, a community of Senegalese Muslims that has been migrating across West Africa, Europe, and the United States for over half a century. More precisely, the book traces the history of Murid migrations and settlement to selected cities in Senegal, Côte d'Ivoire, Gabon, France, and the United States from the end of World War II to the first decade of the twenty-first century. By focusing on Murid use of space, the book uncovers the relationships between place making, religious identity, and the politics of belonging. I argue that for Murid immigrants, the appropriation of space and the public performance of piety serve as instruments for the construction of a diasporic collective identity. This collective identity, in turn, facilitates

Murid immigrants' insertion into the cultural matrix of host societies and their acceptance as members of the citizenry. I explore the contradictions and tensions involved in the construction of a transnational, collective Murid identity and reveal how this process of identity making generates conflicting understandings of the role of Murid ideology and institutions abroad, reframing the relationships between immigrants and the Murid leadership back in Senegal.

The Muridiyya on the Move investigates the transformative power of Murid disciples in the diaspora. In African studies, the word "diaspora" often evokes people of African descent in the New World who share an experience of enslavement and forced displacement. The diaspora I am interested in here is the product of European imperial rule in Africa and postcolonial migration. It is better conceived as a transnational diaspora, which Nina Glick Schiller and Georges Fouron define as a diaspora consisting of "migrants who are fully encapsulated neither in the host-society nor in their native land but who nonetheless remain active participants in the social settings of both locations."[4] As we will see, while Murids share some characteristics of the transnational migrant as described by Schiller and Fouron, Murid immigrants present some of their own unique traits. They are simultaneously present at home and abroad. This double embeddedness is made possible, on the one hand, by the building of networks that allow for continuous movement, back and forth, of people, goods, memories, and ideas between the diaspora and the Muridiyya's holy city of Tuubaa in Senegal. On the other hand, this relation is strengthened by the symbolic transformation of the Muridiyya holy city into a portable sacred site that can be relocated across the diaspora.

Most scholars insist on the "rigid hierarchy" of the Murid order (*tariqa*, or "way," in Arabic); they emphasize the unidirectionality of the flow of power and authority from the leadership in Tuubaa, which is construed as shaping culture and behavior. I argue that Murid migrants have had an equally important role. Migrants are agents of change, and they serve as the ties that bind Tuubaa to the diaspora. They have harnessed the transformative power of mobility and distance from the Shaykhs and holy cities of the Muridiyya in Senegal to put their own stamp on the order. Immigrants, for example, built the first modern hospital in Tuubaa at a time when the Murid leadership was mostly invested in building and refurbishing places of worship.[5] For these migrants, the diaspora offers a discursive space where they articulate aspects of Murid culture that draw from the order's core tenets and rely upon their own interpretations to meet discrete spiritual and existential needs. Diasporic space forms the canvas on which these reinterpretations and refabulations of Murid history, memory, and culture are inscribed. In this book, I use space as an entry point to demonstrate how Murid migrants transform the Muridiyya from the bottom up. By focusing on processes of space making in the diaspora, I document the innovative power, creativity, and influence of a community that scholars of the Muridiyya often portray as passive recipients of change.

The events of September 11, 2001, in New York City and the subsequent attacks in London, Madrid, and Paris have generated unprecedented interest in the study of Muslim immigrants, especially in Western countries. But these studies focus primarily on Muslims of North African, Middle Eastern, and Asian origin. They are mostly concerned with documenting an assumed incompatibility between Islam and "Western culture" or the danger of political Islam. This book offers fresh insight by focusing on an understudied immigrant community. My study is guided by several lines of inquiry: How do Murid immigrants make spaces where they can express their faith and identity? What are the inevitable compromises and concessions that these efforts entail? How are structures of power and authority within immigrant religious organizations affected by a vibrant diaspora? How do home communities and diasporic communities influence each other's practices, identities, and aspirations?

The Muridiyya on the Move challenges three fundamental starting points of many existing histories of African migrations. First, this book deemphasizes the role of external stimulus (e.g., the state, capital) often portrayed as the driving force behind the migration. While recognizing the impact of material incentive to migration, it emphasizes the equally central role of social practices from below developed within the confines of family and religious networks in influencing decisions to migrate. I particularly highlight the role of the *dahira*, an urban prayer circle that for over half a century has functioned as a crucible for the socialization of Murid immigrants.

The dahira was instrumental in the expansion of the Muridiyya in urban areas across Senegal and around the world. It first emerged as an alternative to the *daara* (Murid rural working school), functioning as a site for identity formation and social action for recently urbanized Murid immigrants. Gradually, the dahira incorporated rituals that solidified Murid historical memory through religious commemorations such as pilgrimages and processions. More recently, the dahira has moved beyond mere performance of memory to inscribing this memory in urban space by appropriating and suffusing this space with Murid culture.

Second, the book underscores the role of internal African migration, which is often overlooked in the literature, and scrutinizes the popular media that tend to overdramatize the journey of African refugees and migrants struggling to cross the Mediterranean into Europe. While much emphasis is put on migration out of Africa, two-thirds of African migrants remain on the continent.[6] This is reflected among disciples of the Muridiyya Sufi order in Europe and the United States, most of whom have sojourned in cities in West and central Africa before moving on to their European and North American destinations.

Third, *The Muridiyya on the Move* documents the centrality of space making in Muslim immigrants' strategy for integration with host societies. While some Muslim intellectuals such as Taha Jabir al-Alwani emphasize the role of judicial adjustment by reconfiguring sharia law to adapt to the Western context (*fiqh* of minority Muslims in the West),[7] among the Murids, accommodation is sought through localized efforts at place making that include the appropriation of space and public performance of piety through urban pilgrimages and processions. By appropriation of space, I do not mean taking space that belongs to others. I am pointing to cultural practices that Murids participate in to give meaning to a space they already consider their home. I look at appropriation not as an act of subtraction but as one of addition: a contribution to cultural diversity. To make the countries they settle their own, Murids strive to inscribe their own culture into their living space.

A BRIEF INTRODUCTION TO THE MURIDIYYA

The founding and development of the Muridiyya was intimately associated with the spiritual growth of Ahmadu Bamba and the socioeconomic and political context in the Wolof (Wolof are the majority ethnic group in Senegal and most Murids are Wolof) states of Senegal in the second half of the nineteenth century. Ahmadu Bamba was born in the early 1850s to a family of Muslim clerics, and like his forebears, he devoted his life to earning the credentials that would make him worthy of his ancestry. However, in contrast to the family tradition that advocated cultural conformism, political neutrality, and accommodation of rulers, Bamba had a different vision of the cleric's role in society. He grew up in a period of turmoil in the Wolof states marked by the intensification and then suppression of the slave trade, civil wars, and French colonial conquest. Bamba noted the failure of the Muslim establishment to remedy the situation, whether through jihad or through collaboration with secular rulers.

The solution he offered was rooted in Sufi tradition that emphasizes social and geographical distance from temporal power holders, education of the soul, hard work, and strict submission to the shaykh (spiritual guide). He was convinced that the best way to heal society's sicknesses was to transform the people that composed the society. And for him, the best way to transform the people was religious and social renewal through education.

The Muridiyya that Bamba founded in the late nineteenth century was the educational tool to bring about this renewal. It was a response both to the contemporary sociopolitical situation he detested and to the classical system of education he blamed for its inadequate response to the challenges of the time. For Bamba, the seeds of change had to be sown in peoples' hearts and souls if an enduring impact was to be achieved. The type of education he initiated encompassed body, mind, and soul: he called for a new pedagogy that differed from that of the classical Qur'anic schools, which primarily focused on the transmission of knowledge. The new system was centered on the *daara tarbiyya* (rural working school). It accommodated atypical disciples (grownups), used unconventional teaching methods (work and meditation), and focused on holistic transformation of the disciples.

In the context of aggressive French encroachment and pressure on Wolof economic, political, and social institutions, the Muridiyya became a rallying point for those of different social strata who joined the organization. By 1889, Ahmadu Bamba had attracted a large following, and his increasing popularity in the newly conquered provinces of Bawol and Kajoor made the French and their African auxiliaries increasingly nervous. Between 1895 and 1912, suspected of preparing to wage jihad, Bamba was the target of increasing French repression that eventually sent him into exile in central Africa and Mauritania and kept him under house arrest in Senegal until his death in 1927. The Muridiyya grew dramatically during this period of political conflict, and its popularity was further enhanced when its leader was sent back to his native land of Bawol in 1912.

Furthermore, Murid farmers soon became pillars of the colony's economy as they made substantial contributions to the production of peanuts, which was the only colonial cash crop produced in Senegal. By 1912, the French had worked out a policy of accommodation with the Murids: the cost of suppressing the Muridiyya far outweighed the trust they could earn by establishing stable and peaceful relationships with Bamba and his disciples.[8] By the eve of World War I, the Muridiyya had gained a modicum of recognition from the French, although Muridiyya leaders would remain under close surveillance.[9] Despite French pressure, the order's following continued to grow. After the establishment of Ahmadu Bamba in Diourbel, French sources estimated Murid disciples at over seventy thousand—in the early 1950s colonial estimations put the number of Ahmadu Bamba's followers at three hundred thousand. As of 2019, the Muridiyya had over five million disciples, many of them immigrant workers, scattered across Africa, Europe, and North America.[10]

THE MURIDIYYA AND MIGRATION

Although the history of colonial-era labor migration in Africa has attracted much scholarly interest over the years, postcolonial internal African migration—particularly the cultural dimension of this migration—has been largely overlooked by scholars.[11] Bruce Whitehouse rightly observes, "South-South migration in general and intra-African migration in particular, has been all but invisible to officials, policy makers and researchers."[12] The literature on Murid migration reflects this trend. While there is extensive scholarship on Murid immigrants in France, Italy, Spain, and the United States, we know very little about Murid migration and immigration within the continent of Africa, including Senegal. Here I explore dynamics of rural-rural migration in the Murid heartland of western-central Senegal, the circumstances for the transition to rural-urban migration, and finally the migration out of Senegal. The continuities, discontinuities, similarities, and differences between Murid migration and broader Senegalese migration will be investigated.

Migration is foundational to the Muridiyya. Its role in the development of the Murid order took different forms, which were influenced by changing economic, political, and social circumstances. Some of these transformations were induced by external forces; others were internal to the Murid organization. Before World War II, the Muridiyya was mostly made up of rural peanut farmers, and migrants were often confined to rural areas. Their movement followed the rhythm of the agricultural cycle and the vagaries of rain patterns.[13] Rural-urban migration began in earnest in the postwar era and accelerated in the 1960s after Senegal acquired national sovereignty. The successive droughts of the late 1970s, the drastic structural adjustment programs of the 1980s, and a transformative Murid leadership stimulated migration outside Senegal. Murid migrants headed to countries across West Africa, central Africa, then Europe: and by the mid-1980s, a community of Murid migrants had formed in the United States.

From the Muridiyya's inception, the Murid leadership has used mobility as a political and organizational device. Facing an administration wary of any community with the potential to challenge its authority, Ahmadu Bamba adopted migration as a means to placate colonial rulers, constantly changing his residence to avoid having large gatherings of disciples around him. Between 1884, the year of the Muridiyya's founding, and 1895, the year he was tried and deported to Gabon, Ahmadu Bamba had settled three villages: Daaru Salaam, the Muridiyya holy city of Tuubaa, and Mbakke Jolof. He also elevated many of his senior disciples to the status of shaykhs and encouraged them to form their own communities. Before his exile to Gabon, Bamba had appointed dozens of shaykhs, and many among these were founders of one or more villages. The French administrator, Lieutenant Lucien Nekkach, estimated that in 1952 the Muridiyya had two hundred shaykhs.[14] The actual number might have been larger.

Historians suggest that in the late nineteenth and early twentieth centuries, Murid villages became refuges for freed slaves and defeated Wolof warriors for whom joining the Muridiyya represented a form of passive resistance to colonial rule.[15] There is certainly some truth to these assumptions, but there were also other forces at work that contributed to Murid migration and dispersal.

Guy Rocheteau, who conducted research on Murid migration in the early 1970s, offers insightful analysis of the causes of mobility in Wolof society.[16] Among the Wolof, Rocheteau argues, migration was throughout history a strategy to cope with household dysfunctions and conflicts. These dysfunctions were the result of discordances between the structure of household authority and land management. In polygamous Wolof families, young unmarried males subjected to the authority of their father and older brothers were often torn between their obligation to work on the family farm to support their extended family and the aspiration to achieve economic independence and establish their own household. Tension became particularly intense after the death of the father, and young males became subordinate to an older brother who might have had a different birth mother (and lacked the father's authority). In this situation, migration is often the solution. The older brother would sometimes move out and settle in another village where land was available, or young bachelors might emigrate to start a family elsewhere. Rocheteau argues that Murid villages were particularly attractive to these migrants. These villages were located in newly colonized and sparsely populated areas where access to land was easier for unmarried immigrants who could wed and achieve head-of-household status. The Muridiyya then offered alternative ways to resolve household conflicts caused by demographic pressure, land scarcity, and social dysfunctions.

The transfer of Ahmadu Bamba to Diourbel in 1912 marked an important turning point in Murid migration. Bamba was assigned permanent residence in this colonial town after years of exile and house arrest in and out of Senegal. Diourbel is located in the province of Bawol, Ahmadu Bamba's native land and the heartland of the Muridiyya. Murids understood that their shaykh's settlement in Diourbel marked the dawn of a new era that at least promised peace and stability in the shaykh's relations with the French. Ahmadu Bamba also realized that he might never recover his freedom of movement, but the détente in his relationship with the colonial administration provided an opportunity to build up his organization. Migration and space making were central to the expansion of the Muridiyya. As soon as Bamba was authorized to build his house outside of the colonial quarter where he was initially interned, he invited his senior disciples to join him and build their own houses near his. He also instructed his devotees to create new villages in eastern Bawol, the heartland of the Mbakke clan. Responding to their leader's appeal, Murid shaykhs founded a string of new villages and reoccupied formerly abandoned ones to provide structure and leadership to the growing number of disciples joining them.[17] By 1926, colonial administrators reported, "The Murids had conquered the whole province of Bawol."[18] Murids continued to found new villages, even after the passing of Ahmadu Bamba in 1927.

After Ahmadu Bamba's death, the migration slowed down because of succession disputes. But it picked up again quickly after those disputes were resolved. Murid migration expanded to central and eastern Senegal and took a new form under the guidance of shaykhs engaged in the cultivation of peanuts. Migrants were mostly school age, and the more mature young males (*takder*)[19] confided in Murid shaykhs when it came to their acquisition of a spiritual education (*tarbiyya*), although families, including non-Murids, compelled by droughts, demographic pressure, and soil depletion also joined the movement. Mamadu Mustafa, Ahmadu Bamba's eldest son and first successor—along with some of his brothers and uncles—led the effort by founding a number of new villages in the eastern region of the former precolonial kingdom of Bawol.[20] This migratory movement started what scholars have termed the *front pionnier Murid* (Murid migration frontiers).[21]

French geographer Paul Pélissier notes that from its inception, the migration to eastern Senegal was an initiative of the Murid shaykhs. The colonial administration adopted a hands-off posture, appreciating the contribution that Murid migrant farmers were making to the production of peanuts, which were the backbone of Senegal's economy.[22] This wave of migration was not initiated by Ahmadu Bamba, although he gave his blessings for the creation of the new settlements; the sites targeted were on the margins or outside of the Mbakke's original heartland and most of the time close to the railroad linking Dakar to Bamako in French Soudan.[23] Villages built near train stations along the railroad served as launching pads from which Murid migrants expanded inland. The settlements functioned as *daaras tarbiyya* (working schools) rather than villages; peanut and millet cultivation instead of Qur'anic education occupied the central place in the life of the communities, which were led by ordinary disciples commissioned by their religious guides, not prestigious and learned shaykhs who led during the first phase described earlier.

There is continuity between Murid rural-rural migration and the rural-urban migration that began in earnest in the aftermath of World War II. The first Murids to settle in town were the takder, the young males that populated the rural daara tarbiyya of the front pionnier. During the idle season after the harvest from November to December, many among these disciples moved to cities where they performed menial jobs, returning to their villages before the first rains in June. Their gradual settlement in town as permanent residents was due to three things. First, powerful Murid families established fiefdoms on the frontier zones that other families respected to avoid frictions, limiting possibilities for further expansion. Second, the colonial administration abandoned its laissez-faire policy, encouraging the sedentarization of Murid farmers and enacting environmental policies to protect forested areas.[24] Third, and more significantly, the overhaul of the relationship between France and its colonies brought about transformations that facilitated mobility.

In 1944, at the Conference of Brazzaville, France, under pressure from its colonial subjects (especially the educated elite), enacted a number of reforms to respond to demands for greater freedom and the end of oppressive colonial policies. These reforms removed some of the obstacles that stifled population movement within and between colonies. The mobility of French colonial subjects within and outside Africa was severely constrained by the Indigénat Law of 1887 and the edict of April 24, 1928. The edict mandated that French subjects of the empire obtain official permission to travel even a short distance from their residence. Both laws were rescinded in 1946 when citizenship status was formally granted to all of France's subjects in Africa within the framework of the newly established French Union.[25] Forced labor was also banned the same year. Now, people desiring to travel across the empire needed only an identity card. The impact of these reforms on migration was clearly on display in a memo that the governor general sent to the lieutenant governors throughout French West Africa: "The law of 7 May 1946 which granted citizenship status to all French subjects of overseas France has rendered obsolete all regulations discriminating between French of European extraction and Frenchmen of African roots. . . . For obvious social and economic reasons, everybody should be able to move freely within the borders of each territory of the federation, and freely offers his service without hindrance as he wishes."[26]

Among the Murids, seasonal migration to cities gradually led to permanent settlement in urban areas by a growing number of disciples, some of whom were new local converts. Nekkach estimated that the population of Murids living in the cities of Dakar and Saint-Louis grew from 140 and 150 to 15,000 and 4,000, respectively, between 1916 and 1952.[27] Other medium-sized Senegalese cities such as Thiès, Kaolack, and Rufisque had Murid populations of 15,000, 8,000, and 7,000, respectively, in 1952.[28]

By the 1950s, Murids had started to migrate across Africa, using cities in Senegal as stepping-stones. They headed to cities in West Africa and central Africa, following in the footsteps of the colonial soldiers, civil servants, and professionals that preceded them there. Being the first French colony in West Africa with an advanced educational system, Senegal contributed significantly to the administration of other colonies. Colonially driven migration was clearly behind the subsequent waves of voluntary migration by ordinary Senegalese, including Murids. These voluntary migrants learned from the experience of their predecessors and seized on the opportunity their presence abroad offered.[29]

Although also partly colonially induced, Murid international migration was also different from earlier waves of migration from the Senegal River Valley that mostly involved Haal Pulaar and Soninke speaking people. Mass Murid outmigration began in the postcolonial era at a time when earlier migration streams had slowed or ended. Unlike their predecessors, Murid migrants were not interested in government work or salaried jobs. They created their own economic niches in host countries, working as self-employed merchants, taxi drivers, hair braiders, restaurant owners, and artisans but rarely as wage earners. Among the Murid immigrants, the ubiquitous dahira served as a crucible for brotherhood solidarity. It displaced ethnic affinities and hometown associations, which were central to the lives of sub-Saharan migrants, especially Soninke and Haal Pulaar. Murid immigrants' ties to their villages of origin were more tenuous; emphasis was instead on cultivating relationships with shaykhs and holy cities in Senegal. Additionally, Murid migrants showed great versatility in their destination choices, step migrating from country to country and city to city in an incessant cycle, beautifully captured by scholar Mamadou Diouf: "He [the Murid migrant] is constantly in movement. His stopover points are hotel rooms or overcrowded apartments in the main cities of the world where merchandise is piled up. He is always just stopping off, always in transit, thus erasing the notion of a fixed residence. But a center nonetheless remains: Touba—the place of spiritual and economic investment and the desired last resting place for eternity."[30]

African cities were nodes in this expanding migratory movement that reached destinations in France in the first decades of the 1960s. With the "closing" of the French borders in the mid-1970s, Murid migrants moved to southern Europe and settled in Italy and Spain, where immigration policies were less restrictive. By the mid-1980s, Murid immigrants had found their way to the United States, landing in New York City. But for most of them, this American metropole was their second, third, or even fourth destination. After leaving their villages or small towns in Senegal, they would have transited through the Senegalese capital Dakar, then step migrated to cities in West Africa or central Africa and to one or more European countries before making the journey across the Atlantic Ocean. As scholar D. M. Carter noted, "The world of Mouridism in immigration is vast and extends from the holy city of Touba in Senegal to the major cities of Africa, Europe, the United States, Italy, Spain, France, Germany, Japan, Canada, and Australia: New York, Atlanta, Los Angeles, Turin, Livorno, Milan, Rome, Paris, Toulon, Lyon, Hong Kong, Berlin, London, Yaounde, and Madrid."[31] We will see that these migration trajectories and the experiences they offered were instrumental in shaping the lives of Murids in the diaspora.

SPACE AND PLACE MAKING

One goal of this book is to show the centrality of space making in the spiritual life of Murid disciples and to demonstrate how migrants use space as a canvas to articulate changing interpretations of the Muridiyya. My conception of space and place is informed by the work of cultural geographers, sociologists, historians, and specialists in religious studies who conceive of place as constructed reality.[32] These scholars offer a heuristic definition of space and place that emphasizes the centrality of culture in the process of place making. While space is generally perceived as an abstract geometric entity primarily defined by variables such as size, shape, area, and direction, place appears as a site of "accumulated biographical experiences,"[33] a product of human agency. While space is detached from "material form and cultural interpretation," place, by contrast, draws its significance from infused meaning and value. It is the result of "an agglomeration of meaning."[34] In sum, it is the transformative power of people, practices, objects and symbols that turns space into place. Place then embodies both physical and semiotic qualities. While the analytical distinction between space and place may not reflect the conscious intent of historical actors, it reveals the tangible impact of their culture on their living space.

The history of the Murid holy city of Tuubaa, settled by Shaykh Ahmadu Bamba, provides a good illustration of the power of culture as shaper of space. In "Matlabul Fawzayni" (Quest for happiness in the two worlds), a poem of supplication Bamba wrote soon after discovering in 1889 the site that would eventually become Tuubaa, he beseeched God to make it a sanctified city of light, peace, knowledge, and prosperity: "[God] make of my abode, the blessed city of Tuubaa, a center of knowledge, a place favorable to broadmindedness and healthy meditations that sanctifies Your name permanently. . . . Preserve the inhabitants of Tuubaa against perversion and bless them with an abundant supply of water. . . . Let all that is well-being and a benefit of the heritage from the six sides of the planet flow to my abode, the blessed city of Tuubaa."[35]

Bamba then ordered his disciples to dig a well that he named *ayn rahmati* ("the fountain," or "well of mercy"). Murids believe that water from this well flows from the same source that aliments the spring of Zam-Zam in Mecca, which God made appear to save Hagar, the Prophet Ibrahim's wife, and their son, Ishmael. Bamba envisioned building a mosque, a school to offer advanced Islamic training, and a library. His disciples built these infrastructures after his death. From a small village of a few dozen inhabitants at the close of the nineteenth century, it is now the second-largest city of Senegal after the capital, Dakar, and home to nearly a million people. The exponential growth of Tuubaa reflects its reputation as spatial embodiment of Ahmadu Bamba's prayers.

For Sufis or followers of mystical Islam like the Murids, the effort at place making is intimately associated with the body of the shaykh, or "saint founder." The latter is endowed with *baraka* (God-given gift of grace), which inhabits the shaykh's words, clothes, bodily fluids, photographs, and everything he touches. Although there is disagreement about the meaning of the word, there is a consensus that baraka is a power that emanates from God, which He confers as He wishes but often on uncommonly pious people, on the family of the Prophet Muhammad and on His words enshrined in the Qur'an.[36] The potency of baraka continues even after the shaykh's death. For Sufis, the soul of the dead saint remains alive in his inert but incorruptible body.[37] And it can escape to rush to the aide of disciples or intercede before God in their favor. The shaykh's tomb becomes the focal point from which his baraka radiates and a privileged site of pilgrimage. This capacity to radiate indefinitely allows baraka to transcend space and time and touch the lives of disciples across generations and geographical locations.[38] Thus, Murid residences, businesses, and places of worship across Senegal and the diaspora are often named after Tuubaa and other sacred Murid sites and shaykhs. These names, along with Murid iconography, serve both as talismans and identity markers.

Tuubaa's connection to the diaspora is not, however, limited to its role of sacred space and source of baraka. The city benefits de facto from an extraterritorial status where the power of the state is restricted and authority vested in the caliph, who is Ahmadu Bamba's oldest male heir.[39] This administrative exceptionalism has played a significant role in the settlement and development of the city, as it affords its inhabitants unique advantages such as free water supply, lower taxes, and a relatively low cost of living.[40] Murids see Tuubaa as the perfect realization of Ahmadu's prayer enshrined in his poem "Matlabul Fawzayni." It embodies the morality, values, and ethics of the quintessential Sufi city (alcohol consumption, tobacco, and secular music are prohibited in Tuubaa).[41] From a land of emigration, Tuubaa and its vicinity have become a land of immigration. Besides being a sanctified city, Tuubaa's attraction also stems from the role Murid immigrants ascribe to it. For many among the immigrants who originated from villages in the provinces of Bawol and Kajoor and have lived in Western cities for years, village life is no longer an option. Most have moved their families to the holy city. Tuubaa provides them with the amenities of urban life such as electricity, pipe water, internal plumbing, and modern health-care infrastructures while shielding them against the cultural corruption and high cost of living of Westernized metropolises.[42]

MURID, MOBILITY, AND WORK

The Murids form a third of Senegal's population, yet according to various estimates they account for over half of Senegalese living abroad.[43] The disproportionate representation of Murid disciples among the Senegalese diaspora cannot be explained solely by a traditional macroeconomic approach to migration such as push-pull theory. By overemphasizing cost-benefit calculations, push-pull downplays the impact of migrants' complex circumstances, which cannot be reduced to a formula.[44] Murid migration, for example, does not concern the poor alone but involves disciples of all social statuses, especially the well-off, including shaykhs. Many among those who pioneered the migration were skilled artisans or experienced traders. It took decades before the poor farmers in the Murid heartland of western-central Senegal followed their example. Murid migration intensified in the late 1970s and early 1980s at a time that coincided with economic contraction in the countries they settled in. Murid migrants are mostly self-employed and therefore cannot be counted as part of the "post-industrial migration" that has replaced labor and family reunion. In sum, the Murid migratory experience seems to escape the narrow supply and demand–based labor migration model that informs most theories of international migration.

Without neglecting the impact of global economic, political, ecological, and other factors associated with migration, I suggest that Murid migration and industriousness are better understood by exploring Murid cultural and religious values and some of the historical transformations that have marked the Murid order since its founding in the late nineteenth century. I contend that these values, along with specific historical circumstances, have fostered an ethos of mobility and a spirit of entrepreneurship responsible for Murid disciples' predisposition to migration. I construe this ethos of mobility as a habitus that forms organically, shaped by common belonging in and continued exposure to everyday Murid culture.[45]

The trajectory of Ahmadu Bamba's life and his role as an exemplar reenforces the Murid ethos of mobility. During his many relocations and confinements by the French colonial administration of Senegal, at least from 1895, Bamba attracted a following of both young and old disciples who left their villages behind to congregate around him, thus triggering migratory waves that upset the colonial administration and disrupted traditional household power structures that bound people to the land.

But it was Bamba's exile to Gabon that captured the imagination of Murid disciples and ingrained a culture of mobility symbolized by many of his trunks and suitcases kept as sacred relics in Murid holy places in Tuubaa and Diourbel. Ahmadu Bamba's written account of his exile, along with his hagiographers' depictions of his deportation to Gabon, popularized the shaykh's sacred journey, touting the spiritual rewards he garnered by braving strange and dangerous lands.[46] The most popular version of this narration reads like a vernacular geography of French West Africa and central Africa that later served as a travel guide to faithful Murid pilgrims following in their shaykh's footsteps.[47] It narrates Bamba's transfer from Saint-Louis, the capital of French West Africa (AOF, French acronym), to the port of Dakar. In Dakar he boarded a ship to Gabon, where he would live in exile for seven years.

After returning to Senegal in 1902, Ahmadu Bamba's mobility was severely curtailed by colonial restrictions. But his forced sedentariness, combined with his growing aura as a saint who overcame French machinations, turned Bamba into a magnet for disciples. Faithful Murids from all over Senegal converged to his places of detention in Mauritania and Senegal. I suggest that the waves of short- and long-term devotional migrations unleashed by Ahmadu Bamba's return to Senegal, along with the centrality of mobility in his biography, were instrumental in fostering a culture of migration among Murid disciples.

This culture of migration was wedded to a work ethic. Much has been written about the idea of work's sanctifying virtue among the Murids.[48] But when referring to work in his writings, Bamba often uses the Arabic word *khidma* (service), alongside the words *'amal* (*talabul halal*, "search for the licit"), which means "labor" or "action," and *kasb*, which means "earning," "gain," or "profit."[49]

From the Murid perspective, khidma is a manifestation of the common attachment to the Muridiyya, a way of perpetuating and participating in Ahmadu Bamba's mission or, as Murid disciples put it, "working for Ahmadu Bamba." For Murids, prayer and other forms of worship are duties common to all Muslims; khidma constitutes their distinctive way of expressing love and fidelity to their shaykh, particularly by continuing his mission. The economic implication of khidma is important, as it results in the accumulation of wealth and prestige within the Murid organization. Economic prosperity, in turn, demonstrates the continuing potency of Ahmadu Bamba's baraka even after his death.

But for the disciples, even more important is their ability to contribute through their wealth, investments, and donations to the continuing manifestation of this potency. In other words, Murid disciples consider it their utmost duty to demonstrate through their labor and economic achievements the continuing efficacy of Ahmadu Bamba's prayers. Trust in Bamba's gift of grace and in the power of his prayers creates, in turn, a predisposition for risk taking. Shaykh's guidance has an impact on Murid mobility and economic resourcefulness, but it is not the most important factor.

ISLAM, RACE, GENDER, AND MIGRATION

"In France I was an African, in the United States I discovered that I was black."[50] This statement from one of Malian novelist Mammadou Mahmoud Ndongo's characters echoes certain utterances I have heard from African immigrants across Europe and the United States. It reveals the powerful impact of the racial politics of immigrants' host societies on the construction of their racial consciousness. In France, the Republic purports to be colorblind (the word "race" was removed from the French constitution in June 2018); race is considered irrelevant to the ways the state does business. In the United States, because of a unique historical trajectory, race is central to governance, especially on issues of housing, education, and policing: all areas that have significantly impacted the lives of immigrants. Additionally, the presence of a large transplanted Black population creates a unique racial environment for African immigrants forced to navigate the treacherous and highly politicized terrain of race relations.[51]

In Muslim West Africa, constructions of race stem from the combination of ideas inspired by entrenched Arab racial prejudice against sub-Saharan Africans and European anti-Black racism. Bruce Hall argues that there are African histories of race that do not obey colonial logic. These histories are rooted in the encounter between Arabs who identified as Whites and referred to sub-Saharan Africans as Blacks.[52] "When the Sahel was colonized by France beginning in the late nineteenth century, the colonial administration used these existing local conceptions of racial difference because they corresponded to European denigrations of people defined as black."[53]

In French West Africa, the influence of Arab racial prejudice on the colonial mind is most evident in the construction of sub-Saharan Muslims' identity and the definition of Muslim policies.[54] The encounter between Arab and French race-making ideologies resulted in the formulation by French colonial administrators of the notion of "Islam noir" (Black Islam), of which the Muridiyya is purportedly the perfect representation. "Islam noir" is perceived as an inferior and heterodox form of Islam mired in mysticism that combines aspects of African "pagan religions" and Islam. It is predicated on the idea that because of their skin color and cultures, Black African Muslims cannot understand an abstract God and lack the intellectual capacity to apprehend the intricacies of Islamic theology and Arabic grammar.

Ahmadu Bamba's trips to Mauritania from 1884 marked his first direct exposure to a racially diverse community and shaped his views on race and race relations expressed in his writings and practices.[55] The Mauritanian population is divided into people of Arab and Berber ancestry that identify as *bidan* (White) and a majority Black population.[56] These "Whites" form the religious elite and had many disciples in Senegal and across West Africa. But they harbored an attitude of intellectual and racial superiority and showed little respect for their darker-skinned fellow Muslims. Ahmadu Bamba's family was affiliated with the Shaykh Sidiyya clan, a prominent bidan clerical family, and Bamba paid them multiple visits (he also spent four years with them in exile). But the Sidiyya were not immune to the racial prejudice that affected their fellow bidan. Paul Marty quotes an unspecified work by Sidiyya Baba, Ahmadu Bamba's spiritual guide, in which Baba wrote, "The Blacks think of themselves as Muslims, however, the majority among them do not have the slightest correct notion of what Islam is really about, they ignore the Islamic ethic, its laws and principles. But we [the Moors in our capacity as teachers and spiritual guides] have a lot of responsibility to bear in this situation."[57] On another occasion, Baba expressed his scorn for the uncivilized "little black kinglets" of Senegal who did not deserve the attention the French gave them.[58]

Ahmadu Bamba's biographer, Ahmad Lamine Diop, evokes two events that happened during the former's stay in Mauritania as an exile between 1903 and 1907. These events provide a window into the racial prejudice Bamba confronted. Diop indicates that when one Al-Haaj Ibrahim al-Baghadi [sic], an exceptionally learned scholar from Baghdad, submitted to Ahmadu Bamba and became one of his disciples, some highly regarded Mauritanian clerics (probably White) reproached him for choosing a Black person as his shaykh despite his renown and erudition.[59] When Bamba learned about this reproach, he wrote a poem touting his own status as servant of the Prophet Muhammad. He noted in the poem that no saint had ever suffered the kind of ordeal he experienced for the sake of his devotion to the prophet. He added that his sacrifices earned him the prophet's satisfaction, hinting that what mattered in God's eyes was not skin color but piety.[60] This poem was a polite rebuke to his racially prejudiced hosts. Diop also mentions that Ahmadu Bamba declined many requests from Mauritanians who wished to marry his daughters, arguing that the differences in cultures and customs should discourage such marriages. These events give some insight into the circumstances that shaped Ahmadu Bamba's own understanding of the politics of race and racial relations. He firmly believed that piety and erudition trumped all other considerations, including race, in a Muslim's quest for closeness to God.

In his magnum opus, *Masalik al-Jinan*, a book he wrote soon after returning from his first trip to Mauritania, Bamba criticized those who tied Blackness to intellectual inferiority. He wrote, "Blackness cannot be a sign of stupidity; the best among humans, without discrimination, are those who fear God the most."[61] These two verses, in a book that contains several hundred, have had a disproportionate impact on Murid discourse on race, especially in the diaspora. The verses, some of which are prominently featured by Murid immigrants on posters during public celebrations (especially in the United States), helped them build bridges with African American cultural nationalists and civil rights activists. In France, where immigrants confront the racial biases of fellow North African Muslims, Murid orthodoxy and Bamba's scholarly accomplishments are emphasized to dispel the notion of Black intellectual inferiority.

Just as life in the diaspora contributed to the reshaping of Murid racial consciousness, immigration also reframed the role of women within the Muridiyya. There is extensive scholarship on Muslim women in West Africa, but hardly any of it concerns Murid women.[62] This literature mostly documents Muslim women's resistance to Islamic patriarchy. Reviewing the literature on the politics of Muslim women, and particularly the works of Janice Boddy and Lila Abu-Lughod, Saba Mahmood points to the analytical flaws of binary terms such as "resistance" and "subordination." She cautions against "ascription of feminist consciousness to those for whom it is not a meaningful category."[63] Drawing on her research on the women's mosque movement in Cairo, she emphasizes that it was critically important "to interrogate the practical and conceptual conditions under which different forms of desire emerge, including the desire for submission to recognized norm."[64] She perceptively observes that "agentival capacity is entailed not only on those acts that resist norms but also in the multiple ways in which one inhabits norms."[65]

Mahmood's insights are particularly helpful in examining the role of Murid migrant women. Exploring the experience of women in the diaspora provides insight into how Murid women are able to reconfigure and inhabit norms and chart their own path in the Murid order. I have argued that women are at the center of Murid sociability, especially in the diaspora. However, to better understand the changing roles of women as the Muridiyya transitions from a rural Sufi order of peanut farmers to an urban organization of traders and professionals, it is more productive to adopt a bottom-up approach to gender identity and roles. By a "bottom-up" approach I mean a conception of gender rooted in local constructions of masculinity and femininity (Mahmood's inhabited norms). Looking at gender from within rather than from without helps minimize the mistakes of ascribing meanings that do not always align with the historical actors' perceptions and intents.

The emergence of women as central players in the spiritual and economic life of the Muridiyya can be associated with the rise of Maam Jaara Buso (d. 1866), Ahmadu Bamba's mother, as an iconic figure and saint in the late 1950s. Maam Jaara first appeared on the scene in the context of a struggle for influence between two powerful Murid shaykhs, each of them trying to control her shrine in the village of Poroxaan, where she was buried, and appropriate her memory.[66] But gradually these shaykhs were displaced by women who turned Bamba's mother into a symbol of feminine piety. By the 1990s, they had transformed the pilgrimage at her tomb, which attracts tens of thousands of (mostly women) worshippers annually, into the only religious celebration of its scale dedicated to a Muslim woman in all of Senegal and perhaps West Africa.[67] This event fostered a female consciousness of belonging rooted in Islamized, traditional Wolof family values that is best represented by the feminization of rituals.[68]

Today, there is a global women-only dahira named after Maam Jaara Buso with chapters found across Senegal and throughout the Murid diaspora. This dahira makes their own agenda and holds their own events, sometimes in collaboration with male disciples and sometimes independently.[69] I suggest that the formation of this dahira at a time when Murids were migrating in greater numbers to France and the United States partly explains the greater visibility of Murid women in these two countries. Other factors also helped transform the role of Murid women.[70] One can mention the increasing participation of women in the cash economy in the wake of the adoption of structural adjustment programs, immigration policies that facilitated family reunification, and employment opportunities abroad. These developments suggest that the changing meanings of gender roles within the Muridiyya are reflective of transformations beyond the confines of the order's theology and history in Senegal.

STRUCTURE OF THE BOOK

The book is divided into seven chapters. The first investigates the transformation of the Muridiyya from a marginalized rural religious order of migrant peanut farmers to a powerful economic, political, and social force in the cities of Senegal.[71] It focuses on Murid migration and communities in Saint-Louis and Dakar, both former capitals of French West Africa and Senegal. I then examine Murid efforts to enshrine their culture in the two cities' respective spaces and responses to their initiatives. The second chapter explores the history of Senegalese and Murid migration to Côte d'Ivoire. It documents the continuities and disjunctions between colonial and postcolonial migrations, focusing on the personal and collective experiences of Murid immigrants in Abidjan (capital city of Côte d'Ivoire) and their efforts to build a spiritually meaningful life in a foreign land. The following chapter moves the story to Gabon. I use two Murid projects in Libreville (the capital city of Gabon)—the building of the mosque of Montagne Sainte (Sacred Hill) and the creation of a Murid art market—to explore Murid efforts to appropriate space in Gabon. I begin with an examination of the history of these two projects, and then I explain how Ahmadu Bamba's imagined biography provided a grid for a Murid sacred map of Libreville in the twenty-first century.

Chapters 4 and 5 are set in Paris. Chapter 4 offers a comprehensive reconstruction of the history of Murid migration to France, delineating the entanglement between this migration and earlier migration flows and its specificities. The chapter reveals how Murid institutions in France became contested sites where different perceptions of the Muridiyya competed. These diverging perceptions crystallized around differing conceptions of the Murid organization's vocation and the role of disciples in helping fulfill this vocation. In chapter 5, I use the Murid houses of Aulnay-sous-Bois and Taverny in the region of Ile de France as case studies to investigate Murid experiments at place making in Paris. In doing so, I explore Murid immigrants' motivations for owning property in France and how this affects their lives and specifically impacts their interactions with the French state and the Murid leadership in Senegal. I explain how geographical distance from the Murid heartland creates a discursive space where new ways of being Murid can be imagined.

The last two chapters of the book bring the story to the United States. Here I focus on Little Senegal in Harlem. I conceive of Little Senegal as an expression of the amalgamation of Murid profane and spiritual space. Unlike in France, where religion is mostly confined to the privacy of Murid communal houses, in New York, business and religion are performed in the public sphere, occupying the same space sometimes alternately, sometimes simultaneously. Chapter 6 is concerned with Murid migration and businesses. The chapter examines the unfolding of the postcolonial migration of Senegalese to the United States, focusing on Murid traders and how the entanglement between business practices, cultural performance, and spatial occupation gave birth to Little Senegal. The chapter ends with a discussion of gentrification and the slow death of the Senegalese enclave in Harlem. The last chapter of the book is an exploration of Murid place making in Harlem. It begins with an examination of the relationship between Murid disciples and the African American Muslim community. The last two sections of the chapter concentrate on the history of the Murid house in Harlem and the events surrounding Murid culture week, organized every summer and culminating in the manifestations marking Ahmadu Bamba Day on July 28.

The chapters in this book reconstruct over half a century of Murid history, focusing on mobility and cultural transformations in urban settings.

This reconstruction puts Murid migrants at center stage. By following the footsteps of Murid immigrants, we are able to document the centrality of intracontinental migration and the role of the African continent as primary destination of migrants. We are also able to trace patterns of overlapping migration streams connecting rural areas to cities across Africa and those areas beyond the continent in Europe and North America. In doing so, we are able to chart the continuities and ruptures between Murid migrations and earlier migration waves, delineating the economic, sociopolitical, and other forces that powered these population movements, including colonial rule, the economic crises of the postcolonial era, and natural disasters.

Looking at Murid history from the perspective of its diasporic periphery rather than its core in Tuubaa allows us to uncover the innovative power, creativity, and influence of ordinary disciples. Life abroad impels Murid immigrants to rethink their own positionality within the order to negotiate their adaptation to strange lands. Mobility and distance from Senegal provide space for Murids to reimagine the Muridiyya and refashion their collective identity as disciples. Murid institutions such as the dahira acquire new meanings to respond to the challenges of life in the diaspora. New rituals are invented, and old ones are transformed. Immigrants' creative use of space allows the embedding of Murid culture in the host societies' public sphere while building bridges with host communities. The construction of Murid collective identity abroad is a communal but contested endeavor. Differing conceptions of what should be the mission of Murid institutions in the diaspora spawn fissures that reveal disciples' conflicting politics, challenging the notion of Murid homogeneity. Some insist on the universal dimension of Bamba's calling and emphasize *dawa* (proselytizing), while others prioritize preserving Murid identity abroad by consolidating the linkages with the leadership in Senegal. Similarly, traditional bases of power and authority such as genealogy and affiliation with the Mbakke family are no longer uncontested. Diasporic reimaginings of the Muridiyya abroad, in turn, inspire cultural reconfigurations at home.

SOURCES AND METHOD

This study is based on multisited investigations in three continents: Africa, Europe, and the Americas. It is qualitative in its approach and interdisciplinary in its orientation. The immigrant experience is best understood when examined across disciplinary boundaries harnessing insights from different literatures that intersect but rarely speak to each other. This is particularly true for the study of transnational migrants that straddle different national boundaries and juggle multiple and conflicting identities.

The Muridiyya on the Move relies on a wide array of oral and written sources in multiple languages—Wolof (lingua franca of the Senegalese), French (official language), English, and Arabic—and in different media (written texts, novels). I have explored newspaper articles in Africa and abroad that chronicle important events in the life of Murid immigrants. I have also pored over pamphlets, brochures, hagiographies, films, and ephemeral materials produced by immigrants. These documents are available online or kept in private libraries by immigrant associations and provide invaluable insights into the everyday religious life of immigrants. If sentimental bonds to place reflect "accumulated biographical experiences" as some scholars argue, then an examination of internal sources, and especially oral history, becomes critical for understanding Murid immigrants' effort at place making in the diaspora.

I have visited six archives in Senegal and France and have participated as speaker or observer in dozens of events organized by diasporic Murids in Senegal, Côte d'Ivoire, Gabon, France, Italy, Germany, and the United States. I have also drawn extensively from over 130 interviews recorded across Senegal, Abidjan, Libreville, New York City, Milan, Brescia, Berlin, and Paris. These face-to-face interviews were unscripted and semistructured. I often began with a few questions but generally let my interlocutors direct the interviews themselves, returning to questioning only after they had concluded their clarifying statements. The interviews, conducted in Wolof, French, and English, provided critical information for a reconstruction of the experience of Murid immigrants that takes their voices seriously.

I have been studying the Murids since I defended the first history master's thesis on the Muridiyya at University Cheikh Anta Diop of Dakar in 1991. Since then, I have continued to research diverse aspects of Murid culture, including in the diaspora. As a native of Senegal who grew up in a Murid family, I have built strong connections within the Murid organization, including with members of the leadership. These connections have been vital in providing access to important sources that have allowed for the recovery of Murid voices that are critical for the reconstruction of the organization's internal history. Because of my familiarity with these sources and the internal politics of the order, I was able to disentangle the layers of information and to fill in some of the lacunae. By comparing and contrasting a variety of sources and applying a rigorous internal and external critique to Murid oral reports and written documents, I hope to minimize some of the biases inherent in these types of sources.

The advantage of an insider's view like this can make comprehensible many seemingly bizarre components and interrelations within the

Muridiyya. But one should also be aware of the drawbacks of this position. In effect, the empathy and open collaboration of informants who feel a bond with the researcher does not come without a cost, as the researcher may be subject to manipulations or subconsciously indulge in self-censorship to avoid social sanctions or preserve ties with the community. However, outsiders writing about the history of the Muridiyya face equally daunting challenges. The nature of the challenges may be different, but the struggle is the same: to objectively analyze and interpret a large body of written and oral materials produced by faithful disciples in esoteric religious languages—or by biased colonial administrators or outside observers.

In reality, any historian writing about his or her own culture or society will in some way have to confront the insider's challenge. When scholars write about people whose values they share or cherish, they tend to be less skeptical and more willing to listen to the stories they are told and convey them to others. I claim the position of the listener vis-à-vis the Muridiyya. But I believe that adopting the sympathetic attitude of the listener does not necessarily disable one's ability to write critically and objectively. In other words, the historian's ability to write a critical history of a people does not hinge upon one's position but rather on the scholar's capacity to effectively apply the historical method of inquiry and criticism to the historical sources.

1 ⌣ The Muridiyya in the Cities of Senegal

God has spoken. The statue has fallen. It should never stand again.[1]

The three sentences in the epigraph capture the reactions of Murids in the city of Saint-Louis (Senegal) and around the world when on September 5, 2017, a storm knocked the statue of General Louis Faidherbe off its pedestal. The statue had been standing in the square of the same name since 1887 in this historic city that was once the capital of Senegal and French West Africa (AOF, French acronym).[2] The news of Faidherbe's stumble went viral on the internet. YouTube videos circulated celebrating the fall of one of the most powerful French colonial administrators in the history of Senegal and perhaps the history of Africa itself.[3] Faidherbe is a towering figure in Saint-Louis; in addition to the square, the city's largest bridge bears his name (and until recently, so did the largest high school). Since the 1990s, Murids in Saint-Louis have been demanding the statue be removed and the square named after Ahmadu Bamba. The statue's fall on the anniversary of Bamba's prayer in the office of the French governor, where he stood trial in 1895, was for the Murid faithful an unmistakable sign of God's wish. Murid demands for erasing Faidherbe from the city's landscape and inscribing Ahmadu Bamba in his place reflect growing Murid economic and cultural assertiveness in Senegal's cities, especially Saint-Louis and Dakar, where Murid disciples have recently initiated new pilgrimages and religious celebrations.

What is remarkable about Murid claims over space and commemorations in Saint-Louis and Dakar is how they are tied to the real or imagined physical presence of Ahmadu Bamba at specific places on specific dates. Specialists in hagiographic studies note the importance of combining temporal and topographical evidence of a saint's identity.[4] For the Murids, documenting the bodily imprint of Ahmadu Bamba in the urban land-scape by tracing spatio-temporal proofs of his physical presence is essential to the claim for sacred Murid place. Sites of religious commemoration are not ordinary spaces but a product of the transforming power of hierophany (manifestation of the sacred): these are places where the divine world intersects with the profane world to infuse spiritual value to secular geometric space.[5] For Murids, the painstaking reconstruction of Ahmadu Bamba's footprints in Saint-Louis and Dakar and the reenactment of his activities (real or imagined) are important in the contest for space. These two cities are colonial creations that continue to embody traces of their colonial past, whereas Murid culture and history remain marginalized.

Occupied in 1659, Saint-Louis is the oldest French colony on the Atlantic coast of Africa. Its inhabitants began sending a representative to the French Parliament in 1848. Saint-Louis acquired the status of a French commune in 1872, conferring some constitutional rights to those born in the city.[6] As descendants of French citizens who benefited, in theory, from the same rights as French citizens in metropolitan France, Saint-Louisiens do not always share the nationalist sentiments of their compatriots. This includes the Murids, whose ancestors from the inland protectorates were French subjects ruled by the harsh *indigénat* regime that deprived them of basic rights.[7] Saint-Louisiens tend to consider the French soldiers and administrators who worked and fought alongside their ancestors as compatriots. They also recall the peaceful coexistence of Islam and colonial rule in the old city and do not see a contradiction between the Islamic identity of Saint-Louis and the presence of important vestiges of its colonial past.

Dakar, which is also the capital of Senegal, is more cosmopolitan than Saint-Louis and seems less insecure about its identity and future. The indigenous population, the Lébous, are now in the minority. Unlike the people of Saint-Louis, the Lébous have an identity strongly influenced by traditional African values.[8] Although they, too, acquired French citizenship as inhabitants of a commune, the Lébous were not influenced by French culture and colonial history as much as the elite of Saint-Louis were. Their biggest concern was to maintain the cultural identity of some historic Lébou sites and to assert their control over the few ancestral lands that have thus far escaped the developers and real estate speculators of Dakar.

Murid religious commemorations in Saint-Louis and Dakar are important parts of a strategy to invest the Senegalese urban landscape with cultural and historical meaning. These commemorations deflect ingrained popular perceptions of Murids as interlopers who do not belong in the city and make the case for deeper urban connections. As Murids engage in this ritual mapping of the cities, they aim to provide a new sociological identity to the space that challenges entrenched local claims to spaces. Therefore, beyond the quarrel over the removal of the statue, the renaming of the square, or the legitimacy of Murid commemorations in Saint-Louis and Dakar, what is at stake is the reshaping of each city's memory and the political and potential economic implications of that memory. The dispute has as much to do with the past as it does with the present and future: it represents the clash of two competing postcolonial identities. One of these identities is inscribed in historical continuity, recognizing the colonial origins of these cities and the value of maintaining their present traces for a variety of economic, political, and cultural reasons. Another contests and disrupts official history through revision, rehabilitating the actions and voices of silenced historical actors.

By claiming, rediscovering, and inventing sites of Murid memory in the two cities through religious celebrations, Murids seek to stretch their organization's space beyond its heartland in western-central Senegal to include territory they have been excluded from (at least in cultural terms) but that has become their economic dominion.[9] In trying to turn important symbolic places in Saint-Louis and Dakar into shrines for pilgrimages, Murid disciples met opposition from the state and other institutions intent on protecting official memory—that is, "institutions committed to enshrining moments that are deemed central for the construction of national ideology."[10]

This chapter investigates the transformation of the Muridiyya from a marginalized rural religious order of migrant peanut farmers to a powerful economic, political, and social force in Senegalese cities. It focuses on Murid migration and on communities in Saint-Louis and Dakar, which both served as the capital of AOF and colonial Senegal at different times. I examine Murid efforts to enshrine their culture in the two cities' spaces and the responses to their initiatives. Elsewhere I have demonstrated the centrality of place making in preserving Murid identity and in Murid accommodation to colonial rule.[11] In the postcolonial era, Murid efforts at place making have occurred in urban settings and played a different role. I suggest that the recent assertiveness by Murids in Saint-Louis and Dakar is part of an ongoing effort to translate their growing economic power into cultural and symbolic capital to further legitimize their standing in the cities. The legitimacy acquired could then serve as the basis for claiming power and having a greater say in the management of urban space and affairs. This effort is fraught with tensions and controversies because it requires reading a history of the two cities that inscribes Murid culture in urban space while challenging established histories. As Roger Friedland and Richard D. Hect remind us, "The phenomenon in which memory and identity are fused to place may be an important factor in generating resistance, conflict, and change."[12]

DAHIRA AND THE URBANIZATION OF THE MURIDIYYA

Murids began to move to Senegalese cities in the early twentieth century as seasonal rural-urban migrants.[13] They spent the dry season in urban areas working menial jobs as mattress makers, charcoal sellers, landscapers, porters, and bricklayers but returned to their farms in June, when the first rains fell. Permanent settlement in cities started in earnest after World War II, when Murids relocated to urban areas in larger numbers and worked as smiths, jewelers, tailors, butchers, leatherworkers, low-level civil servants, and traders.[14]

The development of the dahira paralleled the steady migration of Murids to Senegalese cities. The dahira has now become the most recognizable Murid institution in urban Senegal. The *Hans Wehr Dictionary of Modern Written Arabic* gives several definitions of the word *dā'ira* (*daïra* or *dahira*) that revolve around mathematical concepts (ring, circuit, circumference, etc.) and administrative notions (district, bureau, agency, etc.).[15] The Sufi orders of Senegal offer what seems to be a unique example of the use of dahira in a religious context. The word "dahira" among Senegalese Sufis embodies both the mathematical and bureaucratic meanings of the word. "Dahira" originally referred to an organization regrouping a community of disciples living in a city, but it also describes their habit of sitting in circle when reciting the *Wird*, chanting devotional poems, or deliberating.[16]

In Senegal, the word "dahira" entered the Sufi lexicon in the late 1920s. It was first used by disciples of the Tijany shaykh, Ababakar Sy.[17] Among the Murids, the dahira was first conceived as a sort of prayer circle where disciples from the same town or neighborhood would meet on a weekly basis to read the Qur'an, chant Ahmadu Bamba's devotional poems, collect financial contributions, and socialize.[18] In the city, the dahira played a role similar to that of the Murid *daara* (rural working school) at the forefront of Murid expansion to the forest of eastern-central Senegal after the relocation of Ahmadu Bamba in Diourbel in 1912. For many recent urban dwellers, it replaced the *toolu larba* (Wednesday farm) where once a week rural disciples donated their labor to the local Murid shaykh.

Many of my Murid informants living in cities in Africa and abroad see the dahira as an institutionalization, in monetary form, of the labor they donated every Wednesday when living in the Senegalese countryside. Today, the tradition of collecting dahira dues on Wednesdays continues in the Senegalese markets and in the wider diaspora.

The development of the dahira in colonial urban Senegal was met with resistance and controversy. The colonial administration resisted the regulation of religious organizations that it deemed outside the mandate of the secular French republic.[19] For example, the administration refused to officially license dahiras. But when religious activities spilled out in public space in defiance of their expected domestic confinement, they created confusion and anxiety among colonial administrators bereft of administrative tools to deal with these public displays of worship.

Murids held their dahira rituals and meetings in private houses. Loud chanting of Ahmadu Bamba's *qasidas* (devotional poems) is a central part of Murid worship. For most Murids, the chanting of these poems is as important as reciting the Qur'an. The spiritual songs are believed to have the power to sanctify space and bring blessings to worshippers.[20] They also help consolidate the emotional bond between fellow disciples now living in a strange land away from the heartland of the Muridiyya. But the loud chanting was not welcome in the colonial cities where strict regulations were in place to control noise pollution, especially in residential areas. Moreover, in the tradition of French secularism with its insistence on strict separation between church and state, religion had no place in public space,[21] let alone a religion that in the mind of colonizers represented "Islam noir" (Black Islam), a corrupted form of Islam invented by and for benighted Wolof farmers.[22]

Murid leaders of dahiras in Dakar remember the harassment they suffered from the police when they met at Gumaalo Sekk's house in the Medina neighborhood.[23] They recall that their meetings were often dispersed because of the worshippers' loud chanting or because of the crowd that gathered in the street. Elhaaj Njaga Gey, echoing the memory of many fellow Murids in Dakar in the 1950s and 1960s, notes: "I remember that when we started to found dahira at Kër Gumaalo, the police would often come to disperse our meetings. They would ask us to apply for an authorization to meet and we knew that they would not grant us the authorization if we applied."[24]

Murids attempting to organize religious events in the houses of the Murid shaykh, Shaykh Mbakke, in the neighborhoods of Grand Dakar and downtown Dakar suffered the same fate. The applications they submitted to colonial officials to organize sacred music concerts were typically denied. Their neighbors, most of whom were middle-class French and Africans, signed petitions complaining about the noise, citing lack of consideration for sick people and pregnant women who were unable to sleep because of the noise. The colonial administration agreed. The police complained that these concerts, which they described as "screams" and "howls," took place too frequently and constituted a danger to people's mental health because they induced a state of hallucination and hypnosis.[25]

The administration had strict regulations regarding the organization of "noisy events" in public or private space. While they were willing to make exemptions for movie theaters and for the Catholic Church, which was never refused authorization to hold processions in the heart of downtown Dakar, organize fireworks shows, or sing at Mass late at night, the Murids were always held to the letter of the law.[26] The regulations allowed the organization of religious music concerts in private space without the use of loudspeakers between 4:00 and 10:00 p.m. and only on official Muslim holidays. The use of loudspeakers was permitted once a year during the celebration of the birthday of the Prophet Muhammad or *Mawlud* (*Gammu* in Senegal).[27]

There are subtle reasons for the colonial administration's unsympathetic treatment of Murid requests. Since its founding in 1857, Dakar (or more precisely downtown Dakar) was meant to be a city of Europeans and assimilated colonial subjects.[28] Murids were not considered legitimate members of the sophisticated urban community of Dakar and therefore were not considered worthy of a place in the city's public sphere.[29] A look at the leadership of the Murid community in Dakar in the 1940s and 1950s reveals that few among them had a formal French education or held prestigious administrative or private sector jobs. Most of them were merchants, artisans, janitors, or low-level postal workers.[30] Moreover, except for one Murid shaykh who owned houses in the middle-class neighborhood of SICAP and in downtown Dakar, most Murids resided in the indigenous quarters of Medina and Geule Tapée or in the impoverished suburbs of Daaru Xaan and Pikine—spaces that had been created to accommodate unwanted rural migrants.[31]

The first Murid dahira was formed in Dakar in the Medina neighborhood in 1948. It met at the house of Gumaalo Sekk, an employee of a French trading company. Dahira members met on a weekly basis on Sunday evenings to chant Ahmadu Bamba's devotional poems, meditate about his life, collect dues, socialize, and ponder the community's business. Elhaaj Bamba Jaw, who was a longtime resident in Dakar and leader of a federation of dahiras for many years, explains how he helped found the first Murid dahira in Dakar:

> I founded a dahira for Sëriñ Fàllu [second caliph of the Muridi-
> yya, 1945–68] the year when [French president] Vincent Auriol
> visited Senegal [1948]. When I proposed Sëriñ Fàllu to form
> a dahira to help him with the building of the mosque [Great
> Mosque of Tuubaa], he first told me: "what is dahira? Let me
> first confer with my aides." . . . He asked his collaborators to
> listen to me and afterwards he said, "Go ahead and register my
> name." I went to see Gumaalo. . . . He suggested that I consult
> with Yuusu Jóob . . . who was leading a [Tijani] dahira in Dakar.
> I met with the latter and he agreed to lend me his card. I showed
> the card to Sëriñ Fàllu who told me to make one for him. I used
> the card [as a model] for our dahira. I sold the card for 25 CFA
> francs (0.62 cents) [annually]. I sent cards to Bamako, Maurita-
> nia and Côte d'Ivoire.[32]

Jaw's version of the story is not uncontested. Old Murid residents in Dakar mention others as the first founders of the Murid dahira in Dakar.[33] However, they agree with Jaw that the first Murid dahira was founded in the 1940s and that it met in the house of Gumaalo Sekk. This was the sole Murid dahira in Dakar for seven years. Jaw founded another dahira in 1958, which he named Dahiratul Elhaaj Faliilu Mbakke. This was the first Murid dahira officially registered with the administration of Senegal.[34] This license allowed the dahira to buy a hearse and secure government authorization to transport corpses to the Tuubaa cemetery.

As Murid migration to Dakar intensified, the number of dahiras grew. These dahiras were headquartered in the markets of Dakar and in the sub-urbs where most Murids lived. By 1965, the different dahiras were fused into seven federations covering Dakar, Pikine, and the city of Rufisque. Each federation was composed of dozens of dahiras. In 2004, the federa-tion of Sandaga Market dahiras included fifteen units.[35] Gradually, the tra-dition of founding dahiras reached rural Senegal. This marked a reversal of historical trends. Among the Sufi orders of Senegal, and particularly the Muridiyya, the received wisdom was that religious innovation always comes from the seat of spiritual authority—the holy city of Tuubaa—not from disciples and particularly not those living in cities. Urbanization was believed to lead to secularization and ultimately to contestation of the conservative ideology promoted by the leadership in rural Bawol.[36]

Transplantation to the city, where work and lodging imposed distance, and dispersal deprived Murid disciples of the densely textured webs of relationships linking shaykhs, disciples, families, and friends that shaped their lives in rural areas. The dahira emerged as a site for the socialization of newly urbanized Murids and an instrument to cope with the anonymity of city crowds. It was a self-help organization and an instrument for the consolidation of Murid solidarity. In the city, Murid disciples engaged in trade and other occupations that rendered inoperative the traditional mechanisms of solidarity that they developed in the Murid heartland. Moreover, settlement in town also meant separation from the shaykhs who provided moral support and guidance. The dahira thus may be seen as a means of preserving Murid identity and sociability in an urban setting. For the Murids it played a role similar to that of hometown or ethnic associations that helped recently urbanized people in colonial cities in Africa maintain social cohesion.[37]

The dahira was also pivotal in promoting and defending the interests of Murid traders who were newcomers in the city and operated in a sector of the economy that at the time did not have access to collective bargaining and labor unions. Ngañ Caam, an elderly Murid trader, explains the role of the dahira in the Murid urban community: "In Dakar, we were dispersed in different neighborhoods. The dahira allowed us to bond and know each other's problems and concerns. The money we collected served to help the needy among us; support those of us who would run in trouble with the police; contribute to naming ceremonies and funerals; help transport the deceased to the cemetery of Tuubaa for burial."[38] The dahira helped disciples leverage power to influence governmental action. For example, when faced with the threat of eviction from downtown Dakar, the dahira of Murid merchants, with the support of caliph Faliilu, was able to convince the government to abandon the initiative. More recently, the dahira was able to stop a project initiated by a businessman to destroy dozens of shops for the construction of a seven-story building at Sandaga Market. According to one of my sources, if allowed to go forward, the project would have cost four hundred family heads of household their livelihood.[39]

CHANGING ROLES OF THE DAHIRA

As Murid urban migration intensified and the Murid migrant profile transformed, the vocation of the dahira also changed. The dahira has transformed from a conservative institution seeking to shield Murid values from the "corruption" of city life into a dynamic instrument to promote Murid identity in urban and rural settings. Until recently, most dahira activities were geared toward preserving Murid identity in cities that were deemed dangerous to one's faith. Cities are in fact centers for the diffusion of threatening French secular and anticlerical culture over which Islam has no authority. They promote a type of individual freedom that challenges Islamic morality. Murids displayed their religious and cultural identities through the naming of their shops and the exhibition of religious icons and arts in their workplaces and houses, drawing a boundary with the polluted secular city space.[40] They looked to their heartland of Bawol as their real home.

This attitude started to change in the early 1990s, but the transformation can be traced back to the late 1970s.[41] In 1975, Murid students from the city of Saint-Louis, influenced by the teachings of the Murid Shaykh Abdoulaye Dièye, founded a dahira at the University of Dakar. This was the first Muslim religious organization created in this institution known for its left-wing political activism in the postcolonial era.[42] Students were particularly concerned with spreading Ahmadu Bamba's teachings and historical legacy among the youth. They seemed to be less preoccupied with networking and consolidating brotherly bonds than were the traders of Sandaga Market. They focused their activities on transcribing (in Latin script) and translating Bamba's original writings in classical Arabic to French.[43] They offered Arabic classes and gave lectures on the life and teachings of Ahmadu Bamba in the French language. Following their lead, the Federation of Young Murids was founded in Dakar in the late 1970s. This association consisted of students, civil servants, merchants, and artisans. They positioned themselves to be powerful political stakeholders in Dakar and urban centers across Senegal. Every year during the end-of-year celebrations, the federation organized religious ceremonies that brought together thousands of young people to Dakar's Iba Mar Diop Stadium. They organized recruiting drives in cities across Senegal, traveling with modern audiovisual equipment to preach and hold singing sessions.[44]

The increasing visibility of young Murid disciples on the urban cultural scene and the popularity of the third Murid caliph, Abdul Ahad Mbakke (1969–88), seen as a defender of the poor at a time of economic hardship, contributed to changing popular perceptions of the Muridiyya, even among Muslim reformists known for their hostility to Sufi orders. In 1977, the Muslim Cultural Union (UCM, French acronym), an organization founded by Muslim reformists trained in Arabic educational institutions in Senegal and the Muslim world, organized the first cultural week dedicated to Ahmadu Bamba in Dakar to commemorate the fiftieth anniversary of his death.[45] For many city dwellers, this was their introduction to Ahmadu Bamba's teachings beyond the hagiography recounted by devout Murid disciples. Western-educated Murid intellectuals such as Shaykh Abdoulaye Dièye, preaching in French and Wolof, undertook a vigorous campaign to promote the religious and nationalist credentials of the founder of the Muridiyya in a language and style increasingly attractive to urban dwellers, especially the youth.

This dynamic was boosted by the democratizing policies and economic reforms of President Abdou Diouf, who took over after the resignation of the first president of Senegal, Leopold Sédar Senghor, in 1980. By adopting multiparty politics and allowing a free, privately owned press, Diouf's policies energized Senegalese civil society. Muslim organizations became vocal participants in public debates.[46] The neoliberal economic policy imposed by the World Bank and the International Monetary Fund ended the socialist policy of Senghor and created opportunities for Murid businessmen who controlled the informal sector of the Senegalese economy. In Dakar, wealthy Murid traders and transnational migrants started to buy houses, especially in the new neighborhoods of Parcelles Assainies, Scat Urbam, Kër Xaadim, and HLM Sud Foire.[47] In Saint-Louis, Murid migrants gradually became a major economic force led by the Suraŋ family, who monopolized the leadership of the city's chamber of commerce.

One result of the renewed dynamism of the Muridiyya in Dakar was the expansion of the dahira and the diversification of its functions.[48] The youth in the middle-class neighborhoods of SICAP and HLM became increasingly attracted to the Muridiyya, which in the recent past they snubbed as an organization of Bawol-Bawol peasants.[49] This change of perception may be explained by the image of Ahmadu Bamba as a hero of national resistance to colonialism, the postcolonial state's loss of prestige due to continued pauperization, the failure of the Western educational system, and the celebrations of the hardworking Murid entrepreneurs sung by Senegalese pop stars.[50] Renewed interest in the Muridiyya led to the creation of many dahiras and associations founded by young disciples born and raised in the city. These changes gradually transformed the Muridiyya from a religion of transient migrant farmers to that of modern urban citizens.

These transformations generated tensions, especially in the cities where the Muridiyya is in intense competition with more entrenched Sufi orders and reform-minded Muslims. Leaders of the Sy Tijaniyya, which was dominant in Dakar and the large Senegalese cities, felt threatened by the increasing assertiveness of the Muridiyya. Tijani students at the University of Dakar founded their own dahira in 1979, four years after the Murids. The same year, an anonymous tract was circulated at the headquarters of the Senegalese government. The tract attacked the Murids as bad Muslims and branded the Baay Faal, a colorful but controversial subgroup within the Muridiyya, as heretics. It touted the Tijaniyya as an orthodox organization that controlled 99 percent of the mosques in Senegal and deemed Tijani disciples as sincere Muslims who took their religion seriously.[51] Tensions between the two Sufi orders led to physical confrontations in Tivavouane, the holy city of the Sy Tijaniyya, and in other cities. It took the interventions of Abdu Aziz Sy and Abdul Ahad Mbakke, the then heads of the two competing organizations, to calm the situation.[52] The aggressive proselytizing of young urban Murids and their determination to stand against critics of their organization also led to conflicts with reformists critical of what they claimed were heterodox Sufi practices.

Murids and Tijaans have now grown closer, probably motivated by the growing influence of the anti-Sufi movement that represents a threat to both groups. Anthropologist Abdou Salam Fall mentions the existence of an interbrotherhood organization in Pikine.[53] It is not surprising that such an initiative would take place in the suburbs of Dakar, a hotbed of Islamism in Senegal, particularly during its heyday in the 1980s and 1990s. The interviews I recorded among Murid disciples in Dakar in the late 1990s also reveal an ecumenical discourse promoting fraternity and attempting to downplay the rivalries between the two largest Sufi orders of Senegal. In their many religious commemorations in Senegalese cities and their holy cities, dahiras affiliated with different Sufi orders have routinely supported and also collaborated with each other.

THE MÀGGAL OF TWO RAKAAS IN SAINT-LOUIS

Although Murid influence in Dakar has been growing since the 1970s, it was in Saint-Louis where the first major Murid urban event took place. The Murid community of Saint-Louis was smaller than that of Dakar, but the leadership of this community was primarily composed of Murids indigenous to the city, in contrast to Dakar where most of the leaders were recent immigrants. The Muridiyya has a long history in Saint-Louis.[54] Ahmadu Bamba visited the former capital of AOF and Senegal at least six times. Some of his brothers and first companions married in the city. By the late nineteenth century, the Muridiyya had gained a small following among the *doomu ndar* (children of Saint-Louis; *ndar* is the Wolof name for Saint-Louis), as the indigenous inhabitants of the city proudly call themselves. However, the Murid order had not succeeded in building a strong foothold in Saint-Louis until recently.[55]

Here is how Mustafa Cuun, an elderly Murid from Saint-Louis whose father was among Ahmadu Bamba's first disciples in the city, describes the standing of Murid disciples in Saint-Louis: "In the past there were only qadiri and tijani in Saint-Louis: Elhaaj Malick Sy [founder of the Sy Tijani order] studied here. . . . At the time when the Murids would sing, people would close their windows. They used to beat the Murids up. They did not want the Muridiyya to develop. When I was growing up, there was a handful of Murid houses in Saint-Louis. Our family house was the headquarter. The Muridiyya was concentrated in Sancu Suuf."[56]

Aale Faal, another disciple of the Muridiyya from Saint-Louis, tells a similar story:

> At that time, there were not many Murids in Saint-Louis. There was a majority of Tijaan and Qadiir (disciples). In Saint-Louis, they had this tradition of inviting all the communities when they hold religious ceremonies. But since the Murids were the minority, they always sang last. There was the Tijaan first, then the Qadiir. Sometimes, some people would deny the Murids their turn to sing. . . . I remember that many of my friends were kicked out of their houses because they became Murids and their parents believed that they were lost and will fail at school.[57]

The Muridiyya was controversial in Saint-Louis because its key figure in the city was Shaykh Ibra Fall, the head of a subgroup that neglected praying and fasting, two important Islamic canonical rituals. The Murid order had a small following in the city, but its constituency was mostly confined to the impoverished fisherman's neighborhood of Get Ndar and among so-called casted people (bards, smiths, leather- and woodworkers). Unlike the situation in Dakar, however, the core group of Murid disciples in Saint-Louis originated from the city and could claim a double identity as Murids and doomu ndar. This position gave them the legitimacy to push for greater visibility for the Muridiyya in public space.

The idea of starting a Màggal in Saint-Louis originated in 1976 from a small group of Murids led by teacher and former left-wing political activist Madické Wade.[58] Màggal is the typical name Murids give to their religious commemorations. Wade and his fellow disciples formed a *kurel* (Wolof for "association") that intended to commemorate what they perceived as an important but hidden chapter in the confrontation between Ahmadu Bamba and the French colonial administration of Senegal. This was the prayer that Ahmadu Bamba performed in the office of the governor in Saint-Louis where he stood trial on September 5, 1895. Caliph Abdul Ahad, who shared the belief that there was a conscious attempt to hide this fact from the Senegalese people, welcomed the kurel's initiative.[59] Wade's claim that Ahmadu Bamba's prayer in the governor's office was hidden from the populace is intriguing. In fact, this event has been recounted by Murid public preachers, sung by Murid poets, and reenacted in popular plays.[60] There is even a visual representation of the act reproduced by Senegalese artist Alpha Waly Diallo in a famous reverse-glass painting popularized by Oumar Ba.[61]

The first Màggal, called "Màggal of two rakaas," took place in the Mosquée du Nord in June 1976.[62] This mosque was built by the French in 1848, and its convenient location in the city center made it a suitable place for the event. The celebration lasted one day. Mustafa Lo, a grandson of Ahmadu Bamba and eminent Arabic-speaking intellectual, gave a well-attended public lecture, and Murid women fed and housed the guests. This first Màggal may have rekindled the enthusiasm of the Murids of Saint-Louis as Wade argued, but it achieved only limited success. The then famous Murid public preacher Xaadim Mbakke (not to be confused with the IFAN researcher of the same name) declined the invitation to participate, and the kurel also failed to convince renowned Murid religious singers and some of the Murid notables of Saint-Louis to attend the event. Many of these people may have doubted the ability of the Muridiyya to mobilize the Francophile Saint-Louis population, most of whom belonged to the Qadiriyya or the Tijaniyya orders and did not want to be associated with a potential failure.[63] Some elder Murids, who had never thought of organizing an event of that magnitude in Saint-Louis, may have resented the daring initiative of the younger generation, or they wanted to avoid tension with the city's non-Murid Muslim majority.

The Màggal organizers were more successful in the following years. The improvement was due to a new strategy that aimed to make the event a national commemoration of the entire Muridiyya and not of the Murids of Saint-Louis alone. From 1980, every edition of the Màggal was dedicated to a son of Ahmadu Bamba or to one of his early companions. From 1983 on, the late Shaykh Murtada Mbakke (d. 2004), the youngest son of Ahmadu Bamba, became a regular participant. This created an atmosphere of emulation among the different

Murid lineages that competed to make their "day" the most successful. They mobilized their disciples, contributed large sums of money to organize the Màggal, and formed motorcades of dozens of cars that paraded the streets of Saint-Louis. The leaders of the kurel also traveled throughout Senegal to attend Murid religious commemorations and promote their initiative.

From a one-day event, the Màggal has become a weeklong celebration spanning the first week of September[64] and has become increasingly sophisticated over the years. The organizers use modern means of mass advertising such as leaflets, banners, and radio and TV announcements to mobilize the public. Each year the Màggal attracts tens of thousands of Murid disciples. The program has also diversified. In the beginning, the kurel limited itself to convening a public lecture in the evening and a séance of *dhikr* (chanting of religious poems) later in the night. They have recently added a photo exhibit that chronicles the trials and tribulations of Ahmadu Bamba at the hands of the French colonial administration. There is also a newly added procession that departs from Wiltord (now Maître Ababacar Sèye) Stadium in the neighborhood of Sor and ends at Faidherbe Square, in front of the governor's palace. The official ceremony is held in this square, where the leader of the kurel delivers a solemn speech in French to the delegations representing the government and diverse Muslim organizations in Saint-Louis and Senegal. The event culminates in thousands of Murids filling the square and standing in prayer to reenact Ahmadu Bamba's feat in the governor's office. Murids see Bamba's shortened prayer commemorated in the office of the most powerful French administrator in West Africa, where he stood trial, as a daring gesture of defiance to colonial rule and an affirmation of the dignity of colonized Africans.[65]

The Màggal of Saint-Louis displays some characteristics that set it apart from traditional Murid religious events. The organizers preferred to use the Gregorian calendar instead of the Muslim lunar-based calendar commonly favored by Murids. They pioneered the use of banners, leaflets, and an official written program as advertising tools. The parade and photo exhibit they introduced were more typical of secular political and cultural activities. Finally, the adoption of the French language to address the audience of a Murid religious gathering was unprecedented. These innovations may be explained by the profile of the leadership, which was composed of Western-educated Murids but also by the nature of the organizers' agenda, the specific cultural identity of the city of Saint-Louis, and the type of message they wished to convey.

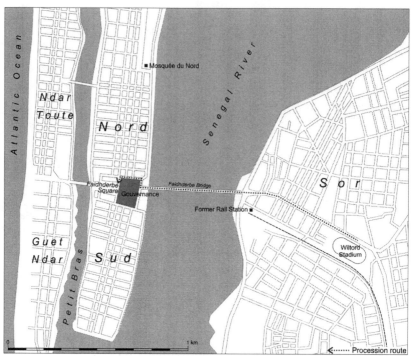

MAP 1.1. Places related to the "Màggal of two rakaas" in Saint-Louis. Map drawn by
Eric Ross.

MURID RELIGIOUS COMMEMORATIONS IN DAKAR

The success of the Màggal of two rakaas became an inspiration to urban
Murids in Dakar and elsewhere. In 1988, Magat Jóob, a Murid merchant
at the Marché du Port (Port Market), a fledging African market near the
Dakar harbor, suggested his fellow disciples organize a ceremony commemorating Ahmadu Bamba's return from exile.[66] Jóob had learned that
when Ahmadu Bamba disembarked at the port of Dakar, returning from
exile in Gabon on November 11, 1902, he had walked on Rue Malan and
Boulevard de la Libération, the two streets that border the market. He
was also informed that Ahmadu Bamba had spent some time under a tree
that is still standing inside the yard of the Catholic School of Immaculate
Conception across from his shop. He convinced a small group of Murid
merchants to form a dahira and travel to Tuubaa to ask for the caliph's authorization to commemorate the anniversary of Ahmadu Bamba's return
from Gabon.

The first commemoration took place in 1988 and lasted two hours.
The disciples read the Qur'an and organized dhikr séances. The following

year the crowd was big enough to warrant pitching a tent on a section of Rue Malan. The disciples' energy was boosted by the involvement of Shaykh Murtada, who attended some of the celebrations, and the support of the fifth caliph of the Muridiyya, Shaykh Saliu (1989–2007), who every year sent the dahira sugar and tea as his symbolic contribution.

Because of the growing size of the Màggal, tents are now pitched along the entire length of the section of Rue Malan that passes in front of the market and part of the Boulevard de la Libération. These two streets are closed to traffic for two to three days every year (against the will of some Murid merchants concerned with the loss of business) to allow for the commemoration.[67] The neighborhood public schools of Berthe Maubert and Libération are also at the Màggal organizers' disposal to accommodate their guests from outside Dakar. Caliph Saliu had particularly recommended that the dahira offer a *beernde* (a sort of thanksgiving-like feast where disciples cook a large amount of food to share with people participating in the celebration) as a way of showing gratitude to God for the safe return of their guide from exile.[68] In addition to reading the Qur'an and singing Ahmadu Bamba's religious odes, new items were added to the commemoration program. Public lectures on themes related to Ahmadu Bamba's teachings and his confrontation with the French are held, and since 2002, a procession has been organized.[69] The parade departs from Independence Square at the heart of the business and administrative district of Dakar and ends at the port. According to the organizers, this march aims to reenact the steps that Bamba took to enter and leave the ship that took him into exile and to share the blessings and rewards he received from God. Jóob denies any hidden agenda in organizing this march, but it is clear that the parade of thousands of Murids in the busiest streets of Dakar cannot go unnoticed by the government, politicians, and Muslims affiliated with other organizations.

Although there may be no firm evidence to doubt Jóob's claim of strict religious motivations, the contested meanings of the date and place in which the Màggal is organized indicate that Murids may be pursuing other goals alongside religion. The manipulation of the symbolic meanings of the date and place suggests Murid efforts to use their newly earned influence to subvert entrenched official memory of the Senegalese capital. This act of subversion could be seen as both an expression and legitimization of Murid power in the capital of Senegal.[70] November 11 coincides with the Armistice that ended the Great War and was one of the most important French colonial holidays.[71] The annual official ceremony marking this event in Senegal was celebrated at the very place (then Place Protêt, now Place de l'Indépendance) where the Murid parade begins. Boulevard de la Libération was named by the French colonial administration of Senegal to memorialize the liberation of Paris from the Nazis. But the word "liberation" carries for the Murids a different symbolic meaning. If for the French it meant liberation from the Nazis, for the Murids it meant their shaykh's liberation from French persecution.[72] Furthermore, while Murids have always associated the port of Dakar with the story of Ahmadu Bamba's deportation to Gabon, it was not until 1988 that this association was considered something worthy of celebration. In reality, it was quite the contrary. The area near the dock named "Bamba's Steps," where the Màggal of Marché du Port takes place, was long considered by Murid disciples a no-go zone, a sort of taboo.[73] This attitude reflecting the marginal position of the Muridiyya in Dakar was reversed when Murids positioned themselves as a major demographic and economic force in the capital of Senegal. The reversal of Murid attitude supports David Chidester and Edward Linenthal's suggestion that "every human attribution of sacrality is always a social construction of reality."[74] We see this social construction of reality at work in the creation of another Murid celebration in Dakar.

One of the largest Murid celebrations in Dakar takes place in the very heart of the commercial quarter of the city: the Sandaga Market.[75] This sprawling open-air market, located on the edge of Dakar Plateau between the administrative district and the indigenous neighborhood of Medina, is the center of Murid economic power in Senegal and a hub in the global network of Murid traders.[76] Sandaga's reputation reached the United States in the 1990s when a Korean businessman catering to African merchants named his store Sandaga, which is located on Broadway in Manhattan. Sandaga Market was inaugurated in 1933 as a modern African market in the center of Dakar to accommodate the growing population of the capital of French West Africa. It was intended to be a meat and vegetable market catering to middle-class Africans discouraged from shopping at the upscale European market of Kermel built in 1910.[77] But it was not long before Sandaga's intended vocation was overturned to the chagrin of colonial urban planners. Sandaga soon turned into a thriving market for the sale of watches, eye glasses, garments, cosmetics, and other merchandise imported by Murid wholesalers from Europe and, later, the United States and Asia.[78] The merchandise was then sold to Murid street vendors who defied municipal prohibition and peddled their wares in Sandaga and surrounding areas. By the 1960s, in an independent Senegal, Murid traders, with the help of their leaders' political muscle, had succeeded in securing market shops. Today, Sandaga is dotted by shops mostly owned by Murid disciples. These shops are easily recognizable, as they are named after Murid holy cities such as Tuubaa, Daaru Muhti, or Daaru Salaam and display pictures of the mosque of Tuubaa or of prominent Murid shaykhs. These same names and pictures grace the façade of Murid businesses around the world. They function both as identity markers and as talismans believed to bring good fortune.

Sandaga, like the port, is also associated with the story of Ahmadu Bamba's exile. The idea of organizing a Màggal in this neighborhood came from young Lébous sympathizers of the Muridiyya.[79] Njuga Jeŋ, a founding member and first head of the organizing committee of the Màggal, recounts that it was in September 1995 that a group of young Lébous from the neighborhood of Cëriñ decided to commemorate Ahmadu Bamba's departure from the port of Dakar into exile. Jeŋ notes that he became involved with the group because he understood that they did not know much about the Muridiyya and did not have strong relationships with the Murid community in the market. Furthermore, they could not count on the support of their parents, who belonged to rival Muslim organizations and were skeptical about the initiative.[80] The Lébous are mostly followers of the Layeen order and the Malick Sy branch of the Tijaniyya.[81] Very few among them are Murid. They have, however, kept alive the memory of the encounter between their ancestors and the founder of the Muridiyya on his way to exile. This memory and the increasing influence of the Murid order in the region of Dakar stimulated the young initiators of the commemoration.

After organizing their first Màggal in 1995, the group decided to form a dahira, which they named after Soxna Aana Fay. Fay was the wife of the Lébou dignitary who, according to Murid and Lébou oral traditions, accommodated Ahmadu Bamba during the two nights he spent in Dakar before boarding the ship to Gabon.[82] Leaders of the new dahira secured the benediction of Shaykh Saliu, who renamed the dahira Silk ul-Jawaahir (Alliance in Precious Beads) from the title of one of Ahmadu Bamba's poems. The word "alliance" suggests the relationships the caliph wished to build between the Muridiyya and the Lébou community of the capital. In 1998, the venue for the Màggal was moved from the corner of Rues Paul Holle and Emile Badiane (which had become too small to accommodate the event) to the corner of Rue Sandinièry and Hotel Clarice. Jeŋ indicated that people first had misgivings about the move, but when they learned that in fact Ahmadu Bamba had walked those streets on his way into exile, everybody agreed that this was the right place to hold the Màggal.[83]

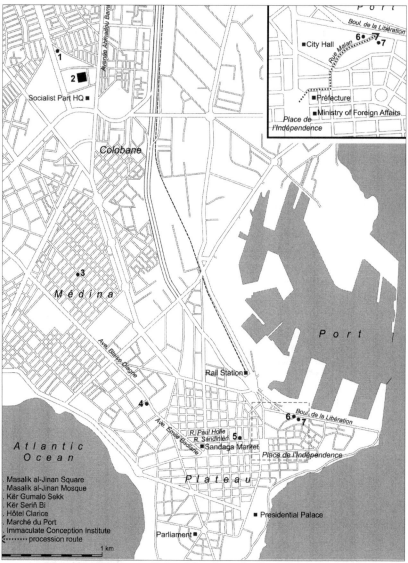

MAP 1.2. Murid historic sites in Dakar. Map drawn by Eric Ross.

The length of the celebration was also extended from one to three days. In 2002, a member of the organizing committee learned from an exhibition put up by the kurel of Saint-Louis that Ahmadu Bamba was not sent to Dakar on September 20 but on September 18. The dahira then decided that henceforth the celebration would be extended from September 18 to 20. During the three-day celebration that began in 2003, tents are pitched on Rue Sandinièry, the Qur'an is read hundreds of times, renowned learned Murids give public lectures, the devotional poems of

Ahmadu Bamba are sung, and large amounts of food are cooked for the guests. The change of dates and venues indicates the impact of continued historical revisions on the creation of Murid sacred space.

RESISTING MURID CLAIMS TO THE CITY

The increasing assertiveness of the Muridiyya in Senegal's cities was met with reactions ranging from open hostility to uncomfortable accommodation. Following Van Gennep, Victor Turner underlined "the peripherality of pilgrimage shrines [and] their locations outside the main administrative centers of the state."[84] Pierre Nora also observes that "sites of memories are refuges for marginalized and threatened memories."[85] If Murid historical memory cannot be construed as threatened because it is deeply imbedded in much of the Senegalese population's collective consciousness, it can certainly be seen as marginalized. The Muridiyya has become a powerful economic and political force in Senegalese cities, but sites of Murid memory are still largely provincialized and confined to its heartland of Bawol.[86] Memories of the precolonial, colonial, and postcolonial states continue to dominate Senegal's urban landscape. Most of the large avenues, squares, and stadiums are named after former French administrators, dead Senegalese state officials, precolonial rulers, or resistors to colonization. This is the case of downtown Dakar, where major streets and buildings bear the names of Gambetta, De Gaulle, Jean Jaurès, and Blaise Diagne.[87] But there is now a thoroughfare named after Ahmadu Bamba, and Murids have built the largest mosque in Dakar at one end of this street at a cost of over $35 million. The site, located on prime real estate and covering fifty-eight hundred square meters, has become the headquarters of the Murids, where all of their major events in the region of Dakar are held. The name given to this place, *Masalik al-Jinan* (Itineraries to Paradise), is reflective of Murid aspiration to stamp their history on the urban landscape. *Masalik al-Jinan* is the title of Ahmadu Bamba's most influential book.

The Muridiyya has experienced the strongest challenge to its expansion in Saint-Louis. The controversy between the Murids and some factions of the population of Saint-Louis revolves around the Màggal of two rakaas held at Faidherbe Square. When this celebration began in 1976, the local government of the city and many of its inhabitants, including some Murids, were skeptical of the initiative. This attitude of indifference soon turned to antagonism. The tension began in 1979 when the organizers added a procession to the program and a public rally in Faidherbe Square in front of the governor's palace. The governor not only banned the parade and rally without notifying the organizers but also sent the police to disperse the small group of disciples involved in the activities. He justified his actions on the grounds that the marchers did not seek proper authorization.[88]

Madické Wade, leader of the kurel, and his fellow disciples saw in the governor's actions evidence of the Senegalese government's hostility toward their organization and initiatives. To support his allegations, Wade referred to the numerous unanswered letters he sent to President Abdou Diouf and to the different ministers of information to seek coverage of the events by the public media.[89] The administration's reluctance to allow media coverage for the Màggal was uncharacteristic. President Diouf was close to the then Murid caliph, who was his staunch supporter. Thus, to understand the administration's attitude, one needs to examine the local politics of the city of Saint-Louis.

The government was certainly aware that the Màggal was unpopular among indigenous Saint-Louisiens, particularly the elite, and did not want to alienate this influential component of its constituency in the city. The government was not enthusiastic about promoting an event that it could not control and was eager to preserve the secular and Francophile identity of the former capital of AOF. Wade recalls that soon after they started the Màggal, the mayor of Saint-Louis decided to remodel and expand the Mosquée du Nord, depriving them of a venue to hold the event. He recognized that the building was old and needed restoration but found the coincidence rather suspect.[90] The kurel was compelled to find an alternative site.

However, the 1990s saw the municipality and members of the larger public expressing openly their opposition to the Màggal. The cause of the intensifying opposition was the demand of the Màggal organizers to rename Faidherbe Square after Ahmadu Bamba. Wade indicated that before making this demand public, he had sent a number of letters to the president of Senegal and to the mayor of the city, neither of whom responded. Finally, under pressure from the Murid youth and with the approval of the organizing committee, Wade made the request publicly in his solemn speech of September 5, 1990.[91]

The demand sparked a public outcry. The mayor's and governor's offices voiced their strong opposition. Some people argued that Ahmadu Bamba was not from Saint-Louis and therefore did not deserve to have his name attached to such a symbolic place. Others mentioned that Faidherbe was part of the historical memory and heritage of Saint-Louis, and as the most influential governor in the history of Senegal, his name should continue to be honored.[92]

The Murids responded by arguing that almost all of the streets, bridges, and squares of Saint-Louis are named after French colonizers and soldiers who were obviously not born in the city. They underscored the nationalist credentials of Ahmadu Bamba by emphasizing his sufferings and heroic resistance at the hands of the colonial administration. They blamed public opposition to their proposal on the works of the alienated Westernized Saint-Louis elite and the Freemasons who were determined to hinder the expansion of the Muridiyya in the city.[93]

As a response to the kurel's criticism, the mayor renamed some streets after prominent notables of Saint-Louis but refused to heed Murid demands.[94] The consul of France in Saint-Louis added his voice to the chorus, warning that the alteration of the French cultural heritage of Saint-Louis could harm the cooperation between the city and his institution.[95] The controversy continued to escalate as each episode of the Màggal became an occasion for Murid disciples to reiterate the demand for the removal of Faidherbe's name and statue from the square. The young and popular Murid Shaykh Moodu Kara, who presided over the Màggal of 1992 that was dedicated to his late father, endorsed the claim to rename Faidherbe Square after Ahmadu Bamba, bringing the controversy to the national stage.

For the two protagonists in the conflict—the city government allied with the French consulate and the majority of Saint-Louisiens on one side and the Murid community on the other—what was at stake was the revision of an important moment in the history of Saint-Louis and its political and economic implications. Saint-Louis had been the capital of the French Federation of West Africa from 1895 to 1902 and of the colony of Senegal from its founding until 1957; both positions it lost to Dakar. It prides itself on being the first modern city along the Atlantic coast of Africa. The city's typical French colonial architecture, picturesque environment (it encompasses an island), and urban culture have become tourist attractions that bring hundreds of thousands of dollars to the municipality annually.[96]

The colonial past also constitutes an important feature of the doomu ndar's identity. The city government's decision in 1995 to organize a grandiose commemoration of the centenary of the French Federation of West Africa—all while the controversy with the Murids was raging—is a testimony to the determination of the Saint-Louisiens to preserve Saint-Louis's colonial heritage.

Murid reading of the city's history was radically different. Their interpretation of the history of Saint-Louis was profoundly shaped by Bamba's odyssey. In the words of Ahmet Fall, president of the kurel since 1997, "Ahmadou Bamba's prayer of 5 September 1895 was an act of defiance to the colonial authority and a resounding defeat of their assimilationist and anti-Islamic policy."[97] In Fall's view, Saint-Louis should strive to make the celebration of this prayer a great moment in the city and the nation's life, "because it was this prayer that sowed the seeds for the independence of Senegal and for the black man's recovery of his dignity." For Fall and his constituency, the colonial past of Saint-Louis is an anachronistic reminder of an era that one should be eager to forget. They see Faidherbe's statue as a powerful symbol of French domination. Removing it and renaming the square after Ahmadu Bamba would be a statement against neocolonialism and an endorsement of Murid cultural nationalism.[98]

In Dakar, the Muridiyya adopted a low profile until the late 1980s perhaps because of their failure to make significant inroads among the indigenous population and because Dakar is the seat of the postcolonial Senegalese government where colonial regulations that stifled Murid commemorations in public space were still enforced. The majority of the Murid population lived (and perhaps still do) in the working-class neighborhoods of Parcelles Assainies, Pikine, Géejaway, and Caaroy and work in the different markets of the city and its suburbs. In Dakar, however, as in Saint-Louis, their increasing demographic and economic ascendancy has encouraged Murid disciples to assert Murid identity and power in some areas of the city they defined as sacred Murid space.

These areas are associated with Ahmadu Bamba's two stays in Dakar (1895 and 1920) but particularly with his arrest and exile in 1895. Lébou and Murid sources say that Ahmadu Bamba stayed for two nights in the house of a Lébou notable in the neighborhood of Cëriñ situated in the business district where Sandaga is located.[99] This event is now commemorated by an annual Màggal. However, even before the Màggal first began in the mid-1990s, wealthy Murids had tried and failed to acquire the house where the cleric is believed to have stayed, as well as a nearby property where he is said to have prayed or rested.[100] Murid dahiras have unsuccessfully tried to rent the same sites where they planned to build a shrine for pious visits. For Jeŋ, one of the leaders of the Lébou dahira, this attitude is understandable. The Lébou, as he observed, are fearful of the Murids because it is impossible to keep them under control once they have established a foothold in a neighborhood.[101] Once the Murids set foot in a place, they may end up imposing their power and influence over the entire area. The building of a four-story shopping mall in Sandaga Market by the Mbuub family and a similar seven-story project by the Sall family (both wealthy Murid business families) seem to confirm this assumption. The Mbuub named their building after Tuubaa, the holy city of the Muridiyya, and incorporated into the complex the first Murid mosque in downtown Dakar. Hundreds of Murids converge to the mosque every Friday. The Sall project, if taken to fruition, will reinforce the already strong Murid presence in downtown Dakar.

Fear of being overtaken by the Muridiyya drives owners of purported Murid sacred places to show ambivalence and reserve toward disciples' claims. The Catholic monks who run the Immaculate Conception school near Marché du Port, for example, deny Murid claims that Ahmadu Bamba sat under the tree in their schoolyard. They insist that he never set foot on the space the school occupies. The Jaañ family that owns the house where Ahmadu Bamba reportedly spent a day is suspected by some Murids of hiding the miracles associated with their shaykh's visit there. They say that there is a secret room in the house where a garden grows on dry sand, but only a small number of people have been allowed to see it.[102]

Besides their reputation for overwhelming their neighbors with their assertive presence, the Murids stir up suspicions in people because of their propensity to seek too much autonomy from the state. Christian Coulon observed that beyond its symbolic significance, the Màggal of Tuubaa constitutes a demonstration of the Muridiyya's autonomy vis-à-vis the state of Senegal.[103] Jean Copans also noted that the different phases in the development of the Murid order's history could be associated with different forms of Murid control of specific social and geographical spaces.[104] This argument is borne out by the history of Masalik al-Jinan square in the neighborhood of Bopp in Dakar. The place was first known as Guy Senghor. The Murid caliph, Faliilu Mbakke, changed the name to Tuubaa-Guy Senghor when the administrator of Dakar granted Murid disciples the permission to use the place for the celebration of *Eid* prayers.[105] When Caliph Abdul Ahad came to power in a context of growing Murid economic and political influence, he renamed the place Masalik al-Jinan, erasing the word "Guy" (meaning "baobab tree" in Wolof) and "Senghor" (the name of the first president of Senegal) to fully claim the space as a Murid place.[106] *Masalik-al-jinan* (Itineraries to paradise), a popular book authored by Ahmadu Bamba, is also the name of a Murid mosque complex in Dakar.

The oldest Murid-owned house in the center of Dakar, Kër Sëriñ Bi (the master or guide's house), is often considered "a state within the state." Murid merchants working in and around the house are frequently accused of fraudulent practices. Kër Sëriñ Bi (KSB) is located on 70 Avenue Blaise Diagne in downtown Dakar, just across from the house where Ahmadu Bamba stayed when he was brought to the city by the colonial administration in 1920.[107] As soon as the shaykh of the Murids left Dakar, Mamadu Mustafa, his elder son and first caliph of the Murids, secured his permission to buy the lot. He built a house there that served as a guesthouse for Murid disciples. KSB still accommodates Murid disciples and shaykhs seeking temporary lodging, but it has become an unregulated market where one can buy anything, particularly prescription drugs. The house has repeatedly been the target of criticism from consumer advocacy groups and members of civil society. It has been raided several times by customs officers and the police, but it has never been closed down.[108]

⤷

The recent history of the Muridiyya is marked by the continuous migration of disciples to urban centers across Senegal. The growth of Murid economic influence and demographic weight in the city is accompanied by a vigorous effort to remake the historical memory of the urban areas they settled. This effort primarily revolves around ritual remapping of the space by tracing Ahmadu Bamba's footprints in the cities and by commemorating heroic feats he has performed. His arrest, trial, and deportation in 1895, which took place between Saint-Louis and Dakar, provide Murid disciples with historical justification for their increasing assertiveness in the urban landscape of Senegal. The wrapping of Murid identity in cities around the memory of Bamba's resistance to the French stresses a dimension of his legacy that resonates well with a growing urban youth and middle class increasingly critical of the weakened postcolonial state and continuing French interference in the internal political and economic affairs of Senegal.

The religious commemorations and ritual practices that mark the public life of the Muridiyya in Saint-Louis and Dakar are not merely peripheral cultural manifestations of interlopers in the city, as Turner's and Nora's works may suggest. Rather, they are alternative sites for the ongoing interpretation of the cities' history and memory. They constitute an attempt to affirm and legitimize Murid presence and power in Saint-Louis and Dakar. This legitimizing enterprise is accomplished through the affirmation of Murid memory and the removal or blurring of competing memories. The personage of Ahmadu Bamba and the events associated with his saga, whether mythical or historical, provide a new grammar with which to read the two cities' histories. Thus, the Murid effort to reinterpret the historical memory of Dakar and Saint-Louis may be viewed as a statement about the present and the future of the two cities. And it is precisely the underlying political significance of Murid urban commemorations (and their potential economic consequences) that explains local opposition to them. In Saint-Louis, important segments of the local population and representatives of the state found themselves on the same side resisting the increasing assertiveness of the Muridiyya. The relative success of the Murids in Dakar, despite their failure to achieve their goals in Saint-Louis, reflects their greater economic power in the more cosmopolitan capital of Senegal and their influence on the central government.

The Murid experience reveals the centrality of space identity in the contest for power and authority in the urban context and how the naming of city landmarks and the events commemorated reflect the power structure of an era. Place-names are fluid and subject to reinvention and negotiation, but they can be a key to decoding the *rapport de forces* in a society at specific moments in history. The pressure of the last three decades to appropriate symbolic places in Saint-Louis and Dakar illustrates the rapid urbanization of the Muridiyya and Murid confidence in their growing power in Senegalese cities. This power is in full display in Dakar, where Masalik al-Jinan mosque (also known as Shaykh Ahmadu Bamba Mosque), the most expensive place of worship in the capital and the largest mosque in sub-Saharan Africa, was inaugurated on September 27, 2019.[109] In Saint-Louis, despite Murid protest, Faidherbe's statue is still standing in the middle of the square of the same name. A few days after the storm knocked the statue down, the municipality diligently put it back up. The fate of these two monuments reflects the diverging fortunes of the Muridiyya in Senegal's two most historic urban centers.

2 ～ Birth of a Diaspora
Murid Migrants in Côte d'Ivoire

> Côte d'Ivoire was the first destination of Senegalese migrants. It was
> a staging ground before moving elsewhere. People of all professions
> settled there.
>
> — Sëriñ Baabu

> [In the 1950s] the dahira of Abidjan was the most active and the
> wealthiest of all Murid dahiras.
>
> — Elhaaj Shaykh Mbuub

THIS CHAPTER explores the history of Murid migration to Côte d'Ivoire,
which is the most popular destination for Murid migrants outside Senegal.
It details the continuities and disjunctions between colonial and postcolonial migrations, focusing on the personal and collective experiences of
Murid immigrants in Abidjan and their efforts to build a spiritually meaningful life in a foreign land. These efforts are conveyed through acts of
personal piety, the building of religious institutions, and the appropriation
of space. This chapter reconstructs the history of the Côte d'Ivoire Murid
community: from the arrival of the first Senegalese immigrants in the late
nineteenth century to more recent developments. The first section offers
a brief discussion of the colonial-era migration that brought Senegalese
soldiers, traders, and civil servants to Côte d'Ivoire. These migrants, most
of them French citizens of the Four Communes, worked as auxiliaries of
French businesses and the colonial administration. An understanding of
this migration's history is important because it paved the way for the mass
migration of Murids to Côte d'Ivoire, an exodus that started in earnest in
the aftermath of World War II.

Many among the Murids who spearheaded the outmigration from
Africa started their journeys in Côte d'Ivoire, the two Congos (Congo
Brazzaville and Democratic Republic of Congo), or Gabon. The African
migration is also important because it provided immigrants the space to

experiment with portable economic and religious practices that facilitated Murid adjustment to the economic and cultural contexts in their host countries outside Africa. In this regard, Côte d'Ivoire played a pivotal role. It was one of the first destinations for Murid international migrants and is still perhaps home to the largest community of Murid disciples abroad. It is the site for the formation of a so-called Murid ethos of migration. Many Murid institutions and practices across the global Murid diaspora were initiated by Murid immigrants in Côte d'Ivoire. Côte d'Ivoire was also the first foreign country visited by a Murid caliph (Mustafa Mbakke, the first successor of Ahmadu Bamba) and was the preferred destination of traveling Murid shaykhs for years.

SENEGALESE IMMIGRANTS IN CÔTE D'IVOIRE

Senegalese migration to Côte d'Ivoire began during the colonial era in the late nineteenth century. The first wave of immigrants comprised military veterans of the wars of conquest, traders working for French companies based in Dakar, and civil servants called to help administer the new French colony. These immigrants played a role comparable to that of the Hausa in the Middle Belt of Nigeria that Moses Ochonu characterizes as "proxy colonialism."[1]

Because of their economic success and intellectual credentials, this first generation of Senegalese immigrants in Côte d'Ivoire helped shape the image of the Senegalese as well-educated and sophisticated citizens of the French Empire.[2] As Cerno Sulay Sall, an Ivorian of Senegalese background, notes: "These professionals and traders raised the profile of Senegalese in this country and even created a feeling of superiority complex. In social standing, the Senegalese came after the French or even were placed on the same plane than them."[3] Murids were not involved in this early migration, which mostly concerned urban dwellers and the Western educated.

From the 1960s, a new generation of Senegalese migrants headed for Côte d'Ivoire, and Murids played an increasingly significant role in this migration. This wave differed from the earlier ones in many respects. It was massive, disconnected from the colonial enterprise, and consisted mostly of younger people from rural Senegal with little Western education. Among them were jewelers and petty traders but also tailors, leather workers, auto mechanics, carpenters, and a host of other workers. The arrival of these immigrants shattered the image fostered by their predecessors of the sophisticated, highly educated Senegalese. The 1988 official census of the Ivoirian government put the number of Senegalese immigrants at 39,727.[4]

There is no breakdown of this number along religious affiliations, but it is likely that the majority were Murid disciples. Côte d'Ivoire was then living its "economic miracle" boosted by the high demand for cocoa and coffee on the international market,[5] while the rest of West Africa was hit by an economic downturn exacerbated by a crippling cycle of droughts.

In the 1980s, there were virtually no households in the small towns of the impoverished Senegalese peanut basin, the heartland of the Muridiyya, without one or more family members who had immigrated to Côte d'Ivoire. The number of Senegalese living in Côte d'Ivoire reached 150,000 in 1994, according to official Senegalese estimates.[6] Unlike the earlier generations discussed previously, for most migrants of the postcolonial era, Côte d'Ivoire was not the primary destination but the last step of a journey that had taken them to the Gambia, Mali, Guinea, or even Haute Volta (now Burkina Faso). Many of these migrants were unskilled or craftsmen/carpenters, blacksmiths, goldsmiths, tailors, and bakers who were not able to make a good living from their trade in Senegal and hedged their bets on migration.

By the 1950s, an increasingly large number of Murid immigrants had joined the migratory trail. Over a decade later, the Murids became the face of Senegalese migration in Côte d'Ivoire. Ibrahima Ngom, who migrated to Côte d'Ivoire in 1955, typifies this new generation of immigrants.[7] Ngom was born in the town of Diourbel in the Murid heartland. He left his job as a baker in Dakar in 1953 and migrated to Bamako in Mali and then to Bobo-Dioulasso in what was then Haute Volta, where he worked for two years. In 1955, he decided to try his luck in Côte d'Ivoire, where he stayed in Bouaké in the north then Abengourou, where he used his savings to open his own African bakery in 1956. Four Senegalese bakers had preceded him in the town. Ngom, who was probably a Murid, could be counted among the precursors of Murid migration across sub-Saharan Africa.

THE ONSET OF MASS MURID MIGRATION TO CÔTE D'IVOIRE

The mass migration of Murids to Côte d'Ivoire began in earnest at the end of the 1950s. The epistolary relations between the leaders of the Muridiyya and disciples in Abidjan and the annual visits they paid them suggest that Murid shaykhs supported (or at least encouraged) this new development in Murid migration. The 1957 Côte d'Ivoire census reveals that ten thousand Senegalese lived in Treichville, the neighborhood dominated by African migrants in Abidjan.[8] Hundreds among them were disciples of the Muridiyya and had their own mosque.[9] However, there is evidence of Murid presence in Côte d'Ivoire as early as the late nineteenth century. Demba Caam, a goldsmith from Rufisque, was probably one of the first Murid disciples to migrate to Côte d'Ivoire. Caam arrived in Agboville in the 1890s. He later resettled in Abidjan.[10] Elhaaj Mayib Sekk, a Murid disciple interviewed by J. L. Triaud in Abidjan in 1969, is another pioneer of Murid migration to Côte d'Ivoire. Sekk was born in 1898 in Louga, a stronghold of the Muridiyya in Senegal. He traveled to Côte d'Ivoire and landed in Cocody in the aftermath of World War I. He then moved to Abidjan in 1920 to join the small but growing community of Senegalese there.[11]

By the 1940s, the Muridiyya started to have greater visibility in Côte d'Ivoire, particularly in the neighborhood of Treichville where Senegalese were concentrated. This transformation was due to the arrival of immigrants with a history of deep connections with the Murid order and its leadership. Sëriñ Ñas and the Jóob brothers were the most influential among these devout Murids.[12] Duudu Jóob was a senior disciple of Mamadu Mustafa Mbakke, then the caliph of the Muridiyya, and Ñas was taught by Bamba's cousin and confidant, Mbakke Buso.[13] Jóob and Ñas began the process for the institutionalization of the Muridiyya in Côte d'Ivoire by founding dahiras and associations that brought disciples together. Ñas became the most high-profile Murid in Côte d'Ivoire. He was decorated several times by the colonial and postcolonial governments of Côte d'Ivoire in recognition of his service to the nation and his skill as a jeweler.[14] This status raised his profile in the eyes of the Murid leadership. Ñas remained the public face of the Muridiyya in Côte d'Ivoire for several decades. The Murid caliph Faliilu Mbakke (d. 1968) appointed him in 1945 as his official representative in Côte d'Ivoire and renewed the appointment even after his authority was fiercely contested by a rival.[15] Ñas's appointment was confirmed by Caliph Abdul Ahad (d. 1988), Faliilu's successor. In 1970, Abdul Ahad upgraded Ñas's status, appointing him as his official representative in eight more countries in both West Africa and central Africa.

Sëriñ Ñas was born in Mbakke Bawol in the first decade of the twentieth century to a devout Murid family. He grew up between Mbakke and Diourbel and studied the Qur'an with Mbakke Buso. Ñas learned his craft with his father and then with a shopkeeper cousin in Dakar, after the former's death. The stay in Dakar was critical in stimulating his interest in migration and providing him with information about traveling. He left Senegal for Côte d'Ivoire in 1933, traveling with another cousin. Following the trail of earlier pioneers of Senegalese migration to Côte d'Ivoire, Ñas opened a jewelry shop in Grand Bassam before moving to Abidjan at a time when this city was establishing itself as the capital of Côte d'Ivoire.

By the 1940s, the Murid community in Côte d'Ivoire was large enough to attract the attention of the highest-ranking leader of the Muridiyya in Tuubaa, Mustafa Mbakke, who paid them an annual visit. Côte d'Ivoire was the only foreign country the caliph had ever visited, and it was also the site of the only Murid mosque outside Senegal at the time. In a letter dated May 3, 1944, and addressed to the governor general of French West Africa, the secretary of Caliph Mustafa Mbakke wrote to seek authorization to travel to Côte d'Ivoire. He stated that he was undertaking the trip because the caliph could not make his annual journey to Côte d'Ivoire that year.[16] Côte d'Ivoire was also one of three countries where Elhaaj Bamba Jaw sent the first dahira membership cards he issued in 1948.[17]

Already by the 1940s several Murid shaykhs had disciples in Côte d'Ivoire. French colonial administrator and writer François Quesnot mentions that Shaykh Murtada Mbakke, the youngest son of Ahmadu Bamba, had bought land in Agboville in 1946, and a small colony of his disciples lived there.[18] This was also the case of Abdul Aziz Mbakke, another son of Ahmadu Bamba, who was represented in Bamako (Mali), Conakry and Kankan (Guinea), and Abidjan.[19]

Elhaaj Shaykh Mbuub, a Murid disciple who migrated to Abidjan in 1959, provides a good description of the Murid community there in the late 1950s: "I was working as a tailor when I traveled to Côte d'Ivoire [for the first time] in 1959. I found there many Senegalese who worked as tailors and in different capacities. There were many Murids. The dahira was led by Daam Sekk then Sëriñ Ñas took over. There were many Senegalese goldsmiths in Abidjan . . . The dahira was very active. Murids of all occupations used to meet there. Sëriñ Shaykh Mbakke [Gaynde Faatma], Sëriñ Murtada and Sëriñ Abdul Ahad used to visit. . . . The dahira of Abidjan was the most active and the wealthiest of all Murid dahiras."[20]

Mbuub's story suggests that before independence in 1960, a relatively large community of Murid disciples resided in Côte d'Ivoire. He notes that the dahira used to invite Murid singers of sacred music to Abidjan to entertain the disciples. He also mentions the dissension present in the dahira where opposing factions coalesced around Daam Sekk and Sëriñ Ñas. The two competed for the position of caliph representative and head of the Murid dahira in Côte d'Ivoire.[21] The caliph of the Muridiyya at the time, Sëriñ Faliilu Mbakke (d. 1968), had to send his secretary and younger brother (and future successor), Shaykh Abdul Ahad, to Abidjan to reconcile the disciples. The involvement of the caliph and the high-level delegation he dispatched to resolve the dispute clearly indicates the influence and respect that the Murid community in Côte d'Ivoire commanded.

In the aftermath of World War II, important shifts in colonial policy and transformations in the economy of Senegal encouraged the outmigration of Senegalese and Murids. The removal of restrictions on mobility encouraged migration that mostly benefited the coastal cities of West Africa, draining the population in the hinterland and the landlocked colonies of French Soudan, Haute Volta, and Niger. These migrants converged on Côte d'Ivoire and Senegal, which were the strongest economies in French West Africa at the time. Senegal had the most developed industrial and transportation infrastructures, and Côte d'Ivoire had the most lucrative cash crop economy. While Côte d'Ivoire was on the receiving end of this migration flow, Senegal was both immigrant and emigrant territory. Seasonal migrants from French Soudan (the so-called *navétanes*) who had been visiting Senegal for decades poured into the country to seek employment in peanut farming,[22] while some found work in the cities as porters, water carriers, or dockworkers. Senegalese migrants headed to the cities of Côte d'Ivoire, especially after the inauguration in 1950 of the port of Grand-Bassam and that of San Pedro in 1971, which boosted the territory's economy. Senegalese migrants mostly departed from the cities on the Atlantic coast, especially Dakar, where the port and airport were located and where information about economic opportunities abroad could be found and transportation was more accessible. Some migrants took ocean liners linking South America to Marseille with stops in Dakar and Abidjan. But most migrants could not afford the cost of travel by sea and instead took the overland route. They boarded the train in Dakar and then landed in Bamako, where they embarked on a six-day truck ride to Abidjan. This migration circuit was dominated by Murid entrepreneurs such as Yaba Laam, who welcomed migrants in Bamako and arranged for their transportation across the border to Côte d'Ivoire. It is likely that Laam also helped migrants find contacts among fellow Murid disciples in Abidjan.[23]

CHANGING PATTERNS OF MIGRATION

The intensification of Murid migration to Côte d'Ivoire that began in the late 1950s was driven by transformations both internal and external to the Murid order. With the death of Shaykh Mustafa Mbakke, the first successor of Ahmadu Bamba in 1945, the internal migration toward eastern Senegal, which had been underway since he became head of the Muridyya in 1927, began to taper off. The peanut economy crisis fueled by the war had rendered peanut farming less attractive. With the end of forced labor and compulsory military conscription, the protection that Murid Shaykhs's remote villages offered was no longer needed. These changes favored redirection of migration flows to the cities of Senegal first, then to the French colonies of western and central Africa, and later to Europe and the United States. By the 1980s, the peanut basin, the heartland of the Murids, had displaced the Senegal River Valley as the primary source of international migrants.[24] The Murid leadership welcomed the monetary contribution of the more affluent urban Murids for the construction of the Mosque of Tuubaa, which started in 1926 and lasted thirty-seven years.

Among those who seized the opportunity to migrate across West Africa were Murid craftsmen and traders who had been migrating to Dakar since the end of World War II and who now could use their status as French citizens to explore other destinations outside Senegal. Living in Dakar allowed them to learn about the potential economic benefits that different foreign territories and countries offered and the vocational niches where their skills could be used profitably. They understood that in some of the French colonies of western-central Africa, artisans were in short supply. This was the case, for example, in Côte d'Ivoire, Congo, and Gabon, where Senegalese goldsmiths, masons, carpenters, bakers, and tailors converged. Not all of these migrants were poor or jobless. Most of them made a relatively decent living but migrated to improve their income or maintain social status. The migratory itinerary of Sëriñ Baabu, a Murid disciple who grew up in Mbacke in western-central Senegal, is illustrative of this migration. Here is the story of his journey to Abidjan:

> I left Senegal for the first time in June 1959. I took an ocean liner named *General Mangin*.[25] In those days, you had ships linking the West African coast to Marseille. . . . I boarded the ship without tickets. When a ship docked in the Dakar harbor, the tourists would disembark for sightseeing and shopping. There was not tight security. The gendarmes would guard the entrance to the ship, but people were allowed onboard to buy stuff or just to visit. . . . The journey from Dakar to Abidjan lasted four days. I stayed in Abidjan for three years. . . . I ate at my brother-in-law's house. . . . I only knew of one dahira in Côte d'Ivoire in the late 1950s and early 1960s. Few shaykhs used to visit. The dahira used to meet weekly to collect the *hadiyas* [monetary contributions]. Côte d'Ivoire was the first destination of Senegalese migrants. It was a staging ground

before moving elsewhere. People of all professions came there, including masons, artisans, traders, etc. . . . There were people who used to sell eyeglasses and some sold fabric. I just continued to sell watches and sunglasses in the streets, the same job I was doing in Senegal before leaving for Abidjan.[26]

Baabu's migratory experience is atypical. He was only nineteen years old when he traveled to Côte d'Ivoire. By then he had lived in Dakar long enough to develop familiarity with port traffic and overcome fears of being caught as a stowaway and tried by the colonial authorities. This was not the case for the majority of Murid migrants who were newcomers in the city and less inclined to take such risks. Most Murid disciples who migrated to Côte d'Ivoire at the time took the overland route. This was the experience of Papa Khouma, a Murid disciple from Dakar, who recounted his 1979 journey from Dakar to Abidjan and then Milan in an autobiographical novel.[27] The price of the trip by sea was out of reach for many would-be immigrants. But Baabu's motivation to migrate and his description of the Murid community and their occupations in Abidjan are consistent with information obtained from other written and oral sources collected in Abidjan and Libreville.

Before leaving for Abidjan, Sëriñ Baabu worked as a street trader at the Sandaga Market, selling watches and eyeglasses. On a good day, he could earn $20, a significant sum of money at the time, particularly for a bachelor. He lived with fellow Murid disciples in the house of the Murid shaykh, Moodu Maamun Mbakke, in the Medina neighborhood. The connections he made while living in the shaykh's house and working at Sandaga allowed him to integrate with networks of disciples and access information about their migration projects and the living and working conditions in potential destinations. This experience also created the incentive to migrate despite his own relatively comfortable economic status. Knowing that his cousin and her husband lived and worked in Abidjan probably influenced his decision to migrate. Baabu's example illustrates the continuity between the earlier internal rural-urban migration of Murid disciples in Senegal and the West African migration that took place in the 1950s.

The pace of Murid migration to Côte d'Ivoire accelerated, especially during the droughts and economic crises of the 1970s and 1980s. The rain shortages that plagued the Sahel dealt a blow to Senegal's agriculture, which was already saddled with depleted soils and low productivity. Drastic structural adjustment and economic reforms imposed by the World Bank and the International Monetary Fund further compounded the burden. These transformations pushed large numbers of farmers to leave the countryside and look for a better life in the cities of Senegal and in foreign countries. The Murid caliph's denunciation of the exploitative cash crop economy of Senegal and his strong connections with Murid immigrants encouraged the migration. People started to migrate directly from their villages, skipping Dakar altogether and taking advantage of family and village connections in the expanding diaspora.

Trade networks developed alongside (and overlapped with) family and village networks. The art trade is a good example of this trend. In the 1960s and 1970s, Aziz Mekouar, a Moroccan-born Senegalese trader based in the town of Mbacke bought masks and other wood carvings in bulk from professional Murid Laobe sculptors and shipped these items to Murid business entrepreneurs in Côte d'Ivoire.[28] These entrepreneurs, in turn, sold the inventory to Senegalese merchants and street vendors who sold the artifacts to European tourists or reexported them to Europe. Khouma, whose journey to Abidjan was previously mentioned, might well have been one of those vendors. He sold Laobe-made antique art objects, ebony masks, and statuettes to French and Italian tourists in Abidjan.

Beyond family and trade networks, there were occupational networks. Murid tailors such as Elhaaj Shaykh Mbuub helped their young Senegalese apprentices migrate. During his fourteen-year sojourn in Mali, Mbuub has helped relocate and train seventy Senegalese apprentices who now live with their families in Bamako.[29] Murid artisans in Abidjan have done the same. During my fieldwork in Abidjan in December 2014, I visited many leatherworkers' and tailors' shops where immigrants from the same family worked together.

From the 1970s, the majority of Murids in Côte d'Ivoire were independent artisans who managed their own shops.[30] Some of the most successful goldsmiths had shops at the upscale market of Bardot or Bardo. Among those were members of the Gey family of Cawaan, a village in the region of Kajoor in Senegal. One family member, Elhaaj Bamba Gey, leader of the Murid community of Treichville, recalls the history of their migration to Abidjan:

> I came here [in 1966] to join my cousin, Shaykh Waaly Gey. His mother is my mother's sister of same father and mother. . . . I am a jeweler. That is what brought me here. Shaykh Waaly must have come to Abidjan in 1949/50. He joined our uncle Ahmad Caam Këkës who was already working and living here. Waaly was trained by Ahmad Caam. He later opened his own shop.

I completed my training with him. At that time, all the space after rue 38 [in Treichville] was a forest. The best dwellings in Treichwille were shoddy wooden shacks.[31]

Another cousin, Elhaaj Medun Gey, migrated to Abidjan but later left for Libreville in Gabon where he opened the first African gold jewelry shop. Traders like Elhaaj Yande Jóob, who dealt in artifacts, and Sëriñ Samb, who imported watches from France, also had shops in downtown Abidjan. Some, like Murid Shaykh Abdul Aziz Mbakke, exported gold from Côte d'Ivoire, which he traded in Antwerp. These businessmen would initiate Murid migration to other African countries and Europe.

MURID DAHIRAS IN CÔTE D'IVOIRE

The settlement of Murid disciples in Côte d'Ivoire predated the formation of the first Murid dahira, but these Murids quickly adopted this innovation. Murid immigrants in Côte d'Ivoire established the first dahira outside Senegal, and this dahira was responsible for building the first house dedicated to Ahmadu Bamba abroad. The attention that the Murid leadership payed to disciples in Abidjan suggests the significance of their contribution to the Murid order. They were the inventors of a Murid diasporic ethos: a means for preserving and consolidating one's Murid identity while living away from the Murid shaykhs and holy sites in Senegal. Now Murids in Côte d'Ivoire have lost the influence they once enjoyed to disciples in France, the United States, and particularly Italy, where Murids are wealthier and more creative culturally. However, it is important to remember that many among the leaders who brought the Muridiyya to Europe and North America started their careers in Côte d'Ivoire. Their experience in this country shaped their spiritual lives and the institutions they helped build in their Western host countries.[32]

The history of Murid dahiras in Côte d'Ivoire is intimately associated with Elhaaj Sëriñ Ñas, the representative of the Murid caliph in Côte d'Ivoire in the 1950s and 1960s. Ñas founded the first official Murid organization outside Senegal. He named the organization Union Fraternelle des Musulmans de la Secte Mouride de la Côte d'Ivoire (Fraternal Union of the Muslims of Murid Sect in Côte d'Ivoire). The organization was officially incorporated in Abidjan on December 5, 1950.[33] Ñas may have been inspired by Elhaaj Bamba Jaw, who had sent him membership cards when he instituted the first Murid dahira in Dakar in 1948.[34] This episode illustrates the circulation of ideas and experiences within the Murid diaspora and the cross-fertilization between home and diasporic cultures.

However, the name that Ñas gave his association suggests an effort to adapt to a religious context significantly different from that of Senegal, where Muslims formed the majority of the population, and the Muridiyya enjoys much influence over the administration. The omission of the word "dahira" in the name of the organization and use of words such as "union" and "fraternal," which are common in naming civil society organizations, can be understood as an effort to communicate with the French colonial administration of Côte d'Ivoire in a familiar language. It is also an illustration of the Murids' willingness to learn from others to adapt to their new environment.

The organization that Ñas founded gradually turned into a conventional Murid dahira with a fixed headquarters, fulfilling the typical role of dahira as a place of worship, education, and socializing. The dahira was also in charge of organizing the Màggal for those who could not afford the travel to Tuubaa and the different Muslim holidays. In addition, it served as a conduit linking disciples in Abidjan to the Murid leadership in Senegal.

The dahira of Abidjan is significant in that it served as a model that inspired Murids across the diaspora. Many of the activities that dahira perform today were inaugurated in Côte d'Ivoire in the 1940s and 1950s. The Abidjan dahira established the tradition of collecting and sending money from the diaspora to the Murid caliph in Tuubaa.[35] The Murids of Abidjan also claim to have built the first house dedicated to Shaykh Ahmadu Bamba outside Senegal. Elhaaj Bamba Gey, a murid disciple who migrated to Côte d'Ivoire in 1966, explains the history of this house, which is still standing in Treichville: "We [Murid disciples] bought this house in 1940. The place was then swampy land where people dumped discarded broken cars and tires. The name of Sëriñ Tuubaa was put on the deed. We gradually built here a *mbaar* and one room plus a crude bathroom. Sëriñ Murtada used to stay in this room."[36]

Gey explains that after acquiring the plot of land, the Murids built a temporary shelter and a room in corrugated iron panels to serve as a mosque, a meeting place, and lodging for visiting shaykhs. Murid communal houses around the world fulfill similar functions. The disciples were initially reluctant to build using durable materials because they thought of their journey in Abidjan as temporary. They also believed that investment should primarily be directed at Tuubaa to support the Murid caliph's project of building a mosque there. Differing visions between generations of Murid immigrants led to tensions in the community over the project: the younger generation favored developing the site, and older disciples preferred maintaining the status quo. In the diaspora, generational con-flicts often pit conservative elder Murids resisting change against younger disciples more open to religious innovations. And these tensions often lead to the breakup of dahiras. Elhaaj Bamba Gey, then among the young Murid disciples, remembers how he was rebuked by Sëriñ Ñas, the then leader of the community, who criticized him for suggesting they destroy the temporary shelter and build a modern brick house in its place.[37]

In the Abidjan dahira, the generational rift started to heal in the 1990s when many of the aging Murid immigrants realized that while they still nourished aspirations to retire in Senegal, this could only realistically be achieved after they had passed away. It is remarkable that while many among the first generation of Senegalese immigrants in Côte d'Ivoire are buried in the cemeteries of Kumasi and Bassam, none among the pio-neers of Murid migration to Côte d'Ivoire have their tombs there. Murids choose to die in Senegal or to have their bodies repatriated after death for burial in the necropolis of Tuubaa or other Murid burial grounds.

Now many Murid disciples are married and have children in Côte d'Ivoire, and their families have put down roots in that country. This is par-ticularly true of artisans (tailors, shoemakers, jewelers) whose skills were not marketable in Europe and who therefore did not appreciate the mobil-ity of traders. In addition, the economic prospects in Senegal were not ap-pealing; therefore, for many, returning home was not an option. Disciples also started to feel that Ahmadu Bamba, who was "the true owner of the Murid house," deserved better. This sentiment dawned on some Murids, especially when the leaky roof of the temporary shelter became a major nuisance in Abidjan's rainy tropical weather.[38]

The arrival of Shaykh Murtada Abdul Ahad (not to be confused with his uncle, who is the youngest son of Ahmadu Bamba), a grandson of Ah-madu Bamba, in Abidjan in the 1980s galvanized the Murid community to raise the necessary funds to rebuild the Murid house. His father, Caliph Abdul Ahad, was nicknamed "the builder" because of his commitment to translate Ahmadu Bamba's vision for Tuubaa, laid out in his poem "Mat-labul Fawzayni," into spatial reality. Relying on substantial contributions from the Murid diaspora, the caliph had spent billions of francs CFA (back then one dollar equaled 250 CFA francs; since 1994, the ratio swings be-tween 500 and 600 CFA) to refurbish the central mosque of the city, built a modern library, a printing press, and a guesthouse. Shaykh Murtada was certainly inspired by his father's example.

Shaykh Murtada started his campaign to rebuild the house in 1991. He sent a letter to members of the Murid community urging them to mobilize and build a house worthy of its owner, Shaykh Ahmadu Bamba. Disciples were solicited to contribute money, labor, or any resources that could help bring the project to fruition. Mangoone Gey, a wealthy jeweler, donated thirty-five grams of gold.[39] Workers whose skills could be useful for the project pledged their labor. Some volunteered to tour the markets of Abidjan to encourage fellow disciples to contribute. The money raised funded the construction of a three-story cement and concrete building comprising a mosque, a library, and a private apartment for visiting shaykhs on the first floor, a Qur'anic school on the second floor, and a large terrace and private rooms on the third floor that serve as living quarters for needy guests. When I visited in December 2014, among these guests were a number of young male migrants looking for work, including some non-Murids. Some are temporary sojourners hoping to save enough money to continue their journey to more potentially prosperous destinations.

The relationship between guests and their hosts is fraught with tension. Members of the dahira criticize the guests for infringing on the dahira's regulations by smoking on the premises of the house, for their reluctance to help with the upkeep of the place, and for their seeming reluctance to come to worship.[40] Some guests are accused of abusing the dahira's hospitality by continuing to benefit from free room and board after they have found a job and have the means to live on their own.[41] These tensions reflect differing values among the leadership and members of the dahira: there were the elderly disciples educated in rural Qur'anic schools, the younger generation consisting mostly of school dropouts, and city boys less motivated by faith and more interested in using the dahira as a source of social capital to fulfill their migration dreams.

The dahira meets every Sunday afternoon in the house, taking up the same agenda replicated in Murid dahira meetings around the world. This ritual practiced at the same time, in the same form, with the same content by Murids in the diaspora contributes to defining Murid immigrants as an imagined community.[42] The session I observed in Treichville mirrors similar gatherings I have attended across the United States and in France, Italy, Germany, and Gabon. Over a hundred disciples were present. The meeting opened with the reading of the Qur'an, followed by the reading and chanting of Ahmadu Bamba's devotional poems. The Imam led the collective dusk prayer, while the latter part of the gathering was devoted to business. At every weekly meeting, three tables are set up by the building's entrance with officers holding registers. Each officer is in charge of collecting money for specific purposes: a portion of monthly dahira dues is sent annually to the caliph to contribute to the Murid order's projects, funerary funds are collected for the repatriation and burial of deceased disciples in Murid necropolises in Senegal, and money for utility bills and groceries is raised to feed people seeking temporary shelter in the house. Exceptional funds are raised for special occasions. The evening I was there, disciples in attendance were asked to contribute money toward the celebration of the Prophet Muhammad's birthday that would take place in a few days. A committee was formed to collect donations from Murid businesses throughout Abidjan. Before closing the meeting, the head of the dahira announced the death of a disciple and invited the people to visit the bereaved family and help prepare for the funeral.

Shaykh Murtada's initiative in Treichville inspired other Murid communities in Abidjan and throughout Côte d'Ivoire to build their own houses dedicated to Ahmadu Bamba. Successful initiatives by a dahira often elicit emulation from peers who strive to prove their worth. Murids in the Abidjan neighborhoods of Adjame and Kumasi, for example, bought a plot of land and built their headquarters to fulfill the same functions as the Treichville house. The Murid community of the nearby old port city of Grand Bassam, where Ahmadu Bamba marked a stop on his way to Gabon, has also built a large mosque and meeting place on a plot of land donated by a female Murid disciple who bequeathed her estate to Ahmadu Bamba after her death.

The dahiras of Côte d'Ivoire, like other Murid dahiras in the diaspora, facilitate the settlement and socializing of fellow Murid disciples. In a country dominated by Christian culture, they offer Murids and other Muslims a place to experience Islamic sociability.[43] Dahiras contribute to making Murid disciples feel at home in Abidjan. However, dahiras can also be a source of strife, especially in the diaspora. There is perhaps not a single Murid dahira abroad in which disciples are not divided by leadership disputes or accusations of embezzlement of funds. Sometimes these tensions are fueled by rivalries between Murid lineages and shaykhs, by the ego of leaders, or by generational frictions.

⌇

Côte d'Ivoire remains a primary destination of Senegalese migrants. An exploration of Senegalese migration history to Côte d'Ivoire offers critical insights for understanding the history of the international migration of Murid disciples across Africa, Europe, and the United States. The story of Murid migration to Abidjan reveals the connections between rural-urban migration in Senegal, internal West African migrations, and migration outside Africa. The migrants who moved from the Murid heartland of western-central Senegal to settle in Dakar, Saint-Louis, and other Senegalese cities were the first to find their way to Côte d'Ivoire in the 1950s.

These migrants followed in the footsteps of the *tirailleurs*, commercial agents, independent traders and artisans, mostly from the Four Communes, who left Senegal to work in the expanding French Empire. While Murid migrants cannot be depicted as auxiliaries of the colonial administration (most Murid migrants are self-employed), they clearly learned from the experience of those auxiliaries and took advantage of the opportunities that the French Empire offered. Therefore, it is possible to discern continuity between colonially induced migration and Murid international migration.

But Murid migration was principally a voluntary migration stimulated by Murid disciples' personal ambition and initiative without interference from the French colonial administration or the Murid leadership. Although the Murid leadership was not the driving force behind migration, Murid shaykhs were quick to appreciate the benefits of a large, wealthy, and faithful diaspora for the Muridiyya, especially at a time when they had undertaken many ambitious projects in Tuubaa. As the site of the oldest, largest, and once most affluent community of Murid disciples abroad, Côte d'Ivoire provided the context for the construction of a Murid diasporic identity on which later diasporas across Africa, Europe, and the United States modeled their own identities. This identity was expressed through the establishment of civil society organizations (licensed dahiras), the appropriation of space (houses dedicated to Ahmadu Bamba), the annual collection and sending of pious donations to the caliph, and the organization of cultural events (Màggals, concerts of Murid sacred music, and pious visits from Murid shaykhs). As we shall see in the following chapters, Murid diasporas in Europe and the United States, while drawing inspiration from their fellow disciples in Côte d'Ivoire, also introduced new innovations to reflect the unique cultural, political, and economic contexts that characterize the countries they settled in.

3 ⌁ Gabon
"Backyard of Tuubaa"

> Gabon is special because we are very close to Sëriñ Tuubaa [another
> name of Ahmadu Bamba]. You cannot spend a day here [Libreville]
> without thinking about him or passing a place where Sëriñ Tuubaa
> once stayed. Gabon is the *tookër* [backyard garden] of Tuubaa.
> All year long, we have people visiting here and telling us that they
> want to visit sites related to the shaykh's exile. . . . There is nothing
> more satisfying than to know that you are walking in Sëriñ Tuubaa's
> footsteps. You are praying on land where Sëriñ Tuubaa once prayed.
>
> —Asan Jóob, Murid immigrant in Libreville

THE SUBTITLE of this chapter, "Backyard of Tuubaa," is an expression
I have heard many times in conversation among Murid disciples in Libreville, the capital of Gabon. This expression illustrates the centrality of
Gabon in Murid imaginaries and collective memory. Murid immigrants
in Gabon see their host country as the most sacred place of the Muridiyya
after Tuubaa, the Murid holy city in Senegal. In the introduction to this
book, I define "place" as a site of "accumulated biographical experiences."
No place in the Murid diaspora fits this description better than Gabon.
Ahmadu Bamba lived in exile there between 1895 and 1902. Murids believe that each of the locations where he was confined was the scene of
an epic battle with the French colonial administration that Bamba won.
Together, these places delineate a spiritual geography. This geography
frames the contour of a narrative that has become central to the construction of Ahmadu Bamba as a *waly* Allah, or "neighbor of God," and a successful resister of colonial oppression.[1]

Murids did not migrate to Gabon for the sole purpose of following
Ahmadu Bamba's footprints (though there is a steady stream of Murid
pilgrims visiting Gabon). However, as soon as they settled in this central
African country, the appropriation and memorializing of places they associate with their shaykh's exile, whether imagined or real, became important for them. No Murid diasporic community has spent as much money
and energy on place making than the Murid community of Gabon. While

the Murid migrants who moved to Gabon from the 1960s onward share the same economic and cultural backgrounds as those who migrated to other destinations, the exceptional place Gabon occupies in the history of the Muridiyya casts these migrants in a unique role. Beyond a search for economic betterment, Murid immigrants in Gabon believe they have a distinctive mission: the revival and preservation of the sacred history of their shaykh's exile. This missionary fervor is instrumental in shaping their religious life and their relationships with the Murid leadership and other fellow Murids. Murid immigrants' aspiration to revive and preserve the memory of Ahmadu Bamba's stay in Gabon influences their perceptions of and relations to space in the central African country.

In this study I use as examples two Murid projects in Libreville: the building of the mosque of *Montagne Sainte* (Sacred Hill) and the creation of a Murid art market to explore Murid efforts to appropriate space in Gabon and the centrality of Ahmadu Bamba's exile stories in these efforts. I reconstruct the history of the two projects, demonstrating how Ahmadu Bamba's hagiography provided a grid for a Murid sacred map of Libreville in the twenty-first century. I explain how the mosque and the market became the two most powerful markers of this sacred space. But before moving on to discuss Murid sacred space in Libreville, we must understand the history of Senegalese and Murid migration to Gabon. The chapter begins with an exploration of this history.

SENEGALESE WORKERS IN GABON

When Murid disciples began migrating to Gabon in the 1960s and 1970s, they were reviving a migratory tradition that was almost a century old, as Senegalese have been migrating to central Africa since the late nineteenth century.[2] This migration, like the migration to Côte d'Ivoire, was connected to the expansion of the French Empire and mostly concerned colonial soldiers who settled in Gabon after completing their tours of duty.

Despite similar beginnings, Senegalese migration to Gabon took a different trajectory. Unlike the migration to Côte d'Ivoire, which continued steadily from the nineteenth to the twenty-first century, early Senegalese migration to Gabon seems to have ebbed quickly. Gabon was mostly a site for the resettlement of freed slaves (the same role Sierra Leone played for Britain) and a sparsely populated penal colony (currently about two million inhabitants, immigrants included) where recalcitrant colonial subjects were sent for punishment.[3] Its administration did not require the continuous supply of African auxiliary civil servants and laborers as was the case in Côte d'Ivoire.

While Senegalese migration to other African destinations (Côte d'Ivoire, Congo) started well before the 1960s, significant migration to Gabon began in the postcolonial era and was partly the result of bilateral initiatives of the Gabonese and Senegalese governments. In 1973, the African heads of state tasked Gabon with organizing the 1977 summit of the Organization of African Unity (OAU, currently the African Union).[4] The country's capital, Libreville, was then a small town lacking the most basic infrastructure to host such an event. Albert Bernard Bongo (later Omar Bongo), then president of Gabon, asked the president of Senegal, Léopold Senghor, to help supply his country with the skilled construction workers it needed to build the necessary infrastructure for the event.[5] Senegal was already sending middle and high school teachers to Gabon in the framework of a cooperative agreement between the two nations. The government of Gabon hired French construction companies to supply the labor needed to carry out President Bongo's projects. Between 1973 and 1977, the Société de Construction et Batîment (SOCOBA) sent hundreds of Senegalese workers to Libreville, Franceville, Port Gentil, and other cities in Gabon.[6] Another French company, Dumez, recruited five thousand Senegalese laborers.[7] Many of these laborers were masons, carpenters, electricians, plumbers, and truck drivers from Dakar and nearby towns where the Muridiyya did not have a large presence. Nevertheless, a few Murid disciples were included in the group. Asan Jóob was one of them:

> I came here [Gabon] in August 18th, 1975 under contract with SOCOBA. I was sent to Franceville. . . . At that time, I was young, about 20–25 years old. I left Franceville to go to Port Gentil where I worked at the naval yard. Then I went to work for SOGEC, a company specialized in energy transportation. I worked there for 9–10 years. After SOGEC, I sought a license as an independent contractor. I know Gabon much better than I do Senegal. I have worked in many different places. I have [also] worked for the government. I settled in Libreville in the years 1992/93.[8]

Besides SOCOBA and Dumez, other French construction companies operating in Gabon such as COLAS, SATOM, and STS also employed Senegalese workers.[9] These companies were hired to build the trans-Gabon railway connecting Franceville, which was located east of Libreville, to the west of the country and the mineral port of Pointe Noire, the port of Owendo, and other infrastructures. All of these companies have been established in Senegal for years and for years relied on skilled and unskilled Senegalese workers to conduct their operations in Gabon. Other immigrants came on their own.[10] The memory of Senegalese labor migration to Gabon is still preserved in the toponomy of Libreville's neighborhoods with names such as "La La La Dakar" and "Camp Sénégalais" marking the places where Senegalese workers once resided.[11]

MURID IMMIGRANTS IN LIBREVILLE

Two things distinguish Murid migration to Gabon from other migrations: first, the symbolism of Gabon as space and its centrality in Bamba's sacred biography; second, the professional occupations of the immigrants. Gabon occupies a special place in the Murid imaginary. Although located two thousand miles from Senegal, Murids have always felt a connection with Gabon because of the time Ahmadu Bamba spent there as an exile. Until the 1960s, this connection was mostly emotional. Most Murids were familiar with the names of Gabonese cities such as Limbëlwëli (Libreville), Maayombe (Mayomba), Lambarna (Lambaréné), and Kablabisa (Cape Lopez). These are cities prominently featured in the written and dramatized narratives of Bamba's life popularized by hagiographers.

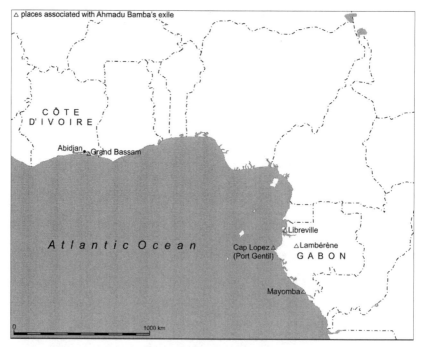

MAP 3.1. Places in Côte d'Ivoire and Gabon associated with Ahmadu Bamba's exile. Map drawn by Eric Ross.

The most influential among these hagiographers is the poet Muusaa Ka, who was literate in classical Arabic but only wrote in Wolofal.[12] Muusaa Ka developed an elaborate master narrative of Ahmadu Bamba's exiles inspired by Bamba's own writings, the Sufi tradition of *manaaqib* (hagiographic literature in which devout disciples tell of their masters' glorious spiritual and material feats), and the West African *griot* style of storytelling.[13] Perhaps the most fascinating aspect of Ka's epic poetry is his depiction of the mystical and physical battles that Ahmadu Bamba waged against the French during his exile in Gabon.

Ka popularized the story about how the crew on the ship headed to Gabon tried to prevent Bamba from fulfilling his religious duty, so he laid down his mat and prayed on the waves of the Atlantic Ocean. Ka also narrated events that took place in the localities of Mayomba, Lambaréné, and Wiir Wiir in Gabon, where Bamba battled infidel genies—converting some of them to Islam—and foiled numerous attempts on his life by French soldiers.[14] Ka's works inspired singers, playwrights, painters, and artists who have figuratively reproduced the stories he recounted to provide more accessible images of Ahmadu Bamba's odyssey to the wider Senegalese and Murid audience that cannot read Wolofal.[15] Ka has been instrumental in keeping alive Bamba's Gabonese journey in Murid memory.

Gabon eventually transformed from imagined land to tangible space as Murid immigrants settled in the central African country. Gabon was sparsely populated and was less developed than most of the French colonies in West Africa and central Africa. After independence, Gabon offered an abundance of work opportunities because so much infrastructure needed to be built: from the presidential palace, to roads, military barracks, hospitals, and schools. In addition, Gabon lacked a skilled workforce, and the French and Lebanese entrepreneurs, who dominated the secondary and tertiary sectors of the former French colonies' economies, had lighter footprints there. Finally, competition for work was less intense in Gabon than in countries such as Côte d'Ivoire or the two Congos, which had long been favored destinations of African and Senegalese migrants.

The first Murid disciples to migrate to Gabon in the 1960s were artisans and traders who were attracted by the economic prospects that the central African nation offered. Most of these migrants moved to Gabon after a stint in Côte d'Ivoire or other former French colonies in central Africa. This was, for example, the case of the goldsmiths Elhaaj Medun Gey, Elhaaj Gey, and Elhaaj Moodu Caam Zaïre, who were believed to be among the first Murid disciples to immigrate to Gabon.[16] Medun Gey first migrated from his village in western-central Senegal to Abidjan and then to Libreville in 1965. He was the personal jeweler of President Omar Bongo, ruler of Gabon from 1967 to 2009. Bongo was known for his love of luxury. He drove customized cars and wore designer clothes and precious jewelry. Gey designed Bongo's watches and eyeglass frames and made jewelry he gave as gifts to his family and important guests.

The 1970s marked the arrival of a new type of Murid migrant in Gabon. Gabon is the sole African country where traders form a minority of the Murid immigrant population. Most Murid immigrants worked in the import/export sector, as car dealers in the transportation sector, and as construction workers and contractors. Murid entrepreneurs collaborated with powerful Gabonese politicians and businessmen who funded their ventures. Construction work gradually became the most lucrative occupation of Murid migrants in Gabon. Asan Jóob, a Murid who migrated to Gabon in the 1970s, observes that "besides the French we [Senegalese] were the only contactors trusted in this country. This was the case until between 1978 and 1980, when some Togolese, Malians, and other Africans started to break out in the business of construction."[17] Jóob's account is corroborated by all those interviewed in this study who moved to Gabon in the 1970s and 1980s.

The most affluent Murid entrepreneurs in Gabon today work in the construction industry. Among these contractors, many were brought to Gabon by French companies as construction workers and ended up creating their own firms. Shaykh Amar, one of the richest Senegalese businessmen abroad, was among these laborers turned entrepreneurs. He built his construction business in collaboration with a Gabonese minister of finance. Despite the economic downturn and the tightening of immigration regulations, Murid disciples continue to see Gabon as a land of opportunity. This is particularly true for construction workers who dominate the Gabonese labor market.[18] According to the Senegalese consul in Libreville, in 2014 forty-five thousand Senegalese immigrants were officially registered with his office, and the majority of the newcomers were disciples of the Muridiyya.[19] The actual number must be larger given that only a fraction of the mostly illiterate and undocumented Senegalese immigrants registered with consular authorities. The professional occupations of Murids in Gabon, and particularly their partnering with the Gabonese ruling class and economic elites, contrast with Murid immigrants in Côte d'Ivoire, France, and the United States, where the majority of immigrants work as merchants, street vendors, or taxi drivers.

But beyond the economic opportunity it presented, Gabon was significant for the Murid disciples for other reasons. Gabon was the first French territory visited by Murid shaykhs. From 1895 to 1902 (the year his deportation order by the French ended), Bamba received a visit from several Murid dignitaries, including some high-profile disciples such as his half-brother Shaykh Anta. Ahmadu Bamba wrote about secret conversations he had with the Prophet Muhammad while in Gabon and that he had buried in Gabonese soil many of his writings related to those conversations.[20] When Murid disciples began to migrate to Gabon in larger numbers in the 1970s, they rekindled the history and memory of Ahmadu Bamba's stay there. There are several sacred sites of the Muridiyya in Gabon, each of them associated with Ahmadu Bamba's journey there. Murid immigrants have worked hard over the years to claim and memorialize those sites. As many of my interviewees in Libreville mentioned, they look upon Gabon as the "backyard of Tuubaa." Asan Jóob, the leader of the dahira of the Batavia neighborhood, expresses this feeling pointedly when he notes:

> Gabon is special because we are very close to Sëriñ Tuubaa. You cannot spend a day here [Libreville] without thinking about him or passing a place where Sëriñ Tuubaa once stayed. Gabon is the *tookër* [backyard garden] of Tuubaa. All year long, we have people visiting here and telling us that they want to visit sites related to the shaykh's exile. . . . There is nothing more satisfying than to know that you are walking in Sëriñ Tuubaa's footsteps. You are praying on land where Sëriñ Tuubaa has once prayed. Sëriñ Abdul Ahad [third caliph of the Muridiyya] told us one day that he would be our witness in the hereafter. He will testify that we did not betray Shaykh Ahmadu Bamba.[21]

When we think of the compression of space and time, we relate this development to the impact of the new information technology, cheap airfares, and the technological revolution in telephony. For the Murids, the imagined proximity between Gabon and Tuubaa rests on shared memories connected by Ahmadu Bamba's journey to central Africa.

SHAYKH MURTADA AND THE SPIRITUAL LIFE OF MURIDS IN GABON

By the late 1970s, a thriving Murid community had emerged in Libreville. Testimonies of informants such as Elhaaj Njaay, who sojourned in Gabon in the 1980s but now lives in New York City, gives a glimpse of this community: "I first travelled to Libreville in 1980. I found many murid disciples in Gabon. They worked as masons, carpenters, electricians, plumbers etc. . . . Many were brought there by SOCOBA. I also found a large dahira where we met every Sunday after lunch near Leo Mbah [he refers to the mauso-leum of the first president of Gabon in downtown Libreville]. . . . At that time, the community was large perhaps over 300 active dahira members."[22]

Today, Libreville has three more dahiras in addition to the dahira that Njaay was referring to and which Medun Gey founded in the 1970s. Seven hundred to a thousand active disciples populate these dahiras.[23] Two have built their own houses dedicated to Ahmadu Bamba, where they hold meetings, organize religious ceremonies, and provide housing for needy disciples and visiting shaykhs. The Libreville dahiras, like those of Abi-djan, are rife with conflicts that revolve around suspicion of parasitic be-havior, leadership disputes, and ethics violation. Asan Jóob, for example, complains that "there are people who we welcome when they first arrive [in Libreville]. We give them shelter, food, pay for electricity, water, ev-erything. Yet when they are well established, they tend to turn their back on the dahira."[24] He also criticizes people in Senegal, including some un-scrupulous businessmen who give the address of the Murid house to po-tentially burdensome would-be migrants with no contacts in Libreville. I have heard such criticisms from dahira leaders across the Murid diaspora. They reveal the difficulties of an institution that was primarily built to cater to cultural and spiritual needs but is now being forced to adapt to increasing economic demands in the diaspora.

Gabon was one of the earliest and most popular destinations of travel-ing Murid shaykhs. Shaykh Murtada (d. 2004), Ahmadu Bamba's young-est son, began his visits to Libreville in the 1970s well before his annual tour across North America and Europe became institutionalized in the 1990s. Beyond the status of Gabon as sacred Murid place, the popularity of Gabon as a destination among Murid shaykhs rested on the prosperity and generosity of Murid disciples there. These disciples donated gener-ously to visiting shaykhs and contributed large sums of money to support the caliph's projects in Tuubaa.[25]

Murid disciples in Gabon, under the leadership of Medun Gey, soon overtook Côte d'Ivoire as the most prosperous Murid community abroad. Gey, the first documented Murid migrant in Gabon, accommodated the first Murid gathering in his home in Libreville. Caliph Abdul Ahad later appointed him as his personal representative in Gabon. This new position, along with the prestige conferred by Gey's proximity with President Omar Bongo, boosted the dahira's dynamism. The annual financial contribution (hadiya) of Gabon disciples to the Muridiyya always topped that of all other Murid diasporas in Africa and rivaled that of communities in Europe and the United States.[26]

Gabon was important for its central role in creating Ahmadu Bamba's sacred biography and the generosity of Murid disciples living there. However, Shaykh Murtada's visit in 1993 further enshrined Gabon as an important node on the web of Murid immigrants' transnational networks. The visit was particularly significant in that it happened at a time when the Murid diaspora had garnered much experience negotiating its insertion in public space in cities in Europe and the United States. Shaykh Murtada leveraged this experience to give the Murid community greater visibility in Gabon. The shaykh's initiative demonstrates the portability of Murid diasporic culture and shows how the circulation of this culture contributes to building a common Murid diasporic ethos.

The institutionalization of the Muridiyya in the diaspora as a community of faith is intrinsically linked with the ministry of Shaykh Murtada Mbakke. He was nicknamed the "Shaykh of the Diaspora" because of his frequent travels to commune with Murid immigrants worldwide and his status as official envoy of the Murid caliph in the diaspora.[27] Shaykh Murtada lived an unusual life for a Murid shaykh and the son of Ahmadu Bamba. Unlike most shaykhs of his time, he did not build his reputation on the number of *daara tarbiyyas* he founded, the size of his peanut harvest, or the size of his community of disciples.[28] While he owned rice fields in the Senegal River Valley and was a certified trader dealing in grains (millet), he was attracted to the modern sector of the Senegalese economy where he invested in transportation, bakeries, and printing.[29] By the 1970s, he was calling for the creation of an exclusive industrial park in the vicinity of Tuubaa.[30] While the Murids are often described as the most traditional and mystical of Senegal's Sufi orders, Shaykh Murtada founded the al-Azhar organization that includes the largest and one of the most progressive private Arabic school networks in Senegal, with an enrollment of thirty-three thousand students in 2004, nearly half of them female.[31]

Shaykh Murtada was atypical in other regards as well. While Murid shaykhs, especially the sons of Ahmadu Bamba, were known for their love of sedentary village life, Shaykh Murtada developed a taste for travel at a time when transportation was problematic. He was one of the rare sons of Shaykh Ahmadu Bamba to travel abroad, and he was known for traveling frequently in punishing conditions and with scant provisions.[32] He took his first trip to North Africa in the late 1950s and early 1960s, and during his lifetime, he visited almost all of the Muslim countries in North Africa and the Middle East, including Iran.[33] He met with such leading Muslim statesmen as Gammal Abd' al-Nasser of Egypt and Muammar Gaddafi of

Libya. Nasser's support was instrumental in the foundation and expansion of Shaykh Murtada's Arabic school networks.[34]

From the late 1970s and 1980s, when a Murid diaspora started to form in Europe and North America, Shaykh Murtada established a tradition of annual visits to those disciples.[35] While some grandsons and great-grandsons of Ahmadu Bamba were frequent visitors of Murid immigrants, he was the highest profile Murid shaykh to engage the diaspora. These trips were always punctuated by religious and cultural events that helped bind disciples together and consolidate their ties with their leaders in Senegal. In his message to Murids abroad, Shaykh Murtada insisted on three things: first, the importance of worship and Islamic education, especially for the second generation of immigrants; second, hard work and honesty; and third, the creation of institutions to strengthen the bonds between the disciples and other Muslims without discrimination. He also emphasized respect for the laws and institutions of the host countries.[36]

Shaykh Murtada's connection with the diaspora allowed him to gain greater relevance and exert significant influence on the Murid organization. As the youngest of many brothers, he was unlikely to access the caliphate. Focusing his ministry on the diaspora, outside the crowded religious scene of Senegal he was able to create a niche where his message about education and cultural preservation had greater purchase.

During Shaykh Murtada's 1993 visit to Gabon, he gathered all the Murids in Libreville and talked to them about the celebrations that Murid disciples around the world hold every year to commemorate the life and work of Shaykh Ahmadu Bamba. He told them that given the centrality of Gabon in Bamba's life, disciples in this country should have been at the forefront of those commemorations.[37] He recommended that Murid disciples plan annual commemorative events to celebrate the end of Ahmadu Bamba's exile in Gabon. Here is how Elhaaj Njaga Jaw, a Murid elder who attended the gathering, remembers the meeting with the Murid shaykh:

> He [Shaykh Murtada] personally told us, "Now all over the world, including in the United States, Italy and everywhere in the world there are special days dedicated to Shaykh Ahmadu Bamba. That initiative should have started in this country where Shaykh Ahmadu Bamba has worked so hard. But perhaps the time for that had not yet come. I recommend that you start such a day of commemoration. I am also asking you to do this in collaboration with the authorities of this country so that you have the necessary official documents that will allow Murids around the world to attend the event."[38]

Jaw's account reveals the connections between Murid communities across continents and how one community's experience can influence another. Disciples living in the United States have emerged as the most influential when it comes to shaping Murid expressions of public piety in urban settings. As we shall see in the last two chapters of this book, the Murid community in Harlem was the first to earn official recognition from a local government in a Western city. This recognition allowed them to build infrastructures and organize religious events in public space. The trust, prestige, and experience that the Muridiyya earned in the United States was, in turn, used by Murids in cities across Europe and Africa to successfully negotiate their acceptance as respected members of civil society and to bolster their presence as a religious community in public space.[39]

The first Ahmadu Bamba commemoration took place in Libreville between March 29 and April 4, 1994, and was presided over by Shaykh Murtada. As stated on the flyer advertising the event, the goal was first to raise awareness about the historic ties between Gabon and Senegal and to cultivate the fraternal relations between the two countries and then to demonstrate the importance of Ahmadu Bamba's contribution to the expansion of Islam worldwide.[40] The events included a tour of the places in Gabon where Ahmadu Bamba stayed during his deportation. Pilgrims visited Montagne Sainte in Libreville, where Ahmadu Bamba is said to have prayed and survived the bullets of a French firing squad. They also traveled to the cities of Lambaréné and Mayomba, where the Murid shaykh was kept under house arrest.

The objective in raising awareness about the historic linkages between Gabon and Senegal stated in the flyer is an invitation to meditate about Ahmadu Bamba's exile in the central African country. The evocation of Bamba's exile reminds Gabonese and Senegalese of their shared history of subjecthood and sufferings under the same colonial power. It is an effort to use history to legitimize claims over space and protect the Murid community against rising nationalist and xenophobic sentiments among some Gabonese who call for a crackdown on West African immigrants.

During the celebration, Shaykh Murtada urged disciples to build a house dedicated to Islam. He had given the same recommendation to disciples in Paris and New York City. The Murids also pledged to erect a mosque on the location where Ahmadu Bamba said his prayers on Montagne Sainte. While the community enthusiastically embraced these projects, their implementation would prove to be a challenge because of leadership disputes that revealed deeply ingrained fissures between Murids of different social statuses and some disciples' resistance to the hegemony of lesser branches of the Mbakke family.

BUILDING A MURID MOSQUE IN LIBREVILLE

If the Murid house of Treichville in Abidjan is the first edifice dedicated to Ahmadu Bamba outside of Senegal, the mosque of Montagne Sainte in Libreville constitutes the most important Murid investment outside of their home country. The magnitude of the building and its cost demonstrate the centrality of Gabon in the Murid imaginary and the entanglement between Bamba's sacred biography and Murid efforts at place making. While the construction of the mosque was completed in 2013, its history is rooted in the nineteenth-century journey of Ahmadu Bamba in Gabon. Murid disciples see the erection of this edifice on the site of Bamba's confinement as a manifestation of their shaykh's ultimate triumph over the French and a sign of the enduring potency of his baraka. Murid disciples in Gabon see themselves as the vessels through which this potency is manifested. Ahmadu Bamba's exile in Gabon has become the signifier that gives meaning to disciples' migratory experiences and to the different collective projects of the Murid community in this central African country.

Montagne Sainte, a hill located in the center of Libreville, was the site of a nineteenth-century Catholic monastery.[41] When Ahmadu Bamba landed in Gabon in 1895, he spent some time in Libreville, kept in military barracks not far from the hill. Murid oral traditions, reportedly collected in the 1960s from older residents of the city, indicate that the hill was Bamba's favored spot where he used to retire for prayers and meditations.[42] Some even cast the hill as the scene of one of the most dramatic encounters between the Murid shaykh and the colonial administration in Gabon. According to Imam Nduur, one of the imams of the Murid mosque, "People believe that the story told by Sëriñ Abdul Ahad that the French threw Ahmadu Bamba in a pit [to be buried alive] happened here."[43] Echoing what has now become standard exile narrative, Njaga Jaw, an elder Murid, affirms: "Montagne Sainte is the site where the French tried to shoot Sëriñ Tuubaa. They brought the sharpest shooters in the French army and asked each of them to target one of the shaykh's body parts. That day the French soldiers saw the warriors from Badr who were protecting him. The French begged the shaykh to remove the Badr warriors from their sight. Sëriñ Tuubaa forgave everybody."[44]

This story is told by Muusaa Ka, but he did not specify where it happened. Disciples living in Gabon, then, are not only custodians of the memory of Bamba's journey in Gabon; they have also become influential coauthors in the ongoing revision of this memory.

The association between Bamba and the hill turned the former Catholic site into a Murid sacred place and a coveted piece of real estate for Murid disciples. As they have done in Saint-Louis, Dakar, and other places where Ahmadu Bamba is believed to have left his bodily imprints, Murid disciples started to conceive the project of buying the plot of land on the hill (where a house was standing) as soon as they arrived in Libreville. Shaykh Mbakke (d. 1975), Ahmadu Bamba's elder grandson, was the first Murid to try to purchase the property without success. A Murid disciple was later able to rent the house, which by then had become a pilgrimage site for disciples and shaykhs. But according to this version of the story, when the owner, who was then living in France, learned that his house had been turned into a "mosque," he expelled the Murids and later put the property on the market for sale with an asking price of $160,000.[45] Maas Njaay, an elder Murid who migrated to Libreville from Abidjan in 1974, recalls the circumstances of the Murids' purchase of the property:

> This place where we are having this conversation [Murid Montagne Sainte Mosque] also belongs to Sëriñ Tuubaa. When the house that was standing here was listed on the market for sale, it was Sëriñ Fallu Buso who contacted Shaykh Amar, who was then in Franceville, to let him know about the asking price of forty million CFA francs [$160,000] and see if he was willing to buy it on behalf [of] the [Murid] community. Shaykh Amar told Sëriñ Fallu to post a deposit of three million [$12,000] to guarantee the sale for two months. . . . At that time, Sëriñ Fallu had built a *mbaar* [a vestibule-looking shelter made of a roof sitting on four pillars] here where we used to meet. A month later, Shaykh Amar returned from Franceville and paid the owner fully and in cash. After the purchase, the notary asked that we put a name on the deed. Sëriñ Murtada proposed the name of Sëriñ Tuubaa but the notary insisted that a deceased person could not own land. Finally, the name of Sëriñ Murtada was put on the deed.[46]

As soon as the deal was closed, Buso proceeded to build a temporary prayer room on the site. Another disciple volunteered to build a well to protect a water hole that Ahmadu Bamba had used to prepare for prayers. Shaykh Murtada contributed seed money for the building of a mosque on the site, as he had done in Europe and the United States. This gesture was meant to challenge and encourage disciples to donate, but it was also understood as a blessing that would help bring the project to fruition. The Shaykh's money is believed to be endowed with sanctifying qualities that can help protect and fructify disciples' investments.

Shaykh Amar played a critical role in the building of the mosque of Montagne Sainte. Amar has become one of the most popular Murid disciples in the diaspora because of the extent of his investment in the Murid order. Amar is from the city of Diourbel in the heartland of the Muridiyya where Ahmadu Bamba was kept under house arrest from 1912 until his death in 1927. Unlike most of his fellow Murids of the time, he attended French schools. His father was the driver of the French commandant (district commissioner) of Diourbel and had close relationships with powerful politicians in postcolonial Senegal. Amar was trained at the Andre Peytavin technical high school in Saint-Louis, where he graduated with an associate's degree in iron carpentry.[47] Amar was brought to Gabon in the mid-1970s by a French contractor specializing in aluminum and glass carpentry. Shaykh Amar is now the owner of a prosperous construction company specializing in road building and in the construction of infrastructure for the Gabonese government.[48] He has won important government contracts around the country to build roads, airstrips, schools, and hospitals.

Years after the acquisition of the house on Montagne Sainte, the Murids were still unable to build the planned mosque. Controversy surrounding the leader of the project, a Murid shaykh notorious for his authoritarianism and bad temper, was a major obstacle in bringing the project to its fruition.[49] Each of the dahiras preferred to invest in their own projects. To fulfill the promise Murid disciples made to Shaykh Murtada to build the mosque, Amar took the lead and pledged to do the heavy lifting. He suggested opening a bank account dedicated solely to financing the construction of the edifice. He also offered his company's assets. Leaders of dahiras and ordinary disciples mobilized to raise funds. Volunteers toured Murid businesses on a daily basis to encourage disciples to donate. Hundreds of thousands of dollars were raised, but Shaykh Amar made the most significant contribution, estimated at least at $2 million. He oversaw the construction of the mosque from start to finish. The Shaykh Ahmadu Bamba Mosque was officially inaugurated on March 12, 2013, in the presence of Senegalese and Gabonese government officials.[50] It is a two-story building with a large prayer hall for male worshippers on the first floor, a prayer space for women on the mezzanine, a library, a basement, additional rooms, and a vast garden where people gather to break the fast during Ramadan.[51]

Murids have also built two houses in Libreville dedicated to Ahmadu Bamba that serve as seats for dahiras. Gabon is the only country outside Senegal where Murids have built infrastructures of such magnitude. The centrality of Gabon in Bamba's spiritual itinerary and the Murid imaginary explains the commitment to ingrain the cultural and religious footprints of the Muridiyya in Gabonese soil and to bear the financial cost of this endeavor. Conversely, Ahmadu Bamba's journey in Gabon became central to his legacy as a saint and innocent victim of colonial injustice.

However, the growing presence of the Muridiyya in Libreville's public space is not welcome by all. As I have witnessed recently during the celebration of Murid cultural week, some Gabonese are irritated by the Murids' display of power through their pilgrimages, parades, long motorcades of luxury vehicles, and loud singing.[52] Murids are also suspected of giving shelter to undocumented immigrants. The leaders of the dahira of Batavia who manage the largest Murid house in Libreville claim they had to change their management style to dispel suspicion of harboring illegal immigrants and to avoid police raids.[53]

Since the mid-1980s, pushed by a grassroots xenophobic movement amplified by greater freedom of expression and an intensifying economic crisis, the Gabonese government has adopted a policy of "Gabonisation" or national preference, not dissimilar to "ivoirité."[54] This policy, specifically directed against the so-called Ouestaf (West African migrants), aims to reserve Gabonese jobs for Gabonese nationals, limit legal immigration, and send undocumented immigrants back home. More recently, this policy has led to the deportation of hundreds of West African immigrants accused of residing in the country illegally, including among them dozens of Senegalese. Hostility toward Senegalese and the Murids in particular may be fueled by the economic crisis in Gabon while Murid businessmen continue to do well, thanks in part to their close association with the ruling class and economic elites.[55] In the most recent Gabonese national elections, where President Ali Bongo Odimba was suspected of having benefited from massive voter fraud, West Africans and particularly Senegalese immigrants were accused of colluding with the ruling party. Whether this accusation is founded or not, Senegalese have suffered less from "Gabonisation" than, for example, the Malians, Nigerians, and Beninese who have been deported in their hundreds. Some argue that this lenient treatment is due to the historically close relationships between the ruling classes of Gabon and those of Senegal. Others cite the fact that many among the Gabonese elite were taught by Senegalese teachers. Still others emphasize the role of Senegalese religious leaders who use their influence on Senegal's government and their proximity with the Bongo family to protect their flock.[56] Nevertheless, the increasing hostility to immigrants in Gabon does not seem to affect current Murid attitudes. The story of the art market of Libreville further illustrates the Murids' continued efforts to inscribe Ahmadu Bamba's sacred biography in Gabonese soil.

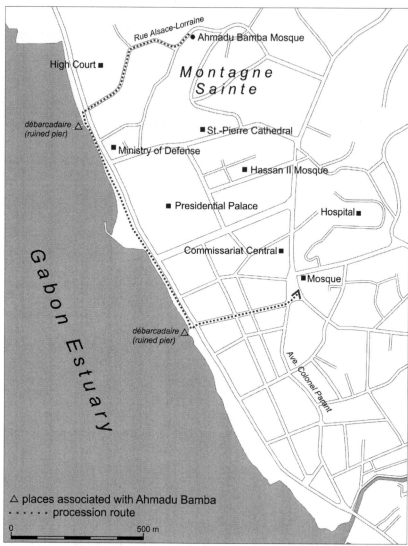

Rue Alsace-Lorraine

● Ahmadu Bamba Mosque

High Court ■

Montagne Sainte

débarcadaire △
(ruined pier)

■ St.-Pierre Cathedral

■ Ministry of Defense

■ Hassan II Mosque

■ Presidential Palace

Hospital ■

Gabon Estuary

Commissariat Central ■

■ Mosque

débarcadaire △
(ruined pier)

Ave. Colonel Parant

△ places associated with Ahmadu Bamba
· · · · · procession route

0   500 m

MAP 3.2. Murid historic sites and procession route in Libreville. Map drawn by Eric Ross.

IN BAMBA'S NAME, WE WILL HAVE OUR MARKET

Senegalese street vendors were the first sub-Saharan Africans to set up shop in downtown Libreville in the 1960s, competing with French and Lebanese storeowners. The Gabonese, like most people in the forested areas of equatorial and central Africa, do not have an established tradition of trade as the Sahel and desert-dwelling West Africans do, who have been involved in long-distance and regional trade networks for centuries. Many among the Senegalese vendors managed stalls or worked out of temporary shelters.[57] They sold a variety of goods but particularly antique arts, African fabrics, jewelry, and other items, targeting French nationals working in Gabon, European tourists, diplomats, and the Gabonese middle class. Elhaaj Medun Gey, the goldsmith and pioneer of Murid migration to Gabon, opened the first jewelry shop in downtown Libreville in 1965. He named his shop SeneGabon, and it is still standing as of this writing. Soon other Murid jewelers, art dealers, tailors, and wage laborers followed suit. Women opened restaurants to feed the growing Senegalese and West African communities. The relationship between these traders and store owners in the prime real estate of downtown Libreville was contentious, especially since many of these traders were undocumented immigrants who did not have proper government licenses.

As the Gabonese government was taking advantage of the country's booming oil economy to develop and modernize Libreville, Murid traders were increasingly becoming a nuisance. They were forced numerous times to move their businesses to make room for the construction of government offices and other buildings to accommodate banks and private sector ventures. In 1998, Murid art traders were forced to evacuate one of the last of downtown Libreville's vacant lots, which they had been squatting for some years. So they set their sights on one of the few remaining lots that could accommodate their trade: the land located on Avenue du Colonel Parant, which belonged to an old family of Senegalese immigrants.[58] When the Murid traders proposed to the owners to use the space for their trade, the latter agreed on the condition that they bear the cost of cleaning the place, which had become a dumping ground for trash, and accept a rent of $2,400 a month. For the Murids, the mere fact that the owners of the land had agreed to rent it to them was a miracle. This sentiment is conveyed by their leader, Njaga Jaw: "The history of this place [market] is telling about the value of believing in Sëriñ Tuubaa. This is not the first place we have settled, we have been to two places and we were not alone in coveting the place where our market is located today. Even the Gabonese government wanted the place."[59]

For the traders, the attraction of the market was not solely due to its convenient location near downtown Libreville. They coveted the place because they believed it was located in the vicinity of the military barracks where Ahmadu Bamba was once held and where he used to bury the monthly stipend that the French allocated to him.[60] Murid disciples see a connection between this story and the fact that this area of Libreville has become the financial district of the city, where the Ministry of Finances, the office of the treasurer, and a number of banks and other financial institutions are located. To put it metaphorically, the money that Bamba sowed in the soil of Libreville over a century ago is now germinating. And having the art market in this neighborhood was critical because it put Murid traders in a position to harvest the rewards of their shaykh's sacrifice.

But the initial excitement soon gave way to anxiety. The family that owned the land was divided. The members of the family living in Senegal, who also happened to be followers of the Muridiyya, wanted to sell the property, while those in Libreville were in favor of continuing the lease. Disputes over land and inheritance are common among polygamous Senegalese diaspora families, especially when family members are split between Senegal and their countries of immigration. Families living in Senegal are often eager to sell shares of their deceased immigrant parents' assets for cash; they rarely agree with their siblings in the diaspora, who often prefer to grow the assets' value over the long term. Cerno Sulay Sall, a son of the first imam of the mosque of Treichville in Abidjan, indicates that his father and his fellow Senegalese immigrants owned many houses and lots in this neighborhood of Abidjan. But because of inheritance disputes between family members based in Senegal and those residing in Abidjan, many of the properties have been sold to Ivorian nationals.[61]

Njaga Jaw explains how the split within the family that owned the land affected their plan to remain in the market:

> We continued to work and pay the rent, but things started to change in 2003. The family [that owned market] was divided. They told us that the place was now for sale and since [they presumed] that we did not have the money to pay [we would have to evacuate the place]. They asked for a million dollars. They sent us a summons and gave us a deadline of six months to pay or leave. . . . Not long after, a member of the family of owners came to me and told me that they were no longer selling the place but they had decided to increase the rent to three thousand dollars from twenty-four hundred. Afterwards, I went to Senegal. [From there] I received a phone call and was told that a member of the family from Dakar [residing in Dakar] had come and had changed the whole deal. They were again talking about selling and expelling us. This happened in 2008.[62]

The Murid shopkeepers who had been operating in the market for ten years were now threatened with eviction if they could not come up with the money to buy the lot. But a million dollars was an immense sum of money for these small-business owners. In fact, many among the merchants did not have bank accounts, and if they did, it was just for savings. For most of them, taking a bank loan was never a part of their business model, but there was no other alternative if they wanted to keep the place. And keeping the lot was of paramount importance to all of them.

Elhaaj Njaga Jaw and his fellow traders were determined to raise the money necessary to acquire the land. On the advice of local leaders of the Murid community, they approached the Senegalese ambassador to Gabon who suggested they form a professional association that would allow them to secure a license from the Gabonese government. Having this license was indispensable for opening a bank account and applying for a loan. One month after founding the association, the traders opened an account at the Industrial and Commercial Bank of Gabon (BICG, French acronym). This bank is a branch of the French bank BNP Paribas, which has branches throughout former French West Africa. But time was running out. Soon after opening the account with very little money, Jaw applied for a loan of $800,000. By then the merchants had raised $200,000 to use as a down payment on the loan and to cover transaction and closing cost fees.

The bankers' reaction to the Murid traders' loan application was a mixture of amazement and respect. The director of the bank wondered how somebody without a banking history and without collateral should dare ask to borrow such a large sum of money. Jaw replied (speaking in Wolof, a language the director did not understand): "I put my trust in Ahmadu Bamba's guidance and I am confident that we will get the loan."[63] One of the loan officers was more supportive. She advised the traders to borrow a lower amount, $700,000, to facilitate the negotiations. A larger sum would have required approval from their superiors in Paris, who would have automatically denied the application because of the traders' weak credentials.

A few days after the initial meeting at the bank, the loan officer called Jaw and asked him to bring all the receipts he had accumulated during the ten years that they had rented the market. The receipts documented the payment of over $300,000, a sum equal to nearly half the total amount the traders wanted to borrow. Later, the loan officer informed Jaw that she needed the receipts to encourage her skeptical colleagues to grant the loan. The receipts helped the sympathetic loan officer convince her colleagues that the Murid traders were serious and trustworthy clients. She assured them that the Murids would not default on the loan and that if they did not lend them the money, another bank would.

The loan officer finally convinced the bank to give the Murid traders a loan of $700,000, repayable over eight years. Her reasoning, based on the credit worthiness of the traders backed by the record of their rental payments, was accurate. Since closing the deal in 2008, the traders have not missed a payment. The market hosts 102 shops; all of them but a few are occupied by Murid disciples.

While the bankers' decision to grant the loan was based on rational calculations that make perfect economic sense, for Jaw and his fellow traders the outcome was nothing short of a miracle. They could not imagine how in normal circumstances a bank could lend such a large sum of money to people without a banking history or collateral. For Jaw, this was "clearly the work of Sëriñ Tuubaa."[64] As soon as the owners of the land were paid and the deed transferred to the traders' association, Jaw flew to Tuubaa to present the document to the caliph of the Murids. He was also invited by the Murid-owned TV network, Tuubaa TV, to tell the story of the market. For Jaw and for his fellow disciples in Senegal, the acquisition of this important piece of real estate in the country where their shaykh was exiled and denied all his rights was evidence of the continuing effectiveness of Ahmadu Bamba's spiritual grace. They see themselves as the agents who made manifest the power of their shaykh's blessings through their hard work and economic achievements.

⌐

Murid migration to Gabon is primarily a postcolonial phenomenon. It is the result of two migratory flows. The first Murids to settle in Gabon step migrated from Côte d'Ivoire, a country that has a long history of hosting Senegalese migrants and where competition among immigrants in the same profession was intense. Gabon became an outlet for the most adventurous in search of better economic opportunities. The second migration was triggered by a bilateral agreement between the Gabonese and Senegalese postcolonial governments for the supply of Senegalese teachers and construction workers to the central African nation. Many Senegalese and Murids took advantage of this opportunity to find their way to cities and towns across Gabon where workers were in high demand.

Murid immigration in Gabon turned this country that occupies a central place in Murid imaginary into tangible space. For Murid immigrants, the stamping of the memory of their shaykh's exile on Gabonese soil was a sacred duty. They used Ahmadu Bamba's sacred biography reconstructed from Bamba's writings and stories narrated by Murid hagiographers as a blueprint to map the contours of his footprints in Libreville. This map allowed them to identify and memorialize space associated with their shaykh's stay in Gabon. The building of Murid space in Libreville also involved annual commemorations that reenact the shaykh's journey.

Gabon is a small country with a relatively small population of Murid immigrants. But Gabon is central for understanding the construction of a Murid diasporic identity. Murid immigrants around the world see their struggle as a symbolic reenactment of Shaykh Ahmadu Bamba's exile and sufferings in Gabon, and they take solace in what they see as his ultimate triumph. Murids in Gabon construe their success in acquiring and memorializing significant places and events associated with Bamba's exile as evidence of this triumph. They see the building of the Ahmadu Bamba mosque on Montagne Sainte and the acquisition of the Murid art market in downtown Libreville as evidence of historical vindication of their shaykh over his French foes and the manifestation of the continuous potency of his baraka. Both of these structures stand on grounds where Shaykh Ahmadu Bamba was once confined against his will.

Beyond Murid migration, this chapter, along with the preceding one on Côte d'Ivoire, sheds light on an important but overlooked dimension of African migration: mobility within the continent. Despite the dramatic media coverage of African migrants and refugees besieging the gates of Europe and dying in the thousands trying to cross the Mediterranean, internal continental African migration mobilizes by far the largest number of migrants. Two out of every three African immigrants stay on the continent. This ratio ranks Africa as the continent with the lowest outmigration.[65] The chapter also calls for an approach to migration that moves beyond conventional models inspired by theories (push/pull, for example) often dissociated from empirical reality. It suggests an approach to migration from within: one that centers the migrants' own values and their perceptions of their migratory experiences. Looking at migration through the eyes of the migrants offers an indispensable corrective to the misrepresentations embedded in quantitative and theoretical models that often value theory over empirical reality.

PLATE 1.1. Ahmadu Bamba teaching his disciples. Picture commissioned by the author.

PLATE 1.2. The trial of Ahmadu Bamba in the office of the governor general of West Africa, in Saint-Louis. Painting by Alpha Wali Diallo, commissioned by Oumar Ba. From Oumar Ba, *Ahmadou Bamba face aux autorités coloniales* (Abbeville, France: Fayard, 1982). Reproduced by permission of Oumar Ba.

PLATE 1.3. Ahmadu Bamba's arrival at the port of Dakar from exile in Gabon. Painting by Alpha Wali Diallo, commissioned by Oumar Ba. From Oumar Ba, *Ahmadou Bamba face aux autorités coloniales* (Abbeville, France: Fayard, 1982). Reproduced by permission of Oumar Ba.

PLATE 1.4. One of the seven minarets of the Great Mosque of Tuubaa. Photo by the author, August 2006.

PLATE 1.5. Well of Mercy in Tuubaa. Photo by the author, August 2006.

PLATE 1.6. The statue of Faidherbe on Faidherbe Square in Saint-Louis. Photo by
Moussa Dieng, February 2019.

PLATE 1.7. Maam Jaara Buso's mausoleum in Poroxaan. Photo by the author, May 2006.

PLATE 1.8. Murid businesses in Dakar. Photo courtesy of Shaykh Baabu, June 2020.

PLATE 1.9. Picture of members of the Dahira Kër Gumaalo Sekk in Dakar in 1954. Standing first from the right, Elhaaj Bamba Jaw; standing in the middle, fifth from the right, Sëriñ Jaañ, singer; sitting first from left, Moor Joób, preacher.

PLATE 1.10. Mosque Masalik al-Jinan in Dakar. Photo by Macoumba Bèye, May 2020.

PLATE 1.11. Library of Kër Sëriñ Tuubaa, Treichville, Abidjan. Photo by the author, December 2014.

PLATE 1.12. A classroom at Kër Sëriñ Tuubaa, Treichville, Abidjan. Photo by the author, December 2014.

PLATE 1.13. Murid preparing qasida books for reading at Kër Sëriñ Tuubaa, at Treichville, Abidjan. Photo by the author, December 2014.

PLATE 1.14. A Murid tailor shop in Treichville, Abidjan. Photo by the author, December 2014.

PLATE 1.15. A Murid-owned restaurant in Treichville, Abidjan. Photo by the author, December 2014.

PLATE 1.16. The Great Mosque of Tuubaa. Photo by the author, May 2006.

PLATE 1.17. Buses parked at the site in Lambaréné in Gabon where Murid pilgrims pay pious visits to the place where Ahmadu Bamba was confined in exile between 1900 and 1902. Photo by the author, September 2015.

PLATE 1.18. Mosque Shaykh Ahmadu Bamba on Montagne Sainte, Libreville. Photo by the author, December 2014.

PLATE 1.19. Murid procession in downtown Libreville. Photo by the author, September 2015.

PLATE 1.20. A stall at the Murid art market of Libreville. Photo by the author, December 2014.

PLATE 1.21. The first Murid-owned business in Libreville. Photo by the author, December 2014.

4 ᔐ The Muridiyya in France

[In France, among the African community,] Islam was confined to immigrant workers' hostels in neighborhoods where African Muslims were concentrated. It did not start to break out of its confinement until the year 1977. The main agents of this transformation were disciples of the Muridiyya brotherhood of Senegal.[1]

—Amadou M. Diop

THE PRESENCE of people of African descent in France dates from the Ancien Régime. But unlike the United States—and to a lesser extent Britain, where there is a rich historiography of ethnic minorities—the study of Black people's lives in France was not considered a legitimate subject for historical inquiry until recently. Pap Ndiaye notes the hostile response of French academia to William Cohen's book *The French Encounter with Africans*, in which Cohen established the long history of interactions between France and Black Africans on French soil and the racial tensions that resulted. Cohen urged historians to take seriously the history of race relations in metropolitan France.[2] Cohen's work was a serious challenge to the notion of White France, transient Black sojourners, and the utopian idea of a colorblind France immune to racial prejudice. His book was dismissed as "patent historical delusion," and his call was not heard until thousands of Afro-French marched in the streets against xenophobia and racial discrimination and forced historians to confront the deep historical roots of Black people in France and the economic, political, and sociocultural implications of this presence.[3]

But even in the context of growing interest in the history of Black people in France, the history of immigrants from the former French colonies in sub-Saharan Africa still remains relatively marginalized compared to the history of Black immigrants from the Caribbean. When looking at the literature on the history of Francophone African immigrants in France, it is possible to distinguish between two types of scholarship defined by fields, chronology, and methodological approach. First, the study of colonial migration is dominated by historians inspired by the American school

99

of African American and African diaspora studies. These historians are primarily interested in issues of race, class, and social movement.[4] The second and more extensive type of scholarship is on postcolonial migration and produced by anthropologists and sociologists interested in ethnic sociability, labor migration, development and village associations, and their interactions with communities left behind in Africa.

This chapter contributes to the historiography of postcolonial Francophone African immigration to France by focusing on the Muridiyya, a community of immigrants that until recently has not attracted much scholarly attention.[5] This omission can be attributed to the invisibility of Murid immigrants in the archives, their absence from the French public sphere, and their confinement to sectors of the French economy that eluded state regulators. The chapter reconstructs the history of Murid migration to France from the 1960s to the close of the twentieth century.

The massive presence of Murid disciples among the Senegalese diaspora has raised questions about the role of the Muridiyya as an institution in the creation and expansion of this diaspora (the Murids form 30.1 percent of the Senegalese population but count for over half of Senegalese living abroad).[6] These statistics raise several questions about the relationship between the Muridiyya and mobility. What makes this migration a Murid phenomenon in the first place? What role, if any, does the Murid leadership play in encouraging migration and organizing the lives of immigrants in countries abroad? There are myths and assumptions surrounding Murid migration. But the key to understanding these migration patterns is why and how migration in itself has both consolidated and challenged Murid forms of organization, beliefs, and sociability. In other words, what does the examination of migration teach us about the Muridiyya? And what insights do the Muridiyya bring to the study of migration? This chapter addresses these questions and demonstrates how the diaspora creates a discursive space that compels Murids to ask and respond to questions that would have been unthinkable at home. It also demonstrates how these responses define competing and conflicting conceptions of what it means to be a Murid in the diaspora.

SENEGALESE MIGRATION TO FRANCE

The Murid migration to France that began in the 1960s is just one chapter in a long history of population movement between France and its West African colonies. The different waves of Senegalese immigrants came from distinct regions of origin, religious affiliations, and class positions within Senegal. They arrived in France for different purposes, thus finding distinct kinds of employment and settling in various parts of France. Yet, these divergent migration streams are also connected.

Since the French occupation of Saint-Louis in northern Senegal in 1659, Senegalese have found their way to France. First among these immigrants were young Senegalese *métis* born of the encounter between Frenchmen and Senegalese women. These young men were sent to France to seek an education.[7] From the nineteenth century, a small number of Senegalese craftsmen, artists, and families hired to be exhibited in so-called African villages managed to settle in France as well. Jean Caam, who hosted Murid shaykhs in Dakar, was instrumental in helping the colonial administration select and send skilled Senegalese craftsmen to France to be displayed in the notorious "human zoos."[8] It is likely that Murid disciples were included among the artisans he sent to France. However, this migration would have only involved a small number of isolated individuals and was not significant. The same can be said of Senegalese veterans of the two world wars and other colonial conflicts: these veterans stayed in France after their service in defiance of the French government's policy of repatriating African soldiers.[9]

In the early twentieth century, a small group of students from the Four Communes and graduates of Senegal's high schools were sent to France to pursue a university education.[10] Many of them married French women and maintained close ties with the metropole when they returned to Senegal. The tradition of sending young Senegalese to study in French universities continues. France remains the primary destination of Senegalese students abroad. According to the French Ministry of Foreign Affairs, Senegalese rank first in sub-Saharan Africa for the number of students studying in France and fifth overall among countries sending students to French universities. We shall see that some of these students were instrumental in shaping the life of the Murid community in France, and their influence was noticeable in Senegal and in the diaspora.

The pace and magnitude of Senegalese migration to France became significant after World War II. But unlike the first wave of immigrants that consisted mostly of students, the postwar migration mostly involved seamen who had lost their jobs and settled near their port of call in Marseille, Le Havre, Toulon, Rouen, or Bordeaux. During World War II, with the conscription of French sailors to staff the navy, Soninke, Haal Pulaar, and Mandjack moved in to fill the vacant posts on merchant ships.[11]

The 1960s marks an important turning point in the migration of sub-Saharan Africans to France. This was also the time when a steady paper trail began to form in the archives, recording the struggle of bureaucrats to document the arrival and settlement of Black African workers and to cope with the problems they associated with "mass" African migration to French cities. Archival sources reveal that "mass" arrival of African immigrant workers in France was first recorded in the late 1950s.[12] Many of these migrants settled in the department of Seine-Maritime. By 1959, the migration started to expand across the whole of France. This expansion was fueled by a steady flow of new arrivals. In 1962, the requests for cheap fourth-class seats on ships that transported the immigrants was so high that the Association of French Shipping Companies (*les chargeurs unis*) met in Abidjan and Dakar to declare their inability to meet the demand. Tickets that were valued at 23,000 francs ($92) were sold for 35,000 francs ($140) around the port of Dakar.[13] From 1962 to 1968, the number of immigrants from Francophone sub-Saharan Africa increased from 15,220 to 27,540. Over 27 percent of these immigrants originated from Senegal.[14] According to official French government estimates (these numbers are to be taken with a grain of salt, since at best they reflect the perceptions of officialdom) from 1957 to 1961, the population of Senegalese living in France grew from 4,000 to between 12,000 and 15,000. This is an average increase of over 2,000 a year. Government records show that 3,000 among them were registered as unemployed due to lack of qualifications.[15]

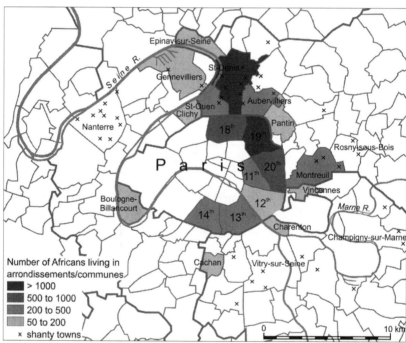

MAP 4.1. Geographic distribution of African immigrants in Paris in the 1960s, based on a map found at the French National Archives of Pierrefitte in box no. AG5 (F) 3384, probably dated from 1963 (the report it illustrates is dated from September 17, 1963). Map drawn by Eric Ross.

The accords that France signed with its former colonies to facilitate the circulation and reciprocal settlement of workers made the French destination even more attractive. Between 1963 and 1971, all of the former French West African colonies except for Guinea signed agreements that made Africans visiting France exempt from visa requirements.[16] The ordinances of 1946 regulating the entry and stay of foreigners in France were not applicable to former French African subjects.[17] To be granted entry, citizens of former French colonies traveling to France were only required to show an identity card along with an international vaccination certificate and enough money for a return ticket. These regulations that facilitated migration from the former colonies were upended in the mid-1970s. But even before then, muted opposition to African immigration was discernible.

Because of the increasing number of job seekers flocking to France, opposition to the migration of Africans mounted among French administrators as early as the 1960s. Yet, Black Africans represented but a small fraction of France's immigrant population, which was dominated by North Africans, people from the Caribbean, and southern Europeans.[18] The hostility toward African immigrants calls into question the master narrative that constructs the *trente glorieuses* (1945–75) as an immigration bonanza in France.[19] Early on, African immigration was treated as a national security issue. This is reflected in the dominant voice of the Ministry of Home Affairs and the Police Prefect of Paris in setting immigration policies despite the discordant moderating voices of the minister of foreign affairs and the minister of cooperation, both of whom opposed harsh measures.[20] From 1960, the biannual reports on immigration filed by the office of the Paris prefecture of police, at the time led by the notorious secretary general of the prefecture of Bordeaux under Vichy, Maurice Papon, continued to lament the dismal living conditions of African workers and the health hazard they represented to the population of France as carriers of tuberculosis, leprosy, and venereal and tropical diseases. African immigrants were also denounced for the supposed threat they posed to public order and the pressure they put on the social welfare budget. These reports unfailingly suggested regulatory measures to curb migration. However, this tough stance did not deter migration. All in all, French factories still needed the cheap, docile African labor, although they complained about its ineffectiveness. Additionally, there were far more French nationals working in the former colonies in sub-Saharan Africa than sub-Saharan Africans in France. In 1963, the number of French nationals working in Africa was estimated at 220,000, while the number of West African immigrants in

France stood at 70,000. The minister of foreign affairs, in particular, kept reminding his more hawkish, anti-immigrant colleagues of this fact.[21]

In 1964, official Senegalese government sources put the number of Senegalese living in France at 25,000, up from 20,000 in 1963: an increase of 5,000 in one year.[22] The majority of these immigrants originated from the regions of Saint-Louis, Senegal Oriental, and Casamance where ethnic groups such as the Soninke and Mandjack had a long tradition of migration to France.

By the late 1960s, over 50 percent of Senegalese immigrants in France were living in Paris.[23] This marked a new turn in migration, which up until then was dominated by sailors living in port cities. Now the majority of immigrants sought employment in the salaried sector of the economy in urban areas. They worked in the steel industry, textiles, chemical, construction, and automobile sectors. For example, in 1969 French automaker Citroën employed 312 Senegalese workers, while Renault had 227 Senegalese in its plants in and around Paris.[24] The number of Senegalese who worked in auto factories in the Havre seemed even larger.[25] The Soninke, and to a lesser extent the Haal Pulaar, who formed the majority of Senegalese immigrants in France, were hired en masse in the urban sanitation sector. Some worked in the hospitality industry or in the restaurant business.[26]

The labor migration of Senegalese and other former West African French colonial subjects is well documented in the French national archives. By the late 1960s, this migration started to attract the attention of mostly sociologists and anthropologists, whose research still dominates the scholarship.[27] Less documented was another migration that was underway simultaneously. This was a migration of self-employed traders and street vendors who entered France using the same tactics as the immigrants who sought salaried jobs; however, unlike the latter, they evaded the eyes of the state. These migrants were invisible to the state because they did not register to look for salaried jobs in the formal sector of the economy or for housing in the hostels built by Société Nationale pour la Construction des Travailleurs Algériens (SONACOTRA) to accommodate African migrant workers. In addition, because of their immigration status—almost all of them were undocumented—they managed to have the least amount of contact possible with the services of the French central and local government. The Murid migrants at the center of this book belong to this category of invisible immigrants—at least invisible to the state.[28] While the Murids are not alone in the business of trading and street peddling, their identity as migrants is defined by this profession.[29] Until very recently,

Murids loathed salaried jobs. Self-employment was the most sought-after occupation by Murid disciples abroad and at home. There was a saying among Murids that "the poor man is the one who knows how much he is able to make in a month."

THE MURID TRADE DIASPORA IN FRANCE

Senegalese migration to France intensified in the late 1960s. There was also a gradual transformation of the ethnic makeup of migrants, their regions of origin in Senegal, and their professional occupations abroad. Although Soninke and Haal Pulaar from the Senegal River Valley have continued to migrate to France, they were gradually surpassed by Laobe and Wolof from the regions of Njambur, Kajoor, and Bawol, who worked as independent traders and self-employed artisans. Most of these traders were farmers, disciples of the Muridiyya, compelled to move because of deteriorating climate conditions and transformation in policies that facilitated mobility.[30]

Gerard Salem's pioneering work on Senegalese traders in France reconstructs the beginning and expansion of Murid migration to France from the late 1960s to the early 1980s.[31] Salem, a geographer, was mostly interested in describing the trade networks connecting Murid traders at the Sandaga Market in Dakar with wholesalers and street peddlers in the cities of France. He was not interested in religious spirituality and did not fully understand the entanglement between religion, ethnicity, and trade networks. However, his research offers a helpful description of early Murid migration to France. Salem identifies Elhaaj Amadi Sow and Elhaaj Yande Jóob as the two key figures in the migration. Sow is also identified in the oral tradition as the man who "opened up" France and convinced his fellow Laobe that the European trade in African artifacts could "make them rich quickly."[32] He was a Laobe *yat* (woodcarver) from Njambur province in the current region of Louga. He left his village after the government of Senegal, concerned by the southward advance of the Sahara in north and northwestern Senegal, banned the cutting down of trees in the area. Sow migrated to Dakar to join family members already established there. By the late 1950s, Sow had completely abandoned the making of wooden utensils (mortar, pestle, benches, and bowls, among other items), the traditional professional occupation of the Laobe *yat*, to specialize in sculpting animals and masks representing a variety of West African ethnic groups and cultures for European tourists. He later became an art dealer, visiting communities across West Africa to buy traditional ethnic masks. Sow took his first trip to Marseille in 1966 and spent two weeks there. One of my sources suggests 1963, but 1966 is more plausible. Sow immediately understood the potential market that France represented for his craft. It is significant that he traveled to France only a few months after the conclusion of the World Fair of Negro Arts that was held in Dakar in April of the same year.[33] This cultural fair, organized by President Léopold Sédar Senghor under the auspices of UNESCO, was the first event of its kind on the African continent. It featured multiple dimensions of African arts and culture, including painting and sculpture but also literature, theater, dance, music, and cinema. Senghor was a poet and patron of the arts, and he invited some of the most influential Black intellectuals and artists of the time, such as Duke Ellington, Josephine Baker, Langston Hughes, and Aimé Césaire, all of whom attended the event. But one of the most lasting impacts of the festival was that it popularized African art, especially sculpture.[34]

Both Elhaaj Amadi Sow and Elhaaj Yande Jóob, who was a Murid art dealer with shops in Dakar and Abidjan, were poised to capitalize on the budding African arts cachet among Europeans. Sow returned to Marseille in April 1967 with two of his relatives (also from Louga) and stayed until August, traveling by train to research the French art market. They also learned about customs procedures and rules of consignment at the port. They started to ship artifacts to France as soon as they returned to Senegal, traveling back and forth between the two countries for many years. Jóob, who was from Diourbel, was a senior disciple and traveling companion of Shaykh Murtada Mbakke. By the late 1960s, he owned a number of art shops in the tourist districts of Dakar and in Abidjan.[35] Jóob also owned shops, run by his nephews, at the Saint-Ouen flea market in Paris. Sources conflict on the time of his settlement in Paris. Salem indicates that Jóob owned businesses in Paris as early as the 1960s, but one of my sources locates him in Abidjan in 1959–60, and other sources suggest that his settlement in Paris dated from 1972.[36] These different versions of the story are not necessarily contradictory. It may well be that while entrusting helpers to run his shops in France, Jóob was also involved in seasonal migration like most Senegalese traders working in France at the time. This is all the more plausible because we know that he had businesses in Dakar and Abidjan in the 1960s. Before the closing of the French borders in the mid-1970s, Senegalese traders spent part of the spring and summer seasons in Europe selling their wares in beach resorts and tourist towns, and they returned to Senegal to tend to their business there in the fall and winter. My sources, however, agree that Jóob, along with a few Murid traders based in Côte d'Ivoire, were the precursors of Murid migration to France. They migrated to Paris from Abidjan in the late 1960s and early 1970s.[37] Their resettlement in Paris illustrates the connection between intra-Africa migration flows and African outmigration.

It was not long until other Murid traders learned about the opportunities that the French market offered their businesses and followed in Sow and Jóob's footsteps. It is important to mention the role of the Laobe from Njambur (region of Louga) as trailblazers of Murid migration to France. It is clear that they were the inspiration behind the larger migratory movement that began in the 1970s. Murid disciples from Njambur are still disproportionately represented among the Murid diaspora. Louga is located on the edge of the semiarid region of Ferlo, and its unforgiving climate and weak economy might have been a factor in the emigration. However, one should not underestimate the influence of the Laobe who first left the region to settle across Africa and in Europe.[38] When the rains continuously failed from the early 1970s and rural-rural migration to Saalum and other more humid areas of Senegal was no longer an option (see introduction and chapter 1), many looked at Laobe emigration as a model to emulate.[39] This was the case of Mama Mbóoj, a Murid immigrant from Njambur, who arrived in Paris in 1975. He recalls, "In Njambur we could not grow anything because of the drought. Some people returned [from France] and they brought money. This was an incentive for us to try to go to France."[40] Salem mentions the examples of Elhaaj Papa Jen, Elhaaj Mbakke Jen, and Yatu Sylla, all of whom were from the region of Louga, as the most important Senegalese wholesalers in Paris and Strasbourg in the 1970s. All three were Murid disciples and arrived in Paris between 1967 and 1970. They worked with dozens of retailers, most of them Murids and most also from Louga. Yatu was based in Strasbourg where he headed an extensive trade network of Murid street peddlers, many of whom he helped migrate to France. He was also the local representative of a powerful branch of the Muridiyya led by Shaykh Mbakke Gaynde Faatma, Ahmadu Bamba's eldest grandson. Yatu dealt in artifacts imported from Senegal (masks, wooden statuettes, bead jewelry) but also in leather goods such as hats and belts imported from Morocco. Traders also sold artifacts made of fake ivory or imitation ebony imported from Hong Kong and other places. Strasbourg is a border city visited by German tourists and, as early as the 1970s, it began attracting a large community of Laobe traders. It was the presence of these traders that alerted Yatu to the city's limitless business potential. Along with Paris and Marseille, Strasbourg became one of the most important hubs of Murid businesses in France. Nice, another touristic border city, also attracted Murid traders.

By the mid-1980s, Murids from the areas of Bawol and Kajoor, heartland of the Murid order, had joined the migratory trail in large numbers, following on the trails of precursors such as Elhaaj Yande Jóob, who is from the same region in Senegal. Most of these new migrants were former farmers who relocated to Dakar and other cities along the Atlantic coast of Senegal following the crippling droughts that devastated rural Senegal in the late 1970s. They migrated from these cities and headed to the streets and beaches of France and later Italy and Spain, inserting themselves into the trade networks founded by their predecessors.

Among the dozens of traders in Salem's sample, only three are non-Murids: two are disciples of the Tijaniyya, and one is Qadiri. It is likely that this distribution was an accurate representation of the position of Murid disciples in the Senegalese trade business in France at the time. There are no reliable statistics on Senegalese international traders, but my own observation and those of scholars of Senegalese migration suggest that Murids continue to form the most visible segment of Senegalese traders living and working in France, Europe, and the United States: although their dominance may be less pronounced than in the 1970s and 1980s.[41]

Given the dominant presence of disciples of the Muridiyya in the Senegalese diaspora, Salem and other scholars raise questions about the role of the Muridiyya as a formative institution in this diaspora. He suggests that the relationships between Elhaaj Papa Jeŋ and Yatu Sylla and their Murid retailers reproduce the hierarchy of power and authority within the Murid order, with the wholesaler playing a role akin to that of the shaykh and the retailer that of the disciple. More recently, French anthropologist Jean P. Dozon argued that the Muridiyya encourages young and recently converted disciples to migrate and provides structure for their life abroad.[42] The popular media that occasionally report on Murid street peddlers in Europe and the United States (or on religious events in Senegal) harbor similar ideas. They assume that given the elaborate organization of Murid trade networks and supply chains there must be some center of power in Senegal responsible for orchestrating the system.[43]

However, such opinions seem to be based more on speculation and myth than hard facts. There is no mystery behind the expansion of Murid trading networks in France and no evidence supporting the involvement of Murid shaykhs in the organization of the trade. As early as 1973, Guy Rocheteau, a researcher at the Office de la Recherche Scientifique et Technique d'Outremer (ORSTOM, now IRD [French acronym]) based in Senegal, had called for a reconsideration of the prominent role that scholars and observers ascribe to the Murid shaykhs as instigators of Murid migration to eastern-central Senegal. He suggested that demographic pressure and an entrenched tradition of mobility in Wolof society play equally important roles in motivating migration.[44] Similarly, in his research on Murid businesses in Dakar, Momar Coumba Diop found that the creation of Murid urban dahiras was not inspired by the Murid leadership but rather the result of disciples' initiatives that responded to their own needs.[45] Salem's own fieldwork in Senegal in 1976 and 1979 revealed to him that the key to understanding Murid trade in France was not to be found in the holy city of Tuubaa where Muridiyya leadership resides but in the markets of Dakar. More recently, Ottavia S. di Friedberg and Sophie Bava concluded that the formation of Murid dahiras in Italy and Marseille was an initiative solely of local Murid disciples without interference from the leadership.[46] Bava rightly observes that the Muridiyya "is not a religious movement which strategically decentralizes its cult. Although the presence of the religious leadership is still felt, the building of places of worship in the diaspora is the result of initiatives by Murid traders to construct decentralized places of worship as a means to maintain and invent spiritual and material links with the holy city of Tuubaa."[47]

Murid traders' migration to France is an extension of the rural-rural then rural-urban migration, which, as chapters 1 and 2 demonstrate, expanded to destinations across West Africa and central Africa after the end of World War II and reached Europe in the late 1960s. It is possible to discern a Murid ethic of mobility inspired by the tradition of mobility within Islam and Ahmadu Bamba's sacred biography of exiles.[48] But as in other contexts in Africa and elsewhere, the decision to migrate is largely dependent on the individual migrant's local circumstances. This explains, for example, why Murids from Njambur dominated the first wave of migration to France in contrast to those living in Bawol, the heartland of the Muridiyya, who only joined the migration years later.

The only Murid institution of relevance in the diaspora is the dahira. The dahira was the creation of newly urbanized disciples that had both religious and secular functions. The Murid hierarchy was rather ambivalent about the initiative as the reaction of Caliph Faliilu Mbakke to the creation of the first Murid dahira in Dakar (discussed in chapter 1) indicates.[49] Similarly, the more recent Murid institutions in the diaspora, such as the kurel and the Kër Sëriñ Tuubaa ("house of Ahmadu Bamba" or "house of Islam") are also creations of disciples that cater to their spiritual and existential needs.[50] This demonstrates that the institutionalization of the Muridiyya abroad is the work of Murid disciples—not that of shaykhs. Disciples selectively reappropriate older institutions or reinvent new ones to help them cope with their difficult lives as workers and immigrants in strange lands.[51] Even in cases where a prominent shaykh has sought to provide guidance to disciples abroad, his recommendations have been resisted until the disciples were convinced of the tangible benefit the advice brought them.

Before the arrival of Caliph Abdul Ahad at the helm of the Muridiyya in 1968, shaykhs were committed farmers who were apprehensive about the corrupting influence of the city on their disciples' faith. Many of my interviewees, among the first generation of Murid migrants to Europe, told me that they had refrained from informing their shaykhs about their intention to migrate because they feared censure. Once the shaykh forbade the journey they would not be able to disregard his injunction.[52] Many recognized that dire economic conditions in their villages left them no other options but to leave in search of a better life.[53]

Like that of most African migrants, the decision of Murids to migrate was a collective decision made in the context of the household or within a circle of friends and coworkers. Likewise, the resources to fund the journey were either raised within the family, borrowed from friends, or came from the migrant's savings. There are disciples that have a particularly close relationship with their shaykhs and can get financial backing. But in general, Murid disciples are reluctant to take money from their spiritual guides. The guides' wealth comes from disciples who donate for the sake of redeeming their sins or fending off misfortunes. Many believe that much rides on taking the shaykh's money and that this indulgence could end up being harmful to the disciple. The shaykh's money can be a blessing but only under particular circumstances.

More importantly, Murid migrants' religious lives in the diaspora do not necessarily reflect their attitude toward the Murid organization prior to their migration. Many among my sources acknowledged they were not particularly religious before they left Senegal but that living in the diaspora enhanced their piety and dedication to the Murid order.[54] This is the case of Cerno Sow, a student in Abidjan in the 1970s:

> I used to party a lot. But one night I went to Adjame and heard people singing the qasidas [Ahmadu Bamba's devotional poems]. This reminded me of Senegal and Sëriñ Tuubaa. I stopped to recognize the people. I went to a shop to buy a lot of candies and crackers to give to the singers. For me, this was a form of atonement for having stayed away from my fellow disciples, living in a boarding school. I stayed with them until late in the night. This event had a cathartic impact. From that day on, I never missed the religious gatherings.[55]

Some recognize that now that they are living away from their families and friends, participating in religious activities has become important for their psychological well-being. For others, going to the dahira is merely a way to spend their spare time for a good cause. Scholars of immigration observe that religious identity and communality take on greater significance for immigrants while away from home. They use religion to connect with others like themselves and find comfort in the teachings and rituals of the faith: in this way, immigrants find a means to negotiate access to public space and earn recognition.[56] This attitude is not specific to African or Senegalese Muslim immigrants. Looking at the religious life of Turkish immigrants in Germany, Werner Schiffauer refers to what he calls "the Islamization of the self," which he describes as withdrawal from the larger society "to enter the religious society," which then becomes "a counterweight, a place of respect."[57] Like Turkish Muslims in Germany, the devotion of Senegalese Murid traders in France tells us little about the intensity of their piety and the influence that the Murid leadership might have had on them before their migration.

SHAYKH ABDOULAYE DIÈYE AND THE TRANSFORMATION OF THE MURIDIYYA IN FRANCE

Studies of Murid immigrants in France in the 1970s and 1980s rarely mention their religious life. As Sophie Bava remarked, scholars in France did not acknowledge immigrant religions until the late 1980s.[58] Research on the Muridiyya mostly focused on the disciples' professional occupations. The privileged sites of field research included the streets, boulevards, beaches, shops, and markets where traders worked: the house and the mosque, which are the primary sites for religious expressions, were overlooked. But it is also true that at its early stage the migration was mostly seasonal, and the Murid community in France mostly comprised young bachelors and single males from rural Senegal who did not speak French, lacked familiarity with city life, and had no organizational know-how. In addition, as scholars of migration have noted, immigrants living without their families are less likely to engage in religious activities. This is also the case of seasonal migrants who do not stay in one place for long. All of this might have hindered research on the religious dimension of Murid migrant lives.[59] The arrival of a new cohort of Murid migrants in the first half of the 1970s transformed the situation.

The Muridiyya gradually moved from the private apartments of the traders to increased visibility in the French public sphere. The architects of this transformation were Shaykh Abdoulaye Dièye and a small group of

Murid students who came to France in the 1970s to pursue graduate education.[60] The process of this transformation was fraught with tension, and as will be shown later, the legacy of this rift still affects Murid communities in France.

Shaykh Abdoulaye Dièye was born in 1938 in Saint-Louis to a family with a long tradition of Islamic learning.[61] Following his forebears' traditions, Dièye received all of his religious education from relatives and principally from his father, who was a teacher and an imam. Later, he deepened his training in *tasawwuf* (Islamic mysticism) with some early disciples of Shaykh Ahmadu Bamba.

Shaykh A. Dièye's education was not, however, limited to religion as was customary in his family. He went to a French school and studied at Lycée Blanchot, a prestigious high school, where many of the leaders of the colonial and postcolonial Francophone West African states were trained. He left Senegal for France in 1977 or 1978 to pursue training as an engineer at the École Supérieure de Paysage de Versailles (High Institute for Landscape Design and Architecture).

Shaykh Abdoulaye Dièye was among the first members of his family to openly claim and promote a Murid identity. At age fourteen, he was a member of dahira Mbaboor, one of the earliest Murid organizations in Saint-Louis, specializing in studying and singing Ahmadu Bamba's devotional poems. In later years, Dièye pledged allegiance to Shaykh S. Ahmad Ismuhu, a Murid shaykh from the Deymani family of Mauritania, who remained his spiritual guide until his death in the early 1970s. After his shaykh's demise, Dièye became the head of his spiritual lineage.

Shaykh Abdoulaye Dièye was one of the rare Murid shaykhs who could articulate Ahmadu Bamba's teachings in French in a knowledgeable and understandable way for Muslim communities in Senegal and beyond. Early in his career, Dièye portrayed himself as a modern Murid intellectual and teacher. He was educated in the French colonial school system and could be considered a member of the emerging elite of the Senegalese civil service. He was among the small minority of Murid disciples to receive an advanced Western education. Although most of his contemporaries in the civil service and in urban Senegal played down their Murid identity to assimilate into the Francophone and Francophile urban culture of newly independent Senegal, he forcefully showcased his Murid identity. Dièye carved out for himself a unique niche in the Muridiyya, which was at the time mostly a rural organization of farmers and seasonal traders educated in the traditional Qur'anic system and the Murid rural working schools (*daara tarbiyya*). He mastered the French language, read the writings of Ahmadu Bamba in classical Arabic, and garnered much oral knowledge through his friendship with old Murid shaykhs and disciples. Dièye also grew up in Saint-Louis where eloquence and civility were highly valued. He was aware of the power of etiquette and adopted an impressive style of dress, body language, and vocabulary that helped him forge a unique identity that would serve him well in his religious and political career.[62] Dièye skillfully exploited his position at the intersection of the Muridiyya, Western culture, and urban sophistication to gradually accumulate symbolic capital, which translated into religious authority.

Abdoulaye Dièye began his career as a shaykh in the 1960s and early 1970s by creating an informal school in Saint-Louis for the dissemination of Ahmadu Bamba's teachings. His style of proselytizing at the time was quite revolutionary. Rather than focusing on hagiography and oral narratives of Bamba's miracles and the use of Wolof (the lingua franca of Senegal), Dièye favored an engagement with Bamba's societal project and thought, comparing it to major ideologies such as Marxism, capitalism, and Maoism. His discourse resonated well with young Senegalese students, particularly those who, in the words of Amadu Dramé (an early disciple of Dièye in France), were on a quest for a "real African hero."[63]

These young men were excited by the leftist and antiestablishment fervor of the late 1960s and early 1970s. They admired Ahmadu Bamba but were uncomfortable with the image of the Muridiyya proliferated in popular discourse and in colonial and scholarly literature. This image was that of a conservative, parochial, and backward organization only fit for the benighted Wolof farmers and traders of Kajoor and Bawol.

Dièye's lectures were among the first attempts to use the French language and the format and setting of a scholarly meeting to disseminate Ahmadu Bamba's teachings. In the words of one of his senior disciples, this was a "scientific approach" to the Muridiyya.[64] The first stage of this approach was research conducted both through the exploration of the internal Murid sources (Bamba and his disciples' writings in Arabic and Wolofal, Murid oral history, and oral tradition through credible sources and field trips) and through a perusal of the colonial and postcolonial literature. The second stage was the delivery of the findings in journal articles and speeches but also through discursive sessions open to the public where Dièye was ready to take on the challenges of his audience. The third stage was the creation of tools (a journal, schools, institutions, and civil society organizations) to promote the approach pioneered by Dièye. He emphasized the concept of *dëggël* (from the Wolof word *dëg*, or "truth"). This means that Ahmadu Bamba's authentic heirs are those who truly embody his teachings and sincerely model their behavior on his.[65] In his view, faithfulness to Bamba's teachings, spiritual fraternity, and brotherhood take precedence over genealogical relationships. Dièye assigned himself the mission to reconstruct and disseminate the "authentic" thought and history of Ahmadu Bamba, which from his perspective had been clouded by the misleading interpretations of Europeans and by the obscurantism of disciples.[66]

Dièye conceived of his ministry as *khidma* or "service." Khidma is central to Murid doctrine. In fact, the name that Ahmadu Bamba coined for himself, Khadim ar-Rasul (Servant of the Prophet), derived from this concept. However, Dièye's innovative style of khidma did not proceed unchallenged. He first faced the skepticism of Murid disciples who reproached him for imitating the French practice of public lectures instead of reading and singing Ahmadu Bamba's *qasidas.* When planning the first Murid culture week at the headquarters of UNESCO in Paris in 1979, he confronted the opposition of Murid disciples and the skepticism of the government of Senegal who suspected him of political maneuvering.[67]

When Dièye arrived in Paris in 1977–78 as a student sent by the government of Senegal to study landscaping and architecture, there was already a sizable Murid community in the city. This was an introverted community of Wolof-speaking traders educated in the traditional Qur'anic schools or working schools in the Murid heartland of Bawol, Kajoor, and Njambur. They maintained strong links with their shaykhs and the holy city of Tuubaa in Senegal but remained largely secluded from French society.[68] Murid disciples, mostly single young men, were concentrated in the neighborhood of Gare de Lyon in the Twelfth Arrondissement between passages Raguinot and Brunoy where they formed a kind of economic enclave not dissimilar to Little Senegal in Harlem, the headquarters of Senegalese and West African migrants in the city of New York.[69] They faced the challenge of housing shortages and residential segregation that confronted all African immigrants in France. Murid traders could not rely on the hostels built by SONACOTRA designated primarily for North African immigrants contracted by French businesses to work in the salaried sector. Most of them were undocumented and self-employed. They lived in cheap but insalubrious long-stay hotels such as Hôtel Madame Boulet on 24 rue de Salamon, Hôtel de France on Passage Brunoy, or La Boule d'Or in the same neighborhood. A few among them settled clandestinely in the hostels reserved for salaried African immigrant workers after La Boule d'Or burned down in 1979 and cost the lives of many African immigrants, including a few Senegalese.[70] Traders were gradually able to rent shops in the neighborhood of the Goutte d'Or in the Eighteenth Arrondissement where they sold their wares. The neighborhood Goutte d'Or continues to be a hub of African trade in Paris. In 2010 there were one hundred shops run by Africans in the market, and 20 percent belonged to Senegalese merchants.[71] My visit to the market in June 2014 revealed that Senegalese are still dominant there. Wolof, the lingua franca of Senegal, could be overheard among the stalls and is even spoken by South Asians hawking their wares.[72] Senegalese vendors also worked the tourist sites, streets, and boulevards of Paris where vending in the streets was prohibited, playing a game of cat and mouse with the police as they would later do in the streets of New York City.

Religious life was organized around dahiras, but these mostly specialized in fundraising on behalf of specific Murid lineages. Some among the few elders in the group would organize meetings in their rooms to tell stories about Ahmadu Bamba, but there was no organization uniting the whole community, nor were there public commemorations or gatherings. Disciples supported each other and collectively celebrated all the major Muslim and Murid holidays. But they limited their religious activities to their homes and refrained from proselytizing in public places. They used Wolof, their native tongue, as the medium of communication and kept their distance from the Francophone Senegalese students and professionals living in France. Here is how Alasaan Mbay, a French-educated Murid disciple from Dakar who migrated to Paris in 1971, describes the life of the Murid community of the neighborhood of Gare de Lyon in the early 1970s.

> A variety of *kërs* [house or Murid lineages] were represented: those of Sëriñ Basiiru, Gaynde Faatma, Sëriñ Murtalla, etc. . . . This taught me a lot about the different Murid families. . . . During the early 1970s, the community was growing, some shaykhs used to visit Gare de Lyon and we could collect easily, in a couple of days, one million CFA [$4,000]. This was the place where you could find Senegalese food, shelter, etc. . . . Soxna Xadi Siiby was among the restaurant owners. Students would go there to eat. Traders would go there to sell their wares. We had similar goals, Sëriñ Tuubaa united us. However, the approaches were different. Early on, I realized that Sëriñ Tuubaa could not be kept in a room. His teachings have universal validity. When you read his writings you feel that he changes you. I used to tell Shaykh Laye [Abdoulaye Dièye], "now the age of the Muridiyya of the hut has passed, we should focus on an international

Muridiyya where you speak to people in a rational and logical language." There were some problems in the beginning. Some would argue that the students were not trained adequately to talk about Shaykh Ahmadu Bamba.[73]

Abdoulaye Dièye took a radically different path. He confronted both the leftist Senegalese students who frowned at religion and the conservative traditional traders of Gare de Lyon who harbored a parochial understanding of the Muridiyya.[74] He proposed Ahmadu Bamba's teachings and the Murid ethic of cultural rootedness, worship, and hard work as an alternative to what he saw as the cultural alienation of Senegalese students in France. Dièye also believed that the Muridiyya had a lot to teach to the Muslim community of Europe, especially on questions related to the true universal message of Islam, religious tolerance, and racial equality. Dièye became a regular visitor of the House of French West Africa on Boulevard Poniatowski, better known by its nickname "Ponia." Since the days of colonial rule, the House has served as headquarters for West African student organizations in Paris.[75]

Dièye's attempt to make space for Islam and the Muridiyya in this abode of leftist and radical thought led to heightened tensions and conflicts with the students, who objected to what they labeled as an obscurantist and backward message. Dièye was accused of serving the interests of the neocolonial state of Senegal by attempting to undermine the students' progressive movement.[76] But Dièye was able to beat the students at their own game, exposing what he saw as their duplicity. Dièye criticized the students for always criticizing the West while displaying in their everyday life their subservience to Western culture and mores. He denounced the students' love for French dress and manners, their habit of drinking alcohol, and their selfishness. He also criticized their adherence to bankrupt Western ideologies (individualism, Marxism, and secularism) that do not reflect the values of the African culture they pretended to defend. Instead Dièye presented the Muridiyya as a system of thought and a praxis invented by a Black African and rooted in African culture. He also underlined the universality of Ahmadu Bamba's message by emphasizing his anti-imperialist and nationalist credentials. The Iranian Revolution, the Rushdie affair, and the controversies over veiling in schools brought Islam to the forefront of French politics and provided an atmosphere favorable to Dièye's calling. The collapse of the Soviet Union in the late 1980s further undermined his leftist opponents and boosted the popularity of his ideas.

In his opposition to the Westernized leftist students of the Poniatowski house, Dièye could count on the support of a small but determined group of Murid students and sympathizers who attended universities in France in the 1970s to pursue graduate education.[77] Some of these students came from the University of Dakar, others from Middle Eastern and North African countries. But the group was united in its embrace of Ahmadu Bamba's teachings and in its willingness to work hard in disseminating said teachings. For Murid Ñaŋ, a former member of the dahira of Murid students of the University of Dakar who migrated to France in 1983, the young people's engagement with the Muridiyya was "more about nationalism than spiritualism but gradually the spiritual side took over."[78] This was also the opinion of Shaykh Sall, a former student at the University of Dakar who moved to Paris in 1977. He observed:

> Our generation was very much influenced by American music and culture and leftist ideology. It was really in 1975–78 that we turned our back to this culture and turned toward religion, an intellectual approach to Islam developed by a black founder of a tariqa. . . . We were proud as students to showcase Shaykh A. Bamba as an authentic African thinker. . . . We wanted to disseminate Shaykh Amadu Bamba's teachings. Many of us were students or interns [in Paris] but many of us also have had an experience in the Muridiyya at the University of Dakar or here. Many had been members of the *dahira* of Murid students. The movement was made up of people from Saint-Louis or former members of the *dahira* of students which in the beginning was also composed mostly of people from Saint Louis.[79]

The role and presence of these students affected the trajectory of the Muridiyya in France in a way that is still palpable.

Dièye labored to forcefully disseminate his message by adopting modern forms of organization and communication, moving away from traditional Murid institutions such as the dahira. He adopted the term *daara* (school) to name sections of his organization and emphasize the educational orientation he privileged. He also imbued his movement with a certain intellectual cachet, targeting Senegalese students and professionals living in France and tackling issues that concerned the global Muslim community. In the words of sociologist Moustapha Diop, Dièye turned the Muridiyya from a popular religion of Wolof-speaking traders into a religion of French-speaking professionals.[80] In 1978–79, Dièye founded the Association of Senegalese Murid Students and Interns in Europe

(Association des Etudiants et Stagiaires Murid d'Europe, AESME [French acronym]) and the following year launched the first international Murid journal, which he named Ndigël (meaning "the recommendation"). This journal became the mouthpiece of the Khidmatul Khadim International Sufi School and of the Muridiyya in Europe and the diaspora. Ndigël was written in French, Arabic, and sometimes Wolofal (Wolof written with Arabic characters), and it had an editorial board that comprised disciples of different ethnicities, nationalities, and professions based in Europe and in Africa. In its fourth issue, the journal editors claimed a circulation of a thousand copies.[81]

In 1983, AESME became the Islamic Movement of the Murids of Europe (MIME [French acronym]). This change was highly significant, happening as it did in the aftermath of the Iranian Revolution and the controversy surrounding the Iraq-Iran war. The coupling of the words "Murid" and "Islamic" and the dropping of the word "Senegalese" was indicative of Dièye's willingness and that of his followers to place their actions in the framework of the broader global Muslim community, or umma. The precedence given to the adjective "Islamic" in the naming of the organization further emphasized the idea that the Murids were part of the global Muslim community and that Bamba's message was directed to Muslims of all nations at all times and not just to the Wolof of nineteenth-century Senegal, as French orientalists argued. These changes also signaled Dièye's aspiration to expand beyond the narrow confines of the Senegalese diaspora that formed the major constituency of the Muridiyya in Europe. Alongside MIME, Dièye founded an organization exclusively reserved for new converts to Islam: the International Islamic Association for the Support of the Dissemination of the Muridiyya in Europe (AIIDME [French acronym]). This organization was led by Ahmad Guy Pépin, a member of Khidmatul Khadim and retired professional athlete from the French Antilles. The founding of the AIIDME clearly indicated the innovative nature of Dièye's work. Pépin, who adopted the name of Ahmad Aïdara, led a community of mostly West Indian disciples. He focused his ministry on building strong marriages and ethical family lives among his flock. Dièye was the first Murid shaykh to make the conversion of foreigners a major dimension of his dawa (calling). Murid shaykhs inside and outside Senegal have primarily directed their effort to nurturing and consolidating the bonds between Senegalese-Wolof disciples and between disciples and masters.[82]

Dièye's message of universalism was not only reflected in the type of organizations he promoted but also embedded in the symbolism of the space where he held meetings and the themes he favored in his writings and conferences. He was literally moving the Muridiyya from the confines of the private rooms where it was kept for decades by its mostly non-Western-educated Wolof-speaking followers to the public sphere where it was exposed to the wider European audience.[83] He convened the first cultural week devoted to the Muridiyya in France at the UNESCO headquarters in 1979.

This event put the Muridiyya on the map of the Parisian cultural landscape, but it did not happen without challenge. The traders of the neighborhood of Gare de Lyon, who were the financial muscle behind the Muridiyya in Paris, opposed the event. Here is how one of Dièye's disciples who worked with him to organize the event recalls their mood after a meeting with Murid elders:

> When we met with the elders and talked to them about our project, they were completely against it. For them the duty of disciples was to work for the shaykh, to revere him, to seek his blessings, not to try to peruse, discuss or spread his teachings, especially in Europe. For them no human being can truly understand the essence of Shaykh Ahmadu Bamba's message or talk on his behalf. . . . There was the problem with Shaykh Abdoulaye Dièye, whom they did not know, many thought that he was a Qadiri because his shaykh was a Moor [White Mauritanian]. He was also a francophone [not believed to be versed in classical Arabic and Islamic thought]. . . . For many we were not qualified to talk about the Shaykh. . . . We were thinking of just giving up. Shaykh Abdoulaye Dièye thought that the time had not come yet for the kind of work we were doing. It was Caliph Shaykh Abdul Ahad who encouraged us to persist.[84]

The cultural week was finally held in 1979 and was successful. It was attended by UNESCO general director Amadu Makhtar Mbow and a slew of famous African intellectuals and writers, including Birago Diop, Amadou Hampaté Ba, and some Arab and French scholars. Shaykh Abdul Ahad sent a delegation and speakers who addressed the large crowd of attendees in Arabic and French. Abdoulaye Dièye gave a presentation. The event was covered by the French and Arabic language media based in Paris.

The following year, Dièye and his group held a conference at the College de France, the most prestigious institution for research and scholarship in the humanities, social sciences, and natural and physical sciences, located in the famed Latin Quarter across from the Sorbonne. Some high-profile French intellectuals such as lawyer Francis Lama and

Le Monde journalist Claude Balta were in attendance. In 1981, they organized a second cultural week dedicated to Ahmadu Bamba at UNESCO headquarters and in Brussels in 1982. Also, in 1981, Dièye led a delegation of his fellow Murids to the international meeting of the Organization of the Islamic Conference in Kuala Lumpur.

These meetings gave Dièye the opportunity to express the universal message of the Muridiyya through exhibits, film projections, and lectures. This message stressed solidarity and respect among Muslims regardless of skin color, the recognition of Ahmadu Bamba as a resister of colonialism and a champion of Islam, and finally the necessity for Muslims to resist Western materialism by strengthening their faith. This view was forcefully articulated by Dièye's disciple and head of AESME, who declared at the Brussels gathering that "his association represented an Islam that escapes race barriers."[85]

Yet, despite his apparent success, Dièye still faced resistance from some Murids. Some objected to his proselytizing methods, while members of the Mbakke family and some disciples contested his religious authority, given that his spiritual guide was not a member of Bamba's family but a "White" Mauritanian. Some contended that Dièye was in reality not a Murid but a member of the Qaridiyya order. Others accused him of usurping his title of shaykh of the Muridiyya.[86] Another underlying complexity derived from the fact that Dièye wore two hats, so to speak. On the one hand, he was the leader of a large proportion of Murid students in Paris who were not his disciples but admired his knowledge, organizational skills, and oratory prowess; on the other, he was the spiritual guide of a few of these followers who developed a special bond with Dièye as disciples seeking spiritual guidance and enlightenment. The type of relationships that these two groups of disciples entertained with Dièye informed the ways they responded to his leadership.

Gradually, it became apparent that Dièye's objectives and his method of proselytizing were incompatible with the practices of the larger Murid community of Paris dominated by the traditionally educated traders operating around Gare de Lyon. Some Western-educated Murids also opposed him because of his lack of genealogical credentials. He was not a descendant of Ahmadu Bamba or renowned shaykhs of the Muridiyya. While both groups appreciated Dièye's contribution in giving greater visibility and prestige to the Muridiyya, they did not share his missionary vision. For them, converting Europeans was not an objective worthy of their time and resources. They preferred to invest in consolidating the ties between disciples in the diaspora and their shaykhs in Senegal and reinforcing communal bonds. They were opposed to the cultural revolution that Dièye was promoting to make the Muridiyya attractive to a non-Wolof-speaking and non-Senegalese constituency. This divide that pitted those who might be called "universalists" against "traditionalists" was not limited to the Parisian context; it also emerged in the United States and affected the relationships between Murid immigrants and their African American brethren in New York City.

The tension led Dièye to create the daara of Chanteloup-les-Vignes where his Paris-based disciples—mostly from Mauritius, Reunion Island, the Antilles, and Europe—held weekly worship sessions. During these sessions, the Qur'an was taught to the youth and those who needed an education; each nationality was given the opportunity to sing spiritual songs using their own tunes and languages, and presentations were given on topics related to Islam and Ahmadu Bamba's teachings.[87] Dièye placed great importance on the rituals of communal dhikr (psalmody of the sacred names of Allah). All of this was accomplished with a great deal of discipline and rigor, unlike the informality that characterized events organized at Gare de Lyon.

Dièye considered the non-Muslim population in Europe as the prime target of his calling. In order to make the Muridiyya attractive to this population, one needed first to show that the Muridiyya was an integral part of mainstream Islam and not an African sect. This meant that the disciples had to strictly follow Bamba's orthodox teachings by abiding by universal Islamic norms and rituals. In addition, one needed to address this population in the Western languages; so, in this regard, the translation, exegesis, and dissemination of Bamba's writings in French and English were crucial. Two features of Dièye's calling were particularly attractive to his Western audience (Black as well as White): his use of sacred music and his ecumenical view of Islam. Already in France in the 1980s he was an influential member of interfaith organizations such as l'Association des Gens du Livre (Association of the People of the Book), l'Association Islam Occident (Association Islam and the West), and la Fraternité d'Abraham (Abrahamic Brotherhood).[88] All of these organizations brought together Roman Catholics, Jews, and Muslims. Later, particularly during his ministry in the United States, Dièye would move his ecumenism beyond the realm of ideas to incorporate interfaith worship through church and synagogue visits and via the sharing of food and the singing of spiritual songs.[89]

Dièye returned to Senegal in 1982, but even before he left Paris, the organization he helped build had started to unravel.[90] The reason for this was not disagreement over spiritual or organizational matters, which as we have seen divided traders and students, but rather Senegalese politics.

Leopold S. Senghor, the first president of Senegal, resigned in 1980 and was succeeded by his prime minister, Abdou Diouf. Diouf acceded to power through constitutional means and was preparing to run for president in 1982. Upon coming to power, Diouf's Socialist Party (PS) officials began courting Dièye's Paris-based Murid movement, whose influence was also felt in Senegal where members traveled every summer to give lectures and mobilize Murid youth. Diouf had the full support of Murid caliph Shaykh Abdul Ahad and appointed Dièye as presidential adviser. He promised to promote Dièye to a ministerial cabinet position if he won the elections. Some of Dièye's disciples in Paris decided to support their leader's political gambit. They proposed to use the journal *Ndigël* to support the president's campaign, arguing that the caliph of the Muridiyya, who was also backing Diouf, would be pleased with the initiative. Some of the students who were committed to the original editorial line of political neutrality and strict focus on religious issues disagreed and were forced to resign. This rift, combined with Dièye's absence from the Parisian scene, gradually weakened the movement. Dièye increasingly turned his attention to his disciples in Mauritius, Reunion Island, and the United States and then to his political activities in Senegal.[91] Gradually the Murid organization in France entered a period of lethargy comparable to the situation in the 1960s and 1970s. The Muridiyya was no longer visible on the Paris public scene. Communal activities again retreated to the private rooms of the traders of Gare de Lyon, while those among the Murid students who still remained in Paris focused on their own spiritual development. It is the arrival of Shaykh Murtada Mbakke on the Parisian scene in the early 1990s that injected new dynamism into the community.

This chapter offers a comprehensive reconstruction of the history of Murid migration to France. Senegalese have a long history of migrating to France, but the nature of this migration changed over time. Earlier migration to France was mostly for educational purposes. Following World War II, labor migration became dominant, pioneered by Soninke- and Pulaar-speaking people from the Senegal River Valley.

Murid migration can be conceived as a form of labor migration, but compared to their compatriots from the Senegal River Valley, Murids were latecomers on the migration trail. Massive Murid migration to France did not start until the late 1970s. Droughts and economic depression prompted an exodus of Murid farmers from their heartland of western-central Senegal to the cities on the Atlantic coast and then later France. Another particularity of Murid migration resides in their professional occupations. While earlier Senegalese immigrants to France sought salaried employment, in continuity with their professional occupations at home, most Murids opted for self-employment in the informal sector of the economy as traders and street peddlers — or in some cases, artisans. This option was not dictated by constraints, it was the result of choice.

The relocation of Murid disciples from Senegal to the cities of France casts the Muridiyya in a new role. While affiliation with the Murid order did not have a major impact in inspiring migration or organizing the journey of the emigrant, Murid institutions became central as sources of identity and a locus of sociability once the Murid became an immigrant settled in France. For the Murid immigrant, these institutions played the same role that ethnicity and village solidarity played in the lives of other Senegalese immigrants.

Because of their preeminent role in the diaspora and the dominant voice of disciples in shaping these institutions, Murid institutions in the diaspora became contested sites where different perceptions of the Muridiyya competed. These diverging perceptions crystallized around differing conceptions of the order's vocation and the role of disciples in helping fulfill this vocation. What was at stake was the power to define what it means to be a Murid abroad. Migration exposed Murid disciples to a new societal reality and forced them to rethink their role within the broader community of Muslims and non-Muslims in France. As the story of Abdoulaye Dièye and the traders of Gare de Lyon demonstrates, visions of the Muridiyya were informed by disciples' educational background, their level of engagement with the global Muslim community and French society, and their reading and interpretations of Ahmadu Bamba's teachings. It demonstrates the influence of preemigration experience on the immigrant's conception of life abroad. While Western-educated Murids promoted innovative forms of cultural interventions and openness to French society, the traditionally educated traders resisted innovations and preached strict fealty to the leadership back in Tuubaa.

The role of Murid religious institutions became even more important with the closure of the French borders in the mid-1970s and the imposition of a visa on Senegalese immigrants in the mid-1980s. These events hampered immigrants' mobility while encouraging naturalization and family reunification. The following chapter investigates how the development of a community of Murid citizens in France transformed these immigrants' religious lives but also led to tensions and had serious implications on their relationship to space.

5 ⤳ Making Murid Space in Paris

> Do not think that because of the distance, you [Murids in France] are farther from Sëriñ Tuubaa. That is not the case. . . . You are far in *zāhir* [the manifest] but close in *bātin* [the hidden or mystical].
>
> —Shaykh Abdul Ahad, third caliph of the Murids

> When Sëriñ Murtada gave us the recommendation to buy the house [Aulnay-sous-Bois], we really did not know the benefit of doing so. It is only now that we realize how important this idea was. . . . Every Sunday when you come here you are able to meet people you need to be in touch with or somebody who can take you to them. . . . We do also have a Qur'anic teacher and you know how difficult it is to have Qur'anic education for our children here [in France]. . . . We will stick to Sëriñ Murtada's recommendations until we join him [in the hereafter] because we have seen the benefit of doing so.
>
> —Ibra Jóob

WHILE MURIDS have been migrating to France since the 1970s, it was only in the 1990s that they began to seek their own places of worship. This initiative coincided with the establishment of a community of Murids who were citizens and permanent residents in France and the arrival of growing numbers of women and children.

The quest for personal space and the creation of civil society associations, especially those promoting cultural and religious values, are some of the means by which immigrants seek acceptance and inclusion among the citizenry of the host nation. Efforts at place making can then be conceived as part of a quest for territorial legitimacy. This legitimacy is achieved by imbuing a space with recognizable material forms and cultural symbols. But the rooting of Murid culture in space can also help consolidate identity and preserve collective memory. As Maurice Halbwachs notes, when "history is rooted in the soil, it becomes a vital part of collective memory. To facilitate remembrance of the past, religious communities stamp space with their imprints and they do this by infusing space with history, customs or traditions."[1] Thus, by stamping space with their imprint, Murids are able to turn this space into a place they can appropriate and call home.

I use the Murid houses of Aulnay-sous-Bois and Taverny as case studies to investigate Murid experiments at place making in Paris. In doing so, I explore their motivations for owning a house in France, the roles of these places in the lives of Murid immigrants, and their impact on the interactions between the immigrants, the French state, and the Murid leadership in Senegal. The Murid house is a means for leaving the imprimatur of the Muridiyya on French soil and a way to claim a place for Ahmadu Bamba in the land of the people who persecuted him for thirty-two years.

The case studies of Aulnay and Taverny present two contrasting visions of the Muridiyya abroad, thus challenging the enshrined discourse that centers on Murid homogeneity, the rigidity of its hierarchy, and the idea that disciples lack agency. I explain how geographical distance from the Murid heartland creates a discursive space where new ways of being Murid can be imagined and experimented with.

The chapter begins with a discussion of the missionary work of Shaykh Murtada Mbakke, a son of Ahmadu Bamba and emissary of the Murid caliph in the diaspora. Perhaps of all the Murid shaykhs he best understood the vulnerabilities of Islamic and Murid values in the diaspora and the importance of creating institutions capable of protecting and promoting those values. I then reconstruct the history of the foundation of the Aulnay and Taverny houses, emphasizing how their diverging trajectories and leaderships shaped two discrete Murid cultures in France.

SHAYKH MURTADA IN PARIS

Shaykh Murtada first appeared on the public Murid scene in France in 1990, two years after he paid his first visit to the Murids of New York.[2] He stopped in Paris during his travels to pay a private visit to his personal disciples. One of them, Elhaaj Yande Jóob, was among the first Murids to settle in France. His house at Porte de Clignancourt served as a meeting place for Murid disciples.[3] Here is how Amadou Dramé, an influential member of the Murid organization in Paris and leader of the community for a decade (1990–2000) recalls the circumstances of Shaykh Murtada's arrival in the city.

> Shaykh Murtada came to Paris with Sëriñ Moodu Maamun Ñaŋ. Sëriñ Moodu Maamun asked me why we no longer organize [religious] events [as used to be the case when Cheikh Abdoulaye Dièye was living in Paris]. He said that he was aware

of my difficulties with Dièye but this should not be a reason to stop working [for Sëriñ Tuubaa]. He asked me if we were ready to work under the guidance of a son of Sëriñ Tuubaa who was a missionary of Islam. I said we were waiting for any guide and would be delighted to work under a son of Sëriñ Tuubaa. This is for us a prayer answered. He told me that Sëriñ Murtada was on his way to Libya for an Islamic conference but on his way back he will stop in Paris. I think that this was in the early 1990s. When he [Shaykh Murtada] came, he asked us to come to meet him. He sent his son Xaasim and Elhaaj Yande Jóob. He asked if it would be possible to do here what he has done throughout the African continent. That is to establish a house of Islam, help the education of the youth and grownups who need an education. I said yes if you give us the order to do so. He also asked us to organize a cultural week that he will preside over in person. I told him that the best time to organize such an event in France is the summer, when the students are on vacations and the traders who were [then] mostly seasonal workers were back [from Senegal].[4]

Dramé's account of the encounter with Shaykh Murtada, which took place in 1990, is highly personalized. It is likely that Sëriñ Moodu Maamun, who was probably acting on the injunction or with the approval of Shaykh Murtada, had also approached other leaders of the Muridiyya in Paris. He probably consulted Elhaaj Yande who was influential among the Goutte d'Or's Murid traders.

However, enlisting Dramé was a strategic decision, for he was an important Muridiyya figure in Paris. He was a notable member of the Dièye movement in the 1970s. But more importantly, Dramé was one of the rare sub-Saharan African Muslims to have a voice in the broader Islamic debate in France.[5] He was the head of the Federation of Islamic Associations of Africa, the Comoros, and the West Indies (FIACWI) and was a founding member of the Representative Council of Islam in France (CORIF [French acronym]). He served on the council for six years. The CORIF was an initiative of Pierre Joxe, the French minister of home affairs under President Mitterrand in 1989. The founding of this institution in the context of the Creil schoolgirl veil affair and increasing affirmation of Islamic identity among young French of North African ancestry, marked a turning point in French Muslim policy.[6] Until then, while France had the largest Muslim population in western Europe, few among these Muslims were devout practitioners or claimed Islam as an important part of their identity.

Religious practice was confined to personal and private spaces. Until the mid-1980s, few mosques existed in France, and many of them were poorly attended.[7] The French government had delegated the management of Muslim affairs in the country to the Paris mosque. This mosque, built in the 1920s as an acknowledgment of the contribution of France's Muslim subjects to World War I, was under the control of the Algerian government. Joxe envisioned the CORIF not as a political body representing the Muslims of France but as a consultative institution independent of foreign control: CORIF was tasked with mediating between the French government and the Muslims living in the country to help solve any problems related to the practice of Islam in France. Some of the notable achievements of CORIF were the allotment of plots for Muslim burial in public cemeteries, the availability of halal food in the army for French soldiers who requested it, and a consensus for deciding the dates of major Muslim holidays: Ramadan, Eid-el-Fitr, and Eid-al-Kabir. In his capacity as head of FIACWI and active member of CORIF, Dramé was the face of African Islam in France in the 1980s and 1990s. His connections at the Ministry of Home Affairs and among Muslim intellectual circles in Paris made him an important asset in achieving Shaykh Murtada's plan to bring the Muridiyya back into the French public sphere.

The establishment of the house of Islam (commonly known as Kër Sëriñ Tuubaa [KST], i.e., Ahmadu Bamba's house) was a centerpiece of this plan. During his trips to Paris, Shaykh Murtada stayed with his disciple Elhaaj Yande Jóob in the latter's house at Porte de Clignancourt. When the shaykh's visits began attracting a large number of Murids across Europe, the disciples moved Shaykh Murtada to hotels. But this created new problems. Hotel managers were unwilling to accommodate the Murid sense of hospitality. They complained about the heavy foot traffic in the hotel lobbies and hallways, sometimes late into the night, with hundreds of disciples lingering for days. There were also complaints about the noise and about the large quantities of food served on hotel grounds. The Murids paid hefty cleaning fees after the shaykh left. As news of Murid nuisance spread throughout the hotel industry, finding an acceptable venue for the shaykh to stay became increasingly difficult.[8] Additionally, neither the shaykh nor the disciples were happy about hotel accommodation. They worried about the ritual cleanliness of the rooms where Shaykh Murtada stayed. As one disciple involved in organizing Shaykh Murtada's visit told me, "You can never know about the morality of the person who was sleeping in the suite where the shaykh stayed and who was going to occupy the room after he had left."[9] Disciples were particularly worried about ritual cleanliness because the hotel lounge where the shaykh was staying served as a temporary mosque. Disciples prayed here and read not only the Qur'an but also Ahmadu Bamba's devotional poems.

However, beyond overcoming the inconveniences inherent in hotel accommodations, having a house for the Murid community in Paris fulfilled even higher spiritual aims. It was this idea that Shaykh Abdul Ahad (1914–89), the third caliph of the Muridiyya, wanted to convey when he told the founders of the Murid dahira in Paris: "Of all the hadiyas [pious donations] I receive, those coming from disciples in France are the ones that amaze me the most. Because if the French's wish were granted then I would not be here to collect them."[10] The caliph was alluding here to the arrest and deportation of his father, Ahmadu Bamba, to Gabon where he stayed for seven years, hinting that the colonial administration's intention was to end his father's life and that the thriving Murid community of Paris in the twentieth century signifies their failure. He was born in 1914, twelve years after his father's return to Senegal in 1902.

In the mind of Murid disciples, the story behind the establishment of Kër Sëriñ Tuubaa is never a question of real estate alone. Everywhere, the establishment of such a house is an effort to turn ordinary space into an extraordinary place and build a bridge to the holy city of Tuubaa. Murids living abroad, and especially those among them whose mobility is curtailed because of their undocumented status, work requirements, or limited resources utilize the space to lament their conditions and express their longing for the time when they can commune with the holy city and its inhabitants. The Murid leadership understands the poignancy of this emotional bond with Tuubaa and has offered different responses to alleviate the disciples' longing. For example, Shaykh Abdul Ahad, responding to the letter of a disciple bemoaning his long absence and the distance separating him from the holy city, wrote the following:

> You may be far physically, but you are always eager to follow our recommendations and stay away from what is proscribed. There are people here under the shadow of the mosque [of Tuubaa] who do neither. They do not listen and do not follow our advice. Therefore, you are closer to us than those people are. Do not think that because of the distance, you are farther from Sëriñ Tuubaa. That is not the case. Those who live here in our neighborhood but do not follow Sëriñ Tuubaa's teachings are farther from him than you who live in France. You are far in *zāhir* [the manifest] but close in *bātin* [the hidden or mystical].[11]

Shaykh Murtada's recommendation to Murids in the diaspora to open houses of Islam should be understood in the context of this struggle to make a home abroad. By emphasizing the superiority of closeness in *bātin*, Shaykh Abdul Ahad, writing in the 1980s when there was not yet a large settled Murid community in the diaspora, seemed to suggest a symbolic erasure of space, collapsing Tuubaa and the diaspora. Instead, by recommending the building of KST to communities of Murid citizens in the West, Shaykh Murtada appears to propose the re-creation of Tuubaa in the diaspora.

Kër Sëriñ Tuubaa serves as a cultural center and typically includes a guesthouse for visiting shaykhs and newly arrived immigrants needing temporary shelter. The space should also include a Qur'anic school, a prayer room, guest rooms, and space for weekly dahira meetings and small religious commemorations. All houses have a kitchen and a modern sound system for the performance of dhikr (Sufi ritual chants) and the loud psalmody of Ahmadu Bamba's poems. Some have a library and a modest printing press facility dedicated to producing the qasidas. They are all decorated with photos and paintings of Ahmadu Bamba, the Great Mosque of Tuubaa, pictures of the deceased caliphs of the Muridiyya, and current leaders of the order. This space-creation strategy is documented by Victoria Ebin's research in which she explains how Murid itinerant traders create sacred space using objects, photos, singing dhikrs, and qasidas wherever they are.[12]

The house is imagined as a receptacle of Ahmadu Bamba's spiritual grace, which emanates from the holy city of Tuubaa and saturates all places associated with his name. For the Murid faithful, the fact that Ahmadu Bamba has been deceased for nearly a century in no way precludes the continued potency of his spiritual power. Disciples believe in his continued presence in their midst, as was the case in Taverny when, during a *mawlid* celebration, a young boy saw the iconic image of the Murid shaykh projected on the wall. Murids from all over Paris converged to the house of Taverny to witness the miracle.[13] There is certainly no greater evidence of a claim to space than to witness a Murid miracle in the Christian and secular French space. Ahmadu Bamba's appearance is, for the Murid faithful, a tangible sign of his presence among them and reinforces the conviction that he has accepted the house dedicated to him in Paris as his own.

Shaykh Murtada understood that it would be difficult to bring his project of a house of Islam to fruition in Paris without a strong organization and a credible leadership capable of mobilizing the disciples to muster the necessary resources. He was also aware of the fractious nature of the Murid order in which multiple and competing lineages maintain a tight hold on their flock. All Murid disciples pledge allegiance to the caliph or paramount leader of the Muridiyya, who is the oldest male descendant of Ahmadu Bamba. But their loyalty goes first to the lineage they are affiliated with and whose leading shaykh acts as their intermediary with the caliph. To overcome the potential obstacle represented by the disciples' divided loyalties, Shaykh Murtada recommended that each disciple remain in their lineage dahira (*dahira Kër*) and continue their activities to support that lineage. But he also recommended the formation of an umbrella dahira uniting all lineages that would be responsible for the organization of community events such as the Great Màggal of Tuubaa, commemorating the beginning of Ahmadu Bamba's exile to Gabon and the mawlid (the birthday of the Prophet Muhammad celebrated by all Muslims, especially Sufis and Shias). This new dahira would also be tasked with raising funds for the acquisition of the house of Islam and for organizing the annual Ahmadu Bamba culture week in Paris. He suggested that the dahira open an account at the Paris branch of Banque de l'Habitat du Sénégal (Senegalese Housing Bank, BHS [French acronym]) and contributed seed money to the account.

When asked by the disciples to appoint the leadership of the new organization, Shaykh Murtada declined and justified his decision by saying, "I do not live with you here. I do not know the people. You live here so you know each other. I ask you to go downstairs to elect your leaders. After you do so, bring the list of the names of those you have chosen and I will come down to pray for you and give you a name [for the new dahira]."[14] He gave the organization the name *Jamaat tahawuni a la tahati lahi* (community that unites in self-help for the sake of pleasing God and avoiding what is wrong). The organization is also known by its French name, Collectif des Mourides de France (Coalition of Murids in France, CMF [French acronym]). The word "self-help" suggests Shaykh Murtada's wish to convey the idea that his initiatives were intended for the disciples' interest alone. He was not animated, as some disciples suspected, by the ambition to build a base in Paris in order to boost his prestige and spiritual authority. This same intention seems to have guided the amendments he made to the list of dahira officers that the assembly presented to him. He ordered that Mustafa Njaay replace his disciple, Elhaaj Yande Jóob, who was appointed general treasurer. Mustafa was a successful Murid trader and leader of the local chapter of the powerful Murid lineage of Daaru Xudoos, founded by the family of Mustafa Mbakke, the elder son and first successor of Ahmadu Bamba. He also proposed the appointment of Amadou Dramé, who was not yet his disciple, to the position of general secretary of the dahira in place of Basiiru Jóob, who was the disciples' pick. Dramé's choice rested on his dual status as both a traditional and a Western-educated Murid disciple and on his familiarity with French bureaucracy and the politics of Islam in France.

However, despite Shaykh Murtada's cautious approach and his prestige as one of the only two living sons of Ahmadu Bamba, there was still resistance. No progress was made on the plan for three years. Here is how one leading member of the Muridiyya involved in carrying out Shaykh Murtada's vision explains the difficulties they faced: "Two to three years passed until people understood and accepted the call for unity. Some thought that Sëriñ Murtada wanted only to boost his own dahira. Some elder Murids were reluctant as well as those disciples who manage funds [of lineage dahira]. Shaykh Saliu [the Murid caliph at the time] intervened telling everybody that Sëriñ Murtada was working under his authority for Sëriñ Tuubaa and that everybody should support him. He told Sëriñ Mbakke Soxna Lo [head of the Daaru Xudoos lineage] and others to spread this message. From then on things started to improve."[15]

Perhaps beyond concerns about Shaykh Murtada's suspected ambition for control, the reluctance of some disciples was dictated by a perceived disconnect between their own migratory project and the shaykh's plan. At the time, a large majority of Murid disciples living in Paris were single males. Although many of them had been living in Europe for decades and some had even united with their families, they still construed their migration as temporary and thus resisted investing in building projects. This attitude was consistent with the behavior of sub-Saharan African Muslims in France. Gilles Kepel, for example, reveals that unlike North Africans and Turks, sub-Saharan Muslims are less likely to contribute funds for the building of mosques in France and prefer instead to build places of worship in their home countries.[16]

Even after the skepticism of disciples was overcome and people started to embrace the project, it took a few more years before the Murids were able to acquire a house. In France since the 1980s, the rise of Islamophobia and grassroots opposition made it difficult for Muslims to find places of worship. As Kepel observes, the inevitable response to Muslims' request for a license to build a mosque in the cities of France is the same everywhere: "refusal, delay, or no response (*classer sans suite*)."[17] Even when Muslim communities have had success buying spaces without external religious signs such as minarets or domes (e.g., abandoned warehouses, a house, a store) to be used as places of worship, mayors have used their right of preemption to purchase the property in order to deny it to Muslim groups. There is no doubt that hostility toward Islam might have affected the Murid disciples' project. However, by and large, Murids and sub-Saharan African Muslims have suffered less Islamophobia than their Middle Eastern and North African counterparts. They have benefited from a certain invisibility, given that until recently sub-Saharan Africa was not associated with Islam in France. Sub-Saharan African Muslims have also managed to remain under the radar by avoiding controversy, staying away from the battles that French Muslims (most of them of North African origin) have waged against the secular state for recognition.[18] The French state—especially local governments that deal with Muslim communities' demands—continues to look at Black African Muslims through the lens of 1970s thinking, when Islam was seen as a positive social force that could help facilitate the socialization and integration in French society of strangers out of the reach of the state.

AULNAY-SOUS-BOIS: THE FIRST MURID HOUSE IN FRANCE

The difficulties that hindered the acquisition of the house were more organizational than administrative in nature. The umbrella dahira responsible for raising funds to buy a house first relied on traditional Murid urban fundraising techniques where collection boxes are placed in Murid-owned shops to receive voluntary contributions. This method proved to be a failure. After collecting donations for over two years, the dahira could not raise more than $20,000.[19] Rumors of embezzlement swirled. In 1996, when the opportunity to buy a house for $130,000 in the commune of Aulnay-sous-Bois presented itself, Shaykh Murtada suggested that Mustafa Njaay lead fundraising efforts. Mustafa and his brother Saer were able to raise $75,000 on their own that year, enough to cover the down payment for the purchase of the house.[20]

Aulnay was not the initial choice of the dahira. Aware of the difficulties of finding an affordable place where Muslim religious practices would be acceptable in Ile de France, nearer to Paris, the dahira had first set its sight on the area behind the rail line that encircles Paris, beyond the city limits.[21] Aulnay, situated only 8.6 miles from the center of Paris and accessible by train and bus, was a particularly convenient site for the planned KST (see map 5.1). The Murids were also attracted to the house because of certain signs that made it especially suitable for a house dedicated to Ahmadu Bamba. The owner of the house was a single male who did not own a dog (an unclean animal in Muslim beliefs), did not drink alcohol (prohibited by Islam), and was believed to be living a moral life.[22] Even the generosity of the notary, who agreed to cut his honorarium in half, asking for 5 percent of the cost of the house instead of the regular 10 percent, was seen by the Murids in charge of the project as a sign of the manifestation of Ahmadu Bamba's baraka (gift of grace) and God's merciful hand.[23]

The small village of Aulnay-sous-Bois, located in the forest on the northeastern side of the Paris agglomeration, was integrated into the French capital during the industrial revolution. In the 1960s and 1970s it became a hub of the automobile industry, attracting immigrants from southern Europe and North Africa who worked for Peugeot and Citroën. A smaller number of West Africans were likely employed in those plants as well. Nowadays the auto industry is no longer an important part of Aulnay's economy, but the population of immigrants has remained, mostly confined to the northern side of the municipality. In 2010, over 26 percent of the population of Aulnay-sous-Bois were immigrants, most of them from Algeria, Morocco, Turkey, and sub-Saharan African countries.[24] At the time, the mayor of northern Aulnay, where the house is located, was a socialist. The presence of a large community of Muslims and a mayor sympathetic to immigrants probably facilitated the purchase of the property.

The excitement following the signing of the contract with the seller in August 1996 and the realization that the Murid community could finally claim a piece of Paris for Ahmadu Bamba galvanized the disciples. In one year, more than enough money was raised to complete the payment of the mortgage on the building and to begin renovation. The three-story building I have visited multiple times since 2010 consists of two prayer rooms for male and female worshippers, a VIP guest room for Murid dignitaries, a library, a Qur'anic school, additional rooms, and internal bathrooms. External bathrooms are found in the courtyard along with a large kitchen under a tent. The property includes five hundred undeveloped square meters, and there are plans to build a mosque and a cultural center. Since its acquisition, Kër Sëriñ Tuubaa (KST) of Aulnay-sous-Bois has become the beating heart of the Muridiyya in Paris. It is a collective property of the Murid community where all religious events are held. Weekly meetings of the umbrella dahira are convened there every Sunday afternoon, coinciding with Qur'anic classes for youth so that parents can meet while their children are learning the Qur'an. Lineage dahiras also have access. The typical dahira meeting starts with Qur'anic recitation followed by *duruus* ("lessons," from the Arabic word *darassa*, meaning "to study"), which are devoted to silent study of Ahmadu Bamba's sacred poetry. Following the silent study there are often loud declamations of Bamba's poems conducted by a kurel (a choir composed of male youths). The *asr* and *maghreb* (late afternoon and dusk) prayers are observed collectively and led by the imam. The weekly congregational Friday prayer is also held there. These religious activities are sanctifying acts that contribute to detaching the house from the surrounding properties with the same external appearance but lack the house's devotional dedication. At the same time, the house is symbolically united with hundreds of other similar places in the Murid diaspora that perform the same rituals on the same day during the same hours, helping to foster an imagined global Murid community beyond geographical borders.[25] The dahira ends with a business session attended by all members where dues are collected and projects debated.

Dahira meetings are also where new additions to the community are welcomed, and the deaths of fellow disciples or their relatives in Senegal are announced and prayers said. Visiting Murid shaykhs are introduced and invited to address the community, and funds are collected to support those in need or to repatriate bodies for burial at the cemetery in Tuubaa. Murids do not bury their deceased brothers abroad. The imam, who is central to the running of the house, is also the Qur'anic teacher and helps maintain cohesion in the community by mediating disputes, including domestic conflicts. Imam Buso is a member of the Mbakke family that Shaykh Murtada sent to Paris to minister to the Murids. Yet dahira talks are not exclusively about religion. Dahira meetings are also occasions to graciously share food and drink offered by fellow disciples and for people to debate Senegalese politics and to comment on the latest wrestling match in the arenas of Senegal.[26] Some take advantage of the moment to share information about business. Thus, for Murid disciples, KST is a home away from home and a safe space, offering protection from police brutality and increasingly violent manifestations of racism, which is the lot of unwanted immigrants. This is especially true in the case of street traders like the Murids whose professional occupation exposes them to everyday face-to-face contact with their unwilling hosts.[27]

The earlier skepticism of some disciples about the utility of the house has now given way to full embrace. Most realize that although their aspiration is to return home someday, there is also the possibility that they may only fulfill this aspiration after their death. Since the French government stopped so-called labor migration in 1974 and imposed draconian conditions for acquiring a visa, undocumented Senegalese immigrants are no longer able to engage in circular migration, leaving them with the choice to return home definitely or to stay in France as undocumented. Most choose to stay. Some have tried to bring their families to France, but this is extremely difficult. Additionally, whether undocumented or legal residents, the children of many Murid immigrants are French citizens and not as emotionally attached to Senegal as their parents are. The house of Aulnay remains the only place where these children can experience Senegalese communal cultural life and get a religious education. Ibra Jóob, one of the elder Murid disciples of Aulnay-sous-Bois (who was probably skeptical about the project in the beginning), explains the centrality of the house in the life of the community:

> When Sëriñ Murtada gave us the recommendation to buy the house, we really did not know the benefit of doing so. It is only now that we realize how important this idea was. People come from everywhere to visit the place. Every Sunday when you come here you are able to meet people you need to be in touch with. And you know, strangers [in a foreign country] are vulnerable like blind people. Here, you will find that person you need or somebody who can take you to him. Every person that comes here and does not have a place to stay, we will allow him to stay for a week. Visiting members of the Mbakke family stay here and disciples come to visit them and bring donations. We do also have a Qur'anic teacher and you know how difficult it is to have Qur'anic education for our children here. Children only have Saturday and Sunday to learn Qur'an. . . . This is what Sëriñ Murtada wanted. There are even some adults who did not know much about religious practice and it is here that they learned how to practice their religion. We will stick to Sëriñ Murtada's recommendations until we join him [in the hereafter] because we have seen the benefit of doing so.[28]

Jóob's appreciation of the services that the house renders to the Murid community is shared by all of my informants. Beyond spiritual solace, the house is a refuge against growing anti-immigrant hostility, especially toward Muslims in France, and a safe space where people find support and empathy as they confront increasing economic hardships and the difficulties of raising a family in foreign land.

TAVERNY: ANOTHER PLACE, ANOTHER FACE OF THE MURIDIYYA IN FRANCE

Taverny, the other communal Murid house in Paris, has a different history than Aulnay-sous-Bois. These diverging histories mark the different paths for the two houses. Aulnay and Taverny represent two distinct faces of the Muridiyya in France and reflect the bifurcated readings of Ahmadu Bamba's teachings by two contrasting constituencies and their divergent perceptions of what it means to be a Murid in the diaspora. We have already seen such a divide play out between Murid students and traders in Paris in the late 1970s and the 1980s, and in some ways the stories of Aulnay and Taverny replicate a similar bifurcation.

Taverny, like Aulnay-sous-Bois, is a municipality located in the Paris region. It is situated in the northwestern suburbs of the French capital, and in 2010 it had a population of 26,440 inhabitants. The immigrant community forms 11.07 percent of the population and includes a significant number of North Africans.[29] The acquisition of the house of Taverny was not an initiative of Murid disciples. It was the culmination of the efforts of Imam Mamadou N'Sangou, a French Muslim of Cameroonian descent (now a Murid disciple), who migrated to Paris in the 1980s.[30] N'Sangou, now in his seventies, is the founder of the Islamic Council of France, an organization dedicated to promoting the interests of the Muslim population in Taverny and France as a whole. Like Amadou Dramé, N'Sangou was actively engaged in the public debate about Islam in France. He has worked with several French ministers of home affairs, beginning with Jean Pierre Chevènement (1997–2000), a former cabinet member in the Mitterrand administration. N'Sangou is credited by some with coining the expression "Islam of France," which relates to the notion of "*Fiqh* of the minority." This is an idea developed by some Islamic institutions and Muslim intellectuals in the West to advocate for the necessity of adapting Islamic law and practices to accommodate the needs of Muslim citizens of the Western world.[31] N'Sangou was involved in interfaith activities and toured Nazi concentration camps around Europe with Jewish, Catholic, and Protestant representatives.

N'Sangou's activism was prompted by the situation he found in Taverny when he moved to the city in the mid-1980s. The locality had no place of worship for Muslims, and one had to drive over a dozen miles to the central Mosque of Paris or to other faraway mosques to take part in Friday prayers. Taverny had a sizable number of first- and second-generation Muslim immigrants of mostly North African origin. These Muslims formed a cultural association, and in 1992 they were able to secure a disused municipal building for use as a mosque. But the escalation of the civil war in Algeria, French military involvement in the First Gulf War, and mounting Islamic radicalism stoked hostility toward Islam in France, and Taverny was no exception. The mayor of the municipality expelled the Muslims from this municipal property they had been using for prayers and had the building destroyed (citing "health hazards") to make space for a park. The Muslim organization sued the municipality but lost.

Imam N'Sangou, who had complicated relations with the North Africans who dominated the Muslim organization of Taverny, took matters into his own hands. He turned his living room into a place for prayers and initiated a policy of rapprochement with the socialist mayor, Maurice Boscavert. He reached out to the mayor's office to explain the orientation of his organization and to plead his cause as a French citizen leading peaceful Muslims solely motivated by their aspiration to practice their religion in full compliance with the laws of the republic. Following the mayor's advice, he mobilized the Muslim community of Taverny to raise the resources necessary to buy their own place of worship. In March 2000, he received a call from the mayor notifying him that there was a house for sale in the city and that the Muslim organization should try to buy it and use it as their mosque.

The house is located not far from downtown Taverny, at 273 rue de Paris, at the intersection of two districts (see map 5.1). The built space occupies 1,045 square meters and consists of a three-story building with twenty rooms, a large kitchen, several toilets, and a basement. The parking space covers 3,000 square meters. The property was owned by two sisters who used the facility as an international school for the education of young girls from wealthy families in the French bourgeois tradition. Later on, the building was turned into an institution for educating underprivileged children. When the sisters died, they bequeathed the house to their foster son, Mr. Desenfants, who decided to sell it. N'Sangou and the Muslim community of Taverny were excited by the prospect of having their own place of worship for the first time, but there was some apprehension. First,

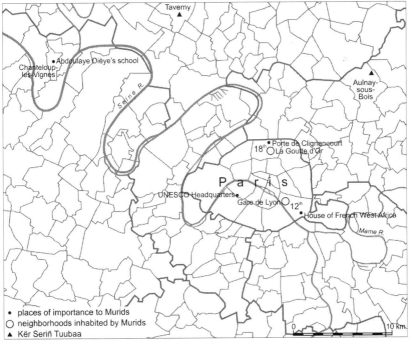

MAP 5.1. Places of importance to Murids in Paris. Map drawn by Eric Ross.

they were unsure that the owner would agree to sell the house to Muslims knowing that it could be turned into a mosque. Second, the asking price of $600,000, although modest compared to normal market value, was still out of reach for the Muslim community.

N'Sangou's misgivings about the willingness of the owner to sell to Muslims were put to rest as soon as he spoke with him:

> When I called him [Mr. Desenfants] he asked me to tell him who I was and what my intentions were. I told him that I was the head of an organization named Islamic Council of France and that we wanted to buy the house for our children's education. I avoided talking about mosque because there were controversies about that. But he indicated that the mayor had told him that we wanted to turn the house into a mosque and that he was pleased to see that happen. He said that he grew up in that property and that he would never sell it to speculators who will cut it into pieces for money. "I am very happy for your proposal." He gave me two years to raise the money to pay him.[32]

N'Sangou was relieved by the owner's willingness to do business with him, but securing the money to buy the house proved to be a challenge. His organization was able to raise the down payment of $60,000, which gave them the right of preemption with the possibility to use the property while collecting additional funds to complete the purchase. For over a year N'Sangou toured Arab embassies in Paris with recommendations from the French Ministry of Home Affairs; he also met with Arab officials visiting mosques in Paris and traveled to Saudi Arabia to look for financial support—but without much success. The terrorist attacks of September 11, 2001, and the US crackdown on Muslim charitable organizations rendered the prospect of getting financial aid from the Middle East even more remote. A few months before the expiration of the preemption deadline, which would have cost them the down payment and the house, a Senegalese acquaintance suggested that N'Sangou travel to Senegal to ask for the support of the caliph of the Muridiyya.

Out of desperation, N'Sangou decided to make the trip to Tuubaa despite the skepticism of his North African constituency, who mockingly wondered how one can expect to receive from a poor country like Senegal the financial help they could not receive from affluent Muslim countries in the Middle East. Here is N'Sangou's description of his meeting with the late Shaykh Saliu, then caliph of the Muridiyya:

I went to Senegal to a place I did not know. I did not even know the shaykh I was visiting. . . . I saw a very nice mosque but I did not know that I was in Tuubaa. I saw many people sitting on the ground, five to six hundred people, some would crawl [to get closer to the shaykh], and nobody was wearing headgear. Yet when we arrived they made way for us until we were in front of the Shaykh. . . . We brought a photo album where we had pictures of the property. He wanted us to explain every page. After he finished looking at the album, he asked me what I wanted to do with the building. I said we wanted the Muslims to use it for the five [daily] prayers, to teach Qur'an, to celebrate the Friday prayer, and also to meet with non-Muslims interested in a dialogue with Muslims. He then asked about the price of the property, I told him that the cost was 3,000,000 francs [$600,000]. He said, "I will buy it for you."[33]

When N'Sangou's party left, Shaykh Saliu handed to Aatu Jaañ the contract for the house N'Sangou had given him. Jaañ is the head of the daara Hizbut Tarqiyya, an organization formed by former Murid students at the University of Dakar in the 1970s.[34] Jaañ, who earned a BA in geography, had been a close adviser to successive leaders of the Muridiyya and was trusted with taking care of the caliph's most important guests, including heads of state and ambassadors. He also played a central role in the organization of the Great Màggal of Tuubaa. Jaañ asked Sulaymaan Juuf, a member of his organization, to study the dossier and provide them guidance as to how to move forward. Juuf studied law and political science at the University of Montpellier and was at the time working on a thesis on the anthropology of law at the Sorbonne.[35] He discovered that the contract brought by N'Sangou included a "substitution provision." This means that Shaykh Saliu could buy the house on behalf of the Muslim community of Taverny and still retain legal ownership of the property. They proposed the formula to N'Sangou, who gladly accepted the arrangement. There was only a month and half left before they would lose the right of preemption and the down payment.

Soon after N'Sangou returned to Paris, Shaykh Saliu sent Aatu Jaañ with a certified check for $600,000 to close the deal. He also tasked Hizbut Tarqiyya with managing the house on behalf of the Muslim community of Taverny. Jaañ suggested the caliph appoint Juuf as manager of the house. The arrival of Juuf and his team was not welcome by all. Some people, especially the North Africans, believed that Shaykh Saliu had bought the house for the Muslim community of Taverny, that the Murids should not interfere with the management of the building and the center's activities, and that it was up to them to continue to run the place as they had done for nearly two years. Most of these North Africans, especially the Algerians and Moroccans, were followers of *salafism*, a culturally conservative and politicized form of Islam that was hostile to Sufism or the mystical Islam professed by the Muridiyya. But Hizbut Tarqiyya did not share their opinions. As Juuf indicates: "When we came here [Taverny], there were a lot of Wahhabis [Saudi tradition of salafism] who were expecting that once the house was bought, they would take control. We found here their books but when I came, I put away those books and brought out other books, including Sëriñ Tuubaa's writings. They were quite unhappy. But since this house is under the name of Shaykh Saliu and the contract says that everything in the house is his property, they could not do anything. We teach the shaykh [Ahmadu Bamba]'s books and religious knowledge we trust."[36]

The tension between the North Africans and the Murids was due not only to doctrinal differences or misunderstandings about the legal status of the house: race also played a role. Imam N'Sangou, who joined the Muridiyya during his trip to Tuubaa, hinted at this when he indicated that the voices of Black African Muslims carried little weight while the Arabs dominated the Muslim organization of Taverny.[37] Juuf noted that some of the North Africans did not want to be led by a Black imam, and some even approached the mayor's office to ask for a different venue for prayers, arguing that sub-Saharan Muslims pray differently.[38] Their demand was dismissed as racially motivated when the mayor's chief of staff, who happened to be of North African origin, attended prayers in the Murid house three times and could see no difference between the way people prayed there and the way Muslims pray everywhere else.

The issue of racial prejudice against sub-Saharans in the Arab world has made headlines in recent years with newspaper articles about the inhumane treatment of stranded African migrants in Algeria and Morocco, the persistent practice of slavery in Mauritania, and the auctioning of enslaved Africans in Libya.[39] However, Arab prejudice against Black African Muslims is not only about race: it is also a reflection of their claim of cultural superiority, as speakers of the language of the Qur'an and originators of Islam. The term *muwallad* (convert) that is applied to Muslims of non-Arab ethnicity connotes this feeling of superiority. Turks in France, who are also muwallad like sub-Saharan Muslims, have tense relations with North Africans, who criticize them for not speaking good Arabic and often prefer to worship separately.[40]

However, the tension was not limited to the relations with the North Africans of Taverny: the Murid leadership of Aulnay also harbored some resentment against Juuf and his team. Their displeasure became manifest when Aatu Jaañ and the delegation sent by Shaykh Saliu to conclude the purchase of the house went to Aulnay to pay a courtesy visit to the community there. Jaañ's delegation immediately noticed the discontent among their hosts. One member of the delegation said the atmosphere was cold and uncomfortable.[41] Later on, rumors circulated that the Aulnay leadership had decided not to set foot in Taverny unless ordered to do so by Shaykh Murtada. When, in 2002, the shaykh came to Paris to preside over the Ahmadu Bamba culture week, some at Aulnay tried to discourage him from visiting the house of Taverny. When he decided to go anyway, they tried to make sure he cut his visit short.

People at Aulnay had many complaints against Taverny. Some of them did not appreciate the fact that they were not consulted or put in charge of buying and managing the Taverny property. They believed that, given their status as the oldest and largest Murid dahira in France, the caliph should have entrusted them with the management of the Taverny house. Others were unhappy about the dominant role of Hizbut Tarqiyya and their management style. Here is how one member of the Taverny team saw the difference between the two communities: "For us the two houses [Aulnay and Taverny] equally belong to Sëriñ Tuubaa but the approach and the way we understand and live the Muridiyya is different. Here everything is structured; we have projects that we try to realize. They [Aulnay] did not have a mosque, but now they have transformed their lounge to turn it into a mosque. The dynamics are different. Here we are open to all Muslims. We are not community driven."[42]

He added: "Some of our Murid brothers are used to doing things a certain way. For example, the sexes mingle. Women go their hair uncovered etc. . . . We brought more rigor and we tried to root our actions in knowledge. Some people reproached us for being too bossy. But this is not the case. We consider this place to be an embassy of Islam, anybody who comes here needs to feel the presence of Islam."

These statements offer a glimpse into the Taverny leadership's conception of their mission. The insistence on the presence of Islam does not mean that they believe that Islam was absent at Aulnay. But for them the house serves a multinational community of Muslims and thus should emphasize the universal dimensions of Islam. Sulaymaan Juuf made this opinion clear to me when he observed, "I was sent here by Hizbut Tarqiyya to manage the place in the spirit of openness and universalism that the Caliph recommended."[43] As discussed previously, the issue of universalism versus parochialism was also central to the controversy between Dièye's disciples and the Murid traders of Gare de Lyon in the late 1970s and 1980s. The divide in Senegal is also felt between disciples who emphasize the universal dimension of Ahmadu Bamba's teachings and appeals and those who put greater value on the consolidation of local communal bonds. But this divide takes on a different significance in the diaspora, where Murid disciples come in contact with a more diverse Muslim community and where different Islamic traditions meet. The dispute seems to crystallize two opposing views of the mission of the Murid diaspora. For some, mostly Western-educated students and professionals, the emphasis should be on *dawa* (calling, preaching) to make the Muridiyya attractive to the people in the host countries and to claim a place for the Muridiyya in the *umma*, the global Muslim community. For the others, mostly non-Western-educated traders and workers of the first generation, the organization must focus on serving the Murid immigrant community abroad and the leadership in Tuubaa. Converting people and engaging others, Muslims or non-Muslims, should not be a priority. These two views have different implications in terms of which image of the Muridiyya to promote, engagement with France's broader Muslim community, the types of activities to organize, and the use of language and modern technologies.

For the Taverny team, although the agenda of the local Murid community remains central, they do not see it as an obstacle for accommodating other Muslims. For example, the mosque is led by imams of different nationalities, the facility is open to all Muslims every day until 11:00 p.m., and it is segregated according to gender. When I visited the house in May 2010, Qur'anic lessons were offered by Yunus Jóob, a Western-educated Murid disciple who was active in the Dièye movement in Senegal and France. Every summer the house organizes a summer camp that attracts on average eighty young girls and boys of mostly Guinean and Malian origins from all over France to study the Qur'an and socialize. There are also classes for adults interested in studying Ahmadu Bamba's qasidas. Three kurels (choirs) are in charge of singing Bamba's devotional poems. The library, which receives special attention from the management, is outfitted with Qur'an texts, books of hadiths (of the Maliki school of jurisprudence dominant in West Africa) in French and Arabic, the writings of Sufi thinkers, and Ahmadu Bamba's books. The house also organizes lectures where scholars of different ethnicities and backgrounds, including those critical of Sufism, are invited to give presentations (in French and Wolof) on dimensions of Islam and the Muridiyya. These events are streamed live on the internet and posted on YouTube.

At Taverny, the highlight of the week is not the dahira meeting but Friday prayer, which attracts worshippers of diverse nationalities, including eastern and central Europeans, Asians, and some North Africans. The imam, who is a young professional, gives his sermon in classical Arabic and French. Major Murid events are celebrated, but unlike in Aulnay, people are discouraged from gathering in the house just for the sake of socializing. As observed by a member of the leadership, one needs to come here for a purpose. Disciples in need of shelter are accommodated just for a few days, and the time of residence is limited, even for members of the Mbakke family. These strict codes have led to tensions, especially with Murid shaykhs who resent the restriction imposed on them, claiming their right to use a property belonging to an organization founded by their ancestor and funded by his disciples.[44]

Another difference resides in the leadership and functions of the two houses. There is no formal dahira in Taverny. Sulaymaan Juuf, who is the *jawriñ* (leader), was appointed by the daara Hizbut Tarqiyya on the order of the late Shaykh Saliu. Hizbut is no longer involved with the house, but Juuf continues to report to the head of Shaykh Saliu's lineage—who is the legal owner of the house. Juuf formed his own team composed of (unlike in Aulnay) former Murid students and professionals, many of whom have a graduate degree. His deputy, Gora Jóob, is a doctoral student in sociology; another member has a doctorate in sociology. Many others are students working on their degrees. This leadership, unlike that of Aulnay, matured in France and developed an understanding of the Muridiyya influenced by the Islamic debate in France and their perception of the spiritual needs of its African Muslim immigrants. Education seems to be at the top of their agenda as they apprehend the threat represented by both the institutions of the French secular state, especially the public school system, and the influence of radical Islamist ideas on the Islamic identity of young African girls and boys. They try to provide an education that will reconcile the multiple identities of these children who are simultaneously African, Muslim, and French. This is the idea that Juuf conveys when he notes, "We want the place [Taverny] to remain a place for the Islamic cult where the Muslims of the future will be trained. There are Muslims in France, but Islamic education is lacking. The most successful in this domain are the Wahhabiyya but their teachings create conflicts and tensions in the country. Worship in peace is impossible without good relationships with the country and its authorities. There are now generations of immigrants that do not have a place to send their children for [religious] education. The shaykh's work is a form of peaceful Jihad to preserve Islamic culture in peace."[45]

The place of women in the houses is another area of difference. In both Aulnay and Taverny women are important members of the community.[46] They play a critical role as fundraisers (they are in fact the most generous donors) and event organizers. They are the backbone of Murid diasporic communities. It is revealing that Murids in the diaspora did not make a concerted effort to acquire their own place and organize communal events until family reunification allowed women a greater presence. *Beernde*, or the cooking and sharing of a large amount of food, is a defining feature of Murid hospitality.[47] No Murid event takes place without beernde, and women are primarily responsible for raising funds and cooking the food. For Murid women like the Ñas Tijani devotees of Dakar studied by Joseph Hill, cooking is a form of worship and an expression of feminine piety from which they expect God's reward.[48] However, if women assume similar roles at Aulnay and Taverny, their presence is not equally felt. They have greater visibility at Aulnay. At Taverny women are a rare sight; at Aulnay, dahira Maam Jaara Buso, a women's-only organization, is quite active in the community. The dahira, which is named after Ahmadu Bamba's mother, is a transnational organization with chapters across the Murid diaspora.[49] The French chapter is based at the Murid house of Aulnay where it holds its meetings. During Ahmadu Bamba culture week, the dahira organizes its own event called "the Night of Maam Jaara Buso." Women are also well represented in all the events organized by the Collectif des mourides de France (Coalition of the Murids in France) headed by the Aulnay leadership. They are a familiar sight in those events where they showcase their own unique ways of being Murids. Many of these women express their gratitude to Ahmadu Bamba for their blessings by donning lavish dresses and gold jewelry and by generously donating to preachers and singers of sacred music.[50]

However, if Aulnay and Taverny differ in their interpretations of Ahmadu Bamba's teachings, their conceptions of the mission of KST in the diaspora, and the place of women, they share a similar vision of their interactions with their French neighbors and local government. Both houses are officially licensed under the 1905 law (the December 9, 1905, Law on the Separation of the Churches and the State) and are denied state funding. The leaders of the houses cultivate openness and good neighborly relations. The leaders of Taverny have installed surveillance cameras in front of the house as a mark of transparency. Both houses inform neighbors about important events and invite representatives of local government to attend public events. Murid dignitaries staying in the house of Aulnay always pay a visit to the local authorities. Shaykh Murtada met with the mayor of Aulnay, and his son and successor, Shaykh Maam Moor, perpetuates this tradition during his annual visit.[51] The mayor of Aulnay hosted a delegation of Murid shaykhs from Senegal, and the municipal official in charge of cooperation has visited Tuubaa. Appreciative of the hospitality of his hosts in Senegal, he proposed establishing official relations between Tuubaa and Aulnay as sister cities.[52] Here is how Abdulaay Ley, the leader of the house of Aulnay at the time, describes the impression that the visit to Tuubaa made on the Aulnay delegation:

> In the month of May, a large delegation from Aulnay traveled to Senegal to visit Tuubaa and meet the religious authorities and members of the local government there. They were hesitant to go but were surprised by the quality of the hospitality. Now they are the ones who are pressuring us to move the cooperation forward. The deputy mayor in charge of decentralized cooperation and local associations led the delegation to Tuubaa. It is true that like elsewhere in the Judeo-Christian world, people are always afraid of Islam. They think that the Muslims are out to convert them, to wage jihad on them, to challenge their culture and values. But with time, when they know us better, they understand that Islam is a peaceful and tolerant religion.[53]

Similarly, the vice mayor of Taverny visited Tuubaa and presented the keys to his city to the head of Tuubaa's rural community.[54] The mayor sends an official representation to attend all the major events organized by the Murid community. Invitations are even extended to the Taverny military base commander, who had recently been a regular participant in some of the events of Ahmadu Bamba culture week organized every July.[55] For both sides, and especially for the Murids working hard to distance themselves from stereotypical portrayals of violent Islam, these interactions are important. They offer the opportunity to display a spirit of openness and tolerance and to demonstrate that a confrontation between Islam and the French secular state is not inevitable. This was made clear to me by the vice mayor of Leu-les-Forêts at the house of Taverny, where he was visiting at the invitation of the Murid community. He praised the Murids for their commitment to the idea of "vivre ensemble" (living together).[56] "Vivre ensemble" seems to be the new orientation of the French government policy toward Islam. This moves the debate away from the notions of integration or assimilation, which suggests the idea of Islam assimilating into the secular French melting pot. "Vivre ensemble" seems to reject the idea of the Muslim as the unassimilable "other" and instead recognizes diversity within French society so long as Muslims play by the rules. However, "vivre ensemble" carries its own contradictions. As the vice mayor observed, "The Republic cannot adapt to the culture of the immigrants. It behooves 'the immigrants' cultures' to adapt to the Republic."[57]

~

This chapter demonstrates the centrality of place making in the lives of Murid immigrants. I explained how the establishment of a community of Murid citizens and permanent residents in Paris transformed their relations to space. The stories of the houses of Aulnay-sous-Bois and Taverny provide insight into how Murids manage to turn secular French space into spiritually meaningful Murid place. Beyond the ownership of land, this effort involves the performance of acts of worship and the organization of activities that sanctify the space. This sanctification symbolically extracts the place from French soil while facilitating its unification with Tuubaa, the holy city of the Muridiyya in Senegal, and other similar Murid places worldwide. But Murid efforts to construct their own place should not be read as a desire for separation. Instead, these efforts signal their aspiration to claim France as their home and to affirm their rights as citizens. Building houses for Ahmadu Bamba in Paris is part of an effort to re-create home abroad and to legitimize the presence of the Muridiyya in France. The symbolic unification with Tuubaa does not preclude belonging to the French citizenry.

However, if Murids agree on the critical importance of owning their own places of worship in France, they differ in their conceptions of the roles of these places. These conflicted visions are also apparent among Murid diasporas in the United States and elsewhere and pose the larger question of what role the missionary plays in the diaspora. While some disciples promote the universalism of Ahmadu Bamba's teachings and emphasize their duty to proselytize and gain new converts, others prioritize the strengthening of communal bonds among Senegalese disciples abroad and between the disciples and the leadership in Tuubaa. Yet this difference sometimes leads to tensions and splits as was the case between the house of Taverny and that of Aulnay-sous-Bois in Paris as well as the divide between supporters of the Murid Islamic Community in America (MICA) based in New York City and Federation Shaykh Ahmadu Bamba based in Detroit.

I have discussed the missionary work of Shaykh Murtada and his central role in helping create a Murid diasporic collective consciousness nourished by a sense of communality built around a network of houses of Ahmadu Bamba and the organization of annual festivities. If at first Murid migrants were skeptical of such initiatives, the transition from sojourners to immigrants committed to building a life abroad has made most of them appreciative of the importance these institutions play in the preservation of cherished religious and cultural values threatened by the assimilatory power of the French state.

The chapter also demonstrates how Murids manage to create a space for themselves in the French secular public sphere while avoiding confrontation with the state and a hostile civil society. The fact that sub-Saharan Muslims, in contrast to North Africans, are not associated with a threatening Islamic tradition facilitated the making of Murid space. But more importantly, the decision of Murid disciples to focus on the creation of cultural centers rather than mosques helped secure their acceptance abroad. Murid communal spaces in the diaspora are simultaneously sacred and profane. Their sanctity is defined by their use. The *musalla* (place for prayers) can be turned into a meeting room, and access is not restricted. The openness of Murid immigrants, and particularly their willingness to engage local government and even encourage relations between French municipal authorities and the leadership in Senegal, alleviates state suspicion. The state is more comfortable when immigrants channel their activities and energy through cultural manifestations rather than political activism.

PLATE 2.1. The Mosque of Paris, built in 1920. Photo by the author, June 2016.

PLATE 2.2. Entrance of the Murid house of Taverny. Photo by the author, May 2010.

PLATE 2.3. Interior furnishing of a room at the Murid house of Taverny. Photo by the author, May 2010.

PLATE 2.4. Crowd at the celebration of Ahmadu Bamba cultural week in Brescia, Italy. Photo by the author, June 2011.

PLATE 2.5. Plaque at the entrance of the Murid house of Aulnay-sous-Bois. Photo by the author, June 2019.

PLATE 2.6. The Murid house of Taverny. Photo by the author, May 2010.

PLATE 2.7. Library of the Murid house of Taverny. Photo by the author, May 2010.

PLATE 2.8. Prayer room of the house of Taverny. Photo by the author, May 2010.

PLATE 2.9. Imam Mamadou N'Sangou, founding member of the Taverny house. Photo by the author, May 2010.

PLATE 2.10. Sulaymaan Juuf, manager of the house of Taverny. Photo by the author, May 2010.

PLATE 2.11. Cheikh Abdoulaye Dièye. Photo by Michelle Farah Kimball.

6 ⇌ Unlikely Migration
Murids in New York City

> We have wasted our time in countries that do not like immigrants. I cannot understand why Senegalese consider France the center of the world, since America is the most powerful country on earth.
>
> —Omar, Senegalese immigrant living in Portland, Oregon

SENEGALESE HAVE been migrating to cities across Africa and to France since at least the nineteenth century. Yet it was only in the mid-1980s that the United States became a popular destination for Senegalese immigrants.[1] History and geography made the United States an unlikely place for the Senegalese to emigrate to. Besides the Atlantic slave trade, whose memory has largely faded among ordinary Senegalese, Senegal has no historical ties with the United States. Moreover, the vast expanse of the Atlantic Ocean that separates West Africa from North America remains an insurmountable barrier even for the most adventurous. More recently, a confluence of push-and-pull factors, along with other circumstances (globalization, revolution in air travel), conspired to turn the United States into a viable immigration destination for the Senegalese.

While the population of Senegalese in France, Italy, and Spain is much larger than the Senegalese diaspora in the United States, Senegalese immigrants in the US have received disproportionate attention from scholars and the media. One reason for this attention is the conspicuous presence of Murids.[2] Murids are not the only Senegalese or Africans to migrate to New York, but their status as "first occupants" (especially in Harlem) and their exuberant culture made them the face of African immigration in New York.[3] Writing in the early 1990s, Michael Fleisher estimated that four out of every five Senegalese residing in New York might be Bawol-Bawol.[4] The legal, economic, and cultural conditions that Murids found in the United States provided fertile ground for the deployment of their economic habitus of traders and the vibrant expression of their culture.

These conditions created an environment that allowed the bifurcation of citizenship and cultural uniformity, encouraging cultural diversity that is widely displayed in Harlem, the nerve center of Murid immigration in the United States.

The Senegalese and Murid immigrant community in the United States shaped and was shaped by the host society in ways not observed anywhere else in the Senegalese diaspora. Three factors played a significant role in shaping their image while at the same time facilitating the stamping of their culture on Harlem: first, the self-perception of America as a country of immigrants; second, the openness to communalism (at least until recently); and third, the presence of an African American community.

The Murid migratory experience in New York City demonstrates how migration can be both a disruptive and creative force. Murid disciples arrived in New York City without the money, skills, or cultural capital (and especially without English-language skills) that would have facilitated their integration into American society. The distance from Senegal and the lack of established commercial and banking connections made it difficult to send remittances back home and to build enduring trade networks, as was the case in France. Yet the Murids were able to garner the social capital and know-how that allowed them to carve out a cultural and economic niche in America.

This chapter reconstructs the history of Senegalese and Murid migration to the United States, focusing particularly on New York City. It explains how the entanglement between business practices, cultural performances, and spatial occupation gave birth to Little Senegal. The chapter ends with a discussion of gentrification, the slow death of the Senegalese enclave in Harlem, and the economic and spiritual losses that this transformation inflicted on Murids.

MURID MIGRATION TO NEW YORK

Murid migrants began arriving in New York City in the mid-1970s. These migrants were embedded in the same networks that facilitated Murid migration to cities in Senegal, West Africa, and France. The extension of these networks to North America demonstrates Murids' ability to take advantage of the opportunities their inclusion in the French imperial dominion made available but also reveals that they are not constrained by imperial boundaries.

The first Murids who arrived in New York were seasonal traders dealing in "antique" artifacts (*jaaykatu bant* or wood merchants). They were the sons of art dealers sent by their fathers who owned shops on Rue

Mohamed V in the tourist district of the Senegalese capital, near Sandaga Market.[5] Elhaaj Yande Jóob, the veteran Murid international trader, was among those dealers. His son, Murtada Jóob, was one of the most successful Senegalese art dealers in New York in in the 1970s and 1980s. These same dealers owned shops in African cities such as Abidjan and in Paris. Encounters with African American and White American tourists in these shops in Senegal and abroad may have created awareness about the potential of the American market for their trade. Moreover, as Joel Millman indicates, the rising African American middle class influenced by Afrocentrist ideas generated a renewal of interest in African crafts, culture, and the continent in general.[6]

Women were active participants in the art trade. Many among these women were middle aged. Before coming to New York City, they had gained experience in international trade, traveling across West Africa and Europe. Fatime Amar was one of them.[7] Amar started in the business of trading when she divorced her husband in 1980. Using a loan from a friend, she bought and sold goods in Mali, Côte d'Ivoire, and France before settling in New York City in 1989.

Historian Sylviane Diouf, who conducted fieldwork among Senegalese immigrants in New York in the 1980s and 1990s, met many women whose stories are similar to that of Fatime Amar.[8] Many among these women began international trading by traveling to Morocco and Las Palmas in Spain where they bought cosmetics, garments, shoes, and other goods they sold wholesale to merchants at Sandaga and other markets in Dakar. As their capital grew, they expanded to France and the Middle East where they bought gold and silver jewelries. By the mid-1970s, they had reached the United States.

By the mid-1980s, Murid migration had taken a new turn. More Murids came to New York and most overstayed their visas, parting with the tradition of seasonal migration established by preceding immigrants. Many among these new immigrants worked as street vendors, cab drivers, wage laborers, and hair braiders. They lived in overcrowded and decaying hotel rooms and apartments, usually cooked their own food, donned traditional clothes whenever weather permitted, used Wolof and Fula (Pulaar) as their lingua franca, and had limited contact with American society. Their living conditions mirrored what some scholars termed "vertical villages," referring to the housing units of Paris where Soninke and Hal Pulaar immigrants from the Senegal River Valley reproduce the societal and family hierarchies of their villages back home.[9] However, although Senegalese and Murid immigrants in New York City shared the lifestyle of their compatriots in Paris, hierarchy did not play a role in their mode of organization. Unlike in France, the tasks of shopping, cooking, and cleaning were democratically distributed and rotated among the mostly male tenants, regardless of age or social status.[10] The difference between Paris and New York can be explained by the contrasting housing accommodations (government-built public hostels in France, private hotels in New York) and ethnicity. While members of the more conservative and hierarchical Soninke and Hal Pulaar ethnic groups formed the majority of Senegalese in Paris, in New York the more urbanized Wolof dominated. Common belonging to the Muridiyya also may have played a role.

The lifestyle and occupations of the new immigrants earned them the label *moodu-moodu*,[11] a derogatory nickname that originated in France in the 1970s but was eventually embraced by these immigrants as a marker of collective identity. The term "moodu-moodu" connotes a classical education in rural Qur'anic schools, professional status as self-employed workers in the informal sector of the economy, cultural conservatism, and identity as both Murid and Wolof. Wolof Murids may have begun the migration, but other Senegalese, including Haal Pulaar (who developed their own migrant identity), soon followed in their footsteps.[12] The dominant presence of moodu-moodu set Senegalese migration apart from other African migratory groups, including the Nigerians, Egyptians, and Ghanaians, which consisted mostly of college-educated and highly trained professionals.[13]

MURID MERCHANTS IN THE STREETS OF NEW YORK

By the late 1980s, the art trade, which was the professional occupation of early Murid immigrants in New York, had diminished. Additionally, most traders shifted from temporal circular migration to permanent residency, although without legal documentation. Street vending became the common occupation of Murids in New York. The presence of Murid merchants in the busy shopping district of Midtown Manhattan soon caught the attention of journalists. The *New York Times*, the *Economist*, *Forbes*, and local newspapers devoted a series of articles to the business of Murid street vendors, traveling shaykhs paying them visits, and their troubles with the police and municipal authorities of New York. These reports presented romantic depictions of the traders, marveling at their resourcefulness, strange sartorial traditions, and uncanny business practices. But Murid migrants were no strangers to city life. Writing about Caribbean immigrants in Harlem in the first half of the twentieth century, Lara Putman argues that their move to New York was not merely a transition from "rural stasis to urban commotion, from local absorption to global connection."[14] The same observation is true regarding the Murids. Before migrating to New York, they were part of a community that was already globally connected — the agents of what historian Mamadou Diouf termed a "vernacular cosmopolitanism."[15]

The migratory histories of Sëriñ Lo and Ahmed Sugu, two Murids who came to New York in the 1980s, give insight into the changing patterns of Murid migration and the dominant role of street vendors. Lo, a merchant at Sandaga Market, heard about New York City for the first time from a fellow trader whose younger brother had recently traveled to the United States. A few days later, he had a visa and airline tickets:

> I took an Air Afrique flight to New York on July 11, 1983. I only knew one person in the United States, my friend's brother, Daam Ndongo, but I did not know his address. Fortunately, I traveled with a trader who was going to New York for his business. When we landed, he told me that a few blocks from his hotel, there was a hotel where some Senegalese reside. It was Bryant Hotel. I proceeded there and met a Senegalese [in the lobby] who told me that Daam was staying in the same hotel. There were only three rooms occupied by Senegalese, two in each room. I arrived on a Tuesday, on Wednesday I was on the street selling sunglasses. There was no time to rest. We paid a weekly rent and if you did not work, you would not be able to pay.[16]

Ahmed Sugu flew to New York from Abidjan on a Saturday in summer 1986.[17] He landed in New York with $40 in his pocket. He proceeded to Hotel Sinton to meet his contact but found the place surrounded by police overseeing the eviction of the undesirable Senegalese tenants. He followed those who had been evicted, and they found rooms at Parkview Hotel on 55 West 110th Street, nicknamed "Le Cent Dix" by West African immigrants. Sugu had touched down in NYC at dawn. But that evening he was already on the streets selling toy cars supplied by a fellow Murid trader. He was hoping to make enough money to pay his weekly rent and contribute to groceries for collective cooking.

Senegalese immigrants were often expelled from hotels because they violated occupancy rules, sometimes doubling the number of guests allowed to occupy one room. They were also accused of disturbing the peace with their heavy foot traffic.[18] These immigrants originated from rural areas or small towns in Senegal, and although most of them had lived in cities before their journey to the United States, they had yet to develop an urban lifestyle. They stayed up late, occupying communal kitchens and socializing after long hours of work and generally becoming a nuisance to their neighbors.

The stories told by Sëriñ Lo and Ahmed Sugu were not atypical; I have heard the same stories many times from the early generation of Murid traders who came to New York City in the mid-1980s. At the time, very few Senegalese had visited the United States. For the urban youth of Senegal, the image of the United States was shaped by Hollywood movies, pop music stars such as James Brown and Jimi Hendrix, and soap operas such as *Dallas, Dynasty,* and the *Cosby Show.* For people in rural areas, there were the occasional interactions with Peace Corps volunteers.[19] For seasoned international Murid traders, Europe was their primary destination; the United States was merely terra incognita. The relative ease of getting a visa and the stories told about business opportunities combined with the "closing" of the European borders to Africans transformed the image of the United States from imagined but unattainable Eldorado into a welcoming land of immigration. Omar, a Senegalese living in Portland, Oregon, in the 1990s, illustrates the changing perception of the United States among Senegalese immigrants when he observed, "We have wasted our time in countries that do not like immigrants. I cannot understand why Senegalese consider France the center of the world, since America is the most powerful country on earth."[20] Migrating to the United States became the goal of most young traders testing their mettle at Sandaga and other markets in Senegal, across Africa, and in Europe.

The growing popularity of the United States as an immigration destination among Senegalese migrants is borne out by official data. Sylviane Diouf-Camara estimates that between 1978 and 1987, the number of Senegalese in New York increased from one thousand to six thousand. Almost all of these migrants entered the country as "non-immigrants," traveling on tourist or student visas.[21] This statement is supported by official US statistics. For example, in 1987, only ninety-two Senegalese crossed US borders with an immigrant visa.[22] Yet, empirical evidence suggests that hundreds more entered the country through other channels. The pace of Senegalese migration to the United States followed the broader trend of African migration. Between 1960 and 2009, the African-born population in the United States increased from 35,355 to nearly 1.5 million.[23] Since the 1960s, more Africans have entered the United States freely than those who were forced to travel there during the three hundred years of the transatlantic slave trade. This is a miniscule number compared to migrations from other continents, but it is significant in the sense that during this period African immigration to the United States grew at the fastest rate.

Most Senegalese immigrants who entered the United States in the 1980s learned about America through the same channels as Sëriñ Lo: by word of mouth or through the migration of an acquaintance. The first Senegalese immigrants began working as street vendors. The streets of New York are no stranger to hawkers, but the arrival of hundreds of Murid itinerant traders transformed the business. The traders emerged in the busy streets of Midtown Manhattan when street vending, common in earlier years, had largely disappeared. Their sheer numbers and the goods they sold also distinguished them. With their suitcases full of merchandise, the new immigrants peddled their wares on Fifth Avenue, Lexington Avenue, Forty-Second and Thirty-Fourth Streets, Times Square, Canal Street, and Broadway. Some operated from sidewalk tables in front of stores. They sold umbrellas, sunglasses, scarves, gloves, pirated movies, CDs, T-shirts, baseball caps, fake Rolex watches, and bootleg name-brand handbags. Unlike their predecessors who dealt in artifacts and mostly targeted African American customers, street vendors sold generic goods to a mostly White clientele. Their "exotic" appearance betrayed their African origin and mitigated the fear and suspicion that animate the relationships between African American males and White Americans. They operated in the shadows of the skyscrapers, glittering office buildings, and designer shops of Midtown Manhattan, offering inexpensive knockoffs of luxury goods sold in upscale stores.

CHALLENGES TO STREET VENDORS

Local government and business operators did not share the empathy that journalists and ordinary New Yorkers showed the Murid merchants. Immigrants resort to jobs in the informal sector of the economy because the formal sector is controlled by the state and private capital; immigrants often lack the skills and financial resources to compete with established business entrepreneurs. Their presence as interlopers in the economies of cities in their host societies in Africa, Europe, and the United States invariably draws hostility from the world of business and state officials. The Murids' business dealings and ubiquitous presence in the heart of Manhattan soon attracted the unwanted attention of the powerful Association of the Merchants of Fifth Avenue and building owners. Powerful businessmen faulted Wolof-Murid merchants and other foreigners "for turning elegant Fifth Avenue into the likes of Istanbul on a Sunday."[24] Donald Trump led the effort to cleanse Manhattan of the Senegalese street peddlers and stall holders, putting pressure on NYC's then mayor, Ed Koch (1978–89), to act.[25]

The police crackdown began in 1986 when the municipality formed a twenty-five-person police task force designed specifically to police street vending. Scores of Murid street vendors were deported. Those who escaped vacated their hotel rooms and fled to the Bronx where they rented apartments. The Bronx brought relief from the police but not safety. Murid traders did not use banks (because banking was not part of their culture, and many were undocumented and suspicious of formal financial institutions), so they stashed money in their rooms and in their pockets, and their neighbors knew this. They became victims of frequent burglaries perpetrated by gangs the traders identified as Dominican youth.[26]

However, contacts with Dominicans and other immigrants from the Global South had a positive impact on the Murids. They learned of the business of gypsy cab driving and how to rent apartments. These two discoveries significantly affected the life of Senegalese and Murid communities when they returned to Harlem in the late 1980s. Like many of his fellow Murids who relocated to the Bronx, Lo acquired a driver's license, rented a car, and started a gypsy cab-driving business. This was a dangerous job. Gypsy cabbies serve violence-ridden neighborhoods in uptown New York where yellow cabs dare not operate. They earned a living and provided invaluable service to underprivileged communities but paid a high price for it. Dozens of West Africans and Senegalese gypsy cab drivers lost their lives resisting robbers and carjackers: in Senegal, a man's honor dictates that he confront rather than flee danger.

Throughout the 1990s, Daam Baabu, a Harlem-based Senegalese journalist and talk-show radio host, documented the murder of forty-three Senegalese cab drivers before giving up on the macabre count.[27] Security improved with the adoption of call centers (or "base" in the cabbies' parlance) where operators identify clients and pickup spots. The killing of African cab drivers has diminished from its peak in the 1990s, but these murders continue. The murder of a Senegalese cab driver in Philadelphia in 2001 prompted the Philadelphia Taxi Association to organize a demonstration that brought together West African cab drivers and their supporters throughout the United States, including Haitians, Latinos, and Dominicans.[28]

Despite the risk involved, gypsy cab driving continues to be one of the most common jobs for Murid immigrants, second only to street vending.[29] The reason is simple. Driving a gypsy cab did not require citizenship or permanent residency status, nor fluency in English: these were all assets that most Murids lacked. Additionally, in the 1980s, a driver did not need a license from the Taxi and Limousine Commission to operate. There was no need for a taxi medallion (permit) as is the case with yellow cab drivers. The only thing that was required was a driver's license and a car.

Bureaucratic flexibility made gypsy cab driving attractive to Murids, but this alone does not explain its popularity. The Murid gypsy cab drivers were driven by a mindset rooted in their life experience and inspiration from Ahmadu Bamba's sacred biography. One of my sources evokes this mindset when he noted, "We were already used to a precarious and difficult life. We did not expect to get anything from anybody. We are survivors. We are not used to writing job applications. . . . You just do what you must do to get by."[30] A Murid street vendor who was arrested by the police the first day he ventured in Manhattan rationalized his trouble as a simple part of the "the trials and tribulations the Mourides expect on their journey towards God. . . . They would confiscated [sic] my goods and arrested me but I managed to save my pennies and keep my faith. I knew that [if] Amadou Bamba prevailed, so could I."[31]

The Murid trader was alluding to Ahmadu Bamba's own experience of exiles and banishment under French colonial rule of Senegal. However, Murid behavioral ethics are also shaped by values they share with most immigrants from the Global South. They are all aware of the lack of alternative economic opportunities at home, and they feel the pressure that society puts on immigrants. Cutting the lifeline that remittances offer to those left behind and returning home empty-handed would bring shame not only to the immigrant but also to his entire family. This moral economy drives many to extraordinary lengths trying to avoid embarrassing themselves and their families. A similar mindset drives the young Africans that brave the Sahara Desert and the Mediterranean Sea, risking and sometimes losing their lives trying to reach Europe.

IMMIGRATION REFORMS AND THE TRANSFORMATION OF MURID BUSINESSES

While family reunion and mobility constitute some of the most visible consequences of immigration reforms, the impact of these reforms on immigrants' employment and economic conditions is equally significant. From the late 1980s, the adoption of a series of immigration reforms by the American administration profoundly affected the lives of Murid immigrants. The reforms allowed many immigrants to escape the semiclandestine situation in which they were living and acquire legal status; the reforms also opened avenues for different types of immigrants. In 1986, the

US Congress passed the Immigration Reform and Control Act (IRCA), known in immigrant circles as the "amnesty."[32] The IRCA offered legal permanent resident status to undocumented immigrants who could prove residency in the United States five years prior to 1986. Immigrants could use their stamped passports, rental and utility bills, or affidavits from their pastors or imams to document their presence in the United States. Although the law was not meant for them specifically, and most among them did not fulfill the residency requirement, many Murids were able to legalize their status. For example, whereas only a hundred Senegalese were registered as legal immigrants in the United States before the adoption of the IRCA, a thousand came out of the blue to apply for permanent residence status.[33] Some, suspicious of the federal government's intention, refused to apply and remained undocumented.

The adoption of the Immigration Act of 1990, which instituted the Diversity Visa Lottery program, affected Senegalese immigration in a different way. This act was designed to increase the number of skilled and employed immigrants and those originating from low-admission regions. It included educational and other requirements that filtered out people like the moodu-moodu while encouraging the emigration of professionals and the Western educated.

From the 1990s, an increasing number of skilled Senegalese immigrants, especially accountants, computer scientists, information technology specialists, and university professors migrated to the United States. According to one estimate, from 1990, 65 percent of Senegalese emigrants who entered the United States had at least a high school diploma.[34] By the beginning of the twenty-first century, most Senegalese entering the United States arrived with a Western education to pursue higher education or take a salaried job in the formal sector of the economy, reversing the trend set by earlier generations of immigrants.[35] The presence of this new category of Murid immigrants is made particularly visible during the annual visit of Shaykh Murtada and now his son, Shaykh Maam Moor Mbakke. A *New York Times* reporter noted that "after nearly 20 years in the city, their [the Murids] profile is changing, evident in the professionals who drove pricey new cars in from the suburbs to pay homage to the sheik, and in the bright presence of toddlers thrust toward him for blessing."[36]

The acquisition of permanent residency and later citizenship status, made possible by the 1986 act, afforded Murid immigrants greater job flexibility. In 1987, when the first green cards were issued, a steady diversification of the economic activities of Murids began. While Murids like Lo moved from gypsy cab driving to the safer job of operating yellow cabs or trucks (or continued in their previous employment), others engaged in new ventures. These entrepreneurs tapped the niche market created by the growing number of Senegalese immigrants in New York and the West African traders traveling back and forth between Europe, New York City, and Africa for business.

African immigrants and traders in New York City were confronted with two pressing problems: first, they needed a secure and simple channel to send remittances back home; second, they lacked effective and affordable means of shipping goods to and from the United States. Immigrants relied on traveling traders to send money to their families left behind. They had also depended on the now-defunct Air Afrique to ship goods to Africa. Neither system was satisfactory. Traveling traders were of no help in case of emergency, and there were disputes arising from the informal exchange of large sums of money without written documents. Similarly, airline freight was not only expensive but also limited the amount of goods traders could ship.

Thanks to their newly earned permanent resident status and the experience they accumulated as street vendors in New York, entrepreneurial Murids were prepared to take advantage of the need for money transfers and international shipping services created by a growing West African diaspora in New York. In 1991, B. S. Njaay opened Kara International Exchange.[37] The same year, two Murids collaborated to launch Touba Mbacke Trading and Lamp Fall Corp. The names given to these businesses feature prominent Murid Shaykhs or holy spaces and function as both blessings and marketing devices.[38] Most offices were located between 1201 and 1225 Broadway in Midtown Manhattan. This address became a favorite hangout for Senegalese and the rendezvous point for first-time Senegalese travelers to the United States and their hosts. I met my wife on the sidewalk in front of a building occupied by a Murid business on a hot morning in August 1996 after she had traveled from Dakar to join me in East Lansing, where I had been a graduate student in history at Michigan State University.

The businesses offered a variety of services, including money transfer, shipping of goods, and wholesale merchandise coveted by African traders such as shoes, garments, cosmetic products, and electronics. Although Murid businessmen worked some of these jobs without a license, they retained their customers' trust, offering an alternative to the costly and complicated procedures of the banks and international shipping companies.[39] This trust is rooted in shared faith and is important in constructing networks, which in turn support the businesses of Murid immigrants.

The success of Murid money transfer businesses was not lost on potential competitors. The government-owned Senegalese Bank de l'Habitat opened offices in Harlem and four other cities in the United States, offering saving accounts and money transfer services. Western Union, MoneyGram, Money Express, and a number of similar companies, working with the Senegalese national postal service and local banks, started to aggressively market their products to Senegalese and West African immigrants. This competition, combined with the tightening of US regulations of money transfers in the aftermath of 9/11, all but killed off the Murid money transfer businesses.

AFRICA IN HARLEM

The encounter between Murid immigrants and mainstream American society mostly took place in the busy streets of Midtown Manhattan. Few New Yorkers were aware of the profound transformation that their presence had unleashed in Harlem.[40] From the mid-1980s, a steady influx of Senegalese immigrants and businesses transformed the portion of West 116th Street between Frederick Douglass Boulevard (Eighth Avenue) and Malcolm X Boulevard (Lenox Avenue). The settlement of Senegalese attracted Malians, Guineans, and immigrants from Niger, Côte d'Ivoire, and other West African countries. The concentration of immigrants infused the space with a unique African flavor. The streets were alive with the languages they spoke (Bamana, Fula, Hausa, Mandingo, Wolof), the smell of the foods they cooked in their restaurants and apartments, the music they played in their stores and cars, and their brightly colored dresses. West 116th Street embodied Africa in a way seen nowhere else in the United States nor perhaps in the wider world. Sounds, smells, and fashion are some of the means by which immigrants turn strange space into familiar place.

The area of Harlem associated with Senegalese and Murids today was not, however, their first destination. If it has ever become a mecca for Black African immigrants, as one scholar argues, it is a mecca mostly of their own making.[41] When the first Murid traders arrived in New York in the early 1980s, they lived in long-stay single-room hotels. The section of West 116th Street they dominate today was a no-go zone. The image of this area that emerges from my interviews with Murids reveals a place then rife with violence and haunted by drug gangs. As one of them stated, "The buildings here were falling apart. You had many liquor stores, some mom-and-pop corner stores selling at prohibitive prices. From Park Avenue to Morningside, there were no stores. One City Bank [branch] on 125th

Street. No CVS, 7-Eleven, Target, or Pathmark. One branch of the New York City Public Library on Twelfth Avenue."[42] Others note that the few buildings in good shape were inhabited by birds because nobody dared to live in the neighborhood wrecked by chronic violence.[43] Some recall the sight of people on street corners clustering around fires burning in steel drums to keep warm during winter. These are images they had seen in American movies set in African American neighborhoods in inner-city America. But these were fictional images to them until they had actually settled in New York. This description of Harlem in the late 1980s and early 1990s is corroborated by scholars such as Linda Beck and Jonathan Gill. Remembering her high school and college days traveling from upstate New York, Beck recalled how she was saddened "to ride through one of the worst ghettos in America, to see the stark difference between impoverished 125th Street juxtaposed to [affluent] 5th avenue."[44] Jonathan Gill titles his chapter on the history of Harlem between 1965 and 1990 "Harlem Nightmare."[45]

Harlem was suffering from over half a century of neglect. The gradual influx of African Americans, West Indians, and Hispanics that began in the early twentieth century ushered in a golden age for Black culture, culminating in the Harlem Renaissance. But it also led to a sustained flight of the Irish, Jewish, Italian, and Greek populations.[46] By 1990, Harlem had lost over three-quarters of its 1950 population, shrinking from 540,000 to 100,000 inhabitants.[47] One-quarter of all houses in central Harlem were abandoned.[48] Unoccupied buildings fell into disrepair, feeding insecurity, bringing down the value of real estate, and discouraging private owners from investing in their properties. A recovery has begun since that low point of 1990. David Dinkins, the mayor of New York from 1990 to 1993, began the revival.[49] Boarded up, dilapidated, and burned-down buildings were auctioned off or rehabilitated and then used as subsidized housing for low-income families or were rented out to tenants at below-market prices. Dinkins also invested heavily in improving security. His successor, Rudolph Giuliani, mayor from 1994 to 2001, continued the effort. Between 1990 and 2006, Harlem's population grew by 14.9 percent.[50]

The Murids were among the first communities to take advantage of the improving situation brought about by municipal initiatives. With its proximity to Midtown, where most of them worked, and the convenient location near subway lines, central Harlem was a particularly attractive neighborhood for Murid immigrants. Fadel Gey was among the first Murids to move to Harlem. His father was a diplomat. Fadel had lived in Saudi Arabia, Italy, and France before coming to the United States in

1985. Refusing to live in crowded hotel rooms like his fellow Murids, Fadel rented an apartment in an upscale neighborhood near Seventy-Ninth Street between Columbus and Amsterdam but soon ran out of money. In 1986, he approached one of the real estate companies in charge of housing in Harlem and leased an apartment from them on West 116th Street. Because of his relationship with an agent working for the real estate company, Gey became a resource for the Murids and members of the Senegalese community in facilitating their access to rental properties.

When the news about the possibility of renting apartments in Harlem spread, Hotel 110, the headquarters of African immigrants and similar hotels, were soon emptied of tenants.[51] Since Harlem was still unattractive for many, rent was cheap. A spacious high-ceilinged, two-bedroom apartment with large windows and a view of 116th Street cost only $500 a month.[52] Rent became even cheaper when four to six adults shared one apartment and split the payment among themselves. The controlled leasing contract included clauses that guaranteed limited rent increases and continued occupancy so long as the tenant paid his rent regularly. Insecurity was still a concern, however. One of my interviewees told me that for the first time in his life he saw a man shot dead while shopping in a deli in Harlem.[53] Sëriñ Lo was held at gunpoint in his restaurant and his partner shot. Africans were routinely assaulted by the bandits who roamed the streets of Harlem.

The insularity of the African immigrant community, cultural misunderstandings, and stereotypes on both sides often led to tense relations between West African immigrants and African Americans.[54] Before coming to the United States, many Africans harbored an idealized image of African Americans, whom they viewed as brothers. But life in the rough neighborhoods of Harlem soon transformed this mindset as they internalized stereotypical depictions of African Americans. Demeaning comments such as "Black Americans are violent"; "They do not want to work"; and "They abuse their women" are frequently heard when Africans converse among themselves. Language barriers and a lack of understanding of the history of Blacks in America, where slavery and racial oppression are strong shapers of identity, further widened the rift between African immigrants and their African American neighbors. Similarly, for African Americans, their perception of African immigrants is shaped by what John Jackson Jr. termed "post-Afrocentric blackness." This is "a blackness that can invoke the African continent as an icon of heritage and history in one context while disavowing personal connections to other parts of the African diaspora in another."[55]

THE BIRTH OF LITTLE SENEGAL

The relocation of African immigrants from long-stay single-room hotels to apartments in central Harlem, a change in lifestyle that began in earnest in the early 1990s, led to the gradual formation of the African cultural and economic enclave known today as Little Senegal.[56] As the number of Senegalese moving to Harlem grew, businesses followed, and a new street culture evolved. Immigrants rented space on the ground floor of their apartment buildings where they opened restaurants specializing in Senegalese and African dishes, and stores selling groceries imported from Senegal, Islamic paraphernalia, halal meats, and other ethnic foods. The Association of Senegalese in America (ASA) opened its office on the same stretch of West 116th Street. Seeking proximity to its constituents, the Senegalese government opened the lone consulate in uptown New York on 125th Street before moving to West 116th Street. The Malcolm Shabazz mosque served as a community center for Murids renting space in the

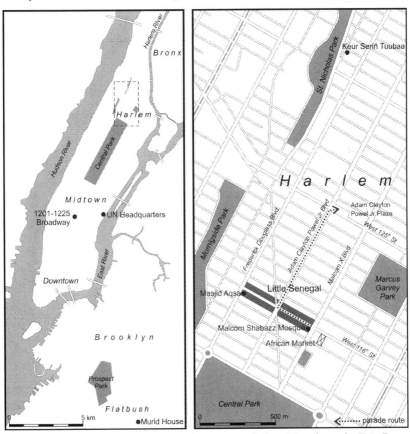

MAP 6.1. Places of importance to Murids in New York City. Map drawn by Eric Ross.

complex for the celebration of Màggals and mawluds and the organization of lectures and other community events.[57] It was this conspicuous physical and cultural presence that earned the area the nickname of Little Senegal (or Le Petit Sénégal), a name popularized by Rachid Bouchareb's 2001 movie of the same name.[58] Murids were not the only Africans to live in the neighborhood, but they were in the majority, and their cultural exuberance overshadowed that of other African immigrants. One scholar even used the name "Little Tuubaa" to emphasize the overwhelming influence of Murids.[59]

In 1990, four years after moving to Harlem, Fadel Gey opened Sunugaal Halal Meats and Poultry on 119 West 116th Street.[60] Sunugaal was one of the first businesses owned by a postcolonial sub-Saharan African in Harlem.[61] Fadel had no personal experience in commerce. However, as he recalled, "With the number of Muslims coming for prayer every Friday at the mosque (Malcolm Shabazz) I thought that selling fresh halal meat would be profitable."[62] Fadel's business not only benefited from the mosque worshippers but also from Arab shopkeepers in the area and the Senegalese restaurants that opened on and around 116th Street. Yuusu Caam, a Murid disciple, launched the restaurant Soumbedioune in 1990; a year later, Sëriñ Lo collaborated with a fellow Murid to start Xeewal, then Keur Sokhna, Africa Kiné, Le Baobab, and more recently, Les Ambassades would follow. All of these eateries were patronized by a Muslim customer base (they do not sell alcohol or pork), but they also drew an African American and White American clientele, especially among the middle class, including former Peace Corps volunteers and students and professors from nearby Columbia University.

The dynamic restaurant business combined with a vibrant social life—where cooking and sharing food is central—stimulated demand for African produce. This demand was met by entrepreneurial Murids and other Africans who opened grocery stores along West 116th Street from Frederick Douglass to Malcolm X boulevards. The businesses sold dried fish, palm oil, the broken rice favored in the Senegalese staple dish *ceebu jen*, couscous, bouillons, peppers, a variety of powdered milks, Nescafé, chocolate, and other items imported from Senegal or bought from Asian wholesalers in New York. Stores also offered suitcases catering to the needs of mobile Senegalese immigrants; there were also Islamic goods, fabrics, cellphones, and other electronics. In addition to the stores and restaurants, there were hair salons managed by African and Caribbean women alongside tailors and barbershops. By the late 1990s, it was estimated that 80 percent of businesses on West 116th Street were owned by Senegalese.[63]

In the words of anthropologist Paul Stoller, the Senegalese became "the aristocracy of West African merchants in New York City."[64]

As in Senegal, some storefronts were converted into *grands-places*, especially when the weather warmed up. In Senegal, especially in rural areas where most Murid immigrants originated from, people spend much of their time outdoors. Rooms are only for sleeping. In Harlem, the *grand-place* plays the role of an urban palaver tree; this is a gendered space where men (and only men) meet when they are retired or not working to chat, gossip, relax, share tea or café Tuubaa, and play the French games of checkerboard or *belote* (card game) with much noisy laughter and arguing. One of those *grands-places* located in front of a tailor's shop was dubbed *Nations-Unies* (United Nations) to connote the ethnic and national diversity of the people who frequented the place.[65] The "African Union" would have been a more fitting name because most of those who patronized the place were from West African countries.

The hair salons that dotted West 116th Street were, likewise, alternative *grands-places* or "United Nations" for women where Africans from a variety of nations interacted with their African American and West Indian customers. The first Senegalese hair-braiding salons opened in New York City and Washington, DC, in the late 1980s.[66] Most owners were wives of Murid immigrants who acquired permanent residence status from the 1986 immigration amnesty. Since then the hair-braiding business has expanded, attracting women of all social statuses, including professionals, students, and even members of the prestigious Mbakke family, defying the stigma attached to a profession often associated with lower-caste groups in Senegal.[67] Hair braiding has been a driving force of Senegalese female migration to the United States, creating the single example in the Senegalese diaspora where the female population is nearly equal to that of men.[68]

The popularity of Senegalese-style braiding opened a large window of opportunity for female immigrants in the United States. Braiding was a lucrative business that brought self-employment and upward mobility to female immigrants. It was not merely a last-resort job that women were compelled to choose because of their immigration situation or because they lacked the professional skills to find employment elsewhere. On a good day during tax-return time (or "busy time" in the language of braiders and the high season for braiding, which is January to April), a fast braider can easily make $200 to $300 a day. Large salons such as those owned by Ndey Astu Aac in Washington, DC, or Asan Gey in Atlanta, which employ dozens of braiders, make six-figure incomes per year. Most female hair braiders earned more than their husbands did. The increase in women's wealth is gradually affecting the distribution of power and authority within the household, upsetting conservative Wolof-Muslim gender roles and straining marriages.[69]

The business of hair braiding was hit hard by the 2008 recession when the African Americans that formed the customer base of hair braiders had less disposable income. The crisis was compounded by the growing number of African (but also African American and West Indian) hair braiders who live in the same American inner-city urban neighborhoods and compete for the same market. Competition brought prices down and gentrification expelled braiders from strategic locations for their businesses. A growing number of Senegalese women are moving to jobs in nursing homes or to restaurants and the hospitality industry. The younger generation, probably inspired by the example of the Ghanaian and Nigerian immigrants, are going to school to train as nurses to work in hospitals and other health-care institutions.[70]

West Africans made a significant contribution to the revival of Harlem. The deputy commissioner for economic development in New York State remarked in a 1999 interview with the *Economist*, "African fabric shops, travel agents and telephone call-centres are internationalizing the economy."[71] Similarly, Linda Beck credits African communities (particularly the Murids) as the catalysts of what she describes as the "astonishing transformation of Harlem in the 1990s."[72] Zain Abdullah, author of a book on Senegalese Muslims in Harlem, relates how "many African Muslim merchants revitalized the area [116th Street] by taking over empty stores."[73]

THE GENTRIFICATION OF LITTLE SENEGAL

While Little Senegal has been the beacon of African and Murid cultures in New York City for three decades, the future of this cultural enclave is in doubt. It remains to be seen if the Murids' ability to adapt to changing economic and sociopolitical circumstances—as evidenced by the resilience of their culture in face of French assimilation policy, postcolonial urbanization, and globalization—will protect them against gentrification.

Already by the late 1980s, at a time when Murids began to move to central Harlem, researchers detected what they called the earliest stages of gentrification in the area.[74] The opening of the office of President Bill Clinton's foundation on 55 West 125th Street in 2001 marked what for many was the most obvious evidence of creeping gentrification. This move was the sign and symptom of changes to come. Recently, Harlem has undergone a profound transformation. This transformation is most visible in the streets, where the sight of young White or Asian people jogging, walking their dogs, or pushing strollers—unimaginable just a few years ago—has become a familiar sight. These new residents are attracted by city tax abatements, new high-end housing, various public improvements, the availability of hip restaurants and fitness studios, stores such as Whole Foods, Victoria's Secret, and other commercial entities catering to the middle class. These investments have ameliorated the quality of life in Harlem considerably, but they have also driven up the price of real estate, squeezing out low-income people and businesses. The Murids and West Africans, who were living and working in Harlem when few dared to visit the neighborhood after dusk, have for three decades now contributed in no small measure to Harlem's revitalization.

Many Senegalese immigrants fear that it is only a matter of time until Little Senegal is lost to gentrification. This is also the opinion of geographer Kathryn Wright: "It [gentrification] is rapidly changing Little Senegal into an extension of the Upper West side (a wealthy, exclusive area of Manhattan) rather than one of the centers of Senegalese social and culture life in the U.S."[75] This observation is supported by the reportage of journalists. Here is how a recent article on Harlem in the *New York Times* begins: "Malcolm X Boulevard in Harlem around 125th Street is now lined with artisanal French restaurants, wood-fired pizza joints and brunch places serving kale salad. A new Whole Foods supermarket shines from the corner. On Sundays, luxury tour buses idle at curbs, unloading foreign tourists who want to experience a gospel church service or a neighborhood meal."[76] New York, like other global cities such as London, Los Angeles, and San Francisco, is experiencing a real estate revolution. Not surprisingly, corporate landlords have set their sights on central Harlem. With the help of likeminded politicians and an often ineffective and underfunded city bureaucracy, corporate landlords have been successful in undermining rent laws put in place to protect low-income tenants. Since 1993, the city of New York has lost 152,000 regulated apartments and 130,000 more have disappeared because of condos and co-op conversions.[77]

In Little Senegal, businesses are the first victims of gentrification because commercial real estate does not benefit from rental protection. In the last ten years, the cost of rent has tripled and, in some cases, quadrupled. The Association of Senegalese in America, which used to pay a monthly rent of $1,500 when it opened its office in 2003, is now paying $5,000, a price that the landlord considers to be a favor for a nonprofit organization.[78] Shopkeepers and restaurant owners who rely on their businesses to cover costs have been pushed out of central Harlem or are struggling to survive. In the last few years, the restaurants La Marmite and Africa Kiné have left Little Senegal to reopen further north where rent is, for the time being, affordable. The buildings they vacated are now occupied by Dunkin' Donuts and 7-Eleven stores. Five Murid-owned grocery stores and most of the hair-braiding salons have closed their doors.[79] The building occupied by Masjul Aqsa and Harlem Car Service was demolished and the place fenced off, the landlord probably just waiting for a building permit to begin construction. The removal of places of worship deeply affects the deeply religious African immigrant community. For the Murids, the most painful loss was the closure of Tuubaa Qassayit store. This shop, among the first to open on West 116th Street in the 1990s, was the anchor of Murid identity in Little Senegal. It specialized in selling Ahmadu Bamba's sacred writings, Qur'ans, prayer beads, cassettes, VHS tapes, and later CDs and DVDs of Murid spiritual music, lectures, and ceremonies. The store was a familiar stop for researchers doing fieldwork on Senegalese in New York, and it was a meeting place for visiting Murid shaykhs and disciples.

Tenants benefiting from rent control or rent stabilization seem to be more successful in resisting gentrification. Although rent prices have been increasing steadily—many among those who were paying $500 a month in the 1990s are now paying more than $1,500 a month—many remain committed to the neighborhood. However, they are also aware of the growing number of tenants, mostly Columbia University students and new western European immigrants, living in the same building and paying twice and sometimes three times as much as they pay for the same apartment. Property owners are deploying a number of tactics, using conciliatory and illegal means to get rid of protected tenants. Some tenants are offered as much as $50,000 and six months of free rent if they agree to vacate their rent-protected apartments.[80] A few have accepted the arrangement. Those who refuse to comply are sometimes subjected to threats and harassment.[81] For example, aggressive landlords refuse to make repairs or to provide pest and rodent control. Some undertake renovations in surrounding vacated apartments using demolition tools and heavy equipment that damage rent-stabilized properties, whose tenants are forced to leave to avoid being saddled with repair costs they cannot afford.[82] The president of ASA, Ibrahima Sow, now spends most of his time advising Senegalese tenants and seeking legal help for those among them facing threats of eviction or mistreatments by their landlords.[83] During the celebration of Ahmadu Bamba Day on July 28, 2018, the president of the Borough of Manhattan, Gale Brewer, and city council member Bill Perkins lauded the role of Senegalese in helping rejuvenate Harlem with their businesses, families, and vibrant culture and vowed to fight gentrification. However, it remains to be seen how these politicians' commitments will fare in face of powerful financial interests.[84]

⌒

The first Murids who came to New York City in the 1980s were already embedded in trade networks linking Senegal to African and French cities. They shared the same economic and cultural ethos as their compatriots across Africa and Europe. When they arrived in New York City, Murids quickly established a monopoly on street vending, paving the way for future Senegalese and African immigrants. The busy sidewalks of Midtown Manhattan became the gateway to their first encounter with American society. Through this encounter emerged a narrative that portrayed the Murids as a strange but honest and hardworking people. They were not dissimilar to earlier generations of immigrants who, like them, came to the United States with hardly any English-speaking ability, scarcely any money, almost no formal education, and a significantly different culture.

The sympathetic reception of Murids by ordinary Americans in the streets of New York is informed, in part, by the role that immigration has historically played in the American imaginary. Likewise, the gradual establishment of Little Senegal from the mid-1980s to the 1990s draws from the American immigration experience as illustrated by established ethnic enclaves such as Chinatown and Little Italy. It demonstrates, in contrast with France, a willingness to encourage the display of cultural diversity in public space—a decoupling of citizenship and cultural cohesion.

However, the Murid practice of street vending did not sit well with established commercial and real estate interests in New York City. The powerful storeowners and real estate magnates in Midtown Manhattan did not share the hospitality and empathy of journalists and commoners who lauded the resourcefulness of Murid itinerant traders. The combination of restrictive municipal regulations and police pressure forced many Murids to leave New York State or find alternative occupations. More recently, gentrification is proving to be a great threat to Murid economic and cultural survival in Harlem. The spread and normalization of toxic xenophobic and Islamophobic rhetoric is becoming the greatest threat to undocumented Murid immigrants, many of whom are even afraid to travel across state borders.[85]

Finally, the presence of a large African American community in New York City affected Murid immigrants in significant ways. Beyond economic considerations (affordable rent, closeness to downtown, convenient public transportation), the attraction of Harlem was due to the presence of a large Black population where Murids could blend in and find support, although the relationships were, at times, contentious. This Black American population was also the consumer of the commodified African culture (artifacts, hair braiding, fabrics, foods) that formed an important part of Murid businesses. Hair braiding, the most sought-after service that Senegalese women provided to African Americans, was particularly instrumental in affecting migration. While braiding remains an occupation of Senegalese across the diaspora, in the United States it is the most popular profession among women. This popularity has demographic and cultural implications. It explains the feminization of Senegalese migration to the United States, where in the last two decades the number of Senegalese women entering the country has surpassed that of men.[86] It also explains the visibility of women among the Murid community in the United States.

7 ～ Making Room for the Muridiyya in New York City

There is something worth learning from the French. Wherever they go they leave traces of their culture. You [Murid disciples] should strive to do the same.

—Statement attributed to Shaykh Murtada Mbakke

IMMIGRANT CULTURES have often been examined through the lenses of host nations' immigration policies and national character. Most scholars of international migration agree with the idea that classic immigration destinations such as the United States, Canada, and Australia, for whom immigration is central to the myth of nation building, are open to multiculturalism and allow the flourishing of diverse immigrant cultures. In contrast, labor migration countries such as France and Germany that claim cultural homogeneity as the foundation of their national identity discourage cultural diversity and encourage assimilation. The presence of large ethnic minorities in France and Germany that have resisted assimilationist policies, and rising xenophobia in North America and countries reputedly welcoming to multiculturalism call into question the divide between immigration-friendly nations open to cultural diversity and labor migration countries opposed to it.

While recognizing the impact of the institutional and cultural environment in receiving countries on the formation of immigrant cultures, it is also critical to note other significant factors. These factors include the culture of the immigrant's country of origin and the cultures of other immigrant communities he or she interacts with in the host society. To better understand the role of these factors, it is important to shift our gaze from the high politics of the state to the immigrant's everyday actions and interactions with people at the local level. My exploration of Murid place making in New York City is informed by this localized approach to immigrant culture. I explain how through building connections with the African American Muslim community of Harlem and the city government,

Murids are able to earn recognition. I then demonstrate how the acceptance they earned facilitated their adaptation to local cultural circumstances and allowed them to carve out their own space in New York City.

This chapter explores the different ways in which New York City is gradually becoming a home for Murids by focusing on Murid strategies of place making. Murid disciples in New York use a variety of media to etch their culture on the city's cultural landscape. Their efforts to produce religiously meaningful places take different forms. These efforts involve the physical occupation of space and the creation of Murid place by infusing Harlem's landscape with cultural and religious meaning. The production of Murid place is achieved through activities such as processions, lectures, the chanting of religious songs, the sharing of food, and the recitation of sacred narratives.

The chapter is inspired by Barbara Metcalf's book on public expressions of religiosity among Muslim immigrants in Europe and North America.[1] Like the contributors to Metcalf's edited volume, I discuss the expansion of Murid religious culture and its role in shaping the life of immigrants around the world. But unlike many of the authors, I emphasize processes of place making, the tensions generated by the debate about ritual and proper practice, and the implications of continued connections with holy places and the religious leadership in Senegal. I particularly stress Murid disciples' efforts to appropriate physical space and their use of sacred words, sacred texts, and bodily performance to turn ordinary space into extraordinary place.

The chapter begins with an exploration of Murid proselytism among African Americans and the challenges they confronted. I highlight the conflicting aspirations among the Murids between "universalists" committed to *dawa* (call for conversion) and "parochialists," who are more interested in identity preservation. The last two sections of the chapter discuss how the purchase of a Murid house in Harlem and the festivities of Ahmadu Bamba Day contribute to a Murid strategy of place making in New York City.

THE MURIDS AND THE MALCOLM SHABAZZ MOSQUE

By the time Murids began to migrate to the United States in greater numbers in the mid-1980s, Sunni Islam was well established in Harlem.[2] In his 1943 book, *New World A-Coming*, journalist Roi Ottley gives a vivid depiction of Harlem's Muslim community:

"Harlem's Moslems," he wrote, "run into several thousand. . . . Since they have no mosque, the faithful worship in private homes and hire halls, where on Saturday mornings their children study the Koran. They live quietly in Harlem, but during their festivals they don rich robes, shawls, turbans, and fezzes of their native land, and the women wear gorgeous brocades and heavy decorative jewelry. Whether they are Africans, Arabs, Tartars or American Negroes, Moors, Persians, or whites, Moslems intermarry. The racial flow back and forth defies classification. . . . They possess a religious fervor that is expressed in much missionary work among American Negroes. Newark, New Jersey, for example, has a congregation of five thousand Negro Moslems and there are several other thousands in the Midwest."[3]

Ottley's account describes a Muslim community mostly composed of immigrants, where Islam was lived as a private religion confined to the home, as the absence of mosques suggests. By the time the Murids began to form a community in Harlem, the situation had significantly transformed. African Americans had become the majority of the Muslim population in the United States. Several Muslim organizations had been formed,[4] each embodying a particular Islamic identity. For some, the appeal of Islam rested on its aspirational message of social justice and equality and the fact that it is essentially a religion of peoples of color. This was the case, for example, of the splinter group led by Minister Louis Farrakhan, after the death in 1975 of Elijah Muhammad, the founder of the Nation of Islam (NOI). The NOI emphasized Black Nationalism, issues of racial inequalities, and Black empowerment. It was less concerned with spirituality, orthodoxy, or connections with the global Muslim community.

In contrast to Farrakhan, Warith Deen Muhammad, the son and successor of Elijah Muhammad, engaged in a reformation that brought his faction of the NOI closer to mainstream Islam. He deemphasized racial politics, rejecting his father's call for Black separatism and urging his followers to embrace the classical teachings of Islam. Under his leadership, the NOI's temples were converted into mosques. He fostered relations with the wider Muslim world while recognizing the specific conditions in the United States that called for an independent American Muslim community. Independence, however, did not mean enacting religious innovations but rather transforming the social role of the mosque, bearing in mind the centrality of the church in the life of African American communities. In other words, independence expresses the need for organizational autonomy to meet the expectations that African Americans historically place on religious institutions.

In addition to the NOI and Warith Deen Muhammad's organization, there were other African American Muslim organizations that cultivated a different Muslim identity. Darul Islam, based in Brooklyn, was one of the most influential among these organizations. Darul Islam adopted an Islamic philosophy profoundly influenced by Islamic reformist movements in the Middle East. Like the Muslim Brotherhood in Egypt and Salafi organizations throughout the Muslim world, they promoted the idea of a universal Muslim creed that transcends race, ethnicity, and national boundaries. They emphasized study of the Arabic language and mastery of the Qur'an and relied on literalist interpretations of the Islamic scriptures (Qur'an and hadiths) to foster this creed. Followers of Darul Islam can be recognized by their raiment: bearded men wearing short baggy pants, skull caps, and flowering robes and women wearing the full body covering.

Two of these African American Muslim organizations had some influence on the development of the Muridiyya in the United States. Most African Americans who joined the Muridiyya were former followers of the NOI. And by the time Murids settled in New York, the Malcolm Shabazz mosque, affiliated with Warith Deen Muhammad, was the anchor of Sunni Islam in Harlem (where most of them lived). This mosque became the nerve center of Murid religious life.

Originally named "Temple 7" of the Nation of Islam, the mosque located on 116th Street and Lenox Avenue was renamed in honor of Malcolm Shabazz (a.k.a. Malcolm X) by Warith Deen Muhammad in 1976. Africans and African American Muslims performed the Friday congregational prayer there. The Murids used the mosque ground to commemorate religious events and offer weekend Qur'anic classes. The mosque also accommodated visiting shaykhs from Senegal. It was there that Senegalese took Sëriñ Abdul Aziz Sy Senior, the leader of the Tijaniyya Malikiyya order and one of the first Senegalese Muslim dignitaries to visit New York City in the early 1980s. He was well received and given the honor of leading prayers as guest imam.[5] Imam Tariq, then the imam of the mosque, extended the same honor to visiting Murid shaykhs and particularly Shaykh Murtada, the Murid caliph's envoy in the diaspora when he began his annual visit to the United States in 1988.

The relationships between African Muslims and the Malcolm Shabazz mosque took a different turn after Imam Tariq's death. His successor, Imam Pasha, who took over the leadership of the mosque in 1993, was less accommodating to African Muslims. Imam Izak-El M. Pasha is a former member of the NOI who followed Warith Deen Muhammad when the latter embraced Sunni Islam. He is a conservative Republican and ally of

Mayor Rudy Giuliani, who appointed him the first Muslim chaplain of the New York Police Department in 1999.[6] Pasha seemed less interested in the idea of Pan-Africanist brotherhood that until then undergirded the relationships between leaders of the African American community in New York and the West African immigrants.

Imam Pasha's distant, and apparently unsympathetic, attitude toward West African immigrants was reflected in his sermons. In one sermon, he admonished West Africans "to spend the money they earned in the United States instead of remitting it back home and to wear decent clothing."[7] Many African worshippers were offended by the comments. These statements echo criticism that Africans often hear from African Americans who denounce what they call "parasitic" behavior of African immigrants. The comment about decent clothing probably refers to the fact that many Africans wear their work clothes to the mosque as they do in their home countries, where Friday is not a holy day and where people are obligated to return to work after prayer. He also might have been objecting to the brightly colored robes, pants, and hats that Africans wear and that for some Muslims depart from Islamic sartorial culture. Feeling insulted by the imam's comments, some West Africans stopped attending the mosque. Others continued to worship there, but many felt it necessary to open their own mosque. Soon after the incident in 1996, the Malian community founded Masjid Aqsa, the first African immigrant mosque in Harlem on Frederick Douglass Avenue between 115th and 116th streets. The Murids, along with other West African Muslims, joined the new mosque where they observed the Friday prayer.[8]

Among the Murids, resentment against Imam Pasha was even stronger, although criticism was muted to avoid confrontation with one of the most powerful political and economic actors in Harlem and a potential ally in times of crisis.[9] The Murids' displeasure was fueled by comments the imam made that most felt were condescending and disrespectful. During a Friday prayer led by Shaykh Murtada on the occasion of a visit in 1995 or 1996, Imam Pasha spoke before and after the Murid shaykh's sermon in a tone that anthropologist Scott Malcolmson, who relates the event, characterized as "dyspeptic."[10] The imam, addressing the two thousand worshippers, most of them Murids, pointed out that "Friday prayers and other mosque activities happen every week and not just when the sheikh visits. . . . You who come here, moved here, live here in the United States, should worship here. You are Senegalese Muslims in the United States." He also stressed that "Islam requires one not to worship a man, any man but to worship God and to honor Muhammad, His messenger and the last of the prophets."[11] During his address the imam did not mention the word "Murid" or the name of Shaykh Murtada, but the Murids understood that the veiled criticism was specifically directed at them.

Imam Pasha may or may not have been aware of it, but he was re-hashing critiques that the Muridiyya and Sufi orders in the Muslim world have confronted all throughout their history. These critiques come from Muslims influenced by the teachings of the conservative Saudi Wahhabi doctrine that rejects the very idea of the necessity of a spiritual guide for Muslims as taught by Sufis, arguing that the Qur'an and hadiths (deeds and sayings of the Prophet Muhammad), accessible to all the faithful, are enough. The Murids are particularly targeted because of the unusual reverence they show their shaykhs and their reliance on the Murid leader-ship in Tuubaa, their holy city, for all things spiritual.

For the beginning and end of Ramadan and the celebration of reli-gious holidays, most Murids in the United States and around the world refuse to follow the lead of local mosques and align with Tuubaa, despite Shaykh Murtada's recommendation that they follow the guidance of local imams. Murid disciples justify their attitude, noting in the words of one disciple living in Harlem that "if you tour the mosques in the area, each follows what is happening in their own country, whether it is Saudi Ara-bia, Kuwait, etc. He [Shaykh Murtada] instructed us to do the search and conform to what the majority of Muslims do."[12] It is likely that the Murid shaykh's recommendation to follow what the majority of Muslims do was an invitation to put forward Islamic universalism rather than national sen-sibilities. But for the Murid immigrants, the connection with Tuubaa is central to the construction of their identity and a means to assert differ-ence in New York's crowded religious environment. Since the founding of the Muridiyya in the late nineteenth century, the bond with Tuubaa has been a defining feature of Murid identity and the foundation of a coun-terculture that has protected them against powerful assimilationist forces, including French culture imposed on them by colonialism, and, more recently, Salafi interpretations of Islam.[13]

BALOZI HARVEY: AFRICAN AMERICAN SHAYKH OF THE MURIDIYYA

The Muridiyya attracted many African Americans who were former fol-lowers of the NOI. But Ahmadu Bamba's teachings were also embraced by Black Muslims who, in the words of scholar Beverly Mack, adopted an ideology in which "Pan Africanism and Pan Islamism converge with a re-ligious focus on African heritage."[14] The highest profile African American to join the Muridiyya, the late Balozi Harvey (d. 2016), fits this ideological orientation. Balozi, along with Mustafa Mbakke, a great-grandson of Ahmadu Bamba who immigrated to the United States in the 1980s, was instrumental in the building of the Murid community of Harlem.

Balozi was a Muslim and Pan-Africanist. He liked to don African clothes, and his living room was filled wall to wall with masks, statues, and artifacts from a variety of ethnic groups across the African continent.[15] Balozi was born in East Orange, New Jersey, in 1940 and grew up in a family where he was immersed in Black Nationalism. Both of his parents were followers of Marcus Garvey.[16] Balozi's encounter with Africa happened at the College of Seton Hall where he befriended a student from Tanzania. This was a time when universities were some of the few places in the United States where African Americans had a chance to meet Africans from the continent. The student, who was the son of the vice president of the recently independent African nation, funded Balozi's tickets to visit his country. Julius Nyerere, the first president of Tanzania, welcomed Balozi as his personal guest in 1964 and gave him the name "Balozi," which means "ambassador" or "statesman" in Kiswahili.

On his return to the United States, Balozi worked as job recruiter for the Tanzanian government, enrolling African American professionals and technicians to help with the development of the young African nation. Throughout his career, Balozi occupied many positions in nongovernmental organizations and local governments in New York and New Jersey to promote economic and cultural cooperation with African countries. In 1982, he was appointed executive director of the Harlem Third World Trade Institute (HTWTI), an agency of the Harlem Urban Development Corporation. HTWTI facilitated trade and investment relations between American minority and women-owned small business firms and developing countries. He led the institute for thirteen years.

It was in his capacity as head of Harlem's Third World Institute that Balozi came to the attention of Senegalese immigrants. In 1987, one Murid shaykh who had befriended Balozi recommended Senegalese street vendors, then under intense pressure from the police, to seek his help.[17] The vendors met with Balozi at his home. He received them well but made clear that in the United States nothing is free and that if the vendors wanted to have their voices heard, they needed to get involved in community activism. At the next Harlem celebration of Marcus Garvey, Balozi called on the Murids to participate in the parade. The African Americans marched holding up placards and shouting nationalist slogans while the Murids, who had never heard of Garvey, sang Ahmadu Bamba's devotional poems in Arabic and waved their shaykh's picture. This event cemented the relationship between Balozi and the West African immigrant community. Later, he facilitated the opening of the enclosed West 125th Street market that accommodated fifty licensed African merchants, half of them Senegalese.[18]

Balozi converted to Islam from Roman Catholicism in 1965 while visiting Tanzania. His introduction to the Muridiyya came later. He recalled, "I was watching Ali Mazrui's documentary on African history, and they were having the Màggal. I saw throngs of people filling train cars, trucks, cars and all kinds of transportation. This reminded me of the Hajj."[19] This would be a "Hajj" to commemorate the life of a Black African Muslim saint. When he traveled to the Gambia for the "Roots festival" in 1987, Balozi spent a few days in Senegal and visited the art market of Rue Muhammad V.[20] There he met with Shaykh Gey, a Murid disciple of Shaykh Murtada. In Gey's art gallery, Balozi recognized the same Murid iconography he saw in Mazrui's film. Gey proposed to take him to visit the Murid shaykh, but Balozi's plane left before he could make the arrangement.

The connection between Balozi's trip to Senegal and the first visit of Shaykh Murtada to New York City, the following year, is unclear. Murids have been traveling to New York since the 1970s. By the mid-1980s, a growing number had settled as permanent immigrants. Just as they had done throughout West Africa and in Paris, these Murids held weekly rotating meetings in their hotel rooms to study and sing Ahmadu Bamba's qasidas, collect donations destined for the caliph in Tuubaa, and socialize in general.

Sëriñ Mustafa Mbakke, the great-grandson of Shaykh Ahmadu Bamba, led the effort to organize the community.[21] After graduating from high school in Senegal, Mustafa migrated to New York in 1981 to work and pursue a college education.[22] He invited the Murid disciples to meet in his apartment on 147th Street and Saint Nicholas Avenue. As the community gathered strength with more disciples arriving, Mustafa suggested that they buy a house dedicated to Shaykh Ahmadu Bamba. The Murid caliph, Shaykh Abdul Ahad, had built such a house in Tuubaa, and this was certainly the inspiration behind Mbakke's proposal. Sëriñ Mustafa, who was married to an African American woman, was one of the rare Murid immigrants with permanent residence in the United States. He also spoke fluent English. Sëriñ Mustafa's Western education and his genealogical credentials as a great-grandson of Ahmadu Bamba made him the natural leader of the NYC Murid community. He oversaw the fundraising and purchase of a house in Brooklyn where he moved with his family. This was the first house in the United States owned by the Murids and dedicated to Ahmadu Bamba.

After completing the purchase of the house in 1987, Mustafa suggested the Murids invite Shaykh Murtada for a visit. There are conflicting explanations of the motivations behind Shaykh Murtada's first trip to New York. The Murid shaykh was a frequent traveler who for two decades had visited many countries throughout West Africa and the Muslim world. However, North America was never among his destinations. Other Murid shaykhs have preceded him in the United States.[23] Some sources suggest that Shaykh Murtada came to New York responding to an invitation from Balozi; others claim that he came to give his blessings and help inaugurate the Murid house.[24] Still, for others, Shaykh Murtada was called to solve an internal dispute that divided the Murid community. A controversy over the legal ownership of the Brooklyn house was brewing, and some Murids had stopped contributing to the mortgage payment. There were also rumors that the caliph had never received donations that the Murid disciples of New York had supposedly sent to him.[25]

Whether Balozi invited Shaykh Murtada to New York or not, their interactions clearly indicate that the Murid shaykh saw him as an important asset for his mission in the United States. Soon after his arrival in New York in summer 1988, Shaykh Murtada demanded a meeting with Balozi.[26] As Balozi recalled, "I received a phone call from Shaykh Mustafa telling me that Shaykh Murtada was here and that he wanted to meet with me. I was a little caught off guard, I never met him. The next day we met in my office in Harlem. And when I asked him what he wanted from me, he replied 'nothing, just to meet you.'"[27] They talked about the Muridiyya and Shaykh Ahmadu Bamba's teachings. Shaykh Murtada revealed to Balozi his father's prediction: "A day is coming in the future when the majority of my disciples will not be native speakers of Wolof." By conveying this message, the Murid shaykh wanted to stress the universality of his father's calling and the universal aspiration of his own mission. Balozi understood Ahmadu Bamba's prediction as an invitation to join the Muridiyya. He later remembered praying, "I wish to be among those non-Wolof speakers who became disciples of Shaykh Ahmadu Bamba."[28] Balozi introduced Shaykh Murtada to his mentor, the New York congressman Charles Rangel, and David Dinkins, then president of the Borough of Manhattan. Both officials later issued proclamations making the day of their meeting with Shaykh Murtada, July 28, Ahmadu Bamba Day in Harlem (see appendix 9).[29]

When Shaykh Murtada arrived in New York, he found two Murid organizations in the city. There was a recently founded dahira based in

Harlem that regrouped the majority of the disciples, and there was the group headquartered in Brooklyn. He urged them to keep the existing dahiras but to form an umbrella organization that would include all disciples. This body would be in charge of organizing communal events such as the Màggal of Tuubaa and Ahmadu Bamba Day. He would later recommend this same formula to Murids in Libreville, Paris, and Milan. On Balozi's recommendation, the organization was named Murid Islamic Community in America (MICA).[30] The pairing of Murid and Islamic cultures clearly indicates the effort to adapt to the American context. In Senegal and throughout Africa, everybody will understand that being Murid is being Muslim. The name might also connote the aspiration for an independent American Murid community. At any rate, MICA, as envisioned by Balozi, reflected the American religious congregational tradition. It was conceived as a culturally oriented institution managed by the laity and catering to disciples' spirituality as well as to their social needs.

A month before his third trip to New York to preside over the commemoration of Ahmadu Bamba Day, Shaykh Murtada sent the Murids a letter asking them to recognize Balozi as their leader: "I want unity to be held around the person of Balozi Muhammad . . . to avoid confusion and disharmony. Every *talibe* [disciple], be him Senegalese, American or any else nationality must follow the guidance, decisions coming from Balozi Muhammad if he wants to deserve my gratefulness, the grace of Allah, His prophet (peace be upon him) and Shaykh Ahmadu Bamba" (see appendix 8).[31] This was an unusual step. As we have seen in the case of Paris, where the shaykh declined involvement in selecting dahira officers, the same is true for Abidjan and Libreville: Shaykh Murtada has always shown discretion when it comes to disciples' choosing leaders. By putting Balozi in a position of leadership, Shaykh Murtada hoped that the former's standing among African Americans as a respected community leader as well as his professional experience and political connections would help the growth of the Murid community in the United States. As one African American disciple close to Shaykh Murtada noted, "Sëriñ Murtada felt that a man like Balozi was critical to make the Muridiyya successful in the diaspora. . . . He wanted Balozi to be a bridge with the African-American community."[32] This opinion is shared by Xaasim Mbakke, who asserts, "My father wanted African Americans to take the leadership of the Murid community in the United States."[33]

Balozi's appointment as the leader of the Murids in America created a controversy.[34] Shaykh Murtada seemed to have been aware of this possibility when in his letter appointing him he insisted on the need "to avoid confusion and disharmony." Some Murid disciples wanted Sëriñ Mustafa to continue to lead the community. Others questioned Balozi's credentials. He is an African American that lacks an understanding of Murid and Senegalese cultures, they argued. Others intimated that because he is not a speaker of Wolof (the lingua franca of Murids in the United States), he would have difficulties communicating with the disciples who do not speak English. Balozi became the public face of the Muridiyya. He led the effort to acquire a tax-exempt nonprofit organization (501c3) status for MICA and to institutionalize Ahmadu Bamba Day. He was MICA's interface with local and state officials. But the day-to-day administration of MICA and the relationships to local Murid disciples and the Murid leadership in Tuubaa were handled by his Senegalese deputies. Balozi's power as leader of the Murids in the United States was limited by his inability to leverage his authority over Murid disciples and to build strong connections with the leadership in Tuubaa, although he had their formal endorsement.

Balozi was not officially made a Murid shaykh during his lifetime.[35] But soon after his death in 2016, Murid disciples informally elevated him to this status, referring to him as Shaykh Balozi Muhammad. The bestowal of this honorific title was a recognition, albeit posthumous, of his significant contribution to the development of the Muridiyya in the United States. As leader of MICA, Balozi gave greater visibility to the Muridiyya among African Americans. One leader of the Murids of New York remembers a trip he took to Balozi's house to preside over a ceremony for the conversion of nine African Americans who joined the Muridiyya.[36] Many among these African American disciples, most of them women, converged on the Brooklyn house where Sëriñ Mustafa held regular meetings every week, and teachers taught parents and their children the Qur'an, Ahmadu Bamba's qasidas, Arabic, and Wolof ajami.[37] The women who brought their offspring to the school were principally concerned about the education and safety of their children exposed to drugs, violence, and the degrading inner-city subculture: they wanted to instill in their children positive Islamic and African values.[38] Balozi's son was among the pupils.

BUILDING BRIDGES WITH ISLAMIC AFRICA

While Balozi's connections to the Murids was initially driven by his Pan-Africanist aspirations, some African Americans were attracted to the Muridiyya for the Pan-Islamic connections, or more precisely, Pan-African Islamic connections. Many among these African American Muslims were in search of deeper connections with the "authentic" Islamic culture of Timbuktu, Jenne, and other renowned centers of Islamic learning in medieval Africa.[39] They saw in Ahmadu Bamba's teachings a bridge to this "authentic" Islamic culture. Most among these African Americans came to the Muridiyya at the end of a spiritual journey that had taken them to many Muslim organizations. Some were disillusioned by perceived cultural insensitivities and racism among Middle Eastern and South Asian Muslim congregations. They saw in the Muridiyya a means to connect to what they saw as their lost Islamic heritage.

The spiritual journey of Muhammad Abdu al-Rahman, a Jamaican-born African American Murid, provides a good illustration of this search for African Islamic authenticity.[40] Al-Rahman grew up in Jamaica, where at a young age his father regaled him with stories about enslaved African Muslims who escaped slavery and formed maroon communities. His father, who was not yet a Muslim, also taught him about Timbuktu and the glorious history of Islam in Africa before the coming of European colonizers. When he came to the United States in the 1970s, al-Rahman enrolled in a seminary to pursue a master's degree in Islamic studies. He also built ties with African Muslims. As he recalled during an interview, "I have always been involved with the African community, with Malians, Nigerians. We were conscious about African Islam. With Dr. Ziad, we founded the Ahmed Baba Research Center." Ahmed Baba, perhaps the most celebrated sub-Saharan Muslim scholar, lived in Timbuktu in the seventeenth century.

Al-Rahman's encounter with the Muridiyya happened in 1988 when he learned about the Murid house in Brooklyn. He became a regular at the house and was particularly impressed by the education given to young pupils and their parents there. Al-Rahman enrolled his son in the school. For al-Rahman, Tuubaa was the genuine modern heir of Timbuktu.[41]

Al-Rahman was particularly preoccupied with the need to build bridges between African American Muslims and West Africa. He conceived of the West African Islamic tradition as the foundation of Black Muslim identity, going back to the era of the Atlantic slave trade, where a large number of West African Muslims were transplanted to the New World.[42] Al-Rahman's most significant initiative when he joined the Muridiyya in 1988 was to build this bridge.

Along with a few African American doctors (he is a licensed clinical psychologist) and professionals, al-Rahman spearheaded the *hijra* project.[43] *Hijra* is an Arabic word that means migration or flight from a hostile to a welcoming land and refers to the Prophet Muhammad's relocation from Mecca to Medina. Among the Muslim diaspora, hijra has a variety of meanings. It relates, among other things, to the struggle of Muslim immigrants to live virtuously as a minority culture and to their duty as privileged citizens of the West to help spread their religion and assist their brethren in the Muslim world. For al-Rahman, the hijra project embodied the idea of returning to African sources of Islam but also giving back to the continent.[44]

The hijra project had two components: an educational one that consisted of sending young African Americans to study the Qur'an in Tuubaa and a medical one through collaboration with Senegalese hospitals and physicians. For al-Rahman, who had turned down a few scholarships to study in North Africa and the Middle East, exposure to the Islamic tradition of West Africa was crucial for the education of African American Muslims. As he stated, they "need to get the African fabric of Islam" because we knew that the "the Islamic education that was given in the Arab World was not adequate."[45]

It is not clear whether Shaykh Murtada was aware of (or understood) the hijra project, but he endorsed the idea of sending young African Americans to study at his school near Tuubaa. African American disciples of Shaykh Hassan Cisse, a Tijani cleric, had started such a project in the city of Kaolack in Senegal.[46]

Shaykh Murtada funded the education of the young Americans, including providing them lodging and food. A small fee was required from the parents but apparently was never collected. From 1990, about thirty young African American boys and a few girls were sent to study in Tuubaa.[47] These young Americans were mixed with fellow Senegalese pupils and lived in conditions that promoted their immersion in Senegalese society and culture. But not all parents embraced this approach. Some objected to the lodging in dormitory-style housing where many pupils shared one room and slept on bunkbeds. Some were unhappy about the Senegalese diet of rice and fish and the fact that the children walked (this was a fifteen- to twenty-minute walk) to their classes. Additionally, the school soon faced logistical and management problems, especially when al-Rahman returned to the United States. The program was ended in 1994. The medical collaboration never took off beyond a fact-finding mission composed of African American doctors from the New York City Health and Hospitals/Harlem Hospital Center that Balozi and al-Rahman led to visit hospitals in Dakar, Tuubaa, and Saint-Louis.[48]

"I CAN HAVE MY AFRICAN-AMERICAN CULTURE AND STILL BE A DISCIPLE OF SËRIÑ TUUBAA"

As this quote from an African American Murid suggests,[49] three decades after the arrival of the first Murids in the United States, the Muridiyya is still struggling to realize the cultural synthesis that would make American disciples comfortable being both Murids and Americans. The difficulties that beset the hijra project magnify the challenges that confront the Muridiyya in its effort to expand beyond its Senegalese constituency. The disconnect rests, in part, on conflicting understandings of what it means to be a Murid in the United States and what should be the primary mission of Murid institutions in the country.

Senegalese disciples see themselves as the custodians and true representatives of Murid teachings and values. They want to build a bridge to America, but this is a one-way bridge that leads back to Senegal. They expect their African American brothers and sisters to adhere to an idealized Murid ethic shaped by Wolof and Senegalese culture. In the classical Sufi way, this ethic demands total surrender of the disciple to the will of the shaykh and selfless giving to the community without expectation of accountability. African Americans, on the other hand, express the need to adapt the Muridiyya to the American cultural context. They prioritize basic Islamic education and the need to introduce disciples to the teachings of Shaykh Ahmadu Bamba. They want their Senegalese brothers to empower themselves by, for example, learning to conduct business in English.

In my discussions with African American Murids, Senegalese "imposition" of Wolof as the lingua franca of the Muridiyya in the United States is a recurring target for criticism. One African American observed, "We will be sitting in events for two to three hours and the speaking will be all in Wolof."[50] Another noted, "We are not accounted for" and "by wanting us to learn Wolof they are not being culturally sensitive."[51] Some construe the exclusive use of Wolof as a major obstacle for the expansion of the Muridiyya among African Americans. As one of my interviewees notes, addressing his fellow Senegalese Murids: "You, Senegalese, have done a good job preserving your culture; you have created communities wherever you go. But you have not expanded your culture."[52] Others lament the failure to separate Ahmadu Bamba's universal teachings from Wolof culture, because they see Wolof culture as merely an imperfect vessel carrying the teachings of Bamba. "They [Senegalese] wrap the Muridiyya up around Senegalese culture, but they are not the same. Shaykh Ahmadu Bamba is greater than Senegal," notes Sister Sultana, an African American Murid in Philadelphia.[53]

Leadership is another area of friction. But this is not solely because African American Murids covet power. They see their "marginalization" as an impediment to the growth of the Muridiyya in the United States. Sister

Sultana, in an interview, said the following: "If you want to keep us on the outskirt of the Muridiyya, you do not know what the shaykh's [Ahmadu Bamba] plan is. The Muridiyya needs to move and if they [Senegalese] do not make it happen, someone else would."[54] African Americans like to recall the time of Shaykh Murtada when he used to surround himself with African American disciples whenever he visited the United States. Aminah Njaay, an elder African American woman who joined the Muridiyya in 1988 or 1989, remarked, "Shaykh Murtada came here for us . . . but after he passed, they [the Senegalese] excluded us. They seem to want to be with themselves."[55]

Differing conceptions of the proper role of the dahira in the United States constitutes another point of contention between Senegalese and African American Murids. Some African Americans even prefer to call the organizations they create *daaras* (schools) to emphasize the need to put education over sociability.[56] African American Murids want the dahira to play both the role of a school and that of a mission. They aspire to use Ahmadu Bamba's teachings as the basis for a religious education and as a guide for daily life.[57]

Most Senegalese Murids, including the leadership, acknowledge their fellow Americans' critiques and complaints and often find them legitimate. They recognize their failure to attract and keep African American disciples.[58] They attribute their shortcomings to "cultural chauvinism,"[59] language barriers, and the lack of an enlightened leadership that understands Shaykh Murtada's vision and mission.

It is important to remember that since its founding, MICA was led by Senegalese elders who drew their legitimacy from classical Murid education and conception of legitimate authority.[60] None of them understood American history and culture, which is something that might have facilitated the adaptation of Murid values and cultures to the American context. The current president of MICA graduated from teacher training school in Senegal and also taught there: he is also the first Senegalese leader of the Murid community in America with a formal education. He speaks of the need to reform MICA and to recognize that "African Americans want to be taught Islam a certain way. A new convert cannot be asked to live [the Muridiyya] the way we [Senegalese] live [it]."[61] It remains to be seen, however, if Senegalese Murids are willing to accept and enact the changes that would make the Muridiyya a truly diasporic religion catering to the specific spiritual and existential needs of a diaspora. It is significant that none of the leaders I interviewed brought up the possibility of putting African Americans in a position of leadership.

The difficulties in attracting and keeping African American disciples reflect the broader issue of universalism and parochialism discussed in previous chapters. Parochial Murid leaders prioritize the relationship with Tuubaa and the need for Senegalese disciples to preserve and consolidate Senegalese Murid identity abroad. They are reluctant missionaries, and they resist the very idea of "diasporic Muridiyya": a Muridiyya open to innovations catering to the spiritual needs of a non-Senegalese constituency. Universalists, on the other hand, put greater emphasis on dawa, or missionary work. These universalists are able to present Ahmadu Bamba's biography and teachings in a way that addresses what they see as issues of relevance to host people. They strive to meet the expectations that their hosts place on religious congregations. The Murid shaykh, Abdoulaye Dièye, is an apt representative of universalist thinking.[62] Dièye achieved much success recruiting disciples in Europe and the United States, both Blacks and Whites, because of his dual cultural outlook as a traditionally trained Murid shaykh and cosmopolitan Western-educated intellectual. He was a prolific writer, and most of his writings in French have been translated into English. He preached ecumenism among interfaith groups and visited churches and synagogues. He promoted Ahmadu Bamba's teachings as therapy for the illnesses that plague American society and families. He intervened to bring peace into dislocated households. Dièye made frequent visits to young Black inmates in prison and proposed Ahmadu Bamba's spiritual poetry, dhikr, and meditation as remedies for their trauma. He addressed issues concerning social and racial injustices, environmental degradation, and the problem of drugs, demonstrating his awareness of the challenges that confront American and Western societies, and particularly a willingness to offer solutions.[63]

MURID HOUSES IN NEW YORK

Shaykh Murtada's call to the Murids to leave traces of their culture on New York's soil seems to have been heard. The Murids established their first house of Ahmadu Bamba in New York in 1987. While the initiative may have been inspired by a similar house built in Tuubaa a few years earlier, the two houses had markedly different roles. The house of Tuubaa is merely a guesthouse where the caliph accommodates important guests. The Murid house located on east Thirty-Seventh Street in Brooklyn had multiple functions that reflect the role of mosque and Islamic centers across America and the influence of American religious congregationalism on Muslim immigrants. As Levent Akbarut perceptively observes, "The American mosque in contrast to the mosques in the countries of origin, needs to be a school, because urban schools are sub-standard; a community center, because the streets are dangerous; and a locus of political activism . . . so that Muslims will have a say in the decision-making processes of this country."[64] One may add to this list that the mosque must also be a recreational space to entertain the youth in a safe environment. The Murid house of Brooklyn, however, only embodied some of these functions. It was a mosque, a living space, a community center, and a school; however, it did not make space available for entertainment or politics. It provided the model for future Murid houses in the United States.

Today, there are over a dozen Murid houses across the United States. These houses represent what Roger Stump calls "bounded segments of secular space" that operate according to the religious principles of the faithful that created them.[65] Although Murid houses, also called Kër Islam (house of Islam) and best known as Kër Sëriñ Tuubaa (house of Sëriñ Tuubaa, Wolof acronym KST), are opened to all, they display typical features of "bounded" space. Besides the few houses located in repurposed churches such as the houses of Detroit and Chicago, nothing externally distinguishes KST from surrounding buildings. The interior, however, tells a different story. When one enters the house, the layout of the rooms, the furnishing, the decoration, and the behavior of the visitors clearly indicate the extraordinary nature of the place. As Gieryn argues, ordinary space becomes meaningful as extraordinary place when people ascribe qualities and values to the material gathered there.[66]

Almost all Murid houses open on a vestibule-like room, reminding one of the *mbaar*, typical of classical Murid-built space in the heartland of the Muridiyya in Senegal.[67] Murid effort to reproduce home-country architectural design in urban America reminds us of the continuing influence of the immigrant's home country on diasporic culture. The vestibule is the largest room in the house. It is furnished with oriental rugs and a few couches, all arranged to leave space for copious seating on the floor. For Murids, walking barefoot and sitting on the floor are signs of modesty and humility, qualities that are highly valued by followers of Sufi Islam. The room serves multiple purposes. It becomes a mosque at prayer times, a meeting room for the local dahiras and lay organizations, a dining room for communal meals, and the site where visiting Murid shaykhs receive disciples. The decorations invariably consist of pictures of sacred Murid sites such as the mosque of Tuubaa, the Well of Mercy, the iconic picture of Ahmadu Bamba (based on his sole known surviving photograph), paintings depicting epic moments during his exile, photographs of Murid caliphs, and sometimes pictures of Muslim holy sites such as the Kaaba or the mosque of Medina. Along with the pictures, there are clocks and calendars illustrated with photos of Murid shaykhs and bookshelves containing Qur'ans and volumes of Ahmadu Bamba's writings kept sometimes in richly decorated leather pouches. These decorations and objects have a purpose. In their work on Murid visual piety, Allen Roberts and Mary Nooter Roberts demonstrate the centrality of sacred pictures and artifacts in the sanctification of Murid space.[68]

Two other things define the Murid house: the sound system and the kitchen. Sophisticated sound-mixing tables, amplifiers, speakers, and microphones now grace all Murid houses in the diaspora. Scholars have written about the role of *adhan*, the Muslim call to prayer, performed five times a day as a way of inscribing Islam in the secular soundscape of Western cities.[69] The sound system in KST serves primarily to convey the chanting of Ahmadu Bamba's sacred poems in Arabic, but sacred Murid music plays a role similar to that of adhan for Murid disciples in cities around the world.[70] All Murid houses have one or more kurels (bands of singers, often young males) specialized in chanting Ahmadu Bamba's devotional poems. The chanting is performed with voice only.[71] This is an area where one can argue that the Murid diaspora has made an original contribution to Murid culture.

The innovation is not in the chanting, which has a long history in the Muridiyya, but in the institutionalization of the act of singing and its elevation to an important act of worship. These innovations are made despite the objection of shaykhs who denounce what they call the disciples' excesses. Qasida Day is one such excess criticized by some shaykhs, particularly Sëriñ Maam Moor Mbakke, the envoy of the Murid caliph in the diaspora.[72] This event has now become an important moment in the cultural calendar of Murid communities across the diaspora. Qasida Day was invented by Murid disciples in Italy in 2004, and it has now spread across the diaspora and in Senegal.[73] It is an annual concert of sacred Murid music that brings together all kurels in a particular country. The concert is often organized on a weekend during the spring or the summer, and groups of singers perform all day and night. The event is not a competition but an act of religious devotion, so no award is given. However, the best performers garner much prestige and symbolic capital.

Along with the musical paraphernalia, the kitchen is another fixture of the Murid house. The kitchen is not for cooking: food is provided by disciples who cook the meals in their houses or restaurants. The kitchen is primarily used to brew café Tuubaa, the favorite drink of Murids. Coffee is not grown in Senegal, but café Tuubaa has become a trademark and a sacred beverage for Murids.[74] There are stories told about Ahmadu Bam-ba's love of coffee and the blessings that come with drinking it.[75] The drink is even ascribed medicinal virtues. Café Tuubaa has displaced Nescafé as the most popular hot street beverage in Senegal. It is consumed by people of all classes and social status, including non-Murids and even foreigners visiting or living in Senegal. Café Tuubaa has now become a ritual drink for most Murid households and is served at all Murid gatherings. Drinking café Tuubaa is becoming such a building block of Murid self-fashioning that even those Murids who do not drink coffee feel compelled to prepare it for random visitors.[76] Café Tuubaa is particularly appreciated as a halal (lawful) stimulant by attendees of sacred music concerts who stay awake all night listening to qasida singers.

Café Tuubaa emerged in the market in Senegal in the 1980s as the Muridiyya was becoming a major economic and political force in urban Senegal.[77] This is another example of expanding Murid culture in the cit-ies of Senegal and now among the Senegalese diaspora. The originality of the drink rests in the delicate portioning and mixing of coffee beans, cloves, and other spices that are grilled at a specific temperature for a specific time and then ground together. The product is then filtered and sweetened. The powdered coffee is imported from Senegal, Montreal, and other places in the Murid diaspora where entrepreneurial disciples pro-duce, package, and commercialize the product.

Of all Murid houses in the United States, and arguably the world, the house situated on 46 Edgecombe Avenue in Harlem occupies a unique place. New York is the Western city where the presence of Murid culture in public space is the most conspicuous. On his third trip to the United States in 1991, Shaykh Murtada recommended the Murids buy a house in Harlem. The Murid cleric wanted the place he called "house of Islam" to serve as a mosque, a school, a guesthouse, and a space where disciples socialize. He contributed $55,000 of his own money to help get the project off the ground.

Two years after the shaykh's recommendation, the Murids were able to raise $100,000 to buy a rundown house in central Harlem. Like the house in Taverny and Aulnay-sous-Bois and the Murid mosque in Libre-ville, the Murids viewed the place as perfectly suited for a house dedicated to Ahmadu Bamba. They learned from their African American neighbors that the building was over a hundred years old. It had always served the Black community, first as a clinic, then as a shelter for homeless people of color, and later a health center.[78] It is irrelevant for the Murids whether the stories told about the house are accurate or not. What is important is that they gave disciples the confidence that the house has always been devoted to serving a noble cause: the same cause it will continue to serve under Murid ownership.

It was a decade before the Murids could complete the renovation and move into the house. They had to deal with complex municipal regulations and unscrupulous contractors. The first contractor asked for $250,000 to do the work, but he severely underestimated the cost and was dismissed. The second was able to finish the project for $350,000, and the house was opened in 2001. The house is now undergoing a second renovation, and the same problems that dogged the first restoration project are recurring. In 2016, the board of MICA decided that it was time to redesign the house to meet the needs of the growing Murid community in New York. The aim was to transform the building into a large mosque that can accommodate seven hundred worshippers and a school, keeping only one apartment for visiting Murid dignitaries from Senegal. The addition of a minaret (one that replicates the large minaret of the mosque of Tuubaa), a dome, and an elevator was planned.[79] One-third of the cost, estimated at two million dollars, was raised and ground broken on January 2017, but the work has stalled amid disputes among the architect, contractor, and city regulators.

Beyond meeting the needs of a growing Murid community, the ambitious renovation project reveals the Murid community's changing relationships with New York City. New York is no longer perceived as a place where one goes just to earn a living. The mentality of transient sojourners reluctant to plant roots in the city that characterized earlier migrants has now given way to enthusiastic settlers eager to leave a permanent cultural imprimatur on the city's landscape. The planned minaret and the dome, in addition to the decorations intended for the mosque's façade, are unmistakable symbols of Islamic and Murid identity. When completed, the mosque will be the first Murid place of worship in any major Western city with external signs of Islamic architecture.

Nearly forty years after the first Murid immigrants settled in New York, and thirty years after Shaykh Murtada's first trip, it is becoming clear that for most Murids, Harlem has now become a home for Ahmadu Bamba and the ideal location for a mosque worthy of him. It is significant that Murid disciples are embracing these ideas at a time when hostility toward Islam is intensifying in the West, including in the United States. Perhaps, the Murids' current attitude signals a dedication to showcase a face of Islam that debunks prejudices and fears and one that calls for mutual understanding. The celebration of Ahmadu Bamba Day represents the same spirit.

AHMADU BAMBA DAY IN HARLEM

Ahmadu Bamba Day came about through the meeting of two traditions: first, there is the tradition of American cities dedicating special days to iconic figures in recognition of their accomplishments; second, for urban Murids, the tradition of celebrating Ahmadu Bamba's memory in public space has long been a means of legitimizing their presence in the city. For the Murids, the symbolic recognition conferred by the official proclamation of Ahmadu Bamba Day by mayors was not enough.[80] They wanted to give tangible significance to the days that local governments in a dozen major US cities dedicated to Shaykh Ahmadu Bamba. And it is to this promotion of Murid cultural significance that Shaykh Maam Moor Mbakke dedicates his tour of the United States, which takes place annually from July 22 to August 15. Shaykh Maam Moor travels to nine states and Washington, DC, to preside over events commemorating Ahmadu Bamba Day. He spends six days in New York City, where the most important commemorations take place.[81] Two major events mark the New York celebrations: the July 28 procession and the lecture held at the headquarters of the United Nations the same day.

Among all the events of Ahmadu Bamba Day, the procession, in the eyes of Shaykh Murtada, is the most important activity. He used to insist that all Murids participate in the march, noting that "this is a day when Muslims are allowed to invoke the name of Allah in the streets of America, and I do not want anybody to stay with me here (in the hotel or house). I want you all to go to the procession. This is a day for Islam that shows that Ahmadu Bamba fought for everybody."[82] Marchers walk along on Adam Clayton Powell Jr. Boulevard from West 116th Street to 163 West 125th Street. The itinerary for the march has changed over time. In the early years, Murid marchers headed to Central Park where they held a rally. Now the march stops at Adam Clayton Powell Jr. State Office Building Plaza (Africa Square) on 125th Street, Harlem's busiest thoroughfare. The circuit is also shorter now, perhaps to accommodate the aging Murid leadership in New York and the shaykhs who lead the procession. The reorientation of the procession's itinerary toward the heart of central Harlem could be understood as a reflection of the Murids' changing self-perception from undocumented interlopers to confident members of the citizenry of Harlem and America.

This Murid procession, which mobilizes between four and five hundred marchers, is unlike any other parade in New York City.[83] It attracts a crowd composed almost entirely of Black African immigrants. There are no floats, no marching bands playing music, no grand marshal, and no baton-twirling girls. The marchers' dress also sets them apart. The men wear brightly colored, floral-print Senegalese style robes and pants. The women who walk behind them are clad all in white. As they walk, men and women perform dhikr (or "remembrance of God") by declaiming the Islamic credo la-ilaha-il-la-lah ("there is no god but God") (The participation of women is another particularity; it is unusual for Muslim women to participate in public performances of religious piety even among more liberal Sufi orders.)[84] Some disciples chant Ahmadu Bamba's sacred poems with their natural voice or using megaphones.

After the procession on July 28, 2018, over a dozen speakers addressed the audience congregated at the Adam Clayton Powell Jr. Plaza, where marchers hold the rally, including representatives of New York's local government, officials dispatched from Senegal, and leaders of local Senegalese organizations.[85] New York City officials, who do not seem to distinguish between Murids and Senegalese, praised Senegalese immigrants for their positive contribution to Harlem's economy and for enriching central Harlem with their culture. A captain from the New York Police Department commended Senegalese immigrants for being peace-loving people, stressing how unusual it was for such a large gathering to happen without disturbance of public order or arrest. The Murid shaykh's speech invariably admonishes the disciples to work hard, respect the law, and follow Shaykh Ahmadu Bamba's teachings.

The Murids like to emphasize that the rather large mobilization of security personnel is not done for fear of violence or disorderly conduct but just to help with traffic. Murids are, in fact, committed to solidifying their positive reputation in the eyes of New York officials. Unlike in Senegal, where such events generate uncollected garbage in the streets for days, in New York Murid youth are mobilized to follow the marchers. Garbage bags in hand, the youths collect plastic bags, empty bottles, napkins, and other trash in order to leave the place as clean as they found it.

In her account of Pakistani Sufi processions across cities in England, Pnina Werbner suggests that Sufi chants and dhikr "not only purif[y] their [the marchers'] hearts and souls, but also sacralize the very earth, the buildings, the streets, and neighborhoods through which they march."[86] This observation is also true for the Murids. Murid disciples believe that the coming of Shaykh Murtada in New York and their processions in the streets of Harlem, chanting the sacred names of God, are a form of therapy. Murids see a direct connection between the healing power of their prayers and the improvement of living conditions in the Black neighborhood since their settlement there in the late 1980s.[87]

Marchers often carry banners and pictures of Shaykh Ahmadu Bamba and other Murid saints, including paintings of Maam Jaara Buso, the mother of the founder of the Muridiyya, conspicuously displayed by women marchers.[88] The texts of the placards displayed at the Ahmadu Bamba Day in July 2018 clearly indicate the Murids' willingness to showcase their triple identity as Blacks in the United States, as Muslims rooted in Senegal's Sufi tradition, and as American citizens aware of the nation's politics. The marchers' slogans are inspired by Qur'anic verses, Ahmadu Bamba's writings, and relevant current events in the United States. In one procession, a placard displayed a quote from Ahmadu Bamba's verse: "Do not let my condition of a black man turn you away from my writings. . . . Blackness is not a sign of weakness of mind."[89] Another read, "Shaykh Ahmadu Bamba is an African Muslim leader of non-violence." Acknowledging the current political climate in the United States, still another banner read: "Islam condemns racism and tribalism."

The lecture at the headquarters of the United Nations begins just a few hours after the end of the procession: this is the other major highlight of Ahmadu Bamba Day. The Murids are keenly aware of the symbolic significance of organizing their forum at UN headquarters. Despite the hefty cost of paying overtime hours for technicians and security personnel, they remain committed to holding the meeting there.[90] Some claim that the Murid gathering is the sole religious event to ever be authorized on UN premises. The Murids see in the United Nations' meetings the fulfillment of Ahmadu Bamba's call to humanity to join him regardless of race or class. I have been reminded many times of Bamba's verse that reads: "O people of the dryland, O people of the sea, come to the virtuous ocean of generosity."[91] Murids see the headquarters of the United Nations as the place where peoples of the sea and land meet. The same spirit informs Shaykh Maam Moor, who insists that speakers give their presentations in official United Nations languages such as Arabic, French, and English alongside Wolof.

The conference has been held in a room in the UN building for over two decades. The aim of this meeting was to educate Americans, and especially African Americans, about Shaykh Ahmadu Bamba's teachings. Speakers were brought from Senegal to develop themes related to the doctrine of the Muridiyya, the Murid economic ethos, Bamba's pedagogy, and his resistance to colonial rule. More recently, especially after the 2001 World Trade Center attacks, Ahmadu Bamba's philosophy on nonviolence has been a recurring theme.[92] Western-educated guests, often drawn from the world of academia, are invited to speak. The emphasis on peace and nonviolence clearly indicates Murid awareness of global politics and their willingness to have their voice heard.

PLATE 3.1. Shaykh Murtada Mbakke with Balozi Harvey. Image courtesy of Murid Islamic Community in America (MICA).

PLATE 3.2. Shaykh Murtada Mbakke with Balozi Harvey and Mayor David Dinkins at New York City Hall. Image courtesy of MICA.

PLATE 3.3. A Murid-owned shop in Harlem. Photo by the author, July 2018.

PLATE 3.4. 7-Eleven store occupying the building where the restaurant Africa Kiné was located. Photo by the author, July 2018.

PLATE 3.5. New location of Africa Kiné, 2267 Seventh Avenue. Photo by the author, July 2018.

PLATE 3.6. A shop for lease formerly occupied by a Murid businessman, West 116th Street, Harlem. Photo by the author, July 2018.

PLATE 3.7. A Murid Qur'anic school on West 116th Street, Harlem. Photo by the author, July 2018.

PLATE 3.8. Malcolm Shabazz mosque in Harlem. Photo by the author, May 2019.

PLATE 3.9. Blueprint of the mosque under construction at the Murid house of Edge-comb Avenue. Image courtesy of MICA.

PLATE 3.10. Interior decoration of the Murid house of Memphis, Tennessee, featuring pictures of Ahmadu Bamba and his five successors as caliphs of the Muridiyya. Photo by the author, March 2011.

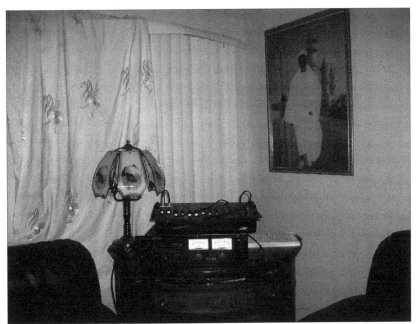

PLATE 3.11. Sound system of the Murid house of Memphis, Tennessee. Photo by the author, March 2011.

PLATE 3.12. A bag of café Tuubaa sold in an African grocery store in Philadelphia. Photo by the author, March 2020.

PLATE 3.13. Singing session, Murid dahira of Philadelphia. Photo by the author, January 2013.

PLATE 3.14. Murid women in the procession of Ahmadu Bamba Day, Harlem, July 2007. Photo by the author.

PLATE 3.15. Aisha McCord, member of the MICA board. Photo by the author, July 2016.

PLATE 3.16. Muhammad Abdu al-Rahman. Photo by the author, May 2016.

PLATE 3.17. Murids singing qasidas at the procession of Ahmadu Bamba Day, Harlem. Photo by the author, July 2007.

PLATE 3.18. Gale Brewer, president of the Borough of Manhattan, addressing the crowd on Ahmadu Bamba Day in Harlem. Photo by the author, July 2018.

PLATE 3.19. The conference room at the United Nations during Ahmadu Bamba Day. Photo by the author, July 2018.

PLATE 3.20. Gare de Lyon (Îlot Chalon), headquarters of Murids and sub-Saharan African immigrants in Paris in the 1970s before the mayor of Paris, Jacques Chirac, evacuated the site to start renovation works in 1984. Photo by the author, June 2019.

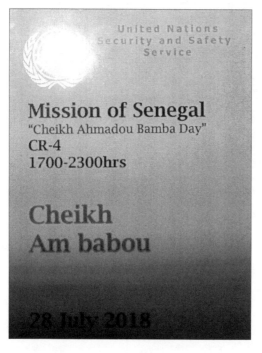

PLATE 3.21. Badge issued for admission to the conference at the United Nations on Ahmadu Bamba Day.

By the time Murid immigrants arrived in the United States in the early 1980s, Sunni Islam had become dominant in New York City. Murid disciples created their own religious networks by founding dahiras, but they also built relationships with African American Muslim institutions, especially the Malcolm Shabazz mosque of Harlem. This mosque became the center of Murid spiritual life. But it soon became clear that shared Sunni creed between the Murids and their African American brethren would not trump cultural differences. These differences and the tensions they fueled pushed Murid disciples to seek their own house of worship. The Murids were, in contrast, relatively successful in attracting lay African Americans, especially those steeped in Pan-Africanist and Afrocentrist sentiments. Converts to the Muridiyya were attracted to the image of Ahmadu Bamba as a Black Muslim saint who founded his own Sufi order and resisted Arab acculturation and French colonial oppression. They admired the Murid ethic of hard work and self-reliance. Others saw in the Muridiyya a genuine representation of the prestigious Islamic tradition of medieval Africa they wished to reconnect with. However, attraction to the image of Ahmadu Bamba and his teachings did not translate into mass adhesion. Language barriers, insufficient knowledge of American history and Black culture, a certain "chauvinism," and perhaps concerns with power and control kept Senegalese Murid disciples from engaging with their fellow African Americans in ways that would have made the latter feel welcome as full members of the Murid community. What resulted was a feeling of alienation among African Americans, some of whom are now trying to form their own organizations independent of Senegalese disciples or have left the Muridiyya altogether.

Murids have been more successful in making their mark on the cultural and religious scene of American cities. They have created houses of Ahmadu Bamba throughout large cities across the United States. These houses are places of worship and cultural centers that are conceived as symbolic replicas of Tuubaa, the holy city of the Muridiyya. All of these places incorporate Tuubaa in their names (Tuubaa New York, Tuubaa Chicago, Tuubaa Cincinnati, etc.).[93] The furniture and decorations in the house, the nature of the events it hosts, as well as the behavior of visitors reflect its status as an extraordinary place and symbolic abode of Ahmadu Bamba. Besides physical presence, Murid efforts at placemaking also include performative acts. The display of photographs of Murid shaykhs (whether deceased or living), of sacred texts and pictures of holy places, and the chanting of Ahmadu Bamba sacred poems allow Murid disciples to convert secular space into Murid place, even for just a day.

Conclusion

My AMBITION for this book was to reconstruct the history of Murid migration from the end of World War II to the turn of the twenty-first century. I wanted to study the interconnectedness between this particular migration and other migrations but also to establish what sets Murid migration apart. Beyond the narrow economic concerns that inform most studies of Murid migration, I wanted to investigate the role of religious culture in immigrants' lives, particularly in urban settings in Senegal and abroad. I was particularly interested in exploring how this culture is reproduced in the diaspora and how it was affected by the changing experiences of Murid immigrants across Africa, Europe, and the United States. Furthermore, I examine how transformations happening in the diaspora influence people left behind in Senegal. My investigation reveals the centrality of place making in the spiritual life of Murid immigrants. Migrants strive to turn ordinary urban space into extraordinary Murid place by infusing this space with spiritual values through the renaming of places, the building of places of worship and sociability, the enactment of processions and pilgrimages, and the display of a sacred iconography. The performance of culture in public space contributes to the construction of a Murid diasporic collective identity. Ordinary Murid disciples played a major role in the formation of this identity. The visible presence of Murid culture, in turn, helps build bridges with local communities and facilitates the acceptance of migrants as legitimate members of the citizenry of host nations. The formation of a Murid collective identity abroad is fraught with tensions and contradictions that reflect conflicting conceptions of the missionary role of disciples.

There is a long tradition of mobility among the Murids. Among the Wolof, migration has historically served as a coping strategy to address overpopulation, land scarcity, and household conflicts. Before colonial rule, migration was seasonal and mostly involved young people, traders, and craftsmen. Young men, mostly those living in the ecologically vulnerable but densely populated areas of Kajoor, western Bawol, and Njambuur (where Murids constitute the majority of the population), migrated to more humid areas during the rainy season to work as sharecroppers (*surga*). Traders who also farmed migrated during the dry season after the harvest. The same was true for itinerant blacksmiths, woodworkers, and leatherworkers who trekked from village to village to offer their services.

Under colonial rule, with the introduction of a cash crop (peanut), a market economy, taxation, and urbanization, French colonization transformed Wolof patterns of mobility. Migrants increasingly headed to cities to participate in the cash economy to earn money to buy manufactured goods, gain resources to fund family ceremonies, or pay their taxes. Among the Murids, migration served multiple purposes. It was initially part of a strategy to mitigate French repression, and then it became an organizing tool that fostered expansion. In the late nineteenth and early twentieth centuries, Ahmadu Bamba and his senior disciples founded dozens of villages in an attempt to achieve autonomy and spatial separation from the colonial administration. Bamba's exile to Gabon between 1895 and 1902 stopped Murid expansion but spawned a narrative of heroism and suffering that sacralized mobility. The end of the exiles and the transfer of the founder of the Muridiyya to Diourbel in 1912 ushered in an era of détente that allowed the resumption and intensification of Murid migration.

The Murid accommodation of the colonial administration created the conditions for the institutionalization of the Muridiyya and its expansion across Senegal. With the encouragement of the colonial rulers, Murid shaykhs engaged in the cultivation of peanuts, which over the next half a century became the engine powering the migration. They founded village farms or working schools (*daara tarbiyya*) in western Bawol and eastern Senegal prompting what scholars have termed the *front pionnier mouride* (Murid pioneer frontiers). These villages also accommodated landless youth yearning to establish a household and served as refuges for young men fleeing conscription in the French colonial army and forced labor. The rural-rural migration tapered off after the end of World War II when migrants set their sights on urban destinations. The rural-urban migration is connected to the earlier pattern of rural-rural migration. Disciples in the rural working schools have long engaged in seasonal migration to cities, and they were the first to settle as permanent residents in urban areas.

Migration to cities was led by craftsmen, whose profession as itinerant artisans has weakened their attachment to the soil, facilitating their transplantation to the new colonial towns. Mass Murid migration to the cities of Senegal, then West Africa, and finally Europe and the United States began in earnest in the aftermath of World War II. A few factors played a key role in the intensification of the urban migration: the stabilization of the *front pionnier*, the discontinuation of colonial policies that stifled mobility, the abolition of forced labor and coerced military conscription, and the droughts of the 1970s and 1980s.

Murids who migrated to cities across West Africa and central Africa followed in the footsteps of the soldiers, employees of French trading companies, and Senegalese civil servants who staffed the administration of the expanding French African Empire. Being the oldest colony with the most advanced educational system, Senegal was relied upon by the French colonial administration to help supply the human resources needed to administer new colonies. The internal African migration mobilizes the largest contingent of Murid migrants and reflects a broader trend of African migration. Despite the disproportionate attention that the popular media and some scholarly circles pay to African irregular migrants, asylum seekers, and refugees trying to cross the Mediterranean to Europe, two-thirds of immigrants remain in the continent. Murid migration illustrates this trend. Most Murid immigrants reside in the neighboring countries of the Gambia, Mauritania, Mali, as well as in Côte d'Ivoire and Gabon. However, Murid migration is distinctive. It differs from classical labor migration that mostly concerns wage laborers. Immigrants create their own economic niche, working in the informal sector of the economy as self-employed traders, hair braiders, artisans, or taxi drivers but rarely as wage earners. Until recently, Murid migration mostly involved artisans, traders, and farmers without a formal Western education; however, these were not among the poorest. Most people migrated to improve the quality of their lives or to preserve social status. African cities provided the staging ground where Murids accumulated the knowledge and experience that facilitated their move to France in greater numbers from the late 1960s and early 1970s.

France has long been a popular destination for Senegalese immigrants, starting from the nineteenth century when young men from the Four Communes (Saint-Louis, Gorée, Dakar, and Rufisque) headed to Europe for their education. France continues to be the primary destination of Senegalese students pursuing higher education. Labor migration to France intensified after Senegal's independence in 1960, stimulated by the accords of freedom of circulation and mutual settlement that France signed with her former colonies (except for Guinea). The first Murids who moved to Paris in the late 1960s benefited from this arrangement. But Murid immigrants were mostly invisible to the French state. Most of them were undocumented. They avoided registering with immigration and social services and worked in sectors of the urban economy that eluded state agents.

When France adopted drastic anti-immigration policies in the mid-1970s, Murids explored new destinations in Italy, Spain, and the United States in the 1980s. Murid migration to the United States, a country with which they have no historical, cultural, or economic ties, demonstrates their ability to transcend the pull of French imperial connections to take advantage of real or imagined economic opportunities. Murid immigrants have a conspicuous presence in New York City, especially Harlem, despite their rather modest numbers compared to Nigerian and Ghanaian immigrants. The reason for this is the visibility of their businesses and culture in public space. This visibility was made possible by the American tradition of multiculturalism, the formation of a West African economic enclave in Harlem, and the Murids' own ambition to claim a space in the lively multicultural scene of urban America.

The dahira, the single most important institution of the Muridiyya in the diaspora, was central in Murid efforts at place making. Murid migrants, like other African and Senegalese migrants, rely on overlapping family, ethnic, and occupational networks to find their way to destinations abroad. The dahira becomes important in their lives once they have settled on foreign soil, giving the diaspora its unique Murid identity. The dahira plays multiple and evolving roles defined by the continuous transformation of immigrant communities wrought by naturalization, demographics, family reunion, gender dynamics, and the changing administrative and cultural environments that Murids find in their host countries. The dahira first provided a crucible for identity formation and preservation as Murid immigrants transitioned from seasonal rural-urban migration to permanent residence in cities. For the recently urbanized Murids who originated from different regions of Senegal, belonged to different ethnic groups, practiced different crafts, and lived in distant areas of large cities, the dahira was the incubator of a collective identity. Dahira meetings and events became sites that helped foster a shared Murid identity that brought disciples together regardless of culture, class, or other differences. However, as Murids consolidated their identity as urbanized citizens, the dahira's role changed. It gradually became an instrument for the promotion and expansion of Murid culture. Dahira activities that revolved around private performance of piety through rituals geared toward social bonding and brotherhood. These activities would shift to public displays of Murid culture aimed at ingraining Murid historical memory in the urban landscape and turning ordinary city space into extraordinary Murid place. Dahiras have now embraced roles traditionally devolved to governmental and nongovernmental organizations to mitigate the failures of the nation-state by building critical infrastructures and providing a safety net to vulnerable communities.

In Senegal, Côte d'Ivoire, and Gabon, the transformation of profane urban space into Murid sacred place was achieved by reconstructing, appropriating, and memorializing places associated with Ahmadu Bamba's sacred biography. The reconstruction was done by tracing Bamba's footprints across West Africa and central Africa, particularly during his exile from 1895 to 1902. In Dakar, Saint-Louis, Grand Bassam, and Libreville, the conversion of secular urban space into sacred Murid place was achieved through the sacralization of time and space. The memory of Bamba's encounter with the colonial administration is enshrined in the cities' landscape through the performance of annual pilgrimages and processions and the building of monuments (mosques, houses of Ahmadu Bamba).

The place-making enterprise became particularly evident in the 1980s, when Murid immigrants emerged as dominant actors in the economy of the cities where they settled. For example, all the Murid religious commemorations in Dakar began in the 1980s and later years whereas Murids have started to settle in the capital of Senegal since the aftermath of World War II. The correlation between enhanced economic status and cultural assertiveness is significant. It reflects a conscious effort to translate the immigrants' economic capital into social and cultural capital. In the context of Senegal, the accumulation of social and cultural capital contributed to legitimizing Murid presence in urban areas and afforded them a voice in the management of cities. Everywhere else, it allowed them to build a discrete identity that distinguished them from other competing identities and to avoid the "radical Muslim" label.

In the United States and in France, where Ahmadu Bamba's bodily imprints could not be traced, place making was achieved through other means. Here, the role of Shaykh Murtada Mbakke, the youngest son of Ahmadu Bamba, was paramount. He was instrumental in helping migrants imagine ways of transforming secular Western space into spiritual Murid place, thus transforming the diaspora into a home. Shaykh Murtada arrived in the diaspora at a time when Murid immigrants were gradually shedding the image of temporary sojourners and becoming accepted as Western citizens. The formation of Murid families abroad, especially the increasing number of women and children born in the diaspora, required a rethinking of the role of Murid institutions in the diaspora. Until then, these institutions were mostly concerned with consolidating the relationships with the Murid leadership in Senegal. Migration was believed to be temporary, and little thought was given to the idea of the formation of a Murid citizenry abroad. In the context of a growing community of Murid citizens in the West, Shaykh Murtada recognized the necessity for the creation in the diaspora of institutions dedicated to the production and dissemination of Islamic and Murid culture. However, he believed that Murids in the diaspora had specific needs. These needs included building infrastructures for the education of future generations of Murids who have looser ties and less emotional attachment to the holy cities and leadership in Tuubaa, adapting Murid culture to local contexts, and creating bridges with host communities and local political and administrative authorities. These needs were not necessarily aligned with those of the disciples, and leadership in Tuubaa and migrants were best equipped to take the lead in addressing them.

The distance from the Murid holy land, the leadership in Tuubaa, and the necessity to attend to the unique existential and spiritual needs of migrants turned the diaspora into a site of cultural innovation. Shaykh Murtada provided guidance, but ordinary Murid disciples were the true agents of change. The most significant among these innovations are the dahira, the Kër Sëriñ Tuubaa (KST), Ahmadu Bamba Day, Murid Cultural Week, and Qasida Day. Some of these innovations are new inventions, while others are old institutions and practices refashioned to adapt to the demands of life in the diaspora. In the diaspora, for example, many dahiras have taken the form of nongovernmental organizations whose missions in Senegal would have been the purview of the Murid leadership or the state. I have alluded above to the Spain-based dahira that built a hospital in Tuubaa, but this is also the case of the Murid Islamic Community in America (MICA), which serves as an interface between the Murids and local government in New York and is raising funds to build a mosque. As I discussed throughout the book, dahiras in Côte d'Ivoire, Gabon, and France play similar roles. Beyond their strictly religious vocation, dahiras embrace the roles of an extended family, mediating disputes and fostering harmony within migrant families and in the community at large. Similarly, unlike in Senegal, KST is invested with multiple tasks. It fulfills the functions of a mosque, Qur'anic school, cultural center, and guest house. It is the beating heart of the community and plays a role similar to that of the church for African American congregations, in which congregants drive the agenda of religious institutions.

On the other hand, cultural innovations made in the diaspora are transforming practices in Senegal, sometimes to the dismay of shaykhs who resent the loss of their monopoly over the production of Murid culture. Qasida Day, invented by Murids in Italy, and Ahmadu Bamba Day, initiated by Murid migrants in Harlem, are now commemorated throughout the Murid diaspora and in Senegal. Probably inspired by the example of migrants in the diaspora, dahiras in Tuubaa are transforming into civil society organizations providing services that local and national governments fail to adequately deliver. There is, for example, a dahira specifically dedicated to enhancing security in the holy city of Tuubaa in collaboration with the national police. This is different from the *hisba* or so-called moral police in charge of enforcing Sharia morality rules in cities in some Muslim countries. Another dahira specializes in sanitation, organizing cleaning days and helping facilitate wastewater and rainwater disposal.

In half a century, Murid immigrants have created a global diaspora. Among the precursors of this diaspora, many have returned to Senegal or have passed away. Now a new generation is emerging. Some members of this generation are recent immigrants, while others are second-generation Murids, born abroad or migrating to diasporas with their families at a young age. Life in non-Muslim-majority countries and exposure to different Muslim traditions is testing the Murids' ability to adapt to change. Diverging conceptions of what should be the primary missions of Murid institutions abroad reveal deep fissures in the Murid diaspora that also reverberate among the leadership back in Senegal. Some emphasize the universal dimension of Ahmadu Bamba's teachings and insist on the missionary role of these institutions, especially toward non-Muslims. Others put forward the need to preserve Murid identity abroad, prioritizing a focus on the spiritual and existential needs of disciples and on the connections with Tuubaa. The future of the Muridiyya in the diaspora will depend on the changing balance of power between these two visions and especially on the attitude of the growing community of second-generation Murids.

This second generation's profile is different from that of their parents. The latter left Senegal in their thirties, already culturally mature with a strong sense of what it means to be a Murid. Their conception of the Muridiyya was shaped by their experience growing up in the Murid heartland in Senegal. They were nurtured in traditional village Qur'anic schools and the rural working schools. Strong bonds with the shaykhs and emotional attachment to Tuubaa formed the core of their identity as Murid disciples, and they were committed to nurturing and preserving this identity in the diaspora. After spending nearly four decades of their lives abroad, this first generation of Murid immigrants is longing for a return. Young Murids who are born in the diaspora or grew up there are cosmopolitans who straddle multiple cultures, as many have received a formal education in global cities where they now raise their families. Some of them enjoy middle-class status and are committed Western citizens for whom the diaspora is increasingly seen as home. This context is reshaping their understanding of the Muridiyya and their own role in its development in Senegal and the diaspora.

However, just as we have seen with earlier generations of Murid immigrants, the second generation is not monolithic. Some among them are increasingly retreating from community engagement and are experimenting with new ways of being Murid. This Murid identity is built around the development of a personal relationship with Ahmadu Bamba by focusing on the study of his qasidas and trying to use his teachings for guidance in life. Pious visits to his tomb in Tuubaa and participation in the Great Màggal, whenever possible, contribute to consolidating the bonds with Bamba. This option can be explained by the unique conditions of these disciples. Unlike first-generation migrants, they are married professionals raising a family, and often they are more integrated into their host societies. Their occupations and lifestyles make it difficult for them to spend the time, energy, and money that Murid communal life in the diaspora requires. Moreover, the death of Ahmadu Bamba's sons and the ushering in of the era of the grandsons and great-grandsons (who have less charisma and spiritual authority than their predecessors) have weakened the appeal of the living leadership, prompting a return to the founder, who is the quintessential source of baraka.

There are members of the second generation who remain committed to community engagement and to preserving and disseminating a collective Murid identity in the diaspora. But even here we see a shift in goals and strategy when compared to the first generation's approach. A new organization founded by Murid youth in New York City, Ndawi Sëriñ Tuubaa (NST),[1] provides a good example of this reorientation. Many among these young men and women are high school or college students, and some are professionals. The founding of NST was a response to the perceived failures of the MICA, the oldest and largest Murid organization in

North America. Since its founding in the late 1980s, MICA has been led by older first-generation Murids, while young people have little to say in its management. Its agenda focusing on strengthening the bonds between Senegalese disciples in the United States and maintaining the linkages with Tuubaa has not changed and neither has its method. While NST members are careful not to openly criticize the elders, they have articulated a vision for their organization that clearly diverges from that of MICA. For them, dawa (proselytizing) is a foremost priority. They are particularly concerned about the situation of young Senegalese of their generation in Harlem, most of them school dropouts who have drifted away from the community and have embraced a street life that, from NST leaders' viewpoint, violates Murid and Senegalese values. They see the members of this youth group as the primary target of their dawa to help resocialize them. But NST is also engaged in outreach toward African Americans. Its members put forward a vision of the Muridiyya that emphasizes empathy, tolerance, and openness, which they consider core principles of Ahmadu Bamba's teachings. Members of NST believe that their deeper integration into American society and their greater understanding of American culture put them in a better position than their parents to successfully translate Ahmadu Bamba's teachings to Americans.

NST innovations are mostly apparent in their use of space and technology and in their interactions with the wider American community. Unlike dahiras, their activities are not confined to Murid cultural centers or private houses. In the tradition of American urban culture, they organize barbecues in public parks where disciples are encouraged to bring families and friends. They make extensive use of social media and the new information technology, as their Facebook pages and Instagram profiles demonstrate.[2] They have faulted MICA for its conservatism, its inability to harness the new information technology, and its failure to understand and attend to the changing needs of the Murid diaspora, especially the youth. Most NST members are fluent in English and steeped in American culture. They are comfortable interacting with the wider American public. While they are active participants in all of MICA's activities, NST members flourish on the internet. They seem to be engaged in an effort to turn cyberspace into Murid place just as earlier generations of Murid migrants have strived to turn secular urban space into sacred Murid place. There are already cyberdaaras[3] devoted to the online teaching of Ahmadu Bamba's qasidas, the NST initiatives may be the precursor to cyberdahiras. Such initiatives will launch Murid culture in the diaspora on an entirely new historical trajectory.

Appendixes

Titre de l'Association. — « Confrérie des Mourides Dahiratoul E. H. Falilou M'Backé ».

Objet. — Transférer les corps des membres décédés, à Touba, aux fins d'inhumation dans le cimetière mouride de cette ville.

Siège social. — Rue 22 × 25, chez E. H. Diaw Bamba, Dakar.

COMPOSITION DU BUREAU
actuellement 'chargé de l'administration et de la direction de l'Association

Président : Diouf Saliou, marchand, quartier Ainoumane;

Vice-président : M'Baye N'Diaye, tailleur, Champ de Courses;

Deuxième vice-président : Dione Moussa, facteur P. T. T., rues 27 × 28 à Médina;

Trésorier général : E. H. Diaw Bamba, *dit* Ousmane, facteur P. T. T., rues 22 × 25, Médina;

}*Trésorier adjoint :* N'Diaye Samba, employé de commerce, Colobane;

Secrétaire général : M'Baye Bounama, planton, Gueule-Tapée;

Secrétaire adjoint : Bèye Moussa, facteur P. T. T. Champ de Courses;

Commissaire aux comptes : Sylla Tall, employé de commerce, Santiaba-Nimjatt;

Chargé des relations administratives : M'Bow Sangone, planton, rues 25 × 26, Médina.

Récépissé de déclaration d'association n° 657 A. G. du 10 avril 1958, du Délégué du Chef du territoire du Sénégal à Dakar.

Appendix 1. Excerpts from Journal Officiel de l'Afrique Occidentale Française authorizing the first licensed Murid dahira in Senegal, May 17, 1958

PROCES-VERBAL

de l'Assemblée Générale Constitutive de l'Union du Dahiratoul
El Hadj Falilou M'BACKHE de la Région du Cap-Vert - Siège
Social Gouye Senghor - DAKAR

_____

ORDRE DU JOUR :

L'Union du Dahiratoul El Hadj Falilou M'BACKHE s'est réunit
le 21 Septembre 1963 pour renouveler son bureau Fédéral chez El Hadj
Bamba DIAO à Wagou-Niayes, Parcelle Nº 2444.

FORMATION du BUREAU FEDERAL

Président d'Honneur   : El Hadj Ousmane M'BAYE
Président Actif   : N' G O M Mamadou.
1º- Vice-Président   : DIONE   Moussa
2º- Vice-Président   : M'BENGUE Moussa (Ouakam)
3º- Vice-Président   : Medoune   DIONE   (Ouakam)
4º- Vice-Président   : N'Diaga   N'DIAYE (Maka Colobane)

Secrétaire Général   : El Hadji Bamba DIAO
1º- Secrétaire Gal Adjoint : TAMBIDOU Mamadou
2º- Secrétaire Gal Adjoint : N'DIAUL   N'Gom

Secrétaire Administratif   : M'BAYE   Bounama
Secrétaires Adm. Adjoints   : Magatte SARR et Matar BA

Trésorier Général   : M o r DIOP
Trésorier Gal Adjoints   : WADE Ousseynou et N'Gouda KEBE

Secrétaire Général à la Revendication : Mor FALL (Yarakh)
Secrétaires Gal Adjoints Revendic. : FALL Sidy (Yarakh) et N'Dongo N'Diay

Secrétaire Général à l'Organisation : N'GOM Cheikh
Secrétaires Gén. Adjoints à l'organ. : Assane THIAW - Babacar M'BAYE
            Modou GUEYE et N'Diaga GUEYE (Ouakam)

Secrétaire Général à la Propagande : DIOUF Ibra
Secrétaire Gén. Adjt à la Propagande : M o r NIANG.

Commissaire aux Comptes : N'Diaga N'DIAYE (Colobane sans fil)
Commissaires aux Comptes Adjoints : Makane N'DOYE - Abdou GUEYE et
            Samba N'DIAYE.

Appendix 2. List of officers of the federation of Murid dahiras of Dakar in 1963

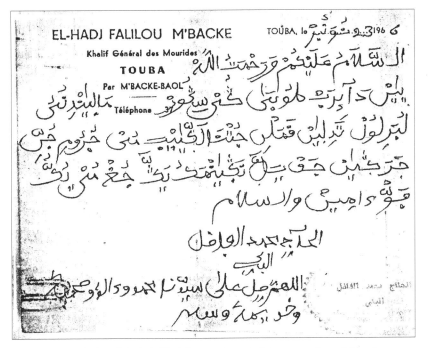

Appendix 3. Caliph Faliilu Mbakke's letter acknowledging reception of donations from the Murid dahira of Dakar, November 23, 1966

Appendix 4. Caliph Abdul Ahad Mbakke's letter acknowledging receipt of donations from the Murid dahira of Dakar, September 13, 1987

Hadj Guèye Bamba
Représentant Officiel du Grand Kalif des Mourides
de passage à Abidjan

- àMonsieur le Chef de la Sûreté du Territoire
de la Côte d'Ivoire

à   ABIDJAN

- s/c. de Monsieur le Chef du Territoire -

_____

Monsieur le Chef de la Sûreté,

        J'ai l'honneur de me permettre de vous adresser
pour information:
- 1º) Procuration faite par le Grand Kalif des Mourides
   de TOUBA Cercle de Diourbel (Sénégal),
- 2º) Copie lettre adressée à Monsieur le Chef du Territoi
   re à ce sujet,
en faveur du nommé Serigne NIASSE, disciple du grand Kalif
demeurant à Trecheville qui désormais est seul habiliter e
agir au nom du Grand Kalif des Mourides de TOUBA - M'BACKE.

        Je vous serais reconnaissant de bien vouloir lui
prêter votre aide agissante sur toutes ses interventions pour les mourides résidant dans ce territoire auprès
des services dépendant de votre Autorité.

        Persuadé qu'il vous sera suffi de prendre connais-
sance des lignes qui suivent pour donner des instructions
au personnel placé sous votre commandement en vue de lui
faciliter sa tache.

        Avec tous mes remerciements anticipés, je vous prie
d'agréer, Monsieur le Chef de la Sûreté l'expression de
mes respectueuses salutations./-

Hadj GUEYE BAMBA

Appendix 5. Caliph Faliilu Mbakke's letter to the governor of Côte d'Ivoire regarding
the appointment of Sëriñ Ñas as his representative, April 14, 1968

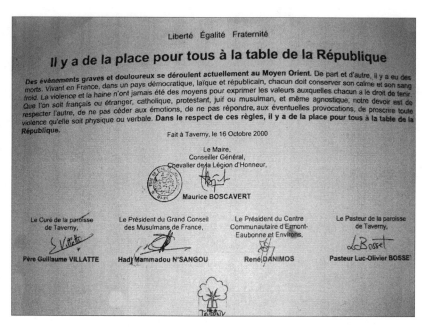

Liberté   Égalité   Fraternité

Il y a de la place pour tous à la table de la République

Des événements graves et douloureux se déroulent actuellement au Moyen Orient. De part et d'autre, il y a eu des morts. Vivant en France, dans un pays démocratique, laïque et républicain, chacun doit conserver son calme et son sang froid. La violence et la haine n'ont jamais été des moyens pour exprimer les valeurs auxquelles chacun a le droit de tenir. Que l'on soit français ou étranger, catholique, protestant, juif ou musulman, et même agnostique, notre devoir est de respecter l'autre, de ne pas céder aux émotions, de ne pas répondre, aux éventuelles provocations, de proscrire toute violence qu'elle soit physique ou verbale. Dans le respect de ces règles, il y a de la place pour tous à la table de la République.

Fait à Taverny, le 16 Octobre 2000

Le Maire,
Conseiller Général,
Chevalier de la Légion d'Honneur,

Maurice BOSCAVERT

Le Curé de la paroisse de Taverny,	Le Président du Grand Conseil des Musulmans de France,	Le Président du Centre Communautaire d'Ermont-Eaubonne et Environs,	Le Pasteur de la paroisse de Taverny,
Père Guillaume VILLATTE	**Hadj Mammadou N'SANGOU**	**René DANIMOS**	**Pasteur Luc-Olivier BOSSE**

Appendix 6. Proclamation by religious community leaders in Taverny, including the Murid Imam Mamadou N'Sangou, regarding the Algerian civil war and violence in the Middle East, October 16, 2000

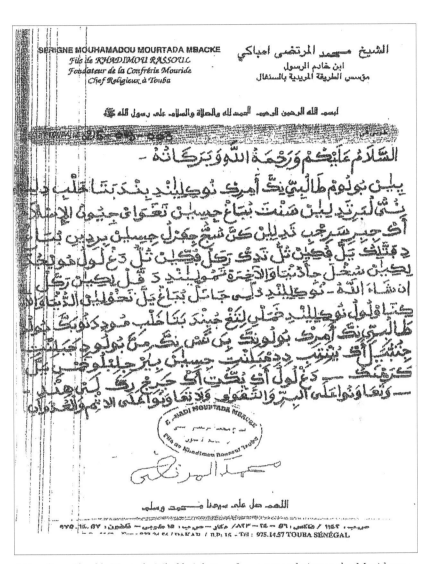

Appendix 7. Shaykh Murtada Mbakke's letter of recommendation to the Murid community in the United States

Seigne Mourtada M Bache

CHEF RELIGIEUX

FILS DE CHEIKH AHMADOU BAMBA

TOUBA (Sénégal)

الشيخ محمد المرتضى المبكي

ابن الشيخ أحمد بمبا

مؤسس الطريقة المريدية

طوبا ــ السنغال

Touba, le   june 28 th   1991

طوبا في

S T A T E M E N T S

       I, CHEIKH MURTADA MBACKE authorizes my talibe BALOZI HARVEY MUHAMMAD to organisze, coordinate and take the best initiatives neces- sary for a succesful celebration dedicated to KHADIMOU RASSOUL.

       I want unity to be held around the person of BALOZI MUHAMMAD.

This to avoid any confusion and disharmony.
Every talibe, be him senegalese, american or any else nationality must follow the guidance, decisions coming from BALOZI MUHAMMAD if he wants to deserve my gratefulness, the grace of ALLAH, his prophet(peace on him) and CHEIKH AHMADOU BAMBA.
Be united, live in brotherhood, faith sincerity and generosity.

All the AHMAD BAMBA Community living in New York has to cooperate without any discrimination and follow the advices, the wisdom of BALOZI HARVEY MUHAMMAD.

I don't forget brothers MALIK, MUHAMMAD AB AL RAHMAN, MUHAMMAD RACHID, AMIR AL MUHAYMIN and the dignitaries of their senegalese brothers.

I hereby certify this with my seal

Appendix 8. Shaykh Murtada Mbakke's letter appointing Balozi Muhammad leader of the Murid Islamic Community in America

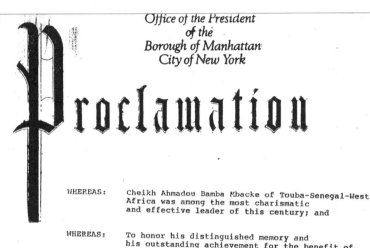

Office of the President
of the
Borough of Manhattan
City of New York

ℙroclamation

WHEREAS: Cheikh Ahmadou Bamba Mbacke of Touba-Senegal-West
           Africa was among the most charismatic
           and effective leader of this century; and

WHEREAS: To honor his distinguished memory and
           his outstanding achievement for the benefit of
           African personality and culture; and

WHEREAS: His venerated son Cheikh Mourtalla Mbacke
           of Touba Senegal has come in Harlem to visit his
           thousands of followers and admirers; and

THEREFORE: The Senegalese Murid Community and the
           people of Harlem are proud to seize this opportuni
           to salute as a great leader Cheikh Mourtalla
           Mbacke and to proclaim this day July 28th, 1988
           to be known as:

           "CHEIKH AHMADOU BAMBA MBACKE "

           in Harlem.

                          IN WITNESS WHEREOF
                          I HAVE HEREUNTO SET
                          MY HAND AND CAUSED
                          THE OFFICIAL SEAL
                          OF THE BOROUGE OF
                          MANHATTAN TO BE
                          AFFIXED THIS 28th
                          DAY OF JULY 1988

                          MANHATTAN BOROUGH
                          PRESIDENT

Appendix 9. Proclamation of Ahmadu Bamba Day in New York City by David Dinkins, President of the Borough of Manhattan

OFFICE OF THE MAYOR

CITY OF CHICAGO

RICHARD M. DALEY
MAYOR

PROCLAMATION

WHEREAS, Cheikh Mourtalla M'Backe, The Second in leadership line of the Mouride Sufi Order, whose headquarters is in Touba-Senegal, West Africa is visiting Chicago; and

WHEREAS, Cheikh Mourtalla M'Backe is the Son of the Founder the Mourdite Sufi Movement, Cheikh Ahmadou Bamba M'Backe; and

WHEREAS, Cheikh Ahmadou Bamba M'Backe of Touba-Senegal-West Africa, was among the most charismatic and effective leaders of this century; and

WHEREAS, the Sufi Brotherhood, Mouridiyyah was formed in 1888 in Senegal by Cheikh Ahmadou Bamba, who advised the Kings of the Wolof and Mandinke to let go of material power so as to attain divine power, uniting the Forces of Resistance against French Colonialism through Islam; and

WHEREAS, Cheikh Mourtalla M'Backe entered an agreement in 1995 with the American Islamic College in Chicago to launch a major student exchange; and

WHEREAS, Cheikh Mourtalla M'Backe, while others seek assistance from the developed countries of the world; he has independently funded more than 400 schools around the world with more than 4,500 teachers; and

WHEREAS, the Senegalese Murid Community and the people of Chicago are proud to seize this opportunity to salute as a great leader, Cheikh Mourtalla M'Backe:

NOW, THEREFORE, I, RICHARD M. DALEY, MAYOR OF THE CITY OF CHICAGO, do hereby proclaim August 13, 1996, to be CHEIKH AHMADOU BAMBA M'BACKE DAY IN CHICAGO, and urge all citizens to be cognizant of the events arranged for this time.

Dated this 31st day of July, 1996.

Mayor

Appendix 10. Proclamation of Ahmadu Bamba Day in Chicago by Mayor Richard M. Daley

Congratulations

Sheikh Ahmadou Bamba Mbacke Day

July 26, 2007

A PROCLAMATION BY THE MAYOR OF THE DISTRICT OF COLUMBIA

WHEREAS, Sheikh Ahmadou Bamba Mbacke was the founder of the Muridiya Sufi order in Senegal; and

WHEREAS, Sheikh Ahmadou Bamba founded the holy city of Touba (Senegal) that attracts millions of people of all races around the world at the annual pilgrimage "Magal" of Touba; and

WHEREAS, the foundation Khadimou Rassoul North America celebrates "Sheikh Ahmadou Bamba Day" on July 26 of each year; and

NOW, THEREFORE, I, THE MAYOR OF THE DISTRICT OF COLUMBIA, do hereby commend the Foundation Khadimou Rassoul North America for your dedication and interfaith dialogue in pursuit of world peace, and I wish you the best during your celebrations today.

Adrian M. Fenty
Mayor, District of Columbia

Appendix 11. Proclamation of Ahmadu Bamba Day in Washington, DC, by Mayor Adrian Fenty

Notes

INTRODUCTION

1. Paul Merles Des Isles, "Contribution à l'Étude du Mouridisme" (brochure ANS1G214) (1949), 23.

2. Des Isles, "Contribution," 23, 26.

3. The one hundred thousand figure is furnished by Des Isles, "Contribution," 36. The four million figure is advanced by journalists, observers, and the Màggal organizers. There are no official estimates of the number of pilgrims attending the Màggal.

4. Quoted by Jill M. Humphries, "Resisting 'Race': Organizing African Transnational Identities in the United States," in *New African Diaspora*, ed. Isidore Okpewho and Nkiru Zwegu (Bloomington: Indiana University Press, 2009), 271.

5. Ellen E. Foley and Cheikh A. Babou, "Diaspora, Faith and Science: Building a Mouride Hospital in Senegal," *African Affairs* 110, no. 438 (2011): 75–95.

6. François Héran, "Europe and the Spectre of Sub-Saharan Migration," *Population et Sociétés* 558 (2018): 1–3, 1; Marie-Laurence Flahaux and Hein De Hass, "African Migration: Trends, Patterns, Drivers," *Comparative Migration Studies* 4, no. 1 (2016): 1–25. In the *Afro-Barometer*, authors Josephine Appiah-Nyamekye Sanny, Carolyn Logan, and E. Gyimah Boadi found that "the most preferred destination for potential [African] emigrants is neither Europe nor the United States, but another African country." See Josephine Appiah-Nyamekye Sanny, Carolyn Logan, and E. Gyimah Boadi, "In Search of Opportunity: Young and Educated Africans, Most Likely to Consider Moving Abroad," *Afro-Barometer* 288 (March 2019): 1–32, 2.

7. Taha Jabir al-Alwani, "Toward a *Fiqh* for Minorities: Some Reflections," in *Muslims' Space in the American Public Square: Hopes, Fears and Aspirations*, ed. Zahid H. Bukhari, Sulayman S. Nyang, Mumtaz Ahmad, and John L. Esposito (Walnut Creek, CA: Altamira, 2004), 3–37. Quoted in Ousmane Kane, *The Homeland Is the Arena: Religion, Transnationalism and the Integration of Senegalese Immigrants in America* (Oxford: Oxford University Press, 2011), 11.

8. See David Robinson, *Paths of Accommodation: Muslim Societies and French Colonial Authorities in Senegal and Mauritania, 1880–1920* (Athens: Ohio University Press, 2000).

9. See David Robinson, "The Murids: Surveillance and Accommodation," *JAH* 40, no. 2 (1999): 13–21.

10. French estimates of the number of Murid disciples come from Paul Marty, *Études sur l'Islam au Sénégal*, 2 vols. (Paris: Leroux, 1917), 259; and Lucien Nekkach, *Le Mouridisme depuis 1912* (Saint-Louis, Senegal: Gouvernement du Sénégal, 1952), ANS, sous-série, 2G. The latest estimates are based on the Senegalese National Census of 2002, which found that 31.70 percent of the Senegalese population (estimated at eleven million) claims to belong to the Murid order. This percentage works out to 4,417,000 persons in total. See National Agency for Statistics and Demography, "Third General Census of Population and Housing, 2002," accessed September 5, 2020, http://anads .ansd.sn/index.php/catalog/9. The five million I suggest is a conservative estimate for 2018 based on a total Senegalese population of fifteen million people, according to the CIA factbook. See Central Intelligence Agency, *CIA World Factbook* (Washington, DC: CIA), accessed March 23, 2019, https://www.cia.gov/library/publications/the-world-factbook /geos/sg.html.

11. See, for example, Abner Cohen, *Custom and Politics in Urban Africa: Hausa Migrants in Yoruba Towns* (Berkeley: University of California Press, 1969); Samir Amin and Darryl Ford, eds., *Modern Migrations in Western Africa* (London: Oxford University Press, 1974); Claude Meillassoux, *Femmes, Greniers et Capital* (Paris: François Maspéro, 1975); Lucy G. Colvin, ed., *The Uprooted of the Western Sahel: Migrants' Quest for Cash in Senegambia* (New York: Praeger, 1981); Catherine Coquery-Vidrovitch, *Histoire des villes d'Afrique noire: Des origines à la colonisation* (Paris: Albin Michel, 1993); Dennis D. Cordell, W. J. Gregory, and V. Piché, *Hoe and Wage: A Social History of Circular Migration System in West Africa* (Boulder, CO: Westview, 1996). Also see François Manchuelle, *Willing Migrants: Soninke Labor Diasporas, 1848–1960* (Athens: Ohio University Press, 1997).

12. Bruce Whitehouse, *Migrants and Strangers in an African City: Exile, Dignity and Belonging* (Bloomington: Indiana University Press, 2012), 5. This is particularly true with regard to historians and humanities scholars in general.

13. The tropical climate of Senegal has two seasons: a rainy season that begins in general in June and ends in September and a dry season. In large extended families where labor shortage is not a concern, young men called *surga* often migrate and work as sharecroppers.

14. Nekkach, *Le Mouridisme depuis*, 15.

15. Martin A. Klein, "The Moslem Revolution in Nineteenth Century Senegambia," in *West African History*, ed. Daniel F. McCall, Norman R.

Bennett, and Jeffrey Butler (New York: Praeger, 1969), 69–101; James Searing, "*God Alone Is King*": *Islam and Emancipation in Senegal: The Wolof Kingdoms of Kajoor and Bawol, 1859–1914* (Portsmouth, NH: Heinemann, 2002), 77.

16. Guy Rocheteau, *Société Wolof et mobilité* (Dakar: ORSTOM, 1973), 6–9.
17. See Cheikh Anta Babou, *Fighting the Greater Jihad: Amadu Bamba and the Founding of the Muridiyya of Senegal, 1853–1913* (Athens: Ohio University Press, 2007), 167.
18. *Rapport politique annuel* (1926), p. 10, ANS 2G 26.
19. *Der* means "leather" in Wolof and refers to the belt that these disciples wear around their waist to symbolize hard work and frugality.
20. Paul Pélissier, *Les paysans du Sénégal: Les civilisations agraires du Cayor à la Casamance* (Fabrègue, France: Saint-Yriex, 1966), 304.
21. Pélissier, *Les paysans du Sénégal*, 304.
22. Pélissier, 302.
23. The construction of this railroad started in 1907 and lasted until 1923. A spur linking Diourbel to Tuubaa completed in 1930 played a particularly important role in facilitating the migration of Murid disciples.
24. See Pélissier, 9.
25. The French Union was conceived as a federation that included France and its colonies, now called "overseas territories." Some measure of power was devolved to the former colonies, but France remained mostly in charge. In *Citizenship between Empire and Nation: Remaking France and French Africa, 1945–1960* (Princeton, NJ: Princeton University Press, 2015), Frederick Cooper offers a more nuanced account of the impact of this law that extended French citizens' rights to colonial subjects.
26. Quoted by Daouda Gary Tounkara, "La dispersion des Soudanais/Maliens à la fin de l'ère coloniale," *Hommes et Migrations* 1279 (2009): 12–23, 14.
27. Nekkach, *Le Mouridisme depuis*, 30.
28. Nekkach, 30. These numbers, like most statistics provided by the colonial administration, have to be taken with a grain of salt. But absent any other data, they offer helpful insights into broader patterns of population movement.
29. The migration to Côte d'Ivoire is a good case in point here. Early Senegalese voluntary immigrants in Abidjan and surrounding areas were Muslim clerics ministering to Senegalese traders and civil servants who had settled there earlier.
30. Mamadou Diouf, "The Senegalese Murid Trade Diaspora and the Making of a Vernacular Cosmopolitanism," trans. Steven Rendall, *Public Culture* 12, no. 3 (Fall 2000): 679–702, 695.
31. Donald M. Carter, *States of Grace: Senegalese in Italy and the New European Immigration* (Minneapolis: University of Minnesota Press, 1997), 73.

32. See, among others, Patrick A. Desplat and Dorothea E. Schultz, eds., *Prayer in the City: The Making of Muslim Sacred Places in Urban Life* (Piscataway, NJ: Transaction, 2012); Oren Baruch Stier and J. Shawn Landres, *Religion, Violence, Memory, and Place* (Bloomington: Indiana University Press, 2006); Kim Knott, *The Location of Religion: A Spatial Analysis* (London: Equinox, 2005); Belden C. Lane, *Landscapes of the Sacred: Geography and Narrative in American Spirituality* (Baltimore: Johns Hopkins University Press, 2002); and Thomas F. Gieryn, "A Space for Place in Sociology," *Annual Review of Sociology* 26 (2000): 463–96.

33. Gieryn, "A Space for Place," 481.

34. See Lawrence Epstein and Peng Wenbin, "Ganjo and Murdo: The Social Construction of Space at Two Pilgrimage Sites in Eastern Tibet," in *Sacred Spaces and Powerful Places in Tibetan Culture: A Collection of Essays*, ed. Toni Huber (Dharamsala, India: Library of Tibetan Works and Archives, 1999), 322–41.

35. Cheikh Ahmadou Bamba Mbacké, *Matlabul Fawzayni: Recherche du bonheur dans les deux demeures*, trans. Cheikhouna Mbacké Abdoul Wadoud (Dakar: Impression Edition Islamique, n.d.).

36. For an extensive discussion of baraka and its role in the Muridiyya and Sufi Islam in general, see Cheikh Anta Babou, *Fighting the Greater Jihad: Amadu Bamba and the Founding of the Muridiyya of Senegal, 1853–1913* (Athens: Ohio University Press, 2007).

37. Emma Aubin-Boltanski, *Pèlerinages et nationalisme en Palestine: Prophétes, héros et ancêtres* (Paris: Edition Ecole des Hautes Etudes en Sciences Sociales, 2007), 36.

38. In their study of the single surviving photograph of Shaykh Ahmadu Bamba, Allen Roberts and Marie N. Roberts explain how this picture illustrates the portability of Amadu Bamba's *baraka*. See Allen Roberts and Mary N. Roberts, "The Aura of Amadu Bamba," *Anthropologie et Sociétés* 22 (1998): 15–38.

39. From its creation, Tuubaa has always enjoyed an exceptional status. It is considered property of the Mbakke family. No law is applicable in the city without the consent of the Murid leadership, and the state allows the city a certain judicial exceptionalism. For example, smoking, drinking alcohol, and drumming are forbidden in Tuubaa.

40. Water is free for the inhabitants of Tuubaa, and some taxes are not collected in the city. The power of law enforcement is restricted.

41. See, for example, Hasan Elboudrary, "Quand les saints font les villes," *Annales ESC* 40, no. 3 (1985): 489–508; and Eric Ross, *Sufi City: Urban Design and Archetypes in Touba* (Rochester, NY: Rochester University Press, 2006).

42. But while hailed as a model city by the United Nations at the meeting of UN Habitat II in Istanbul in June 1996 (Tuubaa then exemplified the meeting's objectives to promote "Adequate shelter for all" and "Sustainable human settlements development in an urbanizing world"),

Tuubaa is now suffering from the same symptoms as other megacities in the world: crime is up, poverty is rife, and waste management is inadequate. See United Nations, Report of the United Nations Conference on Human Settlements (Habitat II, Istanbul, Turkey, June 3 to 14, 1996), accessed February 5, 2020, https://www.un.org/ruleoflaw/wp-content/uploads/2015/10/istanbul-declaration.pdf.

43. Republic of Senegal, *Recensement de la Population et de l'habitat 1988* (Dakar: République du Sénégal, 1993).

44. For a critical assessment of the use of push-pull theory in the scholarship on African migration see Mirjam van Reisen et al., eds., *Roaming Africa: Migration, Resilience and Social Protection* (Bamenda, Cameroon: Langaaa RPCIG, 2019).

45. On the tradition of mobility within Islam, see Dale F. Eckelman and James Piscaroti, *Muslim Travelers: Pilgrimage, Migration, and the Religious Imagination* (Los Angeles: University of California Press, 1990).

46. See Fallou Ngom, *Muslims beyond the Arab World: The Odyssey of Ajami and the Muridiyya* (New York: Oxford University Press, 2016); Cheikh Anta Babou, "Sufi Eschatology and Hagiography as Responses to Colonial Repression: An Examination of the Meanings of Amadu Bamba's Trial and Exiles by the French Colonial Administration of Senegal 1895–1907," in *Practicing Sufism: Sufi Politics and Performance in Africa*, ed. Abdelmajid Hannoum (London: Routledge, 2016), 57–74; Cheikh Ahmadou Bamba Mbacké, *Jazaau Shakuur* [Tribute to the worthy of recognition], trans. and ed. by the Dahira of Murid students of the University of Dakar (Dakar: Bibliothèque du Daara Hizbut Tarqiyya, n.d.). In *Jazaau Shakuur*, Ahmadu Bamba narrates his arrest, trial, and exile to Gabon.

47. Muusaa Ka, *Jazaau Shakuur*, unpublished epic poem in Wolof, sung by Mama Njaay, audio cassette; Diâo Faye, "L'œuvre poétique wolofal de Moussa Ka ou l'épopée de Cheikh Ahmadou Bamba" (PhD diss., Université Cheikh Anta Diop de Dakar, 1999). Also see Sana Camara and R. H. Mitsch, "'A'jami' Literature in Senegal: The Example of Sëriñ Muusaa Ka, Poet and Biographer," in "Arabic Writing in Africa," special issue, *Research in African Literatures* 28, no. 3 (Autumn 1997): 163–82.

48. See Abdoulaye Wade, *La doctrine économique du mouridisme* (Dakar: L'Interafricaine d'éditions, 1970); Jules Brochier, *La diffusion du progrès technique en milieu rural sénégalais*, 2 vols. (Paris: Presse Universitaire de France, 1968); Paul Marty, " Les mourides d'Amadou Bamba: Rapport à M. le gouverneur général de l'Afrique Occidentale," *Revue du Monde Musulman* 25 (1913): 3–164. For a discussion of the literature on the meanings of work among the Murids, see Philippe Couty, *La doctrine du travail chez les mourides* (Dakar: ORSTOM, 1969); and Jean Copans, *Les marabouts de l'arachide* (Paris: L'Harmattan, 1988).

49. In his study of *kazi*, a Swahili word that refers to concepts and practices of work, Johannes Fabian uses linguistic analysis to investigate the

incorporation of African workers' experience in the doctrine of a Christian charismatic movement in the Congo. See "Kazi, Conceptualizations of Labor in a Charismatic Movement among Swahili-Speaking Workers," *Cahiers d'Études Africaines* 50 (1973): 293–325. Although there is not, to my knowledge, a study of the relations between Wolof conceptions of work and the concept of khidma in the Muridiyya, Fabian's work provides a useful beginning point for undertaking such research. It is remarkable that all those who studied the Murid ethic of work insist on its spiritual foundation and fail to consider the possible role of Wolof culture.

50. Quoted in Claire Boulanger and Kevin Mary, "Les Maliens en France et aux Etats Unis: Trajectoires et pratiques transnationales dans les espaces," *E-migrinter* 7 (2011): 17–28, 20.

51. By transplanted Black population, I mean Africans enslaved in the United States through the transatlantic slave trade that lasted from the sixteenth to the nineteenth centuries.

52. The word "White" is capitalized throughout the course of the book. I have done so to highlight that Whiteness is a socially constructed category and to push back against ideas of Whiteness as normative or raceless. See Kwame Anthony Appiah, "The Case for Capitalizing the B in Black," *Atlantic*, June 18, 2020, https://www.theatlantic .com/ideas/archive/2020/06/time-to-capitalize-blackand-white/613159/; Ibram X. Kendi (@DrIbram), "I agree. I capitalize both in my books," Twitter, December 26, 2019, 2:56 p.m., https://twitter.com/DrIbram /status/1210318597849042944.

53. Bruce Hall, *A History of Race in Muslim West Africa, 1600–1900* (Cambridge: Cambridge University Press, 2011), 2. For Hall, the terms "black," "white," and "race" are not meant as objective descriptors of physical or racial difference but merely as social and cultural constructions. The question that remains, then, is the following: Did the changing historical contexts within which these constructions were made have any bearing on their meanings, cultural significance, and impact on people over time? In other words, does Whiteness mean the same thing when it is used to describe the Berber and Arab traders of, for example, fifteenth-century West Africa as the French colonial administrators of the nineteenth and twentieth centuries? I would suggest that the conceptions of race that Europeans found in Africa in the late nineteenth century were the result of evolving processes of construction far from being stable: their own intervention contributed to fostering new reconfigurations of racial relations that drew upon but also transformed "local" conceptions. Michael Gomez has rightly remarked that "any exclusive investment in local configurations of race is . . . ahistorical, as parochial intendment in Savannah and Sahel was clearly influenced by transregional conversations

about race centuries in the making." See Michael Gomez, *African Dominion: A New History of Empire in Early Medieval West Africa* (Princeton, NJ: Princeton University Press, 2018), 55.

54. Jean-Louis Triaud, "Giving a Name to Islam South of the Sahara: An Adventure in Taxonomy," *JAH* 55, no. 1 (2014): 3–15.

55. Bamba rarely directly addresses the issue of race in his writings, but the few statements he made regarding race became powerful shapers of Murid culture.

56. The White community was further divided between *Zawiya* or clerical clans and *Hasan* or warrior clans.

57. See Paul Marty, "Cheikh Sidiyya et sa voie," *Revue du Monde Musulman* 31 (1915–16): 29–133, 39.

58. I refer here to David Robinson who was quoting a conversation between Baba and the interpreter Doudou Seck; see Robinson's *Paths of Accommodation*, 184.

59. Cheikh Muhammad Lamine Diop Dagana, *L'abreuvement du commensal dans la douce source d'amour du Cheikh al-Khadîm, ou la biographie de Cheikh Ahmadou Bamba*, trans. and ed. Khadim Mbacké (Dakar: IFAN, Département d'Islamologie, n.d.), 127.

60. Diop, *L'abreuvement*, 128. Diop reproduces a copy of the poem on this page.

61. Ahmadou Bamba Mbacké, *Masalik al-Jinaan* [Paths to paradise], trans. Serigne Sam Mbaye (Rabat: Dar El Kitab, 1984), 38.

62. Catherine Coles and Beverly Mack, eds., *Hausa Women in the Twentieth Century* (Madison: University of Wisconsin Press, 1991); Barbara Callaway and Lucy Creevey, *The Heritage of Islam: Women, Religion and Politics in West Africa* (Boulder, CO: Lynne Rienner, 1994); Beth Buggenhagen's recent book is an exception. See Beth Buggenhagen, *Muslim Families in Global Senegal* (Bloomington: Indiana University Press, 2011); also see Joseph Hill, *Wrapping Authority: Women Islamic Leaders in a Sufi Movement in Dakar, Senegal* (Toronto: Toronto University Press, 2018).

63. Saba Mahmood, *The Politics of Piety: The Islamic Revival and the Feminist Subject* (Princeton, NJ: Princeton University Press, 2005), 7–10.

64. Mahmood, *Politics of Piety*, 15.

65. Mahmood, 14.

66. Maam Jaara's tomb was rediscovered during the caliphate of Faliilu Mbakke (1945–69). Faliilu's mother is a Buso. The Murid shaykh, Moodu Maamun Mbakke, whose mother is also a Buso, started building the shrine, but his cousin Bachiru Mbakke (and son of Ahmadu Bamba), who had already established his control of the area of the province of Saalum where the Tomb was located, took over the project. See Mustafa Aafe Mbakke, interview by author, June 9, 2000, and Sëriñ Baabu, interview by author, May 25, 2011. Baabu was a disciple of

Moodu Maamun, who remembers traveling with him to Poroxaan in the late 1950s to build a well.

67. It is interesting to note that few Murids know where Ahmadu Bamba's father is buried, and there is no pilgrimage associated with his tomb.

68. See Eva Evers Rosander, "Mame Diarra Bousso: La bonne mère de Porokhane, Sénégal," *Africa* 58, nos. 3–4 (2003): 296–317. The pilgrimage rituals in Poroxaan include drawing water from Maam Jaara's well, pounding millet at the place where she prepared meals, and symbolic washing and drying of clothes.

69. See Ester Guijarro, "The Mame Diarra Dahira in Diaspora: Challenging Murid Patriarchy?,"*Revista de Dialecticologia y Tradiciones Populares* 68, no. 11 (2013): 125–44.

70. Buggenhagen, *Muslim Families*, 163–65.

71. See Copans, *Les marabouts*; and Cheikh Tidiane Sy, *La confrérie sénégalaise des mourides* (Paris: Présence Africaine, 1969).

CHAPTER 1: THE MURIDIYYA IN THE CITIES OF SENEGAL

1. There is no single author for this epigraph. The three sentences are uttered, not necessarily in the order presented here, by many Murid disciples. In the YouTube videos cited in note 3, one can hear Murids uttering these sentences in Wolof.

2. AOF was composed of the eight French colonies in West Africa: Côte d'Ivoire, Dahomey (Benin), Haute Volta (Burkina Faso), Guinea, French Soudan (Mali), Niger, Mauritania, and Senegal. Togo was later incorporated in the federation as a mandate colony that the League of Nations entrusted to France.

3. "La Statue Faidherbe tombe le jour du Magal des deux Rakkas de Saint Louis du Sénégal," Bichri TV International, September 5, 2017, YouTube, https://www.youtube.com/watch?v=tmJ8NFosoVE; "Miracle à Sait Louis: 5 Septembre 2017 la statue de Louis Faidherbe tombe sur terre," 18SaFar TV, September 5, 2017, YouTube, https://www.youtube.com/watch?v=373vq3hsvyY. The controversy around Faidherbe's fall and the heated debate it continues to generate recall the Rhodes Must Fall movement initiated by students in South Africa. The Murid anti-Faidherbe movement dates even further back, but both are inspired by anticolonial and nationalist sentiments. There is another movement based in Lille (Faidherbe's city of birth) led by young Franco-Senegalese not affiliated with the Muridiyya but demanding the removal of the statue. This movement also seems to have been inspired by the Rhodes Must Fall movement and by similar nationalist demands of other former European colonies across and outside the African continent. In the United States, similar protests in southern states call for the removal of Confederate statues from public places.

4. See Hippolyte Delahaye, *Cinq leçons sur la méthode hagiographique* (Brussels: Société des Bollandistes, 1934), especially chapter 1.

5. See Mircea Eliade, *The Sacred and the Profane: The Nature of Religion* (New York: Harcourt, 1987). Eliade has been criticized for his essentialist conception of sacred space as static, uncontested, and unchanging, but his work remains a valuable source.

6. Inhabitants of the Four Communes of Senegal—Saint-Louis, Gorée, Dakar, and Rufisque—acquired full French citizenship rights in 1916 with the adoption of the Blaise Diagne law. For more on the political history of Saint-Louis and Senegal under colonial rule, see Hilary Jones, *The Métis of Senegal: Urban Life and Politics in French West Africa* (Bloomington: Indiana University Press, 2013); and G. Wesley Johnson Jr., *The Emergence of Black Politics in Senegal: The Struggle for Power in the Four Communes, 1900–1920* (Stanford, CA: Stanford University Press, 1971).

7. Saint-Louis, the first French colonial possession in Africa (since the second half of the seventeenth century), was one of the Four Communes of Senegal that benefited from the policy of assimilation. The policy concerned a tiny percentage of French colonial subjects who were given the rights of full citizenship.

8. For more on the Lébous, see Cécile Laborde, *La confrérie Layenne et les Lébous du Sénégal: Islam et culture traditionnelle en Afrique* (Talence, France: Centre d'Études d'Afrique Noire, 1995). Also see Douglas H. Thomas, *Sufism, Mahdism and Nationalism: Limamou Laye and the Layennes of Senegal* (New York: Bloomsbury, 2012).

9. In a recent paper, Jean Copans suggests that in the Muridiyya, building religious and economic spaces where much wealth is generated outside direct state control could incite some Murid shaykhs and subgroups to expand Murid symbolic territory to encompass Senegalese national territory as a whole. See "Les espaces mourides (municipal, régional, national, international et/ou mondial) et les territoires étatiques africains et occidentaux ou comment l'appartenance confrérique interpelle l'instance nationale" (paper presented at the international symposium IFRPDSR, "Stratégies de populations et stratégies de développement: Convergences ou divergences?," Dakar, July 2006), 5.

10. See Marc Michel, "'Mémoire officielle,' discours et pratique coloniale le 14 juillet et le 11 novembre au Sénégal entre les deux guerres," *Revue Française d'Histoire d'Outre-Mer* 77, no. 287 (1990): 145–58.

11. See Cheikh Anta Babou, "Contesting Space, Shaping Places: Making Room for the Muridiyya in Colonial Senegal, 1912–45," *JAH* 46, no. 3 (2005): 405–26.

12. See Roger Friedland and Richard D. Hect, "The Powers of Place," in *Religion, Violence, Memory, and Place*, ed. Oren Baruch Stier and Jonathan Shawn Landers (Bloomington: Indiana University Press, 2006), 23.

13. Paul Marty, "Les mourides d'Amadou Bamba: Rapport à M. le gouverneur général de l'Afrique Occidentale," *Revue du Monde Musulman* 25 (1913): 3–164. Lucien Nekkach, *Le Mouridisme depuis 1912* (Saint-Louis, Senegal: Gouvernement du Sénégal, 1952).

14. Nekkach, *Le Mouridisme*.
15. J. M. Cowan, ed., *The Hans Wehr Dictionary of Modern Written Arabic*, 4th ed. (Ithaca, NY: Spoken Language Services, 1994), 347. Also see Cheikh Anta Babou, "Dahira," in *Encyclopaedia of Islam, THREE*, ed. Kate Fleet, Gudrun Krämer, Denis Matringe, John Nawas, and Everett Rowson (Leiden: Brill, 2017), http://dx.doi.org/10.1163/1573-3912_ei3_COM_27706.
16. *Wirds* are specific prayers revealed by the Prophet Muhammad to the founder of a Sufi order. They consist of excerpts from the Qur'an and are special prayers that disciples of a Sufi order recite collectively or individually at specific times of the day.
17. For the role of Ababakar Sy in the founding of dahira in Senegal see Ibrahima Marone, "Le Tidjanisme au Sénégal," *Bulletin de l'Ifan* 32, no. 1 (1970): 136–215. Ababakar was locked in a dispute with his younger half-brother, Mansuur, since their father's death in 1922. The initiative to organize his urban disciples under the guise of dahira could be understood as part of an effort to consolidate his power as leader of the Sy Tijaaniyya. Among the Murids, the first dahira was formed in the late 1940s, under the guidance of Shaykh Mbakke, oldest grandson of Ahmadu Bamba. Mbakke was then in conflict with his uncle, Faliilu Mbakke, who succeeded his father, Mamadu Mustafa, as caliph of the Muridiyya.
18. M. C. Diop, "La confrérie mouride: Mode d'organization politique et implantation urbaine" (PhD diss., University of Lyon 2, 1980); and Sophie Bava, "Le dahira urbain, lieu de pouvoir du mouridisme," *Les annales de la recherche urbaine* 96 (2004): 135–43.
19. The law of 1901 provided the framework for regulating civil society organizations. But when it came to religion, the law was selectively applied. Educational or charitable organizations could benefit from official license, but those deemed strictly religious were assessed via the 1905 law of separation of church and state and consequently denied administrative approval.
20. Christine Thu Nhi Dang, "Pilgrimage through Poetry: Sung Journeys within the Murid Spiritual Diaspora," *Islamic Africa* 4, no. 1 (2013): 69–101.
21. On the singular nature of French secularism (or *laïcité*) see Olivier Roy, *Secularism Confronts Islam*, trans. George Holoch (New York: Columbia University Press, 2007). Although President Gambetta of France had famously stated that French laïcité was not for export, the anticlerical ideology of the French administration affected the French Empire.
22. For more on "Islam Noir," see Paul Marty, *Études sur l'Islam au Sénégal*, 2 vols. (Paris: Leroux, 1917); and Jean-Louis Triaud, "Giving a Name to Islam South of the Sahara: An Adventure in Taxonomy," *JAH* 55, no. 1 (2014): 1–15.
23. Elhaaj Bamba Jaw, interview by author, April 8 and May 3, 2000; Elhaaj Njaga Gey, interview by author, June 11, 2004; and Basiiru Fall,

interview by author, March 21, 2010. The house of Gumaalo Sekk was located at the corner of Rue 22 and 25 in the Medina neighborhood. It was a popular crossroads. In his novel and movie *The Money Order*, Ousmane Sembène refers to Keur Gumaalo as a popular stop on public transportation routes in Dakar.

24. Gey, interview.

25. Directives from police chief of District V to the security brigade on patrol between 9:00 p.m. and 1:00 a.m., September 29, 1954, Service Regional des Archives de Dakar (henceforth SRDAD), 1D/18bis.

26. From 1950 to 1953, all the requests the Catholic Church made for holding religious events in public space were granted without objection. See for example, the letters of Jean Colombani, representative of the governor of the territory of Senegal in Dakar, December 31, 1950; July 23, 1953; November 1953; December 7, 1953; June 4, 1953. In contrast, between 1955 and 1957 only one authorization was granted to the Murids. See SRDAD, folder Série I, Customary, Lébou community, Muslim, Catholic, and Protestant religious ceremonies affairs. File I/8, Muslim, Catholic and Protestant religious ceremonies, 1953–54; file I/9, Muslim, Catholic and Protestant religious ceremonies, 1955; file I/11, Muslim, Catholic and Protestant religious ceremonies, 1956; file I/17, Muslim religious ceremonies, 1957–59.

27. SRDAD, 1D18 bis, folder "tam-tam, chants religieux, bruits en ville . . . 1954–1963," letter of August 25, 1955, to the police chief of the sixth district. The regulations changed over time and became gradually less stringent, especially on weekends. Although still in the books, they are no longer enforced in the context of independent Senegal.

28. For more on the history of Dakar see Assane Seck, *Dakar, Métropole Ouest-Africaine* (Dakar: Ifan, 1970). Also see Lat Soucabé Mbow, *Quand le Sénégal Fabrique sa Géographie* (Dakar: Dakar University Press, 2017).

29. On French segregationist policies and practices in Dakar, see Luce Beeckmans, "A Toponymy of Segregation: The 'Neutral Zones' of Dakar, Dar Es Salaam and Kinshasa," in *Place Names in Africa: Colonial Urban Legacies, Entangled Histories*, ed. Liora Bigon (New York: Springer, 2016), 105–21.

30. Among seven board members of the first registered Murid dahira (licensed in 1958), two were janitors, one was a tailor, two were low-level postal workers, and two were salesclerks. See *Journal Officiel de l'Afrique Occidentale Française*, May 17, 1958, 921.

31. This is Shaykh Mbakke, Ahmadu Bamba's elder grandson, who was also a businessman and investor. He owned houses built by Société Immobiliaire du Cap Vert's (SICAP) on the lots of Rue 10 and Grand Dakar and also on rue Clémenceau and Blaise Diagne in downtown Dakar. SICAP is a state-owned company in charge of building houses for middle-income patrons in Dakar.

32. Jaw, interview.
33. Ngañ Caam, interview by author, December 9, 1999; and Gey, interview. These interviews name Biraan Ñaan, Moor Caam, and Mandumbe Mbuub as originators of Murid dahiras.
34. The dahira was registered on April 10, 1958, under number 657 A. G. by the representative of the governor of the territory of Senegal in Dakar. See *Journal Officiel de l'Afrique Occidentale Française*, May 17, 1958, 921. It is interesting to note that Jaw omitted the word "dahira" in the application. He presented the organization as an association formed to raise funds and organize the burial of disciples in Murid necropolises.
35. See "Union Fédérale des Dahiratouls El-haj Falilou Mbacke dans la région du Cap vert. Composition de la Délégation du Cap-Vert auprès du Khalif à Touba" [Federation of dahiras affiliated with El-Haj Faliilu Mbakke, list of officers in the region of Cap Vert], January 1, 1965, private archives of Elhaaj Bamba Jaw. Also see Gey, interview.
36. This opinion is shared by scholars of the Muridiyya, especially Donal Cruise O'Brien. See *The Mourides of Senegal: The Political and Economic Organization of an Islamic Brotherhood in Senegal* (Oxford: Clarendon, 1971). This was in line with the secularization theory paradigm that dominated the field of sociology of religion from the 1960s. See Peter L. Berger, *The Sacred Canopy: Elements for a Sociological Theory of Religion* (Garden City, NY: Doubleday, 1969).
37. See Claire Mercer, Ben Page, and Martin Evans, *Development and the African Diaspora: Place and the Politics of Home* (London: Zed, 2008).
38. Caam, interview.
39. Gey, interview. Gey was head of the federation of dahiras of Sandaga Market.
40. See Mouhamed Moustapha Kane, "L'empreinte de l'Islam confrérique dans le paysage commercial sénégalais: Islam et société en Sénégambie," *Islam et sociétés au sud du Sahara* 8 (1994): 17–41. See also Allen Roberts and Mary Nooter Roberts, *A Saint in the City: Sufi Arts of Urban Senegal* (Los Angeles: University of California Fowler Museum of Cultural History, 2003).
41. See Pape G. Mbodj, "Le mouvement des jeunes dans la confrérie religieuse des mourides: Essai d'analyse et d'interprétation" (master's thesis, University of Dakar, 1980).
42. Earlier student Muslim organizations during the colonial era were mostly influenced by modernist ideas and pursued a nationalist and anticolonial agenda. Also see Muriel Gomez-Perez, "The Association des Etudiants Musulmans de l'Université de Dakar (AEMUD) between the Local and the Global: An Analysis of Discourse," *Africa Today* 54, no. 3 (March 2008): 94–117.
43. The result of this work is a two-volume collection of the French translation of some of Ahmadu Bamba's writings. See Abdoul Ahad Mbacké,

ed., *Recueil de poèmes en sciences religieuses de Cheikh A. Bamba*, 2 vols. (Rabat: Dar al-Kitab, 1988–89).

44. Cheikh Anta Babou, "Negotiating the Boundaries of Power: Abdoulaye Wade, the Muridiyya and State Politics in Senegal, 2000–2012," *Journal of West African History* 2, no. 1 (2016): 165–88.

45. On the history of UCM and its impact on Islam in Senegal see Roman Loimeier, "Cheikh Touré, du réformisme à l'islamisme: Un Musulman sénégalais dans le siècle," *Islam et sociétés au sud du Sahara* 8 (1994): 55–66.

46. See Leonardo Villalón, "From Argument to Negotiation: Constructing Democracy in African Muslim Context," *Comparative Politics* 42, no. 4 (July 2010): 375–93.

47. The influence of Murid disciples on these neighborhoods can be gauged by the number of houses that bear front-door plaques engraved with the name of a Murid shaykh or a Murid village, indicating the religious affiliation of the owner. Many of these inscriptions start with the typical Wolof expression *Waa Kër* (The house or family of) followed by the name of a Murid shaykh or his main village. It is also interesting to observe that these days many neighborhoods in Senegalese cities are named after Murid shaykhs or Murid historical sites. This is the case of the neighborhood "Kër Xaadim" (meaning "the servant's house," "The Servant" being one of Ahmadu Bamba's nicknames), which is an upper-middle-class quarter built in the mid-1990s by a Murid developer in Dakar.

48. Elhaaj Njaga Gey indicates that the number of dahiras went from only one in the 1960s to fifteen in the Sandaga Market alone in 2004. See Gey, interview. There are probably dozens of Murid dahiras in the region of Dakar, found in cities like Dakar, Rufisque, Bargny, and others.

49. SICAP and HLM are French acronyms for Société Immobilière du Cap Vert and Habitats à Loyer Modéré, which are the two major state-owned construction companies in Senegal. Bawol is the heartland of the Muridiyya in western-central Senegal. The term "Bawol-Bawol" designates inhabitants of the region of Bawol in western-central Senegal, but it was used pejoratively to refer to Murid traders and merchants in town. The word now has a more positive connotation, signifying toughness, frugality, and business sense.

50. On the aura of Ahmadu Bamba and his new emerging identity fostered through artworks and songs, see Allen Roberts and Mary N. Roberts, "The Aura of Amadu Bamba," *Anthropologie et Sociétés* 22 (1998): 15–38; Roberts and Roberts, *A Saint in the City*. See also Holland Cotter, "Caught in the Aura of Senegalese Saint," *New York Times*, February 16, 2005. This article is an account of the exhibit "Sufi Arts of Urban Senegal" at the Harn Museum of the University of Florida. The exhibit was first organized at the UCLA Fowler Museum of Cultural History by Allen Roberts and M. N. Roberts. Popular Senegalese singers,

including renowned stars of world music such as Grammy winner Youssou N'dour, Baba Maal, the Baobab Band, and others, have dedicated songs to Ahmadu Bamba, praising his resistance to colonial rule.

51. Cited in Momar Coumba Diop, "Fonctions et activités des *dahiras* mourides urbains (Sénégal)," *Cahiers d'Études Africaines* 21, nos. 81/83 (1981): 79–91, 82–83.

52. French translation of Caliph Abdul Ahad's speech, at the occasion of the Tivavouane incident, February 10, 1976, ADN, Ambassade du Sénégal, binder 664, folder "Mourides 1966–1980."

53. Abdou Salam Fall, "Les liens religieux confrériques, réseaux privilégiés d'insertion urbaine à Dakar," in *Islam et villes en Afrique au sud du Sahara*, ed. Adriana Piga (Paris: Karthala, 2003), 325–44, 339.

54. For more on the history of the Muridiyya in Saint-Louis, see Elhaaj Madické Wade, *Le mouridisme à Ndar: De Shaykh Ibra Fall et des pionniers aux audacieux initiateurs du maggal des 2 rakaas de Serigne Touba, tel que j'en ai eu échos et tel que j'en ai vécu* (Saint-Louis, Senegal: published by author, n.d.). I also refer to Wade, interview by author, July 6, 2001, and Mustafa Cuun, interview by author, May 6, 2006.

55. Wade provides estimates of the growth of the Murid population in Saint-Louis, which jumped from thirteen thousand in 1960 (the year of Senegal's independence) to ninety thousand in 1997, when Murids made up roughly 46 percent of the population of the city. See Wade, *Le mouridisme à Ndar*, 15. (It should be noted that Wade does not cite his sources.) Non-Murid informants, such as Abdel Qadr Aidara, chief archivist at the local branch of ANS of Saint-Louis, also confirm the rapid growth of the Murid population of the city, but they do not give estimates. See Abdel Qadr Aidara, interview by author, July 5, 2001. What is certain, however, is that the Muridiyya population started to grow in Saint-Louis only after World War II. The observations made by Elhaaj Masuraŋ Souraŋ (one of the earliest and most prominent leaders of the Muridiyya in this city) about the difficulties of the nascent Murid constituency of Saint-Louis in the 1950s seems to confirm this assumption. See Cheikh Tidiane Sy, *La confrérie sénégalaise des mourides* (Paris: Présence Africaine, 1969), 329.

56. Mustafa Cuun, interview by author, May 9, 2006.

57. Aale Faal, interview by author, May 5, 2010.

58. "Màggal" derives from the Wolof word "màgg," which means "grow," "celebrate," or "elevate." The largest Murid religious celebration is the Màggal of Tuubaa, which commemorates the exile of Ahmadu Bamba to Gabon in 1895. Most Murid religious celebrations are called "Màggal." These events are different from the *eids* and *mawlid* (sing *mawlud*) that the global Muslim community commemorates together. My reconstruction of the history of the Màggal of two *rakaas* of Saint-Louis relies mostly on Wade's *Le mouridisme à Ndar*, newspaper articles, and on

interviews I conducted with Wade, Abdel Q. Aïdara, and Ngóor Sène, in Saint-Louis in July of 2001. For more on the Màggal of Saint-Louis see Cheikh Anta Babou, "Urbanizing Mystical Islam: Making Murid Space in the Cities of Senegal," *International Journal of African Historical Studies* 40, no. 2 (2007): 197–223; and Ferdinand de Jong, "Remembering the Nation: The Murid Maggal of Saint-Louis Senegal (Mémoire de la nation: Les Maggal mourides de Saint-Louis, Sénégal)," *Cahiers d'Études Africaines* 50, no. 197 (2010): 123–51.

59. See Wade's account of his meeting with Caliph Abdul Ahad in *Le mouridisme à Ndar*, 33.

60. Muusaa Ka, the most influential Murid poet and hagiographer writing in Wolofal (Wolof written with Arabic characters), related this event in his *Jazaau Shakuur* (*Les dons du Très Reconnaissant* [Gifts from the most holy]), audio recording sung by Mama Njaay, cassette, in author's possession. This poem of 1,344 verses tells the story of the confrontation between Ahmadu Bamba and the French colonial administration. In the 1970s, a popular play based on Ka's rendition of the trial and the exile of Ahmadu Bamba was created by a group of Murid artists from Kaolack in eastern-central Senegal. One of the most interesting scenes of this play, which toured the Murid heartland, was the confrontation between Ahmadu Bamba and the governor general in the latter's office. However, it is worth noting that neither Ahmadu Bamba (who has written about his exile), his two biographers, his son Basiiru Mbakke, nor his close disciple Ahmad Lamine Jóob mention the prayer in the governor's office.

61. See Oumar Ba, *Ahmadou Bamba face aux autorités coloniales (1889–1927)* (Abbeville, France: Fayard, 1982), 62–63.

62. The prayer of two rakaas, or shortened prayer, is limited to two genuflections and kneeling, in contrast to the normal prayers that Muslims perform five times a day and which require kneeling three or four times. It has great symbolic and political significance and is allowed only when a Muslim feels threatened by adversity or when engaged in a struggle that threatens his or her physical integrity.

63. Saint-Louis has the reputation for being a beacon of civilization in West Africa. This image, popularized by novelists such as Abdoulaye Sadji and Birago Diop, is still claimed by the indigenous inhabitants of the city, which has lost its political preeminence since independence. Saint-Louis also has a strong Islamic tradition and identity, which it still struggles to preserve.

64. The weeklong celebration started in 1983.

65. See Cheikh Anta Babou, *Fighting the Greater Jihad: Amadu Bamba and the Founding of the Muridiyya of Senegal, 1853–1913* (Athens: Ohio University Press, 2007), chapter 5.

66. On the history of the Màggal of Marché du Port, see Magat Jóob, interview by author, June 9, 2004. I have held group interviews with Murid

disciples working at the different markets surrounding the port. I also refer to accounts of the events published in popular Murid magazines and Senegalese newspapers.

67. G. T., a Murid merchant at Marché du Port, while agreeing to contribute money to the event, criticized the Màggal organizers for paralyzing business in this busy area of Dakar for three days. The merchant said that he did not see the necessity of doing this. See G. T., interview by author, June 9, 2004.

68. One important characteristic of Murid social events is the amount of food that is served. Preparing and sharing food is an important dimension of Murid culture. Ahmadu Bamba said when he returned from exile the thing he missed the most during his seven years in Gabon was sharing meals with his disciples. See Galo Mbay, interview by author, March 1, 2000.

69. Processions have become the most typical features of Murid urban commemorations abroad. Even a small Murid community (which is less than a hundred people strong) such as the one in Winston-Salem, North Carolina, organizes a parade as part of the commemorations of Ahmadu Bamba Day.

70. In fact, when I asked Jóob how the non-Murid merchants in the market felt about the commemoration, he responded, "In general, they are supportive" but added, "anyway, we are the majority here and even if they were not happy, they would have to put up with us."

71. See Marc Michel, "'Mémoire officielle,' discours et pratique coloniale le 14 juillet et le 11 novembre au Sénégal entre les deux guerres," *Revue Française d'Histoire d'Outre-Mer* 77, no. 287 (1990): 145–58.

72. One of the speakers at the Màggal du port in 1997 called the attention of the audience to the symbolism of the date and place where the Màggal was being held, referring to the significance of these dates both for the colonial administration of Senegal and the Muridiyya. See Fara Gaye, "Maggal du port de Dakar ou retour d'éxil de Serigne Touba," *Ndigël* (*Sawtoul Mouride, la voix du mouride* [The voice of the Murid]), November–December 1997, 15.

73. Amadu Aly Dieng, face-to-face conversation with author, June 7, 2006. Dieng was a scholar and longtime resident of Dakar.

74. Quoted in Belden C. Lane, *Landscapes of the Sacred: Geography and Narrative in American Spirituality* (Baltimore: Johns Hopkins University Press, 2002), 43.

75. For the history of this Màggal (called the "The Two Nights of Dakar") I rely on my interview with the head of the dahira organizing this event: see Njuga Jeŋ, interview by author, June 8, 2004. Jeŋ was originally from Bawol, in western-central Senegal, but his father had lived in the neighborhood of Cëriñ, in downtown Dakar, since the colonial era. And his family has developed close relationships with the Lébou community.

76. For more on the Murids and the political economy of Sufi orders in Dakar, see Donal Cruise O'Brien and Christian Coulon, eds., *Charisma*

and *Brotherhood in African Islam* (Oxford: Clarendon, 1988); Victoria Ebin, "A la recherche de nouveaux 'poissons': Stratégies commerciales mourides par temps de crise," *Politique Africaine* 45 (1992); and Adriana Piga, *Dakar et les ordres Soufis* (Paris: Harmattan, 2002).

77. Ousseynou Faye, "Les pratiques des talibés de la transaction au marché Sandaga," in *Les économies reélles en Afrique, Real Economies in Africa*, ed. Georges Kobou (Dakar: CODESRIA, 2003), 270–81.

78. Elhaaj Jiily Mbaye, a Murid Shaykh and businessman, was among those wholesalers. His name appeared in a French intelligence report dated December 14, 1962. See ANF, AG (F) 3384. The report reads: "On December 14, 1962, custom officers have arrested two Senegalese in Paris. They had in their possession 5,778 swiss watches valued at 152,520 francs. They were named Elhadj Djili Mbaye and Mbaye Diakhate and they said that they were traders holding shops in Dakar. They were sent to jail [placé sous mandat de dépôt] on December 17, 1962. A third Senegalese, named Elhadj Dramé was also arrested. The fact that two of the arrested men belonged to the Muridiyya sect like president Senghor created some anxiety for the government of Senegal which fears that the incident could be exploited politically in the wake of the crisis that shook the country recently. Cheikh Mbacké, one of the leaders of the Murid Sect, just arrived in Paris to avoid that the incident be publicized. The Senegalese ambassador has also intervened."

79. The Lébou are an ethnic group related to the Wolof. They are the original inhabitants of the Cape Vert peninsula where Dakar is located.

80. Jeŋ, interview.

81. For more on the Lébou, see Cécile Laborde, *La confrérie Layenne et les Lébous du Sénégal: Islam et culture traditionnelle en Afrique* (Talence, France: Centre d'Études d'Afrique Noire, 1995). Also see Douglas H. Thomas, *Sufism, Mahdism and Nationalism: Limamou Laye and the Layennes of Senegal* (New York: Bloomsbury, 2012).

82. The husband's name was Ibra Binta Gey. See Ka, *Jazaau Shakuur*.

83. Jeŋ, interview.

84. Victor Turner, *Dramas, Fields, and Metaphors: Symbolic Action in Human Society* (Ithaca, NY: Cornell University Press, 1974), 195.

85. Pierre Nora, *Les lieux de mémoire*, vol. 1, *La République* (Paris: Gallimard, 1984), xi.

86. Momar Coumba Diop observed that the majority of Murid migrants in Dakar settled in impoverished neighborhoods. See Diop, "La confrérie mouride," 49. This situation started to change in the early 1990s.

87. Hélène d'Almeida Topor notes that after the decolonization of West Africa "very few of the cities changed in terms of place naming." See Hélène d'Almeida Topor, "The Colonial Toponymic Model in the Capital Cities of French West Africa," in *Place Names in Africa: Colonial Urban Legacies, Entangled Histories*, ed. Liora Bigon (New York: Springer, 2016), 93–103.

88. The governor was technically correct, but he was also aware that religious events were routinely organized in the city without securing proper administrative approval.
89. See copies of some of these letters in Wade, *Le mouridisme à Ndar*, 61–68.
90. Wade, interview; Wade, *Le mouridisme à Ndar*.
91. In reality, in 1984 he already had demanded that the governor's palace be renamed "Palace of September 5" (the date of Ahmadu Bamba's trial by the French Privy Council) and that the Faidherbe Square be renamed after Bamba. See a transcript of his speech at the Màggal of September 5, 1984, in the Murid journal *Ndigël* 3 (1984): 25.
92. This position was most recently reiterated by Golbert Diagne, a popular former sportscaster and comedian from Saint-Louis after the call for removing the statue after its fall on September 5, 2017. See Par Papy, "La chute de la statue de Faidherbe relève de la volonté divine," Metro-Dakar, September 5, 2017, https://www.metrodakar.net/societe/chute-de-statue-de-faidherbe-releve-de-volonte-divine-selon-golbert.
93. Wade, *Le mouridisme à Ndar*; Wade, interview.
94. The street Brière de L'Isle became Ablaye Seck Marie Parsine. Neuville became Me Babacar Sèye. Later on Lycée Faidherbe was renamed after Elhaaj Omar Taal, the famous nineteenth-century Senegalese jihadist who fought Faidherbe and founded a short-lived Muslim empire in contemporary Mali.
95. See Wade, *Le mouridisme à Ndar*, 72.
96. The city of Saint-Louis is classified as a UNESCO Heritage Site.
97. See Ahmed Fall, president of the Kureel of two rakaas, interview by Mansour Diop, Sidy Dièye, and Bamba Dièye, *Ndigël* 2 (November–December 1997), 11.
98. This is an opinion shared by the Murids of Saint-Louis and their fellow disciples throughout Senegal.
99. See Ka, *Jazaau Shakuur*; Njuga Jeŋ, interview by author, June 8, 2004.
100. Njuga Jeŋ, lead organizer of the Màggal in downtown Dakar, told me that the late Elhaaj Jiily Mbay, a Murid billionaire, and Elhaaj Bamba Suraŋ, a wealthy transportation entrepreneur from Saint-Louis, have tried to buy the former house of Ibra Binta Gey where Ahmadu stayed in 1895, but the owners refused to sell. See Jeŋ, interview. It might also be that the decision to sell was made difficult because many of these houses are commonly owned by large extended families.
101. Jeŋ, interview. This opinion is shared by other Murids. When I asked Ngañ Caam, one of the oldest Murid merchants in Sandaga, how strong the Murid community was in the market, he responded that it was difficult to tell because "three Murids are worth ten non-Murids." What he meant by this was that because of their activism, Murid influence far outweighs their demographic strength. See Caam, interview.

102. I have been told this story many times by Murid disciples in Dakar. I have visited the Jaañ house in 2000 and 2004, but no mention of this secret room was made.
103. See Christian Coulon, "The Grand Magal in Touba: A Religious Festival of the Mouride Brotherhood of Senegal," *African Affairs* 98, no. 391 (1999): 209, 195–210.
104. See Copans, "Les espaces mourides," 5.
105. In a letter dated May 23, 1953, one Ibra Fall, identifying himself as the representative of the caliph of the Murids in Dakar, wrote the governor's representative of the territory of Senegal in Dakar requesting to use an empty lot in the neighborhood of Bopp to organize the Murid eid prayer. This seems to have been the first time Murids had tried to secure a place for communal worship in Dakar. See Ibra Fall to Governor of Senegal, May 23, 1953, SRDAD, I/17, cérémonies religieuses musulmanes.
106. See Elhaaj Bamba Jaw, interview by author, June 2004. Also see in appendixes, letters from Caliph Faliilu and Abdul Ahad, who respectively mentioned Tuubaa Guy Senghor and Masalik al-Jinan as the new names of Guy Senghor.
107. Mbay Caam, interview by author, December 17, 1999. Mbay Caam was a grandson of Jean Caam, Ahmadu Bamba's host during his trip to Dakar in 1920; Sëriñ Jóob, interview by author, June 11, 2004. Jóob represented the family of Mamadu Mustafa and was manager of the house.
108. See, for example, Mamadou Seck, "La RTS refuse de diffuser un film sur la vente des médicaments à Keur Serigne Bi," *L'Observateur*, July 20, 2005. In this article, Seck tells the story of a documentary about the illegal selling of prescription drugs at Kër Sëriñ Bi, which the state-owned national broadcasting company refused to air.
109. Massalik-al-Jinan is a large, lavishly decorated two-story mosque that can accommodate twelve thousand worshippers.

CHAPTER 2: BIRTH OF A DIASPORA

1. Moses E. Ochonu, *Colonialism by Proxy: Hausa Imperial Agents and Middle Belt Consciousness in Nigeria* (Bloomington: Indiana University Press, 2014).
2. For more on citizenship in the French Empire, see Frederick Cooper, *Citizenship between Empire and Nation: Remaking France and French Africa, 1945–1960* (Princeton, NJ: Princeton University Press, 2015).
3. Cerno Suley Sall, interview by author, December 24, 2014. Sall was a retired teacher and local historian of Senegalese ancestry.
4. The Senegalese government gave the figure of six hundred thousand, which seemed a great overestimation. See Sylvie Bredeloup, "Sénégalais en Côte d'Ivoire, Sénégalais de Côte d'Ivoire," *Mondes en Développement* 23, no. 91 (1995): 13–29.

5. Abou B. Bamba, *African Miracle, African Mirage: Transnational Politics and the Paradox of Modernization in Ivory Coast* (Athens: Ohio University Press, 2016).
6. Bredeloup, "Sénégalais de Côte d'Ivoire," 13.
7. Gnato Zie and Vrih Gbazah, "Les commerçants sénégalais en Côte d'Ivoire de 1880 à 1970," in *Commerce et commerçants en Afrique de l'Ouest—la Côte d'Ivoire,* ed. Pierre Kipré and Leonard Harding (Paris: L'Harmattan, 1992), 262–63.
8. Raymond Delval, "Les musulmans d'Abidjan," *CHEAM* 10 (April 1980): 14.
9. Delval, "Les musulmans d'Abidjan," 44.
10. Mustafa Maar (Caam's grandson), interview by author, December 24, 2014.
11. Jean-Louis Triaud, "Working Paper on Islam and the Muslims in Côte d'Ivoire during the Colonial Era" (unpublished manuscript, n.d.).
12. I am referring to Abdulaay, Mandumbe, Usmaan, and Duudu (also known as Duudu Jóob Murid).
13. Mustafa Maar, interview by author, December 29, 2014. Also see biographical notice of Elhaaj Sëriñ Ñas, from the private papers of Daur Sow, a grandson of Ñas. I thank Dr. Marie Miran Gouyon for making this document available to me.
14. Maar, interview.
15. Between April 1958 and February 1959, the leader of the Muridiyya, Caliph Faliilu Mbakke and his secretary, Elhaaj Bamba Gey, sent a number of letters to the lieutenant governor of Côte d'Ivoire and to a number of local authorities disavowing Daam Sekk, who disputed the role of Sëriñ Ñas as representative of the Murid chief in Côte d'Ivoire but affirmed Ñas's status. I thank Dr. Marie Miran Gouyon for sharing these letters from the National Archives of Côte d'Ivoire.
16. See Governor of Senegal to Governor General, May 3, 1944, ANS 10D3. Touré was Caliph Mustafa Mbakke's representative in Dakar. Letter relates to the trip of marabout Shaykh Touré to Côte d'Ivoire.
17. See chapter 1.
18. François Quesnot, "Les cadres maraboutiques de l'islam sénégalais," in *Notes et Études sur l'Islam en Afrique Noire,* Recherches et documents du CHEAM (Paris: Peyronnet, 1962), 127–29, 164–65.
19. Quesnot, "Les cadres maraboutiques," 164.
20. Elhaaj Shaykh Mbuub, interview with author, May 2, 2014.
21. The archives of the Ministry of Interior in Abidjan hold several letters related to the dispute between 1958 and 1959, suggesting the involvement of the caliph in Tuubaa who called upon the colonial administration in the Ivory Coast to help settle the dispute.
22. Philippe David, *Les Navétanes: Histoire des migrants saisonniers de l'arachide en Sénégambie, des origines à nos jours* (Dakar: Présence Africaine, 1980).

23. The name of Yaba Laam came up in almost all my interviews with Murids who took the overland route to Abidjan in the 1980s and 1990s. He picked the migrants up from the train station in Bamako, provided them with shelter and food while they were in transit, and negotiated their transportation to Abidjan.

24. See Papa Demba Fall, "Eumagine: Imagining Europe from the Outside," in *Project Paper 2: Senegal, Country Research Areas Report* (n.p.: EUMAGINE, 2010). Fall observes that the intensification of international migration flow from Senegal in the 1980s was due to the massive migration of Wolof disciples of the Muridiyya originating from western-central Senegal (19).

25. Baabu is referring to the ocean liner *Mangin* owned by the company Fabre et Fraissinet, which serviced the Marseille-Pointe-Noire (Congo Brazzaville) route with stops along the coast of West Africa and the Gulf of Guinea. See Souleymane Diarra, "Les travailleurs africains noirs en France," *BIFAN* 30, no. 3 (July 1968): 884–1004, 935–36. Several of my interviewees in Abidjan in 2014 said they had traveled on this same ocean liner.

26. Sëriñ Baabu, interview by author, May 25, 2011.

27. Papa Khouma, *IO Venditore Di Elefanti: Una Vita Per Forza Fra Dakar, Parigi e Milano* (Milan: Garzanti Editore, SPA, 2010), 19. I thank my colleague at the Wiko in Berlin, Michele Lopocarno, for help translating passages from Khouma's book into English.

28. Sëriñ Sy, interview by author, February 23, 2014. Sy, a young trader, knew about Mekouar's business and in one of his operations he sold the latter a truck full of sculptures.

29. Elhaaj Shaykh Mbuub, interview by author, May 2, 2014.

30. On information about Murid traders in Abidjan, see Sëriñ Baabu, interview by author, May 25, 2011; Elhaaj Shaykh Mbuub, interview by author, May 2, 2014; Abdulaay Jóob Abidjan, interview by author, December 2014; and Moor Kase, interview by author, June 26, 2011. Kase was a shoemaker who made and sold shoes to Senegalese retailers.

31. Elhaaj Bamba Gey, interview by author, December 28, 2014.

32. In chapters 4 and 6, I discuss the case of Elhaaj Yande Jóob, Ahmed Sugu, and a few other Murids in Paris and New York City who started their migratory journey in Côte d'Ivoire.

33. The organization was registered with the office of the Ministry of Political and Social Affairs under the number 5862, dating from December 5, 1950. See biographical notice of Elhaaj Sëriñ Ñas in the private papers of Daur Sow.

34. Elhaaj Bamba Jaw, interview by author, April 8 and May 3, 2000.

35. Moor Ja, interview by author, December 18, 2014.

36. Gey, interview. The house is located at the corner of Fourteenth and Twenty-Fifth Streets in Treichville. This is the same place that Delval refers to when he notes the existence of a Murid mosque on

Twenty-Fifth Street in Treichville. See Delval, "Les musulmans d'Abidjan," 45.

37. Moor Ja, interview by author, December 28, 2014. Ja indicates that he learned from a son of Shaykh Faliilu, the second caliph of the Muridiyya, that it was in 1956 that the caliph first received *hadiyas* from outside Senegal sent by the Murid dahira of Côte d'Ivoire. Before the tradition of sending money from outside the country was established, Murid shaykhs or their emissaries traveled abroad to collect donations. Lower-level Murid shaykhs still tour the diaspora to collect gifts, but the caliph does not. He is the principal recipient of dahira donations.

38. Elhaaj Bamba Gey recounts the embarrassment that some in the Murid community felt when during a celebration of *Tabaski* (*Eid ul Adha*), the rain came through the shelter's roof and ruined the beautiful attire that people wore for prayer. This moved Gey and another fellow disciple to convince the community to rebuild the site. See Gey, interview.

39. Gey, interview.

40. Unlike the Tijaniyya Sufi order, the Muridiyya discourages smoking but does not formally prohibit it.

41. In my meeting with a group of Murid disciples affiliated with the house, many deplored the attitude of some of these young guests. Group conversation with author, December 28, 2014.

42. Benedict Anderson, *Imagined Communities*, 3rd ed. (London: Verso, 2003).

43. Bredeloup, "Sénégalais en Côte d'Ivoire," 25.

CHAPTER 3: GABON

1. For a discussion of the centrality of Gabon in Ahmadu Bamba's hagiography and biography, see Cheikh Anta Babou, "Sufi Eschatology and Hagiography as Responses to Colonial Repression: An Examination of the Meanings of Amadu Bamba's Trial and Exiles by the French Colonial Administration of Senegal 1895–1907," in *Practicing Sufism: Sufi Politics and Performance in Africa*, ed. Abdelmajid Hannoum (London: Routledge, 2016), 47–74.

2. The French colonial archives reveal that as early as 1888, the government of King Leopold's so-called Congo Free State had authorized recruitment of Senegalese soldiers destined to form the nucleus of the Force Publique (colonial police). Despite strong opposition from French colonial officials, Senegalese workers, swayed by King Leopold's propaganda and the expectation of easy money, found their way to Congo. By December 1891, three hundred emigrants had left the country. In 1894, one Laplène, a demoted French colonial administrator operating from the town of Bathurst in the British colony of the Gambia, was able to recruit and send nine hundred to a thousand Senegalese workers to the Congo Free State. See François Zucarelli, "Le recrutement des travailleurs sénégalais par l'Etat indépendant du Congo (1888–1896)," *Revue*

française d'histoire d'outre-mer 47, nos. 168–69 (1960): 475–81. After completing their contracts, some of these immigrants found their way to other territories in central Africa, including Gabon. Also see Doris Ehazouambela, "Expression mémorielle des mourides et espace public islamique au Gabon," in *Les politiques de l'Islam en Afrique: Mémoires, Réveils et Populismes Islamiques*, ed. Gilles Holder and Jean P. Donzon (Paris: Karthala, 2018), 57–73.

3. Sidiya Leon Jóob, a prince of the precolonial Walo Kingdom in Senegal; Samba Laobé Njaay, the last king of the kingdom of Jolof; and Samory Touré, the Muslim resister who fought the French in Guinea and northern Côte d'Ivoire, among others, were deported to Gabon. The *CIA World Factbook* estimates the population of Gabon in 2017 at 1,772,255.

4. Imam Paap Jaañ, interview by author, December 20, 2014. Jaañ was imam of the mosque of Camp Sénégalais, Libreville; Maam Abdulaay Ba, interview by author, December 16, 2014. Ba was consul to Gabon at the embassy of Senegal, Libreville; and Amadu Basum, interview by author, December 17, 2014.

5. Ba, interview; Basum, interview.

6. See Jaañ, interview. Jaañ migrated to Gabon in the 1970s and is the most important source for SOCOBA. All of my information about the SOCOBA project came from interviews. The Senegalese embassy in Gabon has no archives related to the project.

7. Ehazouambela, "Expression mémorielle," 60.

8. Asan M. Jóob, interview with author, December 16, 2014.

9. See Papa Demba Fall, "Protectionnisme migratoire en Afrique noire: Les migrants sénégalais face à la politique de gabonisation," *Bulletin de l'IFAN* 49, nos. 1–2 (1999–2000): 101–34, 105.

10. This was, for example, the case of Paap Jaañ, a landscaper from Rufisque who migrated to Abidjan in 1968 then moved to Gabon in 1974; Amadu Basum, a welder from Dakar, also migrated to Côte d'Ivoire in 1977 before settling in Libreville in 1981. See Jaañ, interview; Basum, interview.

11. The name *La La La* is a deformation of the Qur'anic verse *laa i laha il lala* (there is no God but God), sung aloud by Sufis, mostly disciples of the Tijaniyya, during the religious ritual of *dhikr* (remembrance of God).

12. Muusaa Ka is the most prolific and influential of all Senegalese writers in Wolofal or Wolof Ajami (Wolof language written with Arabic script). See Fallou Ngom, *Muslims beyond the Arab World: The Odyssey of Ajami and the Muridiyya* (New York: Oxford University Press, 2016). Sana Camara and R. H. Mitsch, "'A'jami' Literature in Senegal: The Example of Sëriñ Muusaa Ka, Poet and Biographer," in "Arabic Writing in Africa," special issue, *Research in African Literatures* 28, no. 3 (Autumn 1997): 163–82.

13. For more on the *griot* see Sory Camara, *Gens de la parole: Essai sur la condition et le rôle des griots dans la société Malinké* (Paris: Karthala, 1992); and Thomas A. Hale, *Griots and Griottes: Masters of Words and Music* (Bloomington: Indiana University Press, 1998).

14. See Muusaa Ka, *Jazaau Shakuur*, unpublished epic poem in Wolof, sung by Mama Njaay, audio cassette. I purchased the recorded version on the market. Also see a French translation of the same poem in Diâo Faye, "L'œuvre poétique wolofal de Moussa Ka ou l'épopée de Cheikh Ahmadou Bamba" (PhD diss., Université Cheikh Anta Diop de Dakar, 1999).

15. Allen and Mary Roberts, in an interesting analysis of the unique picture of Shaykh Ahmadu Bamba, explore some of the themes associated with the exiles and the popular imagery that stemmed from these events. See Allen Roberts and Mary N. Roberts, "The Aura of Amadu Bamba," *Anthropologie et Sociétés* 22 (1998): 15–38.

16. For the history of the first Murid settlers in Gabon, I rely on information provided by Maas Njaay, interview by author, December 19, 2014; Jaañ, interview; Basum, interview; and Elhaaj Sekk, interview by author, November 7, 2015. Jaañ, Njaay, and Sekk arrived in Libreville in the 1970s. Basum moved to Libreville in the early 1980s.

17. Jóob, interview.

18. The unskilled journeyman working in the construction business makes 7,000 CFA francs ($1 = 500/600 CFA francs) a day, which is double what he would earn in Senegal. A qualified mason can earn twice this amount.

19. See Ba, interview. Ba was the Senegalese consul in Libreville. Until recently, the majority of Senegalese immigrants in Libreville were Haal Pulaar Tijaani.

20. See Abdul Ahad Mbakke, ed., *Majmuha: A Collection of Ahmadu Bamba's Correspondence in Arabic* (Touba, Senegal: self-pub., 1985), 21. This is a collection of Ahmadu Bamba's correspondence in Arabic, assembled and published by Shaykh Abdul Ahad. For Sufis, the Prophet Muhammad, who died in 632 CE, continues to communicate with his friends (the *wali* Allah or God's neighbors) through dreams and visions and, even in some circumstances, physically and face to face.

21. Asan Jóob, the leader of the dahira of Batavia, uses the Wolof word *tookër*. *Tookër* is formed by combining the word *tool*, which means "farm," and the word *kër*, which means "house." It refers to a garden often tended by women and used for growing condiments near an inhabited area. The metaphor is used here to refer to the close (imaginary) proximity between Tuubaa and Gabon. See Jóob, interview. Many other interviewees used a similar expression to characterize the connections between Tuubaa and Gabon.

22. Elhaaj Njaay, interview by author, May 2, 2014.

23. Jóob, interview.

24. Jóob, interview.
25. Many among my interviewees in Gabon affirm that under Medun Gey the dahira was able to collect $4,000 in donations every week, and when it fell short of this goal, Gey would donate his own money to make up the deficit. See Njaay, interview; Jóob, interview; and Muusaa Faaty, interview by author, December 16, 2014.
26. In the 1970s and 1980s, the Libreville dahira was first to send the caliph in Tuubaa annual contributions amounting to between $80,000 and $120,000. See Mbay Caam, interview by author, March 13, 2011. I also refer to a phone interview with Elhaaj Sekk, a Murid disciple who migrated to Libreville in 1976. See Sekk, interview by author, November 7, 2015.
27. For information on Shaykh Murtada Mbakke, I rely on my interviews with his son, aide, and traveling companion, Xaasim Mbakke. See Mbakke, interview by author, December 18, 2018. Also see Afia Ñaŋ, interview by author, October 4, 2009. Ñaŋ is a Murid scholar and researcher. There were also interviews with various Murid disciples in Senegal, France, and New York City.
28. It is remarkable that unlike many prominent Murid shaykhs whose names are always associated with the string of villages and daaras they have founded, hagiographers of Shaykh Murtada do not attribute to him the founding of a single locality.
29. Momar Coumba Diop, "Les Affaires mourides à Dakar," *Politique Africaine* 1, no. 4 (November 1981): 90–100, 93.
30. See report by the French ambassador to Senegal, Mr. Xavier Daufresne, to the minister of foreign affairs on the inauguration of the new market of Tuubaa by President Léopold Senghor, April 13, 1977, box no. 664, ADN.
31. See Cheikh Anta Babou, "The al-Azhar School Network: A Murid Experiment in Islamic Modernism," in *Islamic Education in Africa: Writing Boards and Blackboards*, ed. Robert Launay (Bloomington: Indiana University Press, 2016), 173–95.
32. Ñaŋ, interview; Akhma Faal, in discussion with the author, November 2005 (referring to a testimony of one of Shaykh Murtada's sons, Xaasim Mbakke); Amadu Dramé, in discussion with the author, May 30, 2010 (Dramé is the son-in-law and traveling companion of the Shaykh); and Xaasim Mbakke, interview by author, December 18, 2018 (Mbakke is the son and traveling companion of Shaykh Murtada).
33. Mbakke, interview. Mbakke recalls his father's nine-month-long trip across the Arab world in 1966.
34. The government of Egypt sent teachers to Shaykh Murtada's schools across Senegal. Some graduates from al-Azhar also benefited from scholarships to study in Egypt's institutions of higher education.
35. For more on Shaykh Murtada's visits and impact on the Muridiyya in the United States, see chapters 6 and 7.

36. See A. Moustapha Diop, "Les associations Mourides en France," *Esprit* 102 (June 1985): 197–206. These values are also what the son of Shaykh Murtada and director general of the al-Azhar Institute, Saaliu Mbakke, identifies as the core teachings of his father. Mbakke, interview by author, June 1, 2004.
37. All of my Murid interviewees in Libreville remember this injunction.
38. Njaga Jaw, interview by author, December 19, 2014.
39. Mustafa Mbakke, interview by author, August 10, 2018. Mbakke is a great-grandson of Ahmadu Bamba and influential member of the Murid community of New York. He argues that the official certificates for the proclamation of Ahmadu Bamba Day that cities such as New York issued on behalf of the Murid community facilitated Shaykh Murtada's access to city officials in Italy and the ultimate recognition of the Muridiyya as a respected Muslim organization allowed to function in public space.
40. I thank Asan Jóob and the leadership of the dahira of Batavia for providing me with this document.
41. It is more appropriate to call it a "hill." The place is perhaps Libreville's highest point, but it is easily accessible by a number of different means of transportation and does not have steep slopes. While some Murids relate the label "sacred" to Ahmadu's stay in Libreville in 1895, it appears that the name "Sacred Mountain" predated the arrival of the Murid shaykh in Gabon and was associated with the Catholic monastery that once stood on top of the hill. For more on the history of Montagne Sainte, see Ehazouambela, "Expression mémorielle," 61.
42. These older residents are Ignace Mikele, Gora Ñaŋ, and Demba Njaay. Sources are, however, unclear whether the monastery was still standing at the time of Bamba's stay or if it had been moved. For information on the history of the Murid community of Libreville, I rely mostly on my interview with Maasamba (Maas) Njaay, an elder Murid disciple who settled in Libreville in the 1970s. See Njaay, interview. I have collected many slightly different versions of the history of Bamba's sojourn to Gabon; Njaay's was the most complete. Ahmadu Bamba wrote a brief chronicle of his trip to Gabon but did not provide details about what happened to him there. See Cheikh Ahmadou Bamba Mbacké, *Jazaau Shakuur* [Tribute to the worthy of recognition], trans. and ed. by the Dahira of Murid students of the University of Dakar (Dakar: Bibliothèque du Daara Hizbut Tarqiyya, n.d.).
43. Imam Nduur, interview by author, December 16, 2014. The interview was on the site of the Murid mosque of Sacred Mountain, Libreville.
44. Jaw, interview. Interview took place at Murid Art Market in downtown Libreville. Badr is the first battle that the Prophet Muhammad fought with his enemies of Mecca in 624 CE. Standard prophetic hagiography refers to the "army of angels" (warriors of Badr) who came to help the Prophet defeat his more powerful foes. Muslim warriors who fought

and died at this battle are believed to have benefited from immortality, although they are only visible when God wills it.

45. My information about the mosque of "Sacred Mountain" comes from several sources. The most significant of these are Maas Njaay, interview by author, December 19, 2014; and Fallu Buso, interview by author, October 25, 2015. Buso was the leading speaker of the Murid dahira on the occasion of Ahmadu Bamba cultural week in Libreville.

46. Njaay, interview.

47. Amndi Mustafa Saady, interview by author, August 4, 2015. Saady lived in Gabon for a few years in the 1990s.

48. I visited one of Amar's warehouses in Libreville on December 16 and 19, 2014. It stores heavy earth-moving machinery and other construction equipment as well as a carpentry workshop.

49. This leader's name is Fallu Buso; his father's family is related to Ahmadu Bamba's mother, Jaara Buso.

50. The inauguration ceremony was broadcasted by the Senegalese public network Sen 2 on March 12, 2013.

51. I have visited the Murid mosque during field visits in Libreville on December 2014 and October 2015.

52. Ahmadu Bamba cultural week in Gabon was organized from October 22 to 29, 2015, and presided over by the second-most powerful leader of the Muridiyya, who traveled to Libreville with a delegation of fifty Murid dignitaries. He was received by President Ali Bongo. The Murid community visited the different sites associated with Bamba's exile and organized a procession in downtown Libreville that mobilized around one thousand disciples. On three occasions I heard passersby cursing the marchers and drivers, and security agents berated them.

53. Jóob, interview.

54. *Ivoirité* (ivoireness) is a xenophobic ideology promoted by politicians in Côte d'Ivoire in the 2000s. This ideology led to a civil war and pogroms against so-called foreigners. On "Gabonisation," see Papa Demba Fall, "Protectionnisme migratoire en Afrique noire: Les migrants sénégalais face à la politique de gabonisation," *Bulletin de l'IFAN* 49, nos. 1–2 (1999–2000): 101–34.

55. In their relations with the Gabonese elite, Murid businessmen have been inspired by their French predecessors and employers who have built close relationships with postcolonial Gabonese government officials. According to Paap Jaañ, one of my informants, Jean Claude Baloz, a director of SOCOBA, was the son-in-law of President Bongo. Jaañ, interview.

56. These arguments came up in my interview with Amadu Basum and other interviewees. A Senegalese national, Samba Katy Mbuub, was the Qur'anic teacher of President Omar Bongo after the latter converted to Islam on the urging of the late president of Libya, Muammar Gaddafi, in 1973. The same Mbuub introduced Bongo to Shaykh Murtada.

Martin Bongo, President Bongo's cousin, was married to a Muslim woman; Martin's brother, Gustave, was married to a Senegalese Muslim woman. Islam has also made inroads into the Gabonese administration, and Senegalese are said to have contributed to this. Khadime Ouyabi, a general and chief of the Gabonese mobile guard, was converted to Islam by a Senegalese immigrant. Similarly, Abdou Salam Bousougou, a former perfect of Lambaréné who, in 1979, became a disciple of Cheikh A. Dièye, was a Murid. See Moustapha Bousougou, interview by author, June 24, 2006. One of my informants in Libreville, Asan Jóob, tells a story in which President Bongo told a group of Gabonese Wahhabi Muslims complaining about the Murids that he had a robe belonging to Shaykh Ahmadu Bamba and that they should leave Murid disciples alone. See Jóob, interview.

57. Farha Mohamed, interview by author, December 21, 2014.
58. For information related to the history of the Murid market of Libreville, I rely on my interview with Njaga Jaw, chief of the market who led the effort to buy the place. See Jaw, interview.
59. Jaw, interview.
60. See Jaw, interview. This story was also told by many of my Murid informants during my field trip in Libreville between December 11 and 20, 2014.
61. Jaw, interview by author, December 24, 2014.
62. Jaw, interview.
63. Jaw, interview.
64. Jaw, interview.
65. See François Héran, "Europe and the Spectre of Sub-Saharan Migration," *Population et Sociétés* 558 (2018): 1–3; Marie-Laurence Flahaux and Hein De Haas, "African Migration: Trends, Patterns, Drivers," *Comparative Migration Studies* 4, no. 1 (2016): 1–25.

CHAPTER 4: THE MURIDIYYA IN FRANCE

1. A. Moustapha Diop, "Les associations Mourides en France," *Esprit* 102 (June 1985): 197–206.
2. William B. Cohen, *The French Encounter with Africans: White Response to Blacks* (Bloomington: Indiana University Press, 1981).
3. See Pap Ndiaye, *La condition noire: Essai sur une minorité française* (Paris: Calmann Levy, 2008), 111. I am also referring to the March for Equality of 1983. Also see Abdoulaye Guèye, "The Colony Strikes Back: African Protest Movements in Post-colonial France," *Comparative Studies of South Asia, Africa and the Middle East* 26, no. 2 (2006): 225–42.
4. Jean-Philippe Dedieu, *La parole immigrée: Les migrants africains dans l'espace publique en France, 1960–1995* (Paris: Klincksieck, 2012). For history books on the colonial African immigrants in France, see Philippe Dewitte, *Les mouvements nègres en France, 1919–1939* (Paris: L'Harmattan, 1985); Fabienne Guimont, *Les étudiants africains en*

France, 1950–1965 (Paris: L'Harmattan, 1997); Sue Peabody and Tyler Stoval, eds., *The Color of Liberty: Histories of Race in France* (Durham, NC: Duke University Press, 2003); Ndiaye, *La condition noire*, 111. For sociological and anthropological works on the postcolonial migration, see Adrian Adams, *Le long voyage des Gens du Fleuve* (Paris: Maspéro, 1985); Catherine Quiminal, *Gens d'ici, gens d'ailleurs: Migrations So-ninké et transformations villageoises* (Paris: Bourgois, 1991); Mahamet Timéra, *Les Soninké en France: D'une histoire à l'autre* (Paris: Karthala, 1996); Christian Poiret, *Familles africaines en France* (Paris: L'Har-mattan, 1997); and Christophe Daum, *Les associations de Maliens en France: Migration, développement et citoyenneté* (Paris: Karthala, 1998). An exception is Félix F. Germain, *Decolonization and the Republic: African and Caribbean Migrants in Post War Paris, 1946–1974* (East Lansing: Michigan State University Press, 2016).

5. Beyond the pioneering work of geographer Gerard Salem (which is still unpublished), there are a few articles by Moustapha Diop, Victoria Ebin, and Jean Copans. Sophie Bava wrote a dissertation on the Murid community of Marseille and has published a number of articles on the Murid community in France. Diop is a sociologist; Ebin, Bava, and Copans are anthropologists. This book offers the first historical recon-struction of Murid immigration to France.

6. The national census of 1988 indicated that 30.1 percent of the Senega-lese population were Murid. See Republic of Senegal, *Recensement de la Population et de l'habitat 1988* (Dakar: République du Sénégal, 1993); tableau I-15 répartition de la population résidence selon la région et la religion.

7. There is an extensive literature on the cultural and political lives of the métis of Senegal. See for example, Hilary Jones, *The Métis of Senegal: Urban Life and Politics in French West Africa* (Bloomington: Indiana University Press, 2013); Emmanuelle Saada, *Les enfants de la colonie: Les métis de l'empire français entre sujétion et citoyenneté* (Paris: La Découverte, 2007); George E. Brooks, *Euro-Africans in West Africa* (Athens: Ohio University Press, 2003); Owen White, *Children of the French Empire: Miscegenation and Colonial Society in French West Af-rica, 1895–1960* (Oxford: Oxford University Press, 1999); and G. Wesley Johnson Jr., *The Emergence of Black Politics in Senegal: The Struggle for Power in the Four Communes, 1900–1920* (Stanford, CA: Stanford University Press, 1971).

8. Jean Caam was a wealthy gold jeweler who developed close relation-ships with the colonial administration in Dakar in the first half of the twentieth century. He hosted Ahmadu Bamba when the latter was sum-moned to Dakar by the governor of Senegal in 1920. He later became the host of Murid shaykhs visiting the capital of French West Africa. On the so-called villages noirs or human zoos, see Jean-Michel Ber-gougniou, Remi Clignet, and Philippe David, *Villages Noirs et visiteurs*

africains et malgaches en France et en Europe (1870–1940) (Paris: Karthala, 2001).

9. On the history of African soldiers in the French army see Myron Echenberg, *Colonial Conscripts: The Tirailleurs Sénégalais in French West Africa, 1857–1960* (Portsmouth, NH: Heinemann, 1991); Joe Lunn, *Memoire of the Maelstrom: A Senegalese Oral History of the First World War* (Portsmouth, UK: Heinemann, 1999); and Gregory Mann, *Native Sons: West African Veterans and France in the Twentieth Century* (Durham, NC: Duke University Press, 2006).

10. Birago Diop's autobiographical novel, *La plume raboutée* (Paris: Présence Africaine, 1978), offers a glimpse of the life of this community of Senegalese and Black African students in Paris under Nazi occupation.

11. Brigitte Bertoncello and Sylvie Bredeloup, "Le Marseille des marins africains," *Revue européenne de migrations internationales* 15, no. 13 (1999): 177–97, 179. Also see Mahamet Timéra and Jules Garnier, "Les Africains en France viellissement et transformation d'une migration," *Hommes et Migrations* 1286–87 (July–October 2010): 24–36.

12. "Arrivée d'originaires d'Afrique noire dans le département de la Seine," June 25, 1962, ANF, AG (F) 3384. Also see Guy Provost, "Comment et pourquoi les travailleurs sénégalais viennent en France," *Hommes et Migrations* 115 (1970): 90–119, 101.

13. *Les travailleurs d'Afrique Noire en France, Paris*, December 12, 1962, ANF, AG 5(F) 3384.

14. *Rapport du ministre du travail de l'emploi et de la population*, April 6, 1971, ANF, AG 5(F) 3386, 1.

15. Dossier sur le problème de l'immigration des travailleurs sénégalais en France, June 22, 1962, ADN, Dakar Ambassador, box 483, chapter 8, conclusion générale du rapport.

16. "Analyse par nationalités et catégories de ressortissants entre la France et les 15 Etats d'Afrique francophone," 1971, ANF, AG (F) 3386, annexe I, convention de sécurité sociale signée avec les Etats d'Afrique noire francophone.

17. Catherine Quiminal and Mahamet Timéra, "Les mutations de l'immigration africaine (1974–2002)," *Hommes et Migrations* 1262 (July–August 2006): 19–33.

18. In 2004, the population of sub-Saharan African immigrants in France represented 12 percent of the total population of immigrants. See Mahamet Timéra and Jules Garnier, "les Africains," 27. This percentage was much lower in the early 1960s when the sub-Saharan immigrant community was almost exclusively composed of single males. In 1967, the number of sub-Saharan immigrants in France was estimated at forty-one thousand.

19. This is also Félix Germain's opinion. See Félix Germain, *Decolonizing the Republic*, 39, where he invites scholars to revisit the history of

African migration to Paris, noting, "In truth, France never opened its door to African migrants."

20. With regard to African immigration, from the late 1950s to the late early 1970s one can discern two factions within the French government. One faction led by the Ministry of Home Affairs always advocated for harsh anti-immigration measures. The foreign minister, along with the secretary for the community in charge of African and Malagasy affairs then lead by the infamous Jacques Foccart, always opposed those measures. See, for example, "Réunion interministérielle sur les problèmes de l'immigration Africaine," ANF, AG 5(F) 3386, February 1972 and compte rendu de la réunion interministérielle sur le problème de l'immigration Africaine, March 17, 1972.

21. See "Note du conseiller technique Jacques le Cornec à l'attention du premier ministre," February 12, 1973, ANF AG 5(F) 3384.

22. Souleymane Diarra, "Les travailleurs africains noirs en France," BIFAN 30, no. 3 (July 1968): 892.

23. Provost, "Comment et Pourquoi," 118.

24. "Note à monsieur le secrétaire général: Les travailleurs africains en France," May 31, 1969, ANF, AG 5(F) 3385 Paris, 4.

25. Victoria Ebin, email to author, February 28, 2017. Ebin conducted research among Senegalese immigrants in France in the late 1980s.

26. Provost, "Comment et pourquoi," 107; Diarra, "Les travailleurs noirs," 951.

27. See, for example, Diarra, "Les travailleurs noirs"; Adrian Adams, Le long voyage des Gens du Fleuve (Paris: Maspéro, 1985); and Mar Fall, Des Africains noirs en France: Des tirailleurs sénégalais aux Black (Paris: Harmattan, 1986). Also see Jacques Barou, who authored numerous articles on the sub-Saharan African migration and African immigrants in France published in Hommes et migrations.

28. I have reviewed all the records on African immigration to France from the 1960s to the 1970s in the newly released Jack Foccart archives, but there is not a single mention of Senegalese merchants or street vendors.

29. See, for example, Paul Stoller's The Africanization of New York City (Chicago: University of Chicago Press, 2002), which looks at the life of street vendors from Niger working in New York City.

30. Gérard Salem, "De la brousse sénégalaise au Boul'Mich: Le système commercial mouride en France," Cahiers d'Études africaines 21, nos. 81/83 (1981): 267–88; see Papa Demba Fall, "Eumagine: Imagining Europe from the Outside," in Project Paper 2: Senegal, Country Research Areas Report (n.p.: EUMAGINE, 2010). Also see Bruno Riccio, "'Transmigrants' mais pas 'nomades': Transnationalisme mouride en Italie," Cahiers d'Études Africaines 46, no. 181 (2006): 95–114.

31. Gérard Salem, "De Dakar á Paris, des diasporas d'artisans et de commerçants: Étude socio-géographique du commerce sénégalais en France" (PhD diss., École des Hautes Études en Sciences Sociales, 1983). Also

see Brigitte Bertoncello and Sylvie Bredeloup, *Colporteurs africains à Marseille: Un siècle d'aventures* (Paris: Autrement, 2004).

32. I am referring to Elhaaj Ngoone Sow, interview by author, December 26, 2014. Sow is a *Laobe Jula* (trader) and among those influenced by Elhaaj Amadi Sow. He left Senegal at age twenty to travel to Abidjan for the first time in 1966. He started trading in France in 1968.

33. The Festival Mondial des Arts Nègres (World Festival of Negro Arts) was convened in Dakar from April 1 to 24 in 1966 by President Senghor. After the event ended, some of the exhibits traveled to Paris.

34. John F. Povey, "The First World Festival of Negro Arts at Dakar," *New African Literature and the Arts* 1 (1970): 64–75. The discovery of so-called primitive African arts in the museums of Europe inspired Pablo Picasso and Cubism, but this movement did not have the popular impact that the World's Fair achieved.

35. Samir Amin, *Le monde des affaires sénégalais* (Paris: Les Éditions du Minuit, 1969), 165. I am also referring to my interview with Elhaaj Shaykh Mbuub, May 2, 2014.

36. Saer Njaay, interview by author, July 11, 2011.

37. Njaay, interview; Mbuub, interview.

38. In his book, Mboup focuses on Senegalese immigrants from the region of Njambur and refers to the role of the Laobe as precursors of the migration. See Mourtala Mboup, *Les Sénégalais d'Italie. Emigrés, agents du changement social* (Paris: Harmattan, 2001).

39. Migration among the Wolof was seasonal. Young men, mostly those living in populated but ecologically fragile areas, migrated to more humid areas during the rainy season to work as sharecroppers (*surga*). The suggestion that the drought of 1970s triggered the international migration of people from Njambur has been recurrent in my interviews with Murid disciples from Njambur in Europe. Papa Demba Fall also cites the drought of the 1970s as sparking the massive wave of international migration from Senegal in the 1980s. See Fall, *Eumagine*, 19.

40. Mama Mbóoj, interview by author, July 6, 2011.

41. Ottavia Schmidt di Friedberg, "L'immigration africaine en Italie: Le cas sénégalais," *Études Internationales* 24, no. 1 (March 1993): 125–40; Mamadou Diouf, "The Senegalese Murid Trade Diaspora and the Making of a Vernacular Cosmopolitanism," trans. Steven Rendall, *Public Culture* 12, no. 3 (Fall 2000): 679–702; Jean Copans, "Mourides des champs, mourides des villes, mourides du téléphone portable et de l'internet: Les renouvellements de l'économie politique d'une confrérie," *Afrique Contemporaine* 194 (April–June 2000): 24–33; and Sophie Bava, "Routes migratoires et itinéraires religieux: Des pratiques religieuses des migrants sénégalais entre Marseille et Touba" (PhD diss., École des Hautes Études en Sciences Sociales Marseille, 2002).

42. Salem, "De la brousse sénégalaise." See also Victoria Ebin, "A la recherche de nouveaux 'poissons': Stratégies commerciales mourides

en temps de crise," *Politique Africaine* 45 (1992): 86–99; J. P. Dozon, *Saint-Louis du Sénégal, palimpseste d'une ville* (Paris: Karthala, 2012), 106. Also see Malick Ndiaye, *Les Modou-Modou: Ou ethos du développement au Sénégal* (Dakar: Dakar University Press, 1998); Abdoulaye Wade, *La doctrine économique du mouridisme* (Dakar: l'Interafricaine d'éditions, 1970). All these works are inspired implicitly or explicitly by Marx Weber's theory about the relations between the Protestant work ethic and the development of capitalism.

43. See, for example, "'Enquête exclusive': L'enquête sur la multinationale des vendeurs à la sauvette," accessed January 9, 2018, https://www.youtube.com/watch?v=JXE4p8wKiRM; and Tim Judah, "Faith in the Market behind the Street Markets of Italy, There Is a Network of African Muslims Offering a New Response to Globalization," *Economist*, December 19, 2006, http://www.economist.com/node/8450228.

44. See Guy Rocheteau, *Société Wolof et mobilité* (Dakar: ORSTOM, 1973), 1.

45. Momar Coumba Diop, "Fonctions et activités des *dahiras* mourides urbains (Sénégal)," *Cahiers d'Études Africaines* 21, nos. 81/83 (1981): 79–91.

46. Ottavia Schmidt di Friedberg, "Le réseau sénégalais mouride en Italic," in *Exiles et royaumes: Les appartenances du monde arabo-musulman aujourd'hui*, ed. Gilles Kepel (Paris: Presse de la Fondation Nationale des Sciences Politiques, 1994); Sophie Bava, "Le dahira urbain, lieu de pouvoir du mouridisme," *Les annales de la recherche urbaine* 96 (2004): 135–43.

47. Sophie Bava and Cheikh Guèye, "Le Magal de Touba: Exil prophétique, migration et pèlerinage au sein du mouridisme," *Social Compass* 48, no. 3 (2001): 421–38, 422. Author's translation from the French.

48. By "tradition of mobility" in Islam, I refer particularly to the notions of *hijra* (migration for the sake of protecting one's faith), *rihla li talab al-ilm* (migration for the sake of acquiring knowledge), and the many provisions in Islamic law that cater to the needs of the wayfarer.

49. The creation of the first Murid dahira was inspired by Shaykh Mbakke, Faliilu's nephew who was contesting his authority. The latter certainly saw this initiative as an attempt to undermine his power. Additionally, Faliilu headed the Muridiyya at a time when rural-dwelling peanut farmers dominated the organization, and cities were seen as threats to Murid values and ethics.

50. I will show in the following chapter that even when the initiative to organize comes from an important Murid shaykh, it is not immediately accepted. Disciples tend to resist until they are convinced of the benefit of the new initiatives for their life.

51. This idea was first expressed by Momar C. Diop in his work on Murid dahiras in Dakar. It is increasingly shared by scholars of Murid migration. See, for example, a summary of this scholarship in Sophie Bava,

"Migration-Religion Studies in France: Toward a Religious Anthropology of Movement," *Annual Review of Anthropology* 40 (2011): 493–507, 500.

52. This was, for example, the case of Sëriñ Sy. See Sëriñ Sy, interview by author, March 22, 2014.

53. Immigrants interviewed by Mboup, *Les Sénégalais d'Italie*, and Papa Demba Fall, *Des Francenabe aux Modou-Modou: L'émigration sénégalaise contemporaine* (Dakar: L'Harmattan, 2016) similarly emphasize deteriorating economic conditions as their motivation to migrate.

54. Senegalese immigrants in Spain interviewed by Joan Lacomba express a similar view. One of them, for example, indicated "Moi, quand j'étais en Afrique, les confréries ne m'intéressaient pas. Mais en étant ici, on perd ses coutumes, sa culture, alors chaque fois que vient un marabout (chef de la confrérie), j'ai envie d'aller le voir et de l'écouter. Parce que je sais que c'est réellement une aide morale, il te donne plus de force pour te battre" [When I was in Africa, I was not interested in the Muslim orders. However, when you live abroad your customs and culture come under threat. Now I am eager to go to visit and listen to marabouts (Muslim clerics) whenever I hear that one is visiting. They provide you moral strength and encourage you to persevere in your struggle.] See Joan Lacomba, "Immigrés Sénégalais: Islam et Confréries à Valence (Espagne)," *Revue Européenne de migrations internationales* 16, no. 3 (2000): 85–103, 93.

55. Cerno Sow, interview by author, May 9, 2011.

56. See Quiminal and Timéra, "Les mutations," 19–33, 27.

57. Quoted by Barbara Daly Metcalf, ed., *Making Muslim Space in North America and Europe* (Berkeley: University of California Press, 1996), 7–8.

58. Bava, "Migration-Religion Studies in France," 496. This is also the opinion of Jocelyn Cesari, who observes that "it was only in the early 1980s that the French people started to become aware of Islam's presence at the heart of their society; an awareness accompanied by surprise and, sometimes, fear." See Jocelyne Cesari, "Mosques in French Cities: Towards the End of a Conflict?," *Journal of Ethnic and Migration Studies* 31, no. 6 (2005): 1025–43, 1025.

59. It is worth mentioning that the French academy, particularly historians, did not prioritize the study of religion, especially the religion of immigrants—just as they did not emphasize ethnicity or race.

60. For an extensive discussion of Dièye and his role in the expansion of the Muridiyya in the diaspora, see Cheikh Anta Babou, "A West African Sufi Master on the Global Stage: Cheikh Abdoulaye Dièye and the Khidmatul Khadim International Sufi School in France and the United States," *African Diaspora* 4, no. 1 (2011): 27–49. Also see A. Moustapha Diop, "L'émigration murid en Europe," *Hommes et Migrations* 1132 (May 1990): 21–31; Donal Cruise O'Brien, "Charisma Comes to Town,"

in *Charisma and Brotherhood in African Islam,* ed. Donal Cruise O'Brien and Christian Coulon (Oxford: Clarendon, 1988), 135–55.

61. For information related to Dièye's biography, I rely on my interviews with Abdoulaye Dièye's elder son, Bamba Dièye, interview by author, April 2006; and Mustafa Cuun, interview by author, May 9, 2006. Cuun is a Murid disciple originally from Saint-Louis and an amateur archivist.

62. Many among Shaykh Abdoulaye Dièye's American disciples that I interviewed emphasized his impressive physical appearance, especially his body language, his warmth, and his charm. See Chuck Abraham, interview by author, March 19, 2006 (Abraham was a White disciple of Dièye in Santa Barbara); and Rashiida Akbar and Dr. Mark Perrot, interview by author, March 22, 2006 (Akbar and Perrot were African American members of Khidmatul Khadim). Besides being a Murid shaykh, Dièye was also a politician and chief of a political party. He sat for years on the Municipal Council of Saint-Louis and eventually held the position of deputy mayor. He also served as a member of the Senegalese Parliament. Today, his son, Bamba Dièye, is a member of the Senegalese National Assembly representing the party that Dièye founded.

63. Amadu Dramé, interview by author, May 30, 2010.

64. Aale Fall, interview by author, May 16, 2010.

65. My informants in Paris, especially university graduates and early disciples of Dièye, insist on this aspect of his discourse.

66. Bamba Dièye, interview by author, April 14, 2006.

67. The objection of the Murid community of France, dominated by the Wolof-speaking and traditionally educated traders, was related to the method and the leadership, which was composed mostly of students in French institutions of higher education. The Senegalese government objected to the original list of speakers that included Cheikh Anta Diop and Abdoulaye Wade, both leaders of political parties opposed to President Senghor. See Yunus Jóob, interview by author, May 26, 2010; Cheikh Sall, interview by author, May 26, 2010; and Dramé, interview.

68. Diop, "Les associations Mourides," 197–206.

69. For a theoretical analysis of the concept of "economic enclave" and its application to a migrant community, see Alejandro Portes, "The Social Origins of the Cuban Enclave Economy of Miami," *Social Prospect* 30, no. 4 (1987): 340–72.

70. Njaay, interview; Aaly Sidibe, interview by author, May 9, 2011. Hotel de France was destroyed in 1982 because of a sanitary hazard. Finding decent housing was and continues to be a challenge for African immigrants in France.

71. On Senegalese presence in La Goutte d'Or, see Paul Liza Rivers, "La Goutte-d'Or, succursale de l'entrepreuneuriat sénégalais: Un espace intermédiaire dans un commerce circulatoire," *Hommes et Migrations* 1286–87 (July–October 2010): 138–48.

72. I was particularly struck when I heard a South Asian merchant selling roasted peanuts shout the word *gerte*, which means "peanuts" in Wolof.
73. Alasaan Mbay, interview by author, June 3, 2010.
74. Diop, "Les associations Mourides," 199. Diop offers an extensive discussion of Dièye's struggle with the leftist Senegalese students and the conservative Murid traders of the neighborhood of Gare de Lyon.
75. Abdoulaye Guèye, "De la religion chez les intellectuels africains en France: l'Odyssée d'un référent identitaire," *Cahiers d'Études Africaines* 162 (2001): 9–20, http://etudesafricaines.revues.org/documents87.html. Also see Donal Cruise O'Brien, *Symbolic Confrontations: Muslims Imagining the State in Africa* (New York: Palgrave Macmillan, 2003), 85.
76. Diop, "Les associations Mourides," 200.
77. Jacques Barou notes that African students in France numbered 32,398 in 1986. See Jacques Barou, "Les migrations africaines en France: Des 'navigateurs' au regroupement familial," *Revue Française des Affaires Sociales* 1 (1993): 193–205. Many of these students came from Senegal. The University of Dakar, which was the only university in Senegal then, has long been part of the French university network. Students were sent to France to pursue graduate education. In addition, some Senegalese students who graduated from universities in North Africa and the Middle East also joined French universities to complete their doctoral degrees.
78. Murid Ñaŋ, interview by author, July 8, 2011.
79. Sall, interview.
80. Diop, "Les associations Mourides," 197.
81. The concept of Ndigël (order, recommendation) that Dièye used for the title of his journal is central to Murid ideology. It is the instrument through which the leaders of the Murid order (or shaykhs) administer their flock and transform their will into power. The disciple is supposed to strictly follow the leader's commands.
82. Jean Copans, "Espaces mourides, territoires étatiques sénégalais et mondiaux: Comment l'appartenance confrérique interpelle l'instance nationale," *Islam et Sociétés au Sud du Sahara* 2 (2010): 77–94.
83. I emphasize here the geographic dimension of "public sphere." See Cheikh Anta Babou, "Urbanizing Mystical Islam: Making Murid Space in the Cities of Senegal," *International Journal of African Historical Studies* 40, no. 2 (2007): 197–223.
84. Anonymous, interview by author, May 30, 2010. The suggestion that Murid traders opposed the diffusion of Ahmadu Bamba's teachings seems exaggerated. The contention was probably about the content and nature of the teachings and the means by which they were disseminated.
85. Quoted in O'Brien, *Symbolic Confrontations*, 87.
86. Some years ago, a great-grandson of Ahmadu Bamba circulated a mass email denouncing Dièye. And during a visit to Philadelphia in summer 2005 from Shaykh Aale Ndaw, one of Dièye's senior disciples and

successors, Murid disciple Badara Ndaw, probably on his shaykh's instruction, made and distributed tracts accusing Aale Ndaw and Dièye of usurping their status as Murid shaykh.

87. Faal, interview.
88. Faal, interview.
89. As observed by Michelle Farah Kimball, a White disciple from Santa Barbara, and Rashiida Akbar, an African American from Los Angeles, Shaykh A. Dièye was a "musical genius." He knew how to blend tunes from the Indian Ocean, Senegal, the Middle East, Europe, and North America to make beautiful songs based on his own poetry or that of Shaykh Ahmadu Bamba. Dièye's ecumenism was equally appreciated. Michelle F. Kimball, interview by author, March 19, 2006.
90. Sall and Jóob, interview by author, May 26, 2010; Amadu Dramé, interview by author, May 30, 2010; and Faal, interview.
91. Dièye formed a political party and was elected deputy mayor of his native city of Saint-Louis. Later on he was elected member of the Senegalese National Assembly.

CHAPTER 5: MAKING MURID SPACE IN PARIS

1. Quoted by Olivier Chavanon, "La topographie oubliée des immigrés en terre française," *Hommes et Migrations* 1231 (May–June 2001): 92–104, 100. Translation from the French by the author.
2. His first visit to Paris was in the 1950s.
3. Ibra Jóob, interview by author, May 23, 2010.
4. Amadou Dramé, interview by author, May 30, 2010.
5. Dramé is the only Muslim of sub-Saharan descent that Gilles Kepel mentions in his discussion of Islam in France. See Gilles Kepel, *Allah in the West: Islamic Movements in America and Europe* (Stanford, CA: Stanford University Press, 1997), 192. Dramé was for five years the host of a weekly Islamic program entitled *connaître l'Islam* (To know Islam) initiated by the government of Mitterrand and broadcasted by the public TV network TF1. See Dramé, interview.
6. The Creil schoolgirl veil affairs started in September 1989 when three Muslim girls (out of a total enrollment of five hundred Muslim pupils) at the Gabriel-Havez Middle School at Creil, fifty kilometers north of Paris, appeared in class wearing their Muslim head coverings in defiance of school regulation. This event and the controversies it generated gripped the French press and political scene for months and marked the beginning of an acrimonious debate about Islam and immigration in France that continues today. For more on the topic see, Françoise Gaspard and Farhad Khosrokhavar, *Le Foulard de la République* (Paris: La Découverte, 1995).
7. Kepel, *Allah in the West*, 151; Cesari notes that "until the early 1970s, there were no Islamic cultural signs within urban spaces [in France]." See Jocelyne Cesari, "Mosques in French Cities: Towards the End of

a Conflict?," *Journal of Ethnic and Migration Studies* 31, no. 6 (2005): 1025–43, 1027.

8. Saer Njaay, the treasurer of the main *dahira* in charge of organizing Shaykh Murtada's visits, said that on two different occasions he paid a few hundred dollars for cleaning fees. Saer Njaay, interview by author, May 23, 2010.

9. Njaay, interview; and Dramé, interview.

10. See Saer Njaay, interview by author, July 10, 2011. Njaay was the one Caliph Abdul Ahad was talking to.

11. Jóob, interview. Jóob quoted the letter during our interview. The letter dated from 1979, and it was the caliph's response to a letter that Jóob, a leader of the Murid community in Paris, sent him along with a modest sum of money. This was the result of some of the first donations collected from Murid disciples in Paris.

12. See Victoria Ebin, "Making Room vs. Creating Space: The Construction of Spatial Categories by Itinerant Mourids Traders," in *Making Muslim Space in North America and Europe*, ed. Barbara Daly Metcalf (Berkeley: University of California Press, 1996), 92–110.

13. Sulaymaan Juuf, interview by author, May 20, 2010. Juuf was head of the Murid house of Taverny.

14. Jóob, interview. Jóob was present at the meeting, which took place in 1990 or 1991 after Shaykh Murtalla spearheaded a similar initiative in North York City in 1989.

15. Dramé, interview.

16. Gilles Kepel, *Les banlieues de l'Islam* (Paris: Seuil, 1987), 244.

17. Kepel, *Les banlieues*, 294; also see Cesari, "Mosques in French Cities."

18. This perception is changing due to events such as the recent invasion of northern Mali by a mixed group of Black and Arab jihadists and the violent campaign of Boko Haram in Nigeria.

19. There were also suspicions of mismanagement. See Saer Njaay, interview by author, July 11, 2011.

20. Njaay, interview.

21. Abdulaay Ley, interview by author, May 23, 2010.

22. Jóob, interview.

23. Njaay, interview.

24. See INSEE, Commune d'Aulnay-sous-Bois (93005) Population, accessed March 28, 2014, http:// www.Insee.fr/fr/themes/tableau_local .asp?; and Ley, interview. Ley reported the mayor of Aulnay's statement that the commune was home to forty different nationalities. A correspondent of *Le Soleil*, the Senegalese state-owned newspaper, estimated the number of people of Senegalese nationality living in Aulnay in 1999 at 250. See Mouhamadou M. Dia, *Le Soleil*, September 14, 1999.

25. See, for example, Eric Ross, "Globalising Touba: Expatriate Disciples in the World City Network," *Urban Studies* 48, no. 14 (2011): 2929–52. In this article Ross discusses the processes through which the values and

structures of the Murid holy city of Tuubaa are being diffused throughout the Global North.

26. People can now watch these matches live through Senegalese TV channels accessible through commercial satellites or internet streaming.

27. Salem describes the hostile attitude of the merchants and population of Strasbourg toward Murid street peddlers in the 1970s and 1980s. They were not only subject to racist treatment in being refused service by restaurant waiters and bus drivers, but they also suffered violent assaults. See "De Dakar à Paris, des diasporas d'artisans et de commerçants, étude socio-géographique du commerce sénégalais en France" (PhD diss., École des Hautes Études en Sciences Sociales, 1983). More recently, Senegalese vendors were murdered in Italy by angry right-wing extremists. See "Italy: Gunman Kills Two Senegalese Merchants," *New York Times*, December 13, 2011, http://www.nytimes.com/2011/12/14/world/europe/italy-gunman-kills-2-senegalese-merchants.html. These sorts of incidents are so recurrent that they have become almost banal.

28. Jóob, interview.

29. See INSEE, Commune de Taverny.

30. Imam N'Sangou, interview by author, May 22, 2010.

31. Proponents of this idea include the European Council of the Fatwa, based in London, Muslim intellectuals such as Taha Jabir, the chairman of the Fiqh Council of North America, and Tariq Ramadan, a leading Swiss Muslim intellectual and activist who has been influential in the debate on Islam in France and across Europe.

32. N'Sangou, interview.

33. N'Sangou, interview.

34. For more on Hizbut Tarqiyya and Aatu Jaañ, see Cheikh Guèye, *Touba: La capitale des mourides* (Paris: Karthala, 2002), 239–47.

35. Sulaymaan Juuf, interview by author, May 22, 2010.

36. Juuf, interview.

37. N'Sangou, interview.

38. Juuf, interview.

39. See "Migrants Being Sold as Slaves," CNN, November 13, 2017, video, 6:49, https://www.cnn.com/videos/world/2017/11/13/libya-migrant-slave-auction-lon-orig-md-ejk.cnn.

40. Kepel, *Les banlieues*, 129. One needs to be reminded that Turkey was an imperial power that dominated most of the Arab world for centuries, and the memory of this history likely fuels the hostility between the two communities as well.

41. Although my interviewees regarding the tensions between Taverny and Aulnay did not explicitly request anonymity, I have decided to keep them anonymous. Many of them are still involved in running the two houses, and the tensions have not completely subsided.

42. Anonymous, interview by author, May 22, 2010.

43. Juuf, interview.

44. My interviewee recounts an instance where a member of the Mbakke family got angry when the leadership of the house declined to fund and help organize an event he wanted to hold in the house for his disciples. Anonymous, interview by author, July 11, 2011.
45. Juuf, interview.
46. Women play prominent roles in Sufi Islam, and some even enjoy leadership roles as shaykhas (shaykha is the title of a female shaykh). They are particularly visible and active during pilgrimages and pious visits to shrines. See, for example, Catherine Mayeur-Jaouen, *Pèlerinages d'Ègypte: Histoire de la piété Copte et Musulmane XVe-XXe siècles* (Paris: Editions EHES, 2005).
47. The sharing of food is an important ritual in most religions, although Murid emphasis on this practice, especially under their fourth caliph, Shaykh Saaliu, may be unique.
48. Joseph Hill, *Wrapping Authority: Women Islamic Leaders in a Sufi Movement in Dakar, Senegal* (Toronto: Toronto University Press, 2018).
49. On the dahira Maam Jaara Buso, see Eva Evers Rosander, "Mame Diarra Bousso: La bonne mère de Porokhane, Sénégal," *Africa* 58, nos. 3–4 (2003): 296–317.
50. Beth Buggenhagen, *Muslim Families in Global Senegal* (Bloomington: Indiana University Press, 2011); also see Cheikh Anta Babou, "Migration and Cultural Change: Money, 'Caste,' Gender, and Social Status among Senegalese Female Hair Braiders in the United States," *Africa Today* 55, no. 2 (Spring 2009): 1–22.
51. Mouhamadou M. Dia, a correspondent of the Senegalese state-owned daily, *Le Soleil*, reported a meeting between the mayor of Aulnay-sous-Bois and Shaykh Murtada Mbacke, see Mouhamadou M. Dia, *Le Soleil*, September 14, 1999.
52. Ley, interview. Ley is the former head of the house of Aulnay.
53. Ley, interview.
54. Juuf, interview. "Rural community" is the official administrative designation for Tuubaa, although the holy city of the Murids is now the second-largest city in Senegal after the capital, Dakar.
55. Juuf, interview.
56. Personal conversation with author, June 14, 2015.
57. Personal conversation with author, June 14, 2015.

CHAPTER 6: UNLIKELY MIGRATION

1. A small community of Senegalese immigrants resided in the United States during the interwar era. These were seamen in the French merchant marine who debarked in the port of New York by the end of World War I or were captured by the allies during World War II. Battling Siki, a Senegalese from Saint-Louis who was boxing's first African world champion, migrated to New York in the 1920s. From the mid-1960s, a small contingent of Senegalese students enrolled in universities across

the East Coast. See Ira de Augustine Reid, *The Negro Immigrant: His Background, Characteristics and Social Adjustment, 1899–1937* (New York: Columbia University Press, 1939); Lamine Diakhaté, *Chalys d'Harlem* (Paris: L'Harmattan, 1980); Peter Benson, *Battling Siki: A Tale of Ring Fixes, Race and Murder in the 1920s* (Fayetteville: University of Arkansas Press, 2006). See also Mbaye Caam, interview by author, May 17, 1999; and Mamadu Ñaŋ, interview by author, April 14, 2018.

2. The *2009 Yearbook of Immigration Statistics* (Washington, DC: United States Department of Homeland Security, Office of Immigration Statistics, 2010), 69, reveals that twenty-five thousand Senegalese immigrants lived in the New York City area. This figure does not include the large number of undocumented immigrants not accounted for. Sociologist Seydou Kanté, author of a book on Senegalese migration to France and the United States, relying on information from the Senegalese consulate and interviews, estimates that 65 percent of Senegalese in New York are Murid. See *La géopolitique de l'émigration sénégalaise en France et aux Etats Unis* (Paris: L'Harmattan, 2014), 148. Since there is no census of Murids in New York, accurate numbers do not exist, but empirical evidence suggests Murids constitute the majority of Senegalese in New York and the United States. They entered the country in large numbers before the tightening of immigration laws.

3. Nigerians and Ghanaians form the two largest communities of sub-Saharan African immigrants in the United States and in New York, but they have a less prominent presence in Harlem.

4. See Michael L. Fleisher, "Visions of Dallas: A Study of Senegalese Immigration to the United States" (unpublished manuscript, 1991), hard copy, 16. Bawol-Bawol typically refers to Murid traders in the cities of Senegal. The word "Bawol" designates the region of western-central Senegal, the birthplace and heartland of the Muridiyya order. Among Wolof, the inhabitants of a region are named by doubling the name of their region, thus Bawol-Bawol are inhabitants of Bawol; Waalo-Waalo are inhabitants of the region of Waalo.

5. Caam, interview; and Mamadu Ñaŋ, interview by author, May 14, 2018.

6. Joel Millman, "Caste Party: Africa Arrives in America," *APF Reporter* 17 (1996): 1–5.

7. Scott L. Malcolmson, "West of Eden: The Mouride Ethic and the Spirit of Capitalism," *Transition* 71 (1996): 26–45, 33–34.

8. Sylviane Diouf, interview by author, June 10, 2016; also see Sylviane Diouf-Camara, "Senegalese in New York: A Model Minority?," trans. Richard Phicox, *Black Renaissance/Renaissance Noire* 1, no. 2 (1997): 92–116.

9. Diana Ndiaye and G. Ndiaye, "Creating the Vertical Village: Senegalese Traditions of Immigration and Transnational Cultural Life," in *The New African Diaspora in North America*, ed. Kwado Konadu-Agyemang, Baffour K. Takyi, and John A. Arthur (Lanham, MD: Lexington, 2006).

10. Ahmed Sugu, interview by author, April 6, 2018. My own observations confirm the information Mr. Sugu provided.

11. For more on the moodu-moodu, see Malick Ndiaye, *Les Modou-Modou: Ou ethos du développement au Sénégal* (Dakar: Dakar University Press, 1998).

12. See, for example, the work of Abdoulaye Kane on the Haal Pulaar migration to France: Abdoulaye Kane, "Tontines and Village Cash Boxes along the Tilogne-Dakar-Paris Emigration Route," in *Informal Savings Funds from the Global Periphery to the Core?*, ed. Abram de Swann and Marcel van der Linden (Amsterdam: Askant, 2005), 97–120. This chapter is a summary of his dissertation. Also see Benjamin Soares, "An African Muslim Saint and His Followers in France," *Journal of Ethnic and Migration Studies* 30, no. 5 (2004): 913–27.

13. See April Gordon, "The New Diaspora: African Immigration to the United States," *Journal of Third World Studies* 15, no. 1 (1998): 89–91. Also see Marilyn Halter and Violet Showers Johnson, *African and American: West Africans in Post–Civil Rights America* (New York: New York University Press, 2014), 24.

14. Lara Putman, "Provincializing Harlem: The Negro Metropolis as Northern Frontier of a Connected Caribbean," *Modern/Modernity* 20, no. 3 (2013): 469–84, 469.

15. Mamadou Diouf, "The Senegalese Murid Trade Diaspora and the Making of a Vernacular Cosmopolitanism," trans. Steven Rendall, *Public Culture* 12, no. 3 (Fall 2000): 679–702.

16. Sëriñ Lo, interview by author, April 21, 2018.

17. Ahmed Sugu, interview by author, May 6, 2018.

18. One of my interviewees, Sëriñ Baabu, recounts that in June 1986, over the course of fifteen days, they had been expelled from three hotels: Hotel Bryant, Hotel Sinton, and Hotel Rio. They finally found a room at the Parkview Hotel. When they checked into the hotel, they found one Senegalese tenant there. From then on, Parkview, better known as Hotel 110, became the headquarters of Senegalese and Murid immigrants in New York City. See Sëriñ Baabu, interview by author, May 23, 2018.

19. See Fleisher, "Visions of Dallas."

20. Interview quoted by Papa Demba Fall, "Ethnic and Religious Ties in African Emigration: Senegalese Immigrants in the United States," *Studia Africana* 13 (April 2002): 83.

21. Diouf-Camara, "Senegalese in New York," 94.

22. See US Department of Homeland Security, *Department of Homeland Security, Yearbook Immigration Statistics* (Washington, DC: Office of Immigration Statistics, 1999), https://www.dhs.gov/sites/default/files/publications/Yearbook_Immigration_Statistics_1999.pdf.

23. Halter and Johnson, *African and American*, 14; also see Ira Berlin, *The Making of African America* (New York: Viking, 2010).

24. Donna L. Perry, "Rural Ideologies and Urban Imaginings: Wolof Immigrants in New York City," *Africa Today* 44, no. 2 (April–June 1997): 229–59, 234.
25. Ahmed Sugu, Mbacké, interview by author, March 22, 2000; Paul Stoller, *Money Has No Smell: The Africanization of New York City* (Chicago: University of Chicago Press, 2002), 19; Victoria Ebin, "Les commerçants mourides à Marseille et à New York," in *Grands commerçants d'Afrique de l'Ouest*, ed. Emmanual Grégoire and Pascal Labazée (Paris: Karthala, 1993), 101–22, 115; and Donna L. Perry, "Rural Ideologies and Urban Imaginings: Wolof Immigrants in New York City," *Africa Today* 44, no. 2 (April–June 1997): 229–59, 234.
26. Lo, interview.
27. Daam Baabu, interview by author, June 11, 2016.
28. Halter and Johnson, *African and American*, 105.
29. See Seydou Kanté, *Géopolitique de l'émigration Sénégalaise*, 167. I also refer to Ibrahima Sow, interview by author, April 24, 2018. Sow was the president of the Association of Senegalese in America.
30. Daam Baabu, interview.
31. Quoted in "New York and Touba, Senegal," *Economist*, June 17, 1999.
32. Gordon, "New Diaspora," 88.
33. Celia W. Dugger, "Immigrant Influence Rises in New York City in the 1990s," *New York Times*, January 9, 1997.
34. Purnima Erichsen, Halimatou Nimaga, and Hollis Wear, "Harlem's Little Senegal, a Shelter or a Home: A Conversation with Senegalese Immigrants in New York City," Humanity in Action USA, accessed June 8, 2018, https://www.humanityinaction.org/knowledgebase/133-harlem-s-little-senegal-a-shelter-or-a-home-a-conversation-with-senegalese-immigrants-in-new-york-city.
35. Victoria Ebin, "'Little Sénégal' contre la renaissance de Harlem: Les immigrés sénégalais et la gentrification de Harlem," *Revue Asylon(s)*, March 3, 2008, http://www.reseau-terra.eu/article712.html. Also see Sow, interview.
36. See Susan Sachs, "In Harlem's Fabric, Bright Threads of Senegal," *New York Times*, July 28, 2003, https://www.nytimes.com/2003/07/28/nyregion/in-harlem-s-fabric-bright-threads-of-senegal.html.
37. See Serigne Mansour Tall, "Kara International Exchange: Un nouvel instrument financier pour les courtiers mourides de l'axe Dakar-New York" (paper presented at the international colloquium of APAD, June 5–8, 1996, University of Hohenheim [Stuttgart]), 9. Tall notes that in 1994, Kara's office in New York transferred three billion CFA to Senegal ($6 million).
38. See Mouhamed Moustapha Kane, "L'empreinte de l'Islam confrérique dans le paysage commercial sénégalais: Islam et société en Sénégambie," *Islam et sociétés au sud du Sahara* 8 (1994): 17–41; see also Allen Roberts and Mary Nooter Roberts, *A Saint in the City: Sufi Arts of*

Urban Senegal (Los Angeles: University of California Fowler Museum of Cultural History, 2003).

39. See Cheikh Anta Babou, "Brotherhood Solidarity, Education and Migration: The Role of the *Dahiras* among the Murid Muslim Community of New York," *African Affairs* 101, no. 403 (2002): 151–70.

40. Zain Abdullah, *Black Mecca: The African Muslims of Harlem* (Oxford: Oxford University Press, 2010). This is the first monograph devoted to the study of Senegalese in Harlem; Stoller's *Money Has No Smell* has done similar work focusing on immigrants from Niger.

41. See Abdullah, *Black Mecca*.

42. Daam Baabu, interview.

43. Fadel Gey, interview by author, April 13, 2018.

44. Linda Beck, "An American's View of Muridism and the Murids of New York," in *What Is the Muridiyya?* (New York: Murid Islamic Community in America, 2001), 34–35.

45. Jonathan Gill, *Harlem: The Four Hundred Year History from Dutch Village to Capital of Black America* (New York: Grove, 2011), 385–420.

46. Claude McKay, *Harlem: Negrometropolis: An Account of the World's Largest Black Community during the Eventful Years of the Twenties and Thirties* (New York: Harvest, 1968). Also see Gill, *Harlem*, chapter 11.

47. Aly Kheury Ndaw, *Les Sénégalais de New York* (Paris: L'Harmattan, 2012), 104.

48. Richard Schaffer and Neil Smith, "The Gentrification of Harlem?," *Annals of the Association of American Geographers* 76, no. 3 (1986): 347–65, 353.

49. Dinkins has a history with the Muridiyya. As president of the Borough of Manhattan, he met the Murid Shaykh Murtada Mbakke in Harlem in 1988. He proclaimed July 28 as Ahmadu Bamba Day in New York City. More on this in the next chapter.

50. Ndaw, *Les Sénégalais de New York*, 104.

51. Fallu Baabu, interview by author, April 24, 2018.

52. Baabu, interview.

53. Amar Faal, interview by author, July 10, 2017.

54. See Nemata Blyden, "Relationships among Blacks in the Diaspora: African and Caribbean Immigrants and American-Born Blacks," in *Africans in Global Migration: Searching for Promised Lands*, ed. John A. Arthur, Joseph Takougang, and Thomas Owusu (Lanham, MD: Lexington, 2012), 161–74; John L. Jackson Jr., *Harlemworld: Doing Race and Class in Contemporary Black America* (Chicago: University of Chicago Press, 2001); Abdullah, *Black Mecca*; Stoller, *Money*, 23. Fleisher discusses Senegalese immigrants' perceptions of African Americans. See Fleisher, "Visions of Dallas." Umoja, a 2002 media project run by high school students in New York City, was launched to facilitate intercultural communications in Harlem following violent confrontations between African and African American youth. One of

its productions was turned into a movie that was broadcasted on public television.

55. Jackson, *Harlemworld*, 4.
56. For a theoretical analysis of the concept of "economic enclave" and its application to a migrant community see Alejandro Portes, "The Social Origins of the Cuban Enclave Economy of Miami," *Social Prospect* 30, no. 4 (1987): 340–72.
57. *Mawlud* is a Muslim holy day celebrating the birthday of Prophet Muhammad. It is mostly celebrated by Sufis and Shia. More on the relations between the Murids and the Malcolm Shabazz mosque in the next chapter.
58. "Little Senegal" or "Le Petit Sénégal" refers to the portion of West 116th Street between Frederick Douglass and Malcolm X boulevards where immigrants from Senegal form the majority of business owners and the general population. Some people use "Little Africa," but this name designates the area between Fifth Avenue and Morningside, where the African population is more mixed. See Jenna Belhumeur, "You Say Malcolm X Boulevard, They Say Lenox," *Global City, New York City*, October 2, 2014, http://globalcitynyc.com/2014/10/02/you-say-malcolm-x-blvd-they-say-lenox/.
59. The expression "Little Touba" was first used by scholar Linda Beck. See Ousmane Kane, email message to author, January 10, 2019.
60. Gey, interview. *Halal* means "licit" and can be thought of as "kosher" for Muslims. It is food slaughtered or prepared according to Islamic prescriptions.
61. Chalys Leye's restaurant, Leye Luncheonette, opened in New York during the 1920s, was probably the first business opened by a Senegalese national in Harlem. See Diakhaté, *Chalys d'Harlem*.
62. Gey, interview.
63. "New York and Touba."
64. Stoller, *Money*, 19.
65. Ousmane Kane, *The Homeland Is the Arena: Religion, Transnationalism and the Integration of Senegalese Immigrants in America* (Oxford: Oxford University Press, 2011), 69.
66. Cheikh Anta Babou, "Migration and Cultural Change: Money, 'Caste,' Gender, and Social Status among Senegalese Female Hair Braiders in the United States," *Africa Today* 55, no. 2 (Spring 2009): 1–22.
67. Babou, "Migration and Cultural Change," 4
68. See Kanté, *La géopolitique*, 190. Also see Republic of Senegal, Ministry of Finances, *Enquête Sénégalaise auprès des ménages*, Direction de la Prévision et de la Statistique (Dakar: ESAM II, 1999), 154. This official Senegalese government document estimates that from the late 1990s, more Senegalese women migrated to the United States than men. Ibrahima Sow, the president of the Association of Senegalese in America, referring to his organization's records, shares this assessment suggesting

that the population of female Senegalese immigrants in the United States has achieved near parity with their male counterparts. See Sow, interview. The feminization of Senegalese migration is a recent phenomenon. The first generation of Senegalese male immigrants did not encourage their wives to join them in the United States. Most women who joined the migration were divorced, single, or students who migrated to the United States from France or Canada. More recently, the growing number of professionals and students arriving with their wives or marrying locally changed the situation.

69. Babou, "Migration and Cultural Change."
70. Sow, interview. Also see Halter and Jonson, *African and American*, 85–97.
71. See "New York and Touba."
72. Beck, "An American's View," 34
73. Abdullah, *Black Mecca*, 128.
74. Richard Schaffer and Neil Smith, "The Gentrification of Harlem?," *Annals of the Association of American Geographers* 76, no. 3 (1986): 347–365, 352.
75. Kathryn Emily Kendrick Wright, "Senegalese Migrants in Harlem and Denver and a Re-Framing of the Relationships between Development, Transnational Migration, Integration and Place" (PhD diss., University of Colorado Boulder, 2017), 110.
76. See Sharon Otterman, "Malcolm X. Mosque No. 7. Hotel Theresa. Remembering Harlem's Muslim History," *New York Times*, August 12, 2018, https://www.nytimes.com/2018/08/12/nyregion/muslim-history -harlem-nyc.html?.
77. Kim Bakker, "Behind New York's Housing Crisis: Weakened Laws and Fragmented Regulation," *New York Times*, May 20, 2018.
78. Sow, interview.
79. The five stores are as follows: Naawel I and II, which have relocated to Dakar; two stores owned by a merchant named Móodu Wàdd; and Daaru Salaam, a grocery store owned by a prominent member of the Mbakke family.
80. Ibrahima Sow, interview by author, April 24, 2018.
81. The pressure that landlords exert on Black tenants is compounded by some White tenants' racial prejudices. In an opinion piece in the *New York Times*, the New York native and writer Michael Henry Adams refers to what one landlord operating in Little Senegal told him about one of his White tenants: "We're not paying that much money to have black people living in our building!" *New York Times*, May 29, 2016.
82. Bakker, "Behind New York's Housing Crisis."
83. Sow, interview.
84. See Gale Brewer and Bill Perkins, speeches, Adam Clayton Powell Plaza, July 28, 2018, author's field notes. Brewer is president of the Borough of Manhattan and Perkins is a NYC councilman.

85. Persistent but unverified rumors about ICE agents boarding Greyhound buses and train carts to arrest undocumented immigrants have spread among African immigrants since the election of President Trump. Some green-card holders who did not intend to seek naturalization are now doing so, fearing that they could be stopped at the border or might have their card taken back.

86. Senegalese Ministry of Finances, *Enquête*, 1999.

CHAPTER 7: MAKING ROOM FOR THE
MURIDIYYA IN NEW YORK CITY

1. Barbara Daly Metcalf, ed., *Making Muslim Space in North America and Europe* (Berkeley: University of California Press, 1996).

2. By Sunni Islam I refer to the Islamic tradition that follows the Four Rightly Guided Caliphs as opposed to the Shia tradition loyal to Imam Aly. I do not include the so-called proto-Islamic Black organizations such as the Moorish Science Temple and the NOI in the Sunni tradition.

3. Roi Ottley, *New World A-Coming* (Cambridge, UK: Riverside, 1943), 56.

4. For more on African American Islam, see Kambiz GhaneaBassiri, *A History of Islam in the United States: From the New World to the New World Order* (Cambridge: Cambridge University Press, 2010); Michael Gomez, *Black Crescent: The Experience and Legacy of African Muslims in the Americas* (Cambridge: Cambridge University Press, 2005); Aminah Beverly McCloud, *African American Islam* (London: Routledge, 1995); Jane Idleman Smith and Yvonne Yazbeck Haddad, *Muslim Communities in North America* (New York: State University of New York Press, 1994); and Eric Lincoln, *The Black Muslims in America*, 3rd ed. (Trenton, NJ: Africa World, 1994).

5. Abdulaay Caam, interview by author, August 19, 2013.

6. See Masjid Malcolm Shabazz website, accessed August 14, 2018, http://themasjidmalcolmshabazz.com/imam-pasha.php.

7. Ousmane Kane, *The Homeland Is the Arena: Religion, Transnationalism and the Integration of Senegalese Immigrants in America* (Oxford: Oxford University Press, 2011).

8. Murtada Njaay, interview by author, June 10, 2016. Njaay was general secretary of MICA and a long-term resident in Harlem; Caam, interview.

9. A few of my interviewees refer to Imam Pasha as unfriendly but refrain from harsh criticism.

10. Scott L. Malcolmson, "West of Eden: The Mouride Ethic and the Spirit of Capitalism," *Transition* 71 (1996): 26–45.

11. Malcolmson, "West of Eden."

12. Caam, interview.

13. For an extensive discussion of the history of the Muridiyya, see Cheikh Anta Babou, *Fighting the Greater Jihad: Amadu Bamba and the*

Founding of the Muridiyya of Senegal, 1853–1913 (Athens: Ohio University Press, 2007).

14. This is the case, for example, of Balozi Harvey, and Yahya Coats, an African American leader of the Murid community of Cleveland, Ohio, who links his attraction to the Muridiyya with his discovery of the story of Kunta Kinte told by Alex Haley in his novel *Roots* and in the movie about Malcolm X. Victoria Ebin also observes that the African American women who joined the Murid dahira of Brooklyn in the 1980s were fierce cultural nationalists who could not envision following a Muslim leader who was not Black. See Victoira Ebin, "Commerçants et missionnaires: Une confrérie musulmane sénégalaise à New York," *Hommes et Migrations* 1132 (May 1990): 25–31; and Beverly Mack, "Fodiology: African American Heritage Connections with West African Islam," *Journal of West African History* 4, no. 2 (Fall 2018): 103–29, 115.

15. I interviewed Balozi in his living room on July 15, 2007, and was impressed by the rich collection of African arts displayed.

16. See Balozi, interview by author, July 15, 2007, and my interview with his collaborator in the Muridiyya, Muhammad Abdu al-Rahman. Also see Balozi's personal website, accessed August 23, 2015, http://balozirmzharvey.com/. Also see Abdulaay Caam, interview by author, August 19, 2013; Caam, interview by author, July 14, 2017; and Murtada Njaay, interview by author, June 10, 2016. Njaay was general secretary of the Murid Islamic Community of America.

17. See Ahmed Sugu, interview by author, in March 20, 2000, and May 6, 2018.

18. Kane, *Homeland*, 64.

19. Balozi, interview.

20. This must be an early version of the International Roots Festival instituted in 1994 by Yaya Jammeh, the former president of the Gambia. The festival, named after Alex Haley's novel *Roots*, takes place in James's Island and the village of Juffurey, where Haley purports that his ancestor Kunta Kinte was abducted from and brought to the United States as a slave.

21. For more on the origin of this community see Ebin, "Commerçants et missionnaires."

22. Mustafa Mbakke, interview by author, August 10, 2018; also see Mustafa Mbakke, "Moustapha Mbacke, fils de Serigne Cheikh Mbacke Gainde Fatma, candidat a la presidentielle 2012 'Mon père Gaïndé Fatma a remis 35 millions Cfa à Wade pour créer le Pds,'" interview, *l'Observateur*, September 14, 2018, https://www.xibar.net/Entretien-MOUSTAPHA-MBACKE-FILS-DE-SERIGNE-CHEIKH-MBACKE-GAINDE-FATMA-CANDIDAT-A-LA-PRESIDENTI-ELLE-2012-Mon-pere_a39690.html.

23. Those Murid shaykhs are Sëriñ Móodu Buso Jeng Mbakke and Saaliu Mbakke, both grandsons of Ahmadu Bamba and less prestigious Murid clerics.

24. It is unlikely that Balozi invited the shaykh. He told me that he was surprised when he received a call from Shaykh Mustafa telling him that Shaykh Murtada wanted to meet with him. Balozi, interview by author, July 15, 2007.
25. L. C., interview by author, July 14, 2017. Many of my interviewees who evoke these disputes are reluctant to elaborate.
26. On the meeting between Shaykh Murtada and Balozi, I refer to the following interviews: Balozi, interview; Mbakke, interview; Xaasim Mbakke, interview by author, December 18, 2018. Xaasim Mbakke was the son and secretary of Sëriñ Murtada.
27. Balozi, interview.
28. Balozi, interview.
29. Half a dozen cities have either officially recognized Ahmadu Bamba Day or have a day devoted to Shaykh Murtada. These include New York, Chicago, Atlanta, Cincinnati, Philadelphia, Detroit, and Washington, DC.
30. Shaykh Murtada suggested an Arabic name.
31. Shaykh Murtada to the Murid community in America, June 28, 1991. I thank Muhammad Abdu al-Rahman, a close African American disciple of Shaykh Murtada, for sharing this letter with me. See copy in appendixes.
32. Muhammad Abdu al-Rahman, interview by author, June 10, 2016.
33. Xaasim Mbakke, interview with author, December 18, 2018.
34. Opposition to Shaykh Murtada's decision was real but muted. A Murid will never openly admit objecting to his shaykh's command. One of my sources said that he was present at a meeting where the leadership of the Murid community of New York debated the appointment of Balozi as their chief, and he remembers that many were opposed to Shaykh Murtada's recommendation. Anonymous, interview by author, May 30, 2010. This information is now apocryphal. One African American disciple in New York recognized that Senegalese Murids did not heed the shaykh's suggestion because they did not understand his vision. Anonymous, interview by author, May 5, 1999.
35. The Arabic noun "shaykh" refers to the leader of a tribe or to a highly learned Muslim or scholar. Among Sufi Muslims the shaykh is a spiritual guide with the power to initiate new disciples.
36. Sëriñ Lo, interview by author, April 21, 2018.
37. Ajami is a writing system that uses Arabic script (alphabet) to write a foreign language. For more on Wolof ajami see chapter 3.
38. Victoria Ebin estimates there were fifty African American women who frequented the Brooklyn dahira in 1987–89. These African Americans, mostly from working-class backgrounds, gravitated toward the African Muslim Union, an organization founded by African American Muslims in the 1930s for the upliftment of African Americans. See Ebin, "Commerçants et missionnaires," 27.

39. On Timbuktu and its cultural significance in contemporary African Islam, see Ousmane O. Kane, *Beyond Timbuktu: An Intellectual History of Muslim West Africa* (Cambridge, MA: Harvard University Press, 2016).
40. Muhammad Abdu al-Rahman, interview by author, May 1999; and al-Rahman, interview.
41. Al-Rahman, interview.
42. Scholars estimate that between 7 to 20 percent of Africans enslaved in the New World were Muslims. See Michael Gomez, *Black Crescent*. Also see Sylviane Diouf, *Servants of Allah: African Muslims Enslaved in the Americas* (New York: New York University Press, 1998); and Allan D. Austin, *African Muslims in Antebellum America: A Sourcebook* (New York: Garland, 1984).
43. See Muhammad Abdu al-Rahman and Yusuf Abdu al-Rahman, *Journey of the Andu-Sahelian Peoples* (forthcoming). This book discusses the hijra project and engagement with Senegalese and African American Murids.
44. Al-Rahman, interview.
45. Al-Rahman, interview.
46. For more on this see Cheikh Anta Babou, "Globalizing African Islam from Below: West African Sufi Masters in the United States," in *Global Africa into the Twentieth Century*, ed. Dorothy Hodgson and Judith Byfield (Oakland: University of California Press, 2017), 356–66. Also see McCloud, *African America Islam*, 93–94. Two sons of Aminah Njaay, an African American Murid woman who joined the Muridiyya in 1988 or 1989, were enrolled in Shaykh Murtada's school in Ndaam near Tuubaa in the 1990s. See Aminah Njaay, interview by author, October 6, 2018.
47. I visited the school in 1991 while doing fieldwork for my diplôme d'études approfondies (DEA [French acronym], or advanced studies degree) thesis at the University of Dakar.
48. The Murid house, however, continues to collaborate with the New York City Health and Hospitals/Harlem Hospital Center. Until recently, a representative of the house was sitting on the hospital community outreach commission, and the Murids also provide Wolof translators to the hospital. See Njaay, interview. Njaay was secretary of MICA.
49. Sister Aisha McCord, interview by author, August 14, 2018.
50. Shilo Lamp Fall, interview by author, September 7, 2018. Fall was head of an African American Murid dahira in Philadelphia.
51. Sister Sultana, interview by author, September 1, 2018.
52. Fall, interview.
53. Fall, interview.
54. Sultana, interview.
55. Njaay, interview.
56. Fall, interview.

57. This is the project of Sister Aisha McCord, the lone woman on the MICA board who has developed a school curriculum to teach basic Islamic ritual practices based exclusively on Ahmadu Bamba's teachings.
58. I have been attending Ahmadu Bamba Day regularly since at least 2002, and I have seen a steady decline in African American participation.
59. Lo, interview. Lo's opinion is shared by most people I have interviewed, including Xaasim Mbakke, Shaykh Murtada's son, traveling companion, and close aide. See Mbakke, interview.
60. The current leader of MICA, appointed in 2017, was an elementary school teacher in Senegal and is proficient in English.
61. Pape Dramé, interview by author, June 11, 2016. Dramé is the current President of MICA.
62. See chapter 4 for more information on Shaykh Abdoulaye Dièye.
63. Cheikh Anta Babou, "A West African Sufi Master on the Global Stage: Cheikh Abdoulaye Dièye and the Khidmatul Khadim International Sufi School in France and the United States," *African Diaspora* 4, no. 1 (2011): 27–49.
64. Quoted by Susan Slyomovics, "The Muslim World Day Parade and 'Storefront' Mosques in New York City," in Metcalf, *Making Muslim Space*, 209.
65. Roger W. Stump, *Boundaries of Faith: Geographical Perspectives on Religious Fundamentalism* (Lanham, MD: Rowman and Littlefield, 2000), 184.
66. Thomas F. Gieryn, "A Space for Place in Sociology," *Annual Review of Sociology* 26 (2000): 463–96, 465.
67. For more on the Murid built environment, see Babou, *Fighting the Greater Jihad*, chapter 7; Eric Ross, *Sufi City: Urban Design and Archetypes in Touba* (Rochester, NY: Rochester University Press, 2006); Allen Roberts and Mary Nooter Roberts, *A Saint in the City: Sufi Arts of Urban Senegal* (Los Angeles: University of California Fowler Museum of Cultural History, 2003).
68. Roberts and Roberts, *A Saint in the City*.
69. See Regula Burckhardt Qureshi, "Transcending Space: Recitation and Community among South Asian Muslims in Canada," in Metcalf, *Making Muslim Space*, 47–48.
70. Christine Thu Nhi Dang, "Pilgrimage through Poetry: Sung Journeys within the Murid Spiritual Diaspora," *Islamic Africa* 4, no. 1 (2013): 69–101.
71. The Baay Faal, a subgroup within the Muridiyya, use drums in their ceremonies, but in this case the chanting is done in the Wolof language and does not involve the use of Bamba's sacred poetry in Arabic. For more on sacred music see Fiona McLaughlin, "'In the Name of God I Will Sing Again, Mawdo Malick the Good': Popular Music and Senegalese Sufi Tariqas," *Journal of Religion in Africa* 30, no. 2 (2000): 191–207.

72. Sëriñ Maam Moor Mbakke, the spiritual leader of the Murid diaspora, has been critical of kurels and Qasida Day. His critiques sometimes led to polemics on social media and YouTube, as was the case with the dahira of Canada. However, he is not alone in denouncing what some Murids see as excessive. I refer to my interview with Sulaymaan Juuf, the manager of the Murid house of Taverny in France, who criticizes disciples who neglect all other duties, elevating singing the qasida to the utmost form of worship. See Sulaymaan Juuf, interview by author, May 22, 2010.

73. See Saam Jóob, interview by author, June 2, 2011.

74. Cheikh Guèye, "Entre frontières économiques et frontières religieuses: Le café Touba recompose le territoire mouride," in *La ville sénégalaise: Une invention aux frontières du monde*, ed. Jean-Luc Piermay and Cheikh Sarr (Paris: Karthala, 2007), 137–51.

75. In the Majmuha, which is a collection of his correspondence, Ahmadu Bamba wrote a few verses praising God for giving the gift of coffee to humankind. He recommended that coffee drinkers say this prayer before taking a sip: "Praise to God who has sent us the best of beverages and has protected us against our enemies." See Abdul Ahad Mbakke, ed., *Majmuha: A Collection of Ahmadu Bamba's Correspondence in Arabic* (Touba, Senegal: self-pub., 1985), 32. Faliilu Mbakke, the second caliph of the Murids, reportedly recommended that disciples drink tea in the morning and coffee in late afternoon.

76. During research for my first book, *Fighting the Greater Jihad*, I visited a Murid shaykh who was diabetic and did not drink coffee. But he served me café Tuubaa and told me that he felt obligated to have his family prepare the beverage each afternoon because visitors in any Murid household expected it.

77. Café Tuubaa was apparently invented by disciples of Sëriñ Mbakke Soxna Lo, who is the son of Ahmadu Bamba's oldest grandson. His house on Allées du Centenaire in Dakar was the first place in Dakar where seasonal Murid migrants sold café Tuubaa. When on July 17, 2004, I interviewed Xaadim Jóob and Abdu Fatah Mbuub, both makers and sellers of café Tuubaa, our conversations were frequently interrupted by buyers, a few driving expensive Japanese- and German-made cars.

78. Njaay, interview.

79. See "The Community Servant," article by Pape S. Dramé, president of MICA, in the special publication of the Murid Islamic Community in America, Inc. (MICA), published on the occasion of Ahmadu Bamba Day, July 28, 2018. I also refer to Dramé, interview; and Murtada Njaay, interview by author, June 11, 2016.

80. See copies of some of these proclamations in the appendixes.

81. He visits Georgia, California, Illinois, Maryland, Michigan, New York, North Carolina, Ohio, Illinois, and Washington, DC.

82. This is how MICA founding member Ablaay Caam remembers Shaykh Murtada's admonition for Murids to participate in the parade, but all my interviewees agree on the importance that Shaykh Murtada placed on the march of July 28. Caam, interview. I also refer to my interview with Xaasim Mbakke, who particularly emphasizes the significance the parade had for his father. Mbakke said his father appreciated the chanting of Allah's name on the streets of Harlem. See Mbakke, interview.

83. Videos of the last few years of the parade are posted on YouTube. See Bichri TV International, "Bamba Day 2108 | New York City | Marche et Podium," streamed live on July 28, 2018, YouTube video, 3:34:11, https://www.youtube.com/watch?v=D3fCHKnRhvY&t=6581s, for a video of the parade held on July 28, 2018. Also see Zain Abdullah, "Sufis on Parade: The Performance of Black, African, and Muslim Identities," *Journal of the American Academy of Religion* 77, no. 2 (June 2009): 199–237; Monika Salzbrunn, "The Occupation of Public Space through Religious and Political Events: How Senegalese Migrants Became a Part of Harlem, New York," *Journal of Religion in Africa* 34, no. 4 (November 2004): 468–92. Estimates of the number of marchers are based on my observation and that of police officers present at the parade of July 28, 2016. The numbers have gone down in the last few years, reflecting Murid migration out of New York, especially to the southern United States, but also reflecting perhaps waning enthusiasm, especially since the death of Shaykh Murtada in 2004.

84. For more on Murid women and their role in the diaspora, see Beth Buggenhagen, *Muslim Families in Global Senegal* (Bloomington: Indiana University Press, 2011).

85. At the podium on July 18, 2018, speakers included Gale Brewer, president of the Borough of Manhattan, State Councilman Bill Perkins, officials dispatched by the government of Senegal, and local leaders of African religious and secular organizations.

86. Pnina Werbner, "Stamping the Earth with the Name of God: Zikr and Sacralizing of Space among British Muslims," in Metcalf, *Making Muslim Space*, 167–86.

87. I have heard this claim from almost all of my interviewees.

88. On Maam Jaara Buso, see Eva Evers Rosander, *In Pursuit of Paradise: Senegalese Women, Muridism and Migration* (Uppsala, Sweden: Nordistaka Afrikaninstutet, 2015); and Ester Guijarro, "The Mame Diarra Dahira in Diaspora: Challenging Murid Patriarchy?," *Revista de Dialectologia y Tradiciones Populares* 68, no. 11 (2013): 125–44.

89. These are some of the banners displayed during the Ahmadu Bamba Day parade on July 28, 2018. The verse is an excerpt from Ahmadou Bamba Mbacké's magnum opus, *Masalik al-Jinan* [Paths to paradise], trans. Serigne Sam Mbaye (Rabat: Dar El Kitab, 1984), see verses 47–49 on p. 28.

90. For the Ahmadu Bamba Day organized on July 28, 2018, MICA paid over $14,000 to cover overtime pay for UN personnel. Pape Dramé, interview by author, September 12, 2018. With this sum of money the conference could have easily been held in a meeting room in an upscale hotel in New York.

91. In the verse contained in his poem "Mawāhibu n-Nāfi," Bamba refers to the Prophet Muhammad as the "ocean of mercy" (generosity), but for the Murids, Bamba is the "ocean of generosity." See Sana Camara, *Sheikh Ahmadu Bamba: Selected Poems* (Leiden: Brill, 2017), verse 101 on p. 98.

92. See the recent book by an American disciple of the Muridiyya: Michelle R. Kimball, *Ahmadou Bamba: A Peacemaker for Our Time* (Kuala Lumpur: Other Press, 2019).

93. Eric Ross, "Globalising Touba: Expatriate Disciples in the World City Network," *Urban Studies* 48, no. 14 (2011): 2929–52.

CONCLUSION

1. *Ndaw* is a Wolof word with a double meaning: "youth" or "envoy" (messenger). The founders of NST (in 2017) claim both meanings: they are young (most are aged between eighteen and thirty years) and they also believe they are the authentic bearers of Ahmadu Bamba's message and are invested in bettering the Murid and African community in New York, especially those they call the "lost generation." Jonathan Bornman, who is working with me on a dissertation on Murids in New York City, devotes a chapter of his thesis to this group.

2. NST is particularly active online. Its Instagram profile and Facebook page contain hundreds of photos and videos featuring female and male members reading qasidas, worshipping, sharing foods, and socializing. The sites also serve as bulletin boards where events are advertised and fundraising events planned. See Picuki page for Ndawi Serigne Touba (@ndawist), https://www.picuki.com/profile/ndawist, and its Facebook page, Ndawi Serigne Touba Yi—Nst (@NDAWISERIGNETOUBA), https://www.facebook.com/NDAWISERIGNETOUBA.

3. The leading promoter of cyberdaara is Abdul Aziz Mbacké, a great-grandson of Ahmadu Bamba and creator of the Facebook page Majalis. See Majalis (@projetmajalis), Facebook, https://www.facebook.com /projetmajalis, and Cyberdaara, "Majalis introduces Course No. 9 of its e-Learning platform 'CyberDaara' on causes leading to the obligation of washing purification (or Sangu Set)," Facebook, August 5, 2013, https:// www.facebook.com/Cyberdaara/posts/526439640743589/.

Bibliography

INTERVIEWS

Cheikh Anta Babou Interviews, 1999–2018
Chuck Abraham, San Francisco, March 19, 2006
Abdel Qadr Aïdara, Saint-Louis, July 5, 2001
Rashida Akbar, Los Angeles, March 22, 2006
Sabura Abdu al-Kabir, Philadelphia, September 7, 2018
Muhmmad Abdu al-Rahman, New York City, May 5, 1999; June 10, 2016
Yusuf al-Rahman, New York City, June 10, 2016
Shaykh Amar, New York City, May 19, 1999; April 24, 2016,
Mamadu Abdulaay Ba, Libreville, December 16, 2014
Birahim Baabu, Dakar, June 17, 2012
Daam Baabu 1, New York City, May 1999; June 11, 2016
Daam Baabu 2, Cincinnati, April 30, 2011
Fallu Baabu, New York City, April 24, 2014
Sëriñ Baabu, Dakar, May 25, 2011; May 23, 2018
Abdu Karim Baas, Abidjan, December 22, 2014
Fallu Bajaan, Cincinnati, May 1, 2011
Amadu Basum, Libreville, December 16, 2014
Moustapha Boussougou, Dakar, June 24, 2006
Abdulaay Caam, New York City, August 19, 2013; July 14, 2018
Elhaaj Magat Caam, Dakar, February 6, 2012
Mamadu Caam, Cincinnati, April 30, 2011
Mbay Caam, Memphis, March 13, 2011
Ngañ Caam, Dakar, September 12, 1999
Yahya Coats, Cleveland, August 19, 2018
Mustafa Cuun, Dakar, May 9, 2006
Sylviane Diouf, New York City, June 10, 2016
Amadu Dramé, Paris, May 30, 2010
Pape S. Dramé, New York City, June 11, 2016
Aale Faal, Paris, May 16, 2010
Amar Faal, Dakar, July 10, 2015
Basiiru Faal, Dakar, March 21, 2010
Shilo Lamp Faal, Philadelphia, September 7, 2018
Musaa Faaty, Libreville, December 16, 2014
Fara Gay, Philadelphia, October 17, 2007

Abdu Gey, New York City, August 18, 2018
Abdulaay Gey, Dakar, July 6, 2012
Arona Gey, Grand Bassam, December 26, 2014
Elhaaj Bamba Gey, Abidjan, December 28, 2014
Elhaaj Njaga Gey, Dakar, June 11, 2004; June 16, 2004
Fadel Gey, Dakar, April 13, 2018
Mariama Gey, Memphis, March 11, 2011
Moodu Gey, Cincinnati, April 30, 2011
Sëriñ Gey, Dakar, June 17, 2004
Malik Golson, New York City, July 15, 2007
Sister Hadidah, Philadelphia, September 6, 2018
Balozi Harvey, East Orange, NJ, July 15, 2007
Moor Ja, Abidjan, December 18, 2014
Imam Paap Jaañ, Libreville, December 20, 2014
Moortaala Jaañ, Tuubaa, May 22, 2011
Mr. Jallo, Abidjan, December 29, 2014
Abiwa Jaw, Philadelphia, September 6, 2018
Bamba Jaw, Dakar, April 8, 2000; May 13, 2000
Njaga Jaw, Libreville, December 19, 2014
Ibrahima Jaxate, Grand Bassam, December 26, 2014
Sulaymaan Jaxate, Paris, May 16, 2010
Abdulaay Jéey, Paris, May 16, 2010
Bamba Jéey, Dakar, April 14, 2006
Babakar Jeŋ, Libreville, December 18, 2014
Abdulaay Jóob, Abidjan, December 23, 2014
Asan Murtalla Jóob, Libreville, December 16, 2018
Basiiru Jóob, Abidjan, December 19, 2014
Ibra Jóob, Paris, May 23, 2010
Imam Jóob, Libreville, December 16, 2014
Magat Jóob, Dakar, June 9, 2000
Murtala Jóob, Cincinnati, May 1, 2011
Saam Jóob, Pontevico, Italy, June 2, 2011
Sëriñ Jóob, Dakar, June 11, 2004
Xaadim Jóob, Dakar, July 17, 2004
Yunus Jóob, Paris, May 26, 2010
Mariam Judor, Dakar, June 24, 2006
Mbay Juuf, Memphis, March 11, 2011
Mustafa Juuf, Abidjan, December 22, 2014
Sulaymaan Juuf, Taverny, May 22, 2010
Ibra Kan, Cincinnati, May 1, 2011
Mor Kasse, Marseille, June 6, 2013
Ndongo Kebe, Paris, July 6, 2011
Michelle Farah Kimball, San Francisco, March 19, 2006
Abdulaay Ley, Aulnay-sous-Bois, May 23, 2010
Sëriñ Lo, Philadelphia, April 21, 2018

Moustapha Mar, Abidjan, December 24, 2014; December 29, 2014
Baara Mbakke, Abidjan, December 24, 2014
Fallu Mbakke, Brescia, Italy, June 3, 2011
Mustafa Mbakke, Dakar, August 10, 2018
Saaliu Mbakke, Ndaam, June 1, 2004
Xaasim Mbakke, Dakar, December 18, 2018
Alasaan Mbay, Paris, June 3, 2010
Galo Mbay, Tuubaa, March 1, 2000
Ibrahima Jaañ Mbay, Dakar, October 1, 1999
Mama Mbóoj, Paris, July 6, 2011
Musa Mbow, Abidjan, December 22, 2014
Shaykh Mbow, Memphis, March 11, 2011
Abdu Fatah Mbuub, Dakar, July 17, 2004
Elhaaj Shaykh Mbuub, New York City, May 2, 2014
Aisha McCord, New York City, August 14, 2018
Sister Mia, Philadelphia, September 6, 2018
Farha Mohamed, Libreville, December 21, 2014
Sultana Arifah Muhammad, Philadelphia, September 1, 2018
Anwar Muhaymin, Philadelphia, June 28, 2018
Afia Ñaŋ, New York City, August 28, 2012
Basiiru Ñaŋ, Paris, June 7, 2011
Mamadu Ñaŋ, New York City, April 14, 2018
Murid Ñaŋ, Paris, July 8, 2011
Imam Nduur, Libreville, December 16, 2014
Abdulaay Njaay, Treichville, December 23, 2014
Amina Njaay, Philadelphia, October 6, 2018
Asan Njaay, Paris, June 7, 2011
El haaj Njaay, New York City, May 2, 2012
Maass Njaay, Libreville, December 19, 2014
Murtada Njaay, New York City, June 11, 2016
Saer Njaay, Paris, July 11, 2011
Shaykh Njaay, New York City, May 2, 2011
Mamadou N'Sangou, Taverny, May 22, 2010
Mark Perrot, Los Angeles, March 22, 2006
Amndi Mustafa Saadi, Dakar, 5 August 2015
Arfan Saar, Grand Bassam, December 26, 2014
Ibra Saar, Libreville, December 16, 2014
Shaykh Baba Sall, Abidjan, December 25, 2014
Shaykh Sall, Paris, May 26, 2010
Thierno Suley Sall, Abidjan, December 24, 2014; December 25, 2014
Badara Samb, Memphis, March 11, 2011
Moor Samb, New York City, August 2, 1996
Xaadim Samb, Memphis, March 12, 2011
Elhaaj Sekk, Libreville, November 7, 2015
Maxtaar Sekk, Libreville, December 19, 2014

Ngoor Sène, Saint-Louis, July 5, 2001
Ali Sidibé, Paris, May 9, 2011
Musa Siise, Saint-Louis, May 7, 2001
Elhaaj Ngóone Sow, Grand Bassam, December 26, 2014
Pape Ibrahima Sow, New York City, April 24, 2018
Cerno Sow, Paris, May 9, 2011
Ahmed Sugu, Mbacké, March 20, 2000; New York City, May 1999; May 6, 2018
Maxtaar Sugu, Libreville, December 19, 2014
Sëriñ Sy, Berlin, March 22, 2014
Buuba Wàdd, Libreville, December 16, 2014
Usmaan Wàdd, Cincinnati, May 1, 2011
Madické Wade, Saint-Louis, July 6, 2001

ARCHIVAL MATERIALS

Archives Diplomatiques de Nantes (ADN)
Archives Nationales de France (ANF), Pierrefitte (Paris)
Archives Nationales du Sénégal (ANS)
Bamba, Amadou. Dossier. Office of the Director of the National Archives, 10D5-8, Monographie du Cercle de Diourbel 1G214, Paul Merles Des Isles, "Contribution à l'Etude du Mouridisme," 1949. This folder contains most of the archival materials on the relations between Ahmadu Bamba and the colonial administration of Senegal.
Service Regional des Archives de Dakar (SRDAD)

UNPUBLISHED MATERIALS

Babou, Cheikh Anta Mbacké. "Touba, genèse et évolution d'une cité musulmane au Sénégal." DEA thesis, Université de Dakar, 1992.
Bava, Sophie. "Routes migratoires et itinéraires religieux: Des pratiques religieuses des migrants sénégalais entre Marseille et Touba." PhD diss., École des Hautes Études en Sciences Sociales Marseille, 2002.
Copans, Jean. "Les espaces mourides (municipal, régional, national, international et/ou mondial) et les territoires étatiques africains et occidentaux ou comment l'appartenance confrérique interpelle l'instance nationale." Paper presented at the international symposium IFRPDSR, "Stratégies de populations et stratégies de développement: Convergences ou divergences?," Dakar, July 2006.
Diop, M. C. "La confrérie mouride: Mode d'organization politique et implantation urbaine." PhD diss., University of Lyon 2, 1980.
Faye, Diâo. "L'œuvre poétique wolofal de Moussa Ka ou l'épopée de Cheikh Ahmadou Bamba." PhD diss., Université Cheikh Anta Diop de Dakar, 1999.
Fleisher, Michael L. "Visions of Dallas: A Study of Senegalese Immigration to the United States." Unpublished manuscript, 1991. Hard copy.
Ka, Muusaa. Jazaau Shakuur. Unpublished epic poem in Wolof. Sung by Mama Njaay. Audio cassette. I purchased the recorded version on the market.

Kendrick Wright, Kathryn Emily. "Senegalese Migrants in Harlem and Denver and a Re-Framing of the Relationships between Development, Transnational Migration, Integration and Place." PhD diss., University of Colorado Boulder, 2017.

Mbacké, A. Bamba. *Les Dons du Digne de Reconnaissance.* Translated by Dahira des Etudiants Mourides de l'Université de Dakar. Dakar: Library of the Cultural Center of the "Daara" Hizbut-Tarqiyya, n.d.

Mbakke, Abdul Ahad, ed. *Majmuha: A Collection of Ahmadu Bamba's Correspondence in Arabic.* Touba, Senegal: self-pub., 1985.

Mbakke, Shaykh Ahmadu Bamba. *Matlabul Fawzayni: Recherche du bonheur dans les deux demeures.* Translated by Cheikhouna Mbacké Abdoul Wadoud. Dakar: Impression Edition Islamique, n.d.

Mbodj, Pape G. "Le mouvement des jeunes dans la confrérie religieuse des mourides: Essai d'analyse et d'interprétation." Master's thesis, University of Dakar, 1980.

Salem, Gérard. "De Dakar à Paris, des diasporas d'artisans et de commerçants: Étude socio-géographique du commerce sénégalais en France." PhD diss., École des Hautes Études en Sciences Sociales, 1983.

Sylla, Khadime. "Immigration et confrérie." DEA thesis, Institut National des Langues et Civilisations Orientales, Paris, 1992–93.

PUBLISHED SOURCES

Abdullah, Zain. *Black Mecca: The African Muslims of Harlem.* Oxford: Oxford University Press, 2010.

——. "Sufis on Parade: The Performance of Black, African, and Muslim Identities." *Journal of the American Academy of Religion* 77, no. 2 (June 2009): 199–237.

Adams, Adrian. *Le long voyage des Gens du Fleuve.* Paris: Maspéro, 1985.

Alba, Richard, and Nancy Foner. *Strangers No More: Immigration and the Challenges of Integration in North America and Western Europe.* Princeton, NJ: Princeton University Press, 2015.

Amin, Samir. "La bourgeoisie d'affaires sénégalaise." *L'homme et la société* 2 (1969): 29–41.

——. *Le monde des affaires sénégalais.* Paris: Les Éditions du Minuit, 1969.

Amin, Samir, and Darryl Ford, eds. *Modern Migrations in Western Africa.* London: Oxford University Press, 1974.

Anderson, Benedict. *Imagined Communities.* 3rd ed. London: Verso, 2003.

André, P. J. *L'Islam Noir.* Paris: P. Geuthner, 1924.

Appiah-Nyamekye Sanny, Josephine, Carolyn Logan, and E. Gyimah Boadi. "In Search of Opportunity: Young and Educated Africans, Most Likely to Consider Moving Abroad." *Afro-Barometer* 288 (March 2019): 1–32.

Aubin-Boltanski, Emma. *Pèlerinages et nationalisme en Palestine: Prophétes, héros et ancêtres.* Paris: Edition Ecole des Hautes Études en Sciences Sociales, 2007.

Austin, Allan D. *African Muslims in Antebellum America: A Sourcebook*. New York: Garland, 1984.

Ba, Oumar. *Ahmadou Bamba face aux autorités coloniales (1889–1927)*. Abbeville, France: Fayard, 1982.

Babou, Cheikh Anta. "The al-Azhar School Network: A Murid Experiment in Islamic Modernism." In *Islamic Education in Africa: Writing Boards and Blackboards*, edited by Robert Launay, 173–95. Bloomington: Indiana University Press, 2016.

———. "Brotherhood Solidarity, Education and Migration: The Role of the *Dahiras* among the Murid Muslim Community of New York." *African Affairs* 101, no. 403 (2002): 151–70.

———. "Contesting Space, Shaping Places: Making Room for the Muridiyya in Colonial Senegal, 1912–45." *JAH* 46, no. 3 (2005): 405–26.

———. "Dahira." In *Encyclopaedia of Islam, THREE*, edited by Kate Fleet, Gudrun Krämer, Denis Matringe, John Nawas, and Everett Rowson. Leiden: Brill, 2017. http://dx.doi.org/10.1163/1573-3912_ei3_COM_27706.

———. "Educating the Murid: Theory and Practices of Education in Amadu Bamba's Thought." *Journal of Religion in Africa* 33, no. 3 (2003): 309–27.

———. *Fighting the Greater Jihad: Amadu Bamba and the Founding of the Muridiyya of Senegal, 1853–1913*. Athens: Ohio University Press, 2007.

———. "Globalizing African Islam from Below: West African Sufi Masters in the United States." In *Global Africa into the Twentieth Century*, edited by Dorothy Hodgson and Judith Byfield, 356–66. Oakland: University of California Press, 2017.

———. "Migration and Cultural Change: Money, 'Caste,' Gender, and Social Status among Senegalese Female Hair Braiders in the United States." *Africa Today* 55, no. 2 (Spring 2009): 1–22.

———. "Negotiating the Boundaries of Power: Abdoulaye Wade, the Muridiyya and State Politics in Senegal, 2000–2012." *Journal of West African History* 2, no. 1 (2016): 165–88.

———. "Sufi Eschatology and Hagiography as Responses to Colonial Repression: An Examination of the Meanings of Amadu Bamba's Trial and Exiles by the French Colonial Administration of Senegal 1895–1907." In *Practicing Sufism: Sufi Politics and Performance in Africa*, edited by Abdelmajid Hannoum, 57–74. London: Routledge, 2016.

———. "Urbanizing Mystical Islam: Making Murid Space in the Cities of Senegal." *International Journal of African Historical Studies* 40, no. 2 (2007): 197–223.

———. "A West African Sufi Master on the Global Stage: Cheikh Abdoulaye Dièye and the Khidmatul Khadim International Sufi School in France and the United States." *African Diaspora* 4, no. 1 (2011): 27–49.

Bakker, Kim. "Behind New York Housing Crisis: Weakened Laws and Fragmented Regulation." *New York Times*, May 20, 2018.

Bamba, Abou B. *African Miracle, African Mirage: Transnational Politics and the Paradox of Modernization in Ivory Coast*. Athens: Ohio University Press, 2016.

Barou, Jacques. "Les migrations africaines en France: Des 'navigateurs' au regroupement familial." *Revue Française des Affaires Sociales* 1 (1993): 193–205.

Barry, Boubacar, and Leonard Harding, eds. *Commerce et commerçants en Afrique de l'Ouest, le Sénégal*. Paris: L'Harmattan, 1992.

Bava, Sophie. "De la baraka aux affaires: Ethos économico-religieux et trans-nationalité chez les migrants sénégalais mourides." *Revue Européenne de Migrations Internationales* 19, no. 2 (2003): 69–84.

———. "Le dahira urbain, lieu de pouvoir du mouridisme." *Les annales de la recherche urbaine* 96 (2004): 135–43.

———. "Migration-Religion Studies in France: Toward a Religious Anthropology of Movement." *Annual Review of Anthropology* 40 (2011): 493–507.

———. "Les Shaykhs mourides itinérants et l'espace de la ziyâra à Marseille." *Anthropologie et Sociétés* 27, no. 1 (2003): 149–66.

Bava, Sophie, and Cheikh Guèye. "Le Magal de Touba: Exil prophétique, migration et pèlerinage au sein du mouridisme." *Social Compass* 48, no. 3 (2001): 421–38.

Beck, Linda. "An American's View of Muridism and the Murids of New York." In *What Is the Muridiyya?*, 34–35. New York: Murid Islamic Community in America, 2001.

Beeckmans, Luce. "A Toponymy of Segregation: The 'Neutral Zones' of Dakar, Dar Es Salaam and Kinshasa." In *Place Names in Africa: Colonial Urban Legacies, Entangled Histories*, edited by Liora Bigon, 105–21. New York: Springer, 2016.

Belhumeur, Jenna. "You Say Malcolm X Boulevard, They Say Lenox." *Global City, New York City*, October 2, 2014. http://globalcitynyc.com/2014/10/02/you-say-malcolm-x-blvd-they- say-lenox/.

Benson, Peter. *Battling Siki: A Tale of Ring Fixes, Race and Murder in the 1920s*. Fayetteville: University of Arkansas Press, 2006.

Berger, Peter L. *The Sacred Canopy: Elements for a Sociological Theory of Religion*. Garden City, NY: Doubleday, 1969.

Bergougniou, Jean-Michel, Remi Clignet, and Philippe David. *Villages Noirs et visiteurs africains et malgaches en France et en Europe (1870–1940)*. Paris: Karthala, 2001.

Berlin, Ira. *The Making of African America*. New York: Viking, 2010.

Bertoncello, Brigitte, and Sylvie Bredeloup. *Colporteurs africains à Marseille: Un siècle d'aventures*. Paris: Autrement, 2004.

———. "Le Marseille des marins africains." *Revue européenne de migrations internationales* 15, no. 13 (1999): 177–97.

Blyden, Nemata. "Relationships among Blacks in the Diaspora: African and Caribbean Immigrants and American-Born Blacks." In *Africans in Global*

Migration: Searching for Promised Lands, edited by John A. Arthur, Joseph Takougang, and Thomas Owusu, 161–74. Lanham, MD: Lexington, 2012.

Boilat, Abbé David. *Esquisses sénégalaises*. Paris: Karthala, 1984.

Boulanger, Claire, and Kevin Mary. "Les Maliens en France et aux Etats Unis: Trajectoires et pratiques transnationales dans les espaces." *E-migrinter* 7 (2011): 17–28.

Bourdieu, P. "The Forms of Capital." In *Handbook of Theory and Research for the Sociology of Education*, edited by J. G. Richardson, 249–58. New York: Greenwood, 1986.

Böwering, Gerhard. "Règles et rituels soufis." In *Les voies d'Allah*, edited by Alexandre Popovic and Gilles Veinstein, 139–56. Paris: Fayard, 1996.

Bredeloup, Sylvie. "Sénégalais en Côte d'Ivoire, Sénégalais de Côte d'Ivoire." *Mondes en Développement* 23, no. 91 (1995): 13–29.

Brochier, Jules. *La diffusion du progrès technique en milieu rural sénégalais*. 2 vols. Paris: Presse Universitaire de France, 1968.

Brooks, George E. *Euro-Africans in West Africa*. Athens: Ohio University Press, 2003.

Brou, Kouadi et Yves Charbit. "La politique migratoire de la Côte d'Ivoire." *Revue Européenne des migrations internationales* 10, no. 3 (1994): 33–59.

Buggenhagen, Beth. *Muslim Families in Global Senegal*. Bloomington: Indiana University Press, 2011.

———. "Prophets and Profits: Gendered Generational Visions of Wealth and Value in Senegalese Murid Households." *Journal of Religions in Africa* 31, no. 4 (2001): 373–401.

Callaway, Barbara, and Lucy Creevey. *The Heritage of Islam: Women, Religion and Politics in West Africa*. Boulder, CO: Lynne Rienner, 1994.

Camara, Sana. *Sheikh Ahmadu Bamba: Selected Poems*. Leiden: Brill, 2017.

Camara, Sana, and R. H. Mitsch. "'A'jami' Literature in Senegal: The Example of Sëriñ Muusaa Ka, Poet and Biographer." In "Arabic Writing in Africa," special issue, *Research in African Literatures* 28, no. 3 (Autumn 1997): 163–82.

Camara, Sory. *Gens de la parole: Essai sur la condition et le rôle des griots dans la société Malinké*. Paris: Karthala, 1992.

Carter, Donald M. *States of Grace: Senegalese in Italy and the New European Immigration*. Minneapolis: University of Minnesota Press, 1997.

Castles, Stephen, and Mark J. Miller. *The Age of Migration: International Population Movements in the Modern World*. New York: Guilford, 1993.

Central Intelligence Agency. *CIA World Factbook*. Washington, DC: CIA. https://www.cia.gov/library/publications/the-world-factbook/geos/sg.html.

Cesari, Jocelyne. "Mosques in French Cities: Towards the End of a Conflict?" *Journal of Ethnic and Migration Studies* 31, no. 6 (2005): 1025–43.

Chavanon, Olivier. "La topographie oubliée des immigrés en terre française." *Hommes et Migrations* 1231 (May–June 2001): 92–104.

Cohen, Abner. *Custom and Politics in Urban Africa: Hausa Migrants in Yoruba Towns*. Berkeley: University of California Press, 1969.

Cohen, William B. *The French Encounter with Africans: White Response to Blacks*. Bloomington: Indiana University Press, 1981.

Coles, Catherine, and Beverly Mack, eds. *Hausa Women in the Twentieth Century*. Madison: University of Wisconsin Press, 1991.

Colvin, Lucy G., ed. *The Uprooted of the Western Sahel: Migrants' Quest for Cash in Senegambia*. New York: Praeger, 1981.

Cooper, Frederick. *Citizenship between Empire and Nation: Remaking France and French Africa, 1945–1960*. Princeton, NJ: Princeton University Press, 2015.

Copans, Jean. "Espaces mourides, territoires étatiques sénégalais et mondiaux: Comment l'appartenance confrérique interpelle l'instance nationale." *Islam et Sociétés au Sud du Sahara* 2 (2010): 77–94.

———. *Les marabouts de l'arachide*. Paris: L'Harmattan, 1988.

———. "Mourides des champs, mourides des villes, mourides du téléphone portable et de l'internet: Les renouvellements de l'économie politique d'une confrérie." *Afrique Contemporaine* 194 (April–June 2000): 24–33.

Coquery-Vidrovitch, Catherine. *Histoire des villes d'Afrique noire: Des origines à la colonisation*. Paris: Albin Michel, 1993.

Cordell, Dennis D., W. J. Gregory, and V. Piché. *Hoe and Wage: A Social History of Circular Migration System in West Africa*. Boulder, CO: Westview, 1996.

Cotter, Holland. "Caught in the Aura of Senegalese Saint." *New York Times*, February 16, 2005.

Coulon, Christian. "The Grand Magal in Touba: A Religious Festival of the Mouride Brotherhood of Senegal." *African Affairs* 98, no. 391 (1999): 195–210.

Couty, Philippe. *La doctrine du travail chez les mourides*. Dakar: ORSTOM, 1969.

Cowan, J. M., ed. *The Hans Wehr Dictionary of Modern Written Arabic*. 4th ed. Ithaca, NY: Spoken Language Services, 1994.

Cruise O'Brien, Donal. "Don divin, don terrestre: L'économie de la confrérie mouride." *Archives Européennes de Sociologie* 15, no. 1 (1974): 82–100.

———. *The Mourides of Senegal: The Political and Economic Organization of an Islamic Brotherhood in Senegal*. Oxford: Clarendon, 1971.

———. *Symbolic Confrontations: Muslims Imagining the State in Africa*. New York: Palgrave Macmillan, 2003.

Cruise O'Brien, Donal, and Christian Coulon, eds. *Charisma and Brotherhood in African Islam*. Oxford: Clarendon, 1988.

d'Almeida Topor, Hélène, "The Colonial Toponymic Model in the Capital Cities of French West Africa." In *Place Names in Africa: Colonial Urban Legacies, Entangled Histories*, edited by Liora Bigon, 93–103. New York: Springer, 2016.

Dang, Christine Thu Nhi. "Pilgrimage through Poetry: Sung Journeys within the Murid Spiritual Diaspora." *Islamic Africa* 4, no.1 (2013): 69–101.

Daum, Christophe. *Les associations de Maliens en France: Migration, développement et citoyenneté*. Paris: Karthala, 1998.

David, Philippe. *Les Navétanes: Histoire des migrants saisonniers de l'arachide en Sénégambie, des origines à nos jours*. Dakar: Présence Africaine, 1980.

Dedieu, Jean-Philippe. *La parole immigrée: Les migrants africains dans l'espace publique en France, 1960–1995*. Paris: Klincksieck, 2012.

de Jong, Ferdinand. "Remembering the Nation: The Murid Maggal of Saint-Louis Senegal (Mémoire de la nation: Les Maggal mourides de Saint-Louis, Sénégal)." *Cahiers d'Études Africaines* 50, no. 197 (2010): 123–51.

Delahaye, Hippolyte. *Cinq leçons sur la méthode hagiographique*. Brussels: Société des Bollandistes, 1934.

Delval, Raymond. "Les musulmans d'Abidjan." *CHEAM* 10 (April 1980).

Desplat, Patrick A., and Dorothea E. Schultz, eds. *Prayer in the City: The Making of Muslim Sacred Places in Urban Life*. Piscataway, NJ: Transaction, 2012.

Dewitte, Philippe. *Les mouvements nègres en France, 1919–1939*. Paris: L'Harmattan, 1985.

Dia, Mouhamadou M. *Le Soleil*, September 14, 1999.

Diakhaté, Lamine. *Chalys d'Harlem*. Paris: L'Harmattan, 1980.

Diarra, Souleymane. "Les travailleurs africains noirs en France." *BIFAN* 30, no. 3 (July 1968): 884–1004.

Dièye, Cheikh Abdoulaye. *Dialogue: 5 Selections from the Teachings of Sheikh A. Dièye with an Introduction by Rabbi Rami Shapiro*. Wynnewood, PA: Khidmatul Khadim International Sufi School, 2002.

———. *Divine Non-Violence: A Dialogue with Rabbi Seidler-Feller at Royce Hall, UCLA*. Wynnewood, PA: Khidmatul Khadim International Sufi School, 2003.

———. "Du Sénégal a New York: Quel avenir pour la confrérie mouride?" *Hommes et Migrations* 1224 (2000): 36–45.

———. *The Healing of America*. Transcript of a speech delivered in Los Angeles, May 1997, brochure. N.p.: Mauritius Printing Specialists, 1997.

———. *L'exil au Gabon: sur les traces de Cheikh Ahmadou Bamba*. Dakar: Editions Ndigël, 1985.

———. *Ocean of Wisdom*. Saint-Louis: School of the Venerated Master Sheikh Dièye, Réunion Islands, n.d.

———. *Sufism and Self-Discovery*. N.p.: published by the author, n.d.

———. *Touba, signes et symbols*. Paris: Khidmatoul Khadim School, 1997.

di Friedberg, Ottavia Schmidt. "L'immigration africaine en Italie: Le cas sénégalais." *Études Internationales* 24, no. 1 (March 1993): 125–40.

———. "Le réseau sénégalais mouride en Italie." In *Exiles et royaumes: Les appartenances du monde arabo-musulman aujourd'hui*, edited by Gilles Kepel, 301–29. Paris: Presse de la Fondation Nationale des Sciences Politiques, 1994.

Diop, A. Moustapha. "Les associations Mourides en France." *Esprit* 102 (June 1985): 197–206.

——. "L'émigration murid en Europe." *Hommes et Migrations* 1132 (May 1990): 21–24.

Diop, Birago. *La plume raboutée.* Paris: Présence Africaine, 1978.

Diop, Momar Coumba. "Fonctions et activités des *dahiras* mourides urbains (Sénégal)." *Cahiers d'Études Africaines* 21, nos. 81/83 (1981): 79–91.

——. "Les Affaires mourides à Dakar." *Politique Africaine* 1, no. 4 (November 1981): 90–100.

Diop Dagana, Cheikh Muhammad Lamine. *L'abreuvement du commensal dans la douce source d'amour du Cheikh al-Khadîm, ou la biographie de Cheikh Ahmadu Bamba.* Translated and edited by Khadim Mbacké. Dakar: IFAN, Département d'Islamologie, n.d.

Diouf, Mamadou. "The Senegalese Murid Trade Diaspora and the Making of a Vernacular Cosmopolitanism." Translated by Steven Rendall. *Public Culture* 12, no. 3 (Fall 2000): 679–702.

Diouf, Sylviane. *Fighting the Slave Trade.* Athens: Ohio University Press, 2003.

——. *Servants of Allah: African Muslims Enslaved in the Americas.* New York: New York University Press, 1998.

Diouf-Camara, Sylviane. "Senegalese in New York: A Model Minority?" Translated by Richard Phicox. *Black Renaissance/Renaissance Noire* 1, no. 2 (1997): 92–116.

Dozon, J. P. *Saint-Louis du Sénégal, palimpseste d'une ville.* Paris: Karthala, 2012.

Dugger, Celia W. "Immigrant Influence Rises in New York City in the 1990s." *New York Times*, January 9, 1997.

Ebin, Victoria. "Camelots à New York, les pionniers de l'immigration sénégalaise." *Hommes et Migrations* 1160 (December 1992): 32–37.

——. "Commerçants et missionaires: Une confrérie musulmane sénégalaise à New York." *Hommes et Migrations* 1132 (May 1990): 25–31.

——. "Les commerçants mourides à Marseille et à New York." In *Grands commerçants d'Afrique de l'Ouest,* edited by Emmanuel Grégoire and Pascal Labazée. Paris: Karthala, 1993.

——. "Little Sénégal contre la renaissance de Harlem: Les immigrés sénégalais et la gentrification de harlem." *Revue Asylon(s)* 3 (March 2008).

——. "Making Room vs. Creating Space: The Construction of Spatial Categories by Itinerant Mourids Traders." In Metcalf, *Making Muslim Space,* 92–110.

——. "A la recherche de nouveaux 'poissons': Stratégies commerciales mourides par temps de crise." *Politique Africaine* 45 (1992): 86–99.

Echenberg, Myron. *Colonial Conscripts: The Tirailleurs Sénégalais in French West Africa, 1857–1960.* Portsmouth, NH: Heinemann 1991.

Eckelman, Dale F., and James Piscaroti. *Muslim Travelers: Pilgrimage, Migration, and the Religious Imagination.* Los Angeles: University of California Press, 1990.

Economist. "New York and Touba, Senegal." June 17, 1999.

Ehazouambela, Doris. "Expression mémorielle des mourides et espace public islamique au Gabon." In *Les politiques de l'Islam en Afrique: Mémoires, Réveils et Populismes Islamiques*, edited by Gilles Holder and Jean P. Donzon, 57–73. Paris: Karthala, 2018.

Elboudrary, Hasan. "Quand les saints font les villes." *Annales ESC* 40, no. 3 (1985): 489–508.

Eliade, Mircea. *The Sacred and the Profane: The Nature of Religion*. New York: Harcourt, 1987.

Epstein, Lawrence, and Peng Wenbin. "Ganjo and Murdo: The Social Construction of Space at Two Pilgrimage Sites in Eastern Tibet." In *Sacred Spaces and Powerful Places in Tibetan Culture: A Collection of Essays*, edited by Toni Huber, 322–41. Dharamshala, India: Library of Tibetan Works and Archives, 1999.

Erichsen, Purnima, Halimatou Nimaga, and Hollis Wear. "Harlem's Little Senegal, a Shelter or a Home: A Conversation with Senegalese Immigrants in New York City." Humanity in Action (website). https://www.humanityinaction.org/knowledgebase/133-harlem-s-little-senegal-a-shelter-or-a-home-a-conversation-with-senegalese-immigrants-in-new-york-city.

Evers Rosander, Eva. *In Pursuit of Paradise: Senegalese Women, Muridism and Migration*. Uppsala, Sweden: Nordistaka Afrikaninstutet, 2015.

——. "Mame Diarra Bousso: La bonne mère de Porokhane, Sénégal." *Africa* 58, nos. 3–4 (2003): 296–317.

Fabian, Johannes. "Kazi, Conceptualizations of Labor in a Charismatic Movement among Swahili-Speaking Workers." *Cahiers d'Études Africaines* 50 (1973): 293–325.

Fall, Abdou Salam. "Les liens religieux confrériques, réseaux privilégiés d'insertion urbaine à Dakar." In *Islam et villes en Afrique au sud du Sahara*, edited by Adriana Piga, 325–44. Paris: Karthala, 2003.

Fall, Mar. *Des Africains noirs en France: Des tirailleurs sénégalais aux Black*. Paris: Harmattan, 1986.

Fall, Papa Demba. "Ethnic and Religious Ties in African Emigration: Senegalese Immigrants in the United States." *Studia Africana* 13 (April 2002): 81–90.

——. "Eumagine: Imagining Europe from the Outside." In *Project Paper 2: Senegal, Country Research Areas Report*. N.p.: EUMAGINE, 2010.

——. *Des Francenabe aux Modou-Modou: L'émigration sénégalaise contemporaine*. Dakar: L'Harmattan, 2016.

——. "Protectionnisme migratoire en Afrique noire: Les migrants sénégalais face à la politique de gabonisation." *Bulletin de l'IFAN* 49, nos. 1–2 (1999–2000): 101–34.

——. "Stratégies et implications fonctionnelles de la migration sénégalaise vers l'Italie." *Migration-Société* 10 (December 1998): 7–33.

Faye, Ousseynou. "Les pratiques des talibés de la transaction au marché Sandaga." In *Les économies reélles en Afrique, Real Economies in Africa*, edited by Georges Kobou, 270–81. Dakar: CODESRIA, 2003.

Flahaux, Marie-Laurence, and Hein De Haas. "African Migration: Trends,

Patterns, Drivers." *Comparative Migration Studies* 4, no. 1 (2016): 1–25.

Foley, Ellen E., and Cheikh A. Babou. "Diaspora, Faith and Science: Building a Mouride Hospital in Senegal." *African Affairs* 110, no. 438 (2011): 75–95.

Friedland, Roger, and Richard D. Hect. "The Powers of Place." In *Religion, Violence, Memory, and Place*, edited by Oren Baruch Stier and Jonathan Shawn Landers, 17–37. Bloomington: Indiana University Press, 2006.

Gaspard, Françoise, and Farhad Khosrokhavar. *Le Foulard de la République.* Paris: La Découverte, 1995.

Gaye, Fara. "Maggal du port de Dakar ou retour d'éxil de Serigne Touba." *Ndigël* (*Sawtoul Mouride, la voix du mouride* [The voice of the Murid]), November–December 1997.

Geoffroy, Éric. "Hagiographie et typologie spirituelle à l'époque mamelouke." In *Saints orientaux*, edited by D. Aigle, 83–98. Paris: De Boccard, 1995.

Germain, Félix F. *Decolonization and the Republic: African and Caribbean Migrants in Post War Paris, 1946–1974.* East Lansing: Michigan State University Press, 2016.

GhaneaBassiri, Kambiz. *A History of Islam in the United States: From the New World to the New World Order.* Cambridge: Cambridge University Press, 2010.

Gieryn, Thomas F. "A Space for Place in Sociology." *Annual Review of Sociology* 26 (2000): 463–96.

Gill, Jonathan. *Harlem: The Four Hundred Year History from Dutch Village to Capital of Black America.* New York: Grove, 2011.

Glancy-Smith, Julian. "Barakah." In *The Oxford Encyclopedia of the Modern Islamic World*, edited by John L. Esposito. Vol. 1. New York: Oxford University Press, 1995.

Gomez, Michael. *African Dominion: A New History of Empire in Early Medieval West Africa.* Princeton, NJ: Princeton University Press, 2018.

———. *Black Crescent: The Experience and Legacy of African Muslims in the Americas.* Cambridge: Cambridge University Press, 2005.

Gomez-Perez, Muriel. "The Association des Etudiants Musulmans de l'Université de Dakar (AEMUD) between the Local and the Global: An Analysis of Discourse." *Africa Today* 54, no. 3 (March 2008): 94–117.

Gordon, April. "The New Diaspora: African Immigration to the United States." *Journal of Third World Studies* 15, no. 1 (1998): 89–91.

Gouyon, Marie Miran. *Islam, histoire et modernité en Côte d'Ivoire.* Paris: Karthala, 2006.

Gril, Denis. "Le saint fondateur." In *Les voies d'Allah*, edited by A. Popovic and G. Veinstein, 104–20. Paris: Fayard, 1996.

Guèye, Abdoulaye. "The Colony Strikes Back: African Protest Movements in Post-colonial France." *Comparative Studies of South Asia, Africa and the Middle East* 26, no. 2 (2006): 225–42.

———. *Les intellectuels africains en France.* Paris: L'Harmattan, 2001.

——. "De la religion chez les intellectuels africains en France: l'Odyssée d'un référent identitaire." *Cahiers d'Études Africaines* 162 (2001): 9–20.

Guèye, Cheikh. "Entre frontières économiques et frontières religieuses: Le café Touba recompose le territoire mouride." In *La ville sénégalaise: Une invention aux frontières du monde*, edited by Jean-Luc Piermay and Cheikh Sarr, 137–51. Paris: Karthala, 2007.

——. *Touba: La capitale des mourides*. Paris: Karthala, 2002.

Guèye, Mbaye. "Les exils de Cheikh Bamba au Gabon et Mauritanie, 1895–1907." *Annales de la Faculté des Lettres et Sciences Humaines de l'Université de Dakar* 25 (1995): 41–57.

Guijarro, Ester. "The Mame Diarra Dahira in Diaspora: Challenging Murid Patriarchy?" *Revista de Dialectologia y Tradiciones Populares* 68, no. 11 (2013): 125–44.

Guimont, Fabienne. *Les étudiants africains en France, 1950–1965*. Paris: L'Harmattan, 1997.

Hale, Thomas A. *Griots and Griottes: Masters of Words and Music*. Bloomington: Indiana University Press, 1998.

Hall, Bruce. *A History of Race in Muslim West Africa, 1600–1900*. Cambridge: Cambridge University Press, 2011.

Halter, Marilyn, and Violet Showers Johnson. *African and American: West Africans in Post–Civil Rights America*. New York: New York University Press, 2014.

Hanretta, Sean. *Islam and Social Change in French West Africa: History of an Emancipatory Community*. Cambridge: Cambridge University Press, 2009.

Héran, François. "Europe and the Spectre of Sub-Saharan Migration." *Population et Sociétés* 558 (2018): 1–3.

Hill, Joseph. *Wrapping Authority: Women Islamic Leaders in a Sufi Movement in Dakar, Senegal*. Toronto: Toronto University Press, 2018.

Humphries, Jill M. "Resisting 'Race': Organizing African Transnational Identities in the United States." In *New African Diaspora*, edited by Isidore Okpewho and Nkiru Zwegu, 271–301. Bloomington: Indiana University Press, 2009.

Jackson, John L., Jr. *Harlemworld: Doing Race and Class in Contemporary Black America*. Chicago: University of Chicago Press, 2001.

Jackson, Sherman. *Islam and the Blackamerican: Looking toward the Third Resurrection*. Oxford: Oxford University Press, 2005.

Johnson, G. Wesley, Jr. *The Emergence of Black Politics in Senegal: The Struggle for Power in the Four Communes, 1900–1920*. Stanford, CA: Stanford University Press, 1971.

Jones, Hilary. *The Métis of Senegal: Urban Life and Politics in French West Africa*. Bloomington: Indiana University Press, 2013.

Journal Officiel de l'Afrique Occidentale Française, May 17, 1958.

Ka, Muusaa. "Jaaraama." Translated by Amar Samb. *Bulletin de L'Institut Fondamental de l'Afrique Noire* 36 (1974): 592–612.

Kaag, Mayke. "Mouride Transnational Livelihoods at the Margins of a European Society: The Case of Residence Prealpino, Brescia, Italy." *Journal of
Ethnic and Migration Studies* 34, no. 2 (2008): 271–85.

Kane, Abdoulaye. "Tontines and Village Cash Boxes along the Tilogne-
Dakar-Paris Emigration Route." In *Informal Savings Funds from the
Global Periphery to the Core?*, edited by Abram de Swann and Marcel
van der Linden, 97–120. Amsterdam: Askant, 2005.

Kane, Mouhamed Moustapha. "L'empreinte de l'Islam confrérique dans le
paysage commercial sénégalais: Islam et société en Sénégambie." *Islam
et sociétés au sud du Sahara* 8 (1994): 17–41.

Kane, Ousmane. *The Homeland Is the Arena: Religion, Transnationalism and
the Integration of Senegalese Immigrants in America*. Oxford: Oxford University Press, 2011.

Kane, Ousmane O. *Beyond Timbuktu: An Intellectual History of Muslim West
Africa*. Cambridge, MA: Harvard University Press, 2016.

Kanté, Seydou. *La géopolitique de l'émigration sénégalaise en France et aux
Etats Unis*. Paris: L'Harmattan, 2014.

Kepel, Gilles. *Allah in the West: Islamic Movements in America and Europe*.
Stanford, CA: Stanford University Press, 1997.

———. *Les banlieues de l'Islam*. Paris: Seuil, 1987.

Khouma, Papa. *IO Venditore Di Elefanti: Una Vita Per Forza Fra Dakar,
Parigi e Milano*. Milan: Garzanti Editore, SPA, 2010.

Kimball, Michelle R. *Ahmadou Bamba: A Peacemaker for Our Time*. Kuala
Lumpur: Other Press, 2019.

Klein, Martin A. "The Moslem Revolution in Nineteenth Century Senegambia." In *West African History*, edited by Daniel F. McCall, Norman R.
Bennett, and Jeffrey Butler, 69–101. New York: Praeger, 1969.

Knott, Kim. *The Location of Religion: A Spatial Analysis*. London: Equinox,
2005.

Laborde, Cécile. *La confrérie Layenne et les Lébous du Sénégal: Islam et
culture traditionnelle en Afrique*. Talence, France: Centre d'Etudes
d'Afrique Noire, 1995.

Lacomba, Joan. "Immigrés Sénégalais: Islam et Confréries à Valence (Espagne)."
Revue Européenne de migrations internationales 16, no. 3 (2000): 85–103.

Lane, Belden C. *Landscapes of the Sacred: Geography and Narrative in American Spirituality*. Baltimore: Johns Hopkins University Press, 2002.

Lincoln, Eric. *The Black Muslims in America*. 3rd ed. Trenton, NJ: Africa
World, 1994.

Loimeier, Roman. "Cheikh Touré, du réformisme à l'islamisme: Un Musulman sénégalais dans le siècle." *Islam et sociétés au sud du Sahara* 8 (1994):
55–66.

Low, Anthony D., and John Lonsdale. "Introduction: Towards a New Order,
1945–1963." In *History of East Africa*, edited by A. D. Low and Alison
Smith, 1–63. Vol. 3. Oxford: Oxford University Press, 1976.

Lunn, Joe. *Memoire of the Maelstrom: A Senegalese Oral History of the First World War*. Portsmouth, UK: Heinemann, 1999.

Mack, Beverly. "Fodiology: African American Heritage Connections with West African Islam." *Journal of West African History* 4, no. 2 (Fall 2018): 103–29.

Mahmood, Saba. *The Politics of Piety: The Islamic Revival and the Feminist Subject*. Princeton, NJ: Princeton University Press, 2005.

Malcolmson, Scott L. "West of Eden: The Mouride Ethic and the Spirit of Capitalism." *Transition* 71 (1996): 26–45.

Manchuelle, François. *Willing Migrants: Soninke Labor Diasporas, 1848–1960*. Athens: Ohio University Press, 1997.

Mann, Gregory. *From Empires to NGOs in the West African Sahel: The Road to No Governmentality*. Cambridge: Cambridge University Press, 2015.

——. *Native Sons: West African Veterans and France in the Twentieth Century*. Durham, NC: Duke University Press, 2006.

Marone, Ibrahima. "Le Tidjanisme au Sénégal." *Bulletin de l'Ifan* 32, no. 1 (1970): 136–215.

Marty, Paul. "Cheikh Sidiyya et sa voie." *Revue du Monde Musulman* 31 (1915–16): 29–133.

——. *Études sur l'Islam au Sénégal*. 2 vols. Paris: Leroux, 1917.

——. "Les mourides d'Amadou Bamba: Rapport à M. le gouverneur général de l'Afrique Occidentale." *Revue du Monde Musulman* 25 (1913): 1–164.

Mayeur-Jaouen, Catherine. *Pèlerinages d'Égypte: Histoire de la piété Copte et Musulmane XVe-XXe siècles*. Paris: Editions EHES, 2005.

Mbacké, Abdoul Ahad, ed. *Cheikh Amadou Bamba: Fondateur de la confrérie des mourides*. 2 vols. Paris: Editions d'Art des Heures Claires, 1984.

——. *Recueil de poèmes en sciences religieuses de Cheikh A. Bamba*. 2 vols. Rabat: Dar al-Kitab, 1988–89.

Mbacké, Cheikh Ahmadou Bamba. *Jazaau Shakuur* [Tribute to the worthy of recognition]. Translated and edited by the Dahira of Murid students of the University of Dakar. Dakar: Bibliothèque du Daara Hizbut Tarqiyya, n.d.

——. *Masalik al-Jinan* [Paths to paradise]. Translated by Serigne Sam Mbaye. Rabat: Dar El Kitab, 1984.

——. *Matlabul Fawzayni: Recherche du bonheur dans les deux demeures*. Translated by Cheikhouna Mbacké Abdoul Wadoud. Dakar: Impression Edition Islamique, n.d.

Mbacké, Cheikh Bachir. *Les bienfaits de l'éternel ou la biographie de Cheikh Amadou Bamba Mbacké*. Dakar: Saint-Paul, 1995.

Mbakke, Mustafa. "Moustapha Mbacke, fils de Serigne Cheikh Mbacke Gainde Fatma, candidat a la presidentielle 2012 'Mon père Gaïndé Fatma a remis 35 millions Cfa à Wade pour créer le Pds.'" Interview. *l'Observateur*, September 14, 2018. https://www.xibar.net/Entretien-MOUSTAPHA -MBACKE-FILS-DE-SERIGNE-CHEIKH-MBACKE-GAINDE -FATMA-CANDIDAT-A-LA-PRESIDENTIELLE-2012-Mon-pere _a39690.html.

Mboup, Mourtala. *Les Sénégalais d'Italie. Emigrés, agents du changement social*. Paris: Harmattan, 2001.

Mbow, Lat Soucabé. *Quand le Sénégal Fabrique sa Géographie*. Dakar: Dakar University Press, 2017.

McCloud, Aminah Beverly. *African American Islam*. London: Routledge, 1995.

McKay, Claude. *Harlem: Negrometropolis: An Account of the World's Largest Black Community during the Eventful Years of the Twenties and Thirties*. New York: Harvest, 1968.

McLaughlin, Fiona. "'In the Name of God I Will Sing Again, Mawdo Malick the Good': Popular Music and Senegalese Sufi Tariqas." *Journal of Religion in Africa* 30, no. 2 (2000): 191–207.

Meillassoux, Claude. *Femmes, Greniers et Capital*. Paris: François Maspéro, 1975.

Mercer, Claire, Ben Page, and Martin Evans. *Development and the African Diaspora: Place and the Politics of Home*. London: Zed, 2008.

Metcalf, Barbara Daly, ed. *Making Muslim Space in North America and Europe*. Berkeley: University of California Press, 1996.

Michel, Marc. "'Mémoire officielle,' discours et pratique coloniale le 14 juillet et le 11 novembre au Sénégal entre les deux guerres." *Revue Française d'Histoire d'Outre-Mer* 77, no. 287 (1990): 145–58.

Millman, Joel. "Caste Party: Africa Arrives in America." *APF Reporter* 17 (1996): 1–5.

Ndaw, Aly Kheury. *Les Sénégalais de New York*. Paris: L'Harmattan, 2012.

Ndiaye, Diana, and G. Ndiaye. "Creating the Vertical Village: Senegalese Traditions of Immigration and Transnational Cultural Life." In *The New African Diaspora in North America*, edited by Kwado Konadu-Agyemang, Baffour K. Takyi, and John A. Arthur. Lanham, MD: Lexington, 2006.

Ndiaye, Jean-Pierre. *Enquête sur les étudiants noirs en France*. Paris: Réalités Africaines, 1962.

Ndiaye, Malick. *Les Modou-Modou: Ou ethos du développement au Sénégal*. Dakar: Dakar University Press, 1998.

Ndiaye, Pap. *La condition noire: Essai sur une minorité française*. Paris: Calmann Levy, 2008.

Nekkach, Lucien. *Le Mouridisme depuis 1912*. Saint-Louis, Senegal: Gouvernement du Sénégal, 1952.

Neveu-Kringelbach, Hélène. "Gender Educational Trajectories and Transnational Marriage among West African Students in France." *Identities* 22, no. 3 (2015): 288–302.

New York Times. "Italy: Gunman Kills Two Senegalese Merchants." December 12, 2011. http://www.nytimes.com/2011/12/14/world/europe/italy-gunman-kills-2-senegalese-merchants.html.

Ngom, Fallou. *Muslims beyond the Arab World: The Odyssey of Ajami and the Muridiyya*. New York: Oxford University Press, 2016.

Nora, Pierre. *Les lieux de mémoire*. Vol. 1, *La République*. Paris: Gallimard, 1984.

Ochonu, Moses E. *Colonialism by Proxy: Hausa Imperial Agents and Middle Belt Consciousness in Nigeria*. Bloomington: Indiana University Press, 2014.

Otterman, Sharon. "Malcolm X. Mosque No. 7. Hotel Theresa. Remembering Harlem's Muslim History." *New York Times*, August 12, 2018. https://www.nytimes.com/2018/08/12/nyregion/muslim-history-harlem-nyc.html?.

Ottley, Roi. *New World A-Coming*. Cambridge, UK: Riverside, 1943.

Peabody, Sue, and Tyler Stoval, eds. *The Color of Liberty: Histories of Race in France*. Durham, NC: Duke University Press, 2003.

Péllissier, Paul. *Les paysans du Sénégal: Les civilisations agraires du Cayor à la Casamance*. Fabrègue, France: Saint-Yriex, 1966.

Perry, Donna L. "Rural Ideologies and Urban Imaginings: Wolof Immigrants in New York City." *Africa Today* 44, no. 2 (April–June 1997): 229–59.

Piga, Adriana. *Dakar et les ordres Soufis*. Paris: Harmattan, 2002.

Poiret, Christian. *Familles africaines en France*. Paris: L'Harmattan, 1997.

Porcheron, Hélène. "Les *dahiras* mourides du marché Sandaga à Dakar." *Plein Sud* 2 (1992): 18–25.

Portes, Alejandro. "The Social Origins of the Cuban Enclave Economy of Miami." *Social Prospect* 30, no. 4 (1987): 340–72.

Povey, John F. "The First World Festival of Negro Arts at Dakar." *New African Literature and the Arts* 1 (1970): 64–75.

Provost, Guy. "Comment et pourquoi les travailleurs sénégalais viennent en France." *Hommes et Migrations* 115 (1970): 90–119.

Putman, Lara. "Provincializing Harlem: The Negro Metropolis as Northern Frontier of a Connected Caribbean." *Modern/Modernity* 20, no. 3 (2013): 469–84.

Quesnot, François. "Les cadres maraboutiques de l'islam sénégalais." *Notes et Études sur l'Islam en Afrique Noire*, Recherches et documents du CHEAM (Paris: Peyronnet, 1962), 127–95.

Quiminal, Catherine. *Gens d'ici, gens d'ailleurs: Migrations Soninké et transformations villageoises*. Paris: Bourgois, 1991.

Quiminal, Catherine, and Mahamet Timéra. "Les mutations de l'immigration africaine (1974–2002)." *Hommes et Migrations* 1262 (July–August 2006): 19–33.

Reid, Ira de Augustine. *The Negro Immigrant: His Background, Characteristics and Social Adjustment, 1899–1937*. New York: Columbia University Press, 1939.

Republic of Senegal. *Recensement de la Population et de l'habitat 1988*. Dakar: République du Sénégal, 1993.

Republic of Senegal, Ministry of Finances. *Enquête Sénégalaise auprès des ménages*. Direction de la Prévision et de la Statistique. Dakar: ESAM II, 1999.

Riccio, Bruno. "'Transmigrants' mais pas 'nomades': Transnationalisme mouride en Italie." *Cahiers d'Études Africaines* 46, no. 181 (2006): 95–114.

Rivers, Paul Liza. "La Goutte-d'Or, succursale de l'entrepreuneuriat sénégalais: Un espace intermédiaire dans un commerce circulatoire." *Hommes et Migrations* 1286–87 (July–October 2010): 138–48.

Roberts, Allen, and Mary N. Roberts. "The Aura of Amadu Bamba." *Anthropologie et Sociétés* 22 (1998): 15–38.
———. *A Saint in the City: Sufi Arts of Urban Senegal.* Los Angeles: University of California Fowler Museum of Cultural History, 2003.
Robinson, David. "French 'Islamic' Policy and Practice in Late Nineteenth Century Senegal." *JAH* 29, no. 3 (1988): 415–35.
———. "The Murids: Surveillance and Accommodation." *JAH* 40, no. 2 (1999): 13–21.
———. *Paths of Accommodation: Muslim Societies and French Colonial Authorities in Senegal and Mauritania, 1880–1920.* Athens: Ohio University Press, 2000.
Robinson, David, and Jean-Louis Triaud, eds. *Le temps des marabouts: Itinéraires et stratégies islamiques en Afrique Occidentale Française v. 1880–1960.* Paris: Karthala, 1997.
Rocheteau, Guy. *Société Wolof et mobilité.* Dakar: ORSTOM, 1973.
Ross, Eric. "Globalising Touba: Expatriate Disciples in the World City Network." *Urban Studies* 48, no. 14 (2011): 2929–52.
———."Marabout Republics Then and Now: Configuring Muslim Towns in Senegal." *Islam et Sociétés au Sud du Sahara* 16 (2002): 35–65.
———. *Sufi City: Urban Design and Archetypes in Touba.* Rochester, NY: Rochester University Press, 2006.
———."Touba, a Spiritual Metropolis in the Modern World." *Canadian Journal of African Studies* 29, no. 2 (1995): 222–59.
Roy, Olivier. *Secularism Confronts Islam.* Translated by George Holoch. New York: Columbia University Press, 2007.
Saada, Emmanuelle. *Les enfants de la colonie: Les métis de l'empire français entre sujétion et citoyenneté.* Paris: La Découverte, 2007.
Sachs, Susan. "In Harlem's Fabric, Bright Threads of Senegal." *New York Times,* July 28, 2003. https://www.nytimes.com/2003/07/28/nyregion/in-harlem-s-fabric-bright-threads-of-senegal.html.
Salem, Gérard. "De la brousse sénégalaise au Boul'Mich: Le système commercial mouride en France." *Cahiers d'Études africaines* 21, nos. 81/83 (1981): 267–88.
Salzbrunn, Monika. "The Occupation of Public Space through Religious and Political Events: How Senegalese Migrants Became a Part of Harlem, New York." *Journal of Religion in Africa* 34, no. 4 (November 2004): 468–92.
Samb, Amar. "Touba et son Magal." *Bulletin de l'IFAN* 33, no. 3 (1969): 733–53.
Schaffer, Richard, and Neil Smith. "The Gentrification of Harlem?" *Annals of the Association of American Geographers* 76, no. 3 (1986): 347–65.
Schimmel, Anne Marie. *Mystical Dimensions of Islam.* Chapel Hill: University of North Carolina Press, 1975.
Schmidt, Jean. "Le souffle de la parenté: Mariage et transmission de la *baraka* chez les clercs musulmans de la vallée du fleuve Sénégal." *L'Homme* 154 (2000): 241–78.

Searing, James. "*God Alone Is King*": *Islam and Emancipation in Senegal: The Wolof Kingdoms of Kajoor and Bawol, 1859–1914*. Portsmouth, NH: Heinemann, 2002.

Seck, Assane. *Dakar, Métropole Ouest-Africaine*. Dakar: Ifan, 1970.

Seck, Mamadou. "La RTS refuse de diffuser un film sur la vente des médicaments à Keur Serigne Bi." *L'Observateur*, July 20, 2005.

Sembène, Ousmane. *Le docker Noir*. Paris: Présence Africaine, 1973.

———, dir. *Le mandat*. Paris: Filmi Domirev, Comptoir Français du Film Production, 1968.

Slyomovics, Susan. "The Muslim World Day Parade and 'Storefront' Mosques in New York City." In Metcalf, *Making Muslim Space*, 204–16.

Smith, Jane Idleman, and Yvonne Yazbeck Hadda. *Muslim Communities in North America*. New York: State University of New York Press, 1994.

Smith, Steve. *La ruée vers l'Europe: La jeune Afrique en route vers le vieux continent*. Paris: Grasset, 2018.

Soares, Benjamin. "An African Muslim Saint and His Followers in France." *Journal of Ethnic and Migration Studies* 30, no. 5 (2004): 913–27.

Stier, Oren Baruch, and J. Shawn Landres. *Religion, Violence, Memory, and Place*. Bloomington: Indiana University Press, 2006.

Stoller, Paul. *Money Has No Smell: The Africanization of New York City*. Chicago: University of Chicago Press, 2002.

Stump, Roger W. *Boundaries of Faith: Geographical Perspectives on Religious Fundamentalism*. Lanham, MD: Rowman and Littlefield, 2000.

Sy, Cheikh Tidiane. "Ahmadou Bamba et l'Islamisation des Wolof." *BIFAN* 32 (1970): 414–33.

———. *La confrérie sénégalaise des mourides*. Paris: Présence Africaine, 1969.

Tall, Serigne Mansour. "Kara International Exchange: Un nouvel instrument financier pour les courtiers mourides de l'axe Dakar-New York." Paper presented at the international colloquium of APAD, June 5–8, 1996, University of Hohenheim [Stuttgart].

Tamari, Tal. *Les castes de l'Afrique Occidentale: Artisans et musiciens endogames*. Nanterre, France: Société d'Ethnologie, 1997.

Thomas, Douglas H. *Sufism, Mahdism and Nationalism: Limamou Laye and the Layennes of Senegal*. New York: Bloomsbury, 2012.

Timéra, Mahamet. *Les Soninké en France: D'une histoire à l'autre*. Paris: Karthala, 1996.

Timéra, Mahamet, and Jules Garnier. "Les Africains en France: Le viellissement et transformation d'une migration." *Hommes et Migrations* 1286–87 (July–October 2010): 24–36.

Tounkara, Daouda Gary. "La dispersion des Soudanais/Maliens à la fin de l'ère coloniale." *Hommes et Migrations* 1279 (2009): 12–23.

Triaud, Jean-Louis. "Giving a Name to Islam South of the Sahara: An Adventure in Taxonomy." *JAH* 55, no. 1 (2014): 1–15.

———."Khalwa and the Career of Sainthood: An Interpretive Essay." In Charisma and Brotherhood in African Islam, edited by Donal C. Obrien and Christian Coulon, 53–67. Oxford: Clarendon, 1988.

———."Lignes de force de la pénétration islamique en Côte d'Ivoire." Revue des Études Islamiques 62, no. 1 (1974): 123–60.

———. "La question musulmane en Côte d'Ivoire (1893–1939)." Revue Française d'Histoire d'Outre-Mer 61, no. 225 (1974): 542–71.

Trimigham, John Spencer. The Sufi Orders in Islam. Oxford: Clarendon, 1971.

Tuan, Yi-Fu. "Sacred Space: Exploration of an Idea." In Dimensions of Human Geography: Essays on Some Familiar and Neglected Themes, edited by Karl W. Butzer, 84–85. Chicago: Committee on Geographical Studies, 1978.

Turner, Richard B. Islam in the African-American Experience. Bloomington: Indiana University Press, 1997.

Turner, Victor. Dramas, Fields, and Metaphors: Symbolic Action in Human Society. Ithaca, NY: Cornell University Press, 1974.

———. The Ritual Process. Chicago: Aldine, 1969.

United States Department of Homeland Security. Department of Homeland Security, Yearbook Immigration Statistics. Washington, DC: Office of Immigration Statistics, 1999. https://www.dhs.gov/sites/default/files/publications/Yearbook_Immigration_Statistics_1999.pdf.

United States Department of Homeland Security, Office of Immigration Statistics. 2009 Yearbook of Immigration Statistics. Washington, DC: United States Department of Homeland Security, Office of Immigration Statistics, 2010.

van Reisen, Mirjam, Munyaradzi Mawere, Mia Stokmans, and Kinfe Abraha Gebre-Egziabher, eds. Roaming Africa: Migration, Resilience and Social Protection (Bamenda, Cameroon: Langaaa RPCIG, 2019).

Villalón, Leonardo. "From Argument to Negotiation: Constructing Democracy in African Muslim Context." Comparative Politics 42, no. 4 (July 2010): 375–93.

———. Islamic Society and State Power in Senegal: Disciples and Citizens in Fatick. Cambridge: Cambridge University Press, 1995.

Wade, Abdoulaye. La doctrine économique du mouridisme. Dakar: L'Interafricaine d'éditions, 1970.

Wade, Elhaj Madické. Le mouridisme à Ndar: De Shaykh Ibra Fall et des pionniers aux audacieux initiateurs du maggal des 2 rakaas de Serigne Touba, tel que j'en ai eu échos et tel que j'en ai vécu. Saint-Louis, Senegal: Published by author, n.d.

Ware, Rudolph T., III. The Walking Qur'an: Islamic Education, Embodied Knowledge, and History in West Africa. Chapel Hill: University of North Carolina Press, 2014.

Weber, Max. The Theory of Social and Economic Organization. Edited by Talcott Parsons. New York: Free Press, 1964.

Werbner, Pnina. "Stamping the Earth with the Name of God: Zikr and Sacralizing of Space among British Muslims." In Metcalf, *Making Muslim Space*, 167–86.

White, Owen. *Children of the French Empire: Miscegenation and Colonial Society in French West Africa, 1895–1960*. Oxford: Oxford University Press, 1999.

Whitehouse, Bruce. *Migrants and Strangers in an African City: Exile, Dignity and Belonging*. Bloomington: Indiana University Press, 2012.

Zie, Gnato, and Vrih Gbazah. "Les commerçants sénégalais en Côte d'Ivoire de 1880 à 1970." In *Commerce et commerçants en Afrique de l'Ouest — la Côte d'Ivoire*, edited by Pierre Kipré and Leonard Harding, 235–71. Paris: L'Harmattan, 1992.

Zucarelli, François. "Le recrutement des travailleurs sénégalais par l'Etat indépendent du Congo (1888–1896)." *Revue française d'histoire d'outre-mer* 47, nos. 168–69 (1960): 475–81.

Index

Page numbers in italics signify graphics.

Islamophobia, 131–32, 175
Ismuhu, Shaykh S. Ahmad, 112

Jaañ, Aatu, 139, 140
Jabir, Taha, 273n31
Jackson, John, Jr., 168
Jammeh, Yaya, 282n20
Jaw, Elhaaj Bamba, 29–30, 54, 59, 92 (plate 1.9)
Jaw, Elhaaj Njaga, 74–75, 76, 81, 82, 83–84
Je , Elhaaj Mbakke, 107
Je , Elhaaj Papa, 107, 108
Je , Njuga, 41
Jóob, Asan, 70, 71, 72, 258n21, 262n56
Jóob, Basiiru, 131
Jóob, Duudu, 53
Jóob, Elhaaj Yande, 59, 105, 106, 108, 125, 126, 127, 130, 157
Jóob, Gora, 143
Jóob, Ibra, 135
Jóob, Magat, 38, 39
Joób, Moor, 92 (plate 1.9)
Jóob, Murtada, 157
Jóob, Sidiya Leon, 257n3
Jóob, Yunus, 142
Jóob, Yuusu, 30
Joxe, Pierre, 126, 127
Juuf, Sulaymaan, 139, 140, 141–42, 143, 153 (plate 2.10)

Ka, Muusaa, 69, 76, 249n60, 257n12
Kanté, Seydou, 275n2
Kaolack, Senegal, 10, 189, 249n60
Kara, Shaykh Moodu (Mbakke, Shaykh Moodu Kara), 45
Kepel, Gilles, 131
Kër Sëriñ Bi (KSB), 47
Kër Sëriñ Tuubaa (KST): as innovation, 109, 219; layout and design of, 193–95; multiple tasks of, 195–96, 219–20; photos of, 93 (plate 1.11), 94 (plates 1.12, 1.13); raising money for, 132–33, 138, 195–96. See also Aulnay-Sous-Bois Murid house
khidma, 15, 114
Khouma, Papa, 57, 58
Koch, Ed, 162
kurel, 35–37, 44–45, 109, 133, 142, 194

Laam, Yaba, 55, 255n23
Lama, Francis, 119–20
Lébou ethnic group, 25, 41, 46, 251n79

Ley, Abdulaay, 145
Libreville (Limbëlwëli), Gabon: art market in, 80–84, 98 (plate 1.20); Montagne Sainte in, 75, 76, 260n41; Murid commemorations in, 72, 75, 80, 97 (plate 1.19), 98 (plate 1.21); Murid immigrants in, 67, 68–71; Murid mosque in, 76–79
Linenthal, Edward, 40
"Little Senegal," 169–72, 175, 279n58. See also Harlem
Lo, Sëriñ, 159, 162, 168, 170

Mack, Beverly, 182
Màggal: in Côte d'Ivoire, 60; in Dakar, 39, 40, 41, 250n67; Great Màggal of Tuubaa, 1, 130, 139, 221, 248n58; in Harlem, 170
Màggal of two rakaas, 249n62; in Saint-Louis, Senegal, 34–37, 38, 248n58
Mahmood, Saba, 18
Malcolm Shabazz Mosque, 180, 204 (plate 3.8); as Murid community space, 169–70, 213; relationship of African Muslims with, 180–82
Malcolmson, Scott, 181
manaaqib, 69
Marty, Paul, 17
Masalik al-Jinan mosque (Shaykh Ahmadou Bamba Mosque), 49, 93 (plate 1.10)
Masalik al-Jinan square, 47
Masjid Aqsa, 181
Mauritania, 15, 16–17
mawlid, 129, 130, 248n58
mawluds, 170, 279n57
Mbakke, Abdul Ahad, 36
Mbakke, Bachiru, 241n66
Mbakke, Caliph Abdul Ahad, 36, 47, 53, 76, 110, 119, 128–29, 184, 226; and Dièye, 122; popularity of, 32; reconciliations by, 34, 54–55; as "the builder," 61
Mbakke, Caliph Faliilu, 47, 53, 54, 225, 227, 241n66, 254n15; and Dakar dahira, 30, 31, 109
Mbakke, Sëriñ Mbakke Soxna Lo, 131
Mbakke, Shaykh Abdul Aziz, 54, 59
Mbakke, Shaykh Ahmadu Bamba: artwork and songs about, 33, 36, 247n50, 249n60; chanting of devotional poems by, 28, 42–43, 62, 129, 133, 194; and colonial administration,

7, 8, 14–15, 76; as colonialism resister, 45, 65, 120; in Dakar, 38, 46–47, 87 (plate 1.3), 252n100; in Diourbel, 6, 8, 27, 78, 215; and founding of Muridiyya, 4–5; in Gabon, 7, 14, 65, 68, 68, 69, 71, 85, 215; on gift of coffee, 286n75; and Murid mobility, 7, 14–15; and place making, 12, 61, 215; on race, 16–18; in Saint-Louis, 34, 36; translation of writings of, 32, 121, 246n43; trial of, 36, 48, 86 (plate 1.2)

Mbakke, Shaykh Ahmadu Bamba, works of: *Masalik al-Jinan*, 17–18; "Matlabul Fawzayni," 12, 13, 61

Mbakke, Shaykh Gaynde Fatma (grandson of Bamba), 29, 54, 77, 107, 245n31

Mbakke, Shaykh Maam Moor (son of Shaykh Murtada), 145, 164, 194, 197, 286n72

Mbakke, Shaykh Moodu Maamun, 126, 241n66

Mbakke, Shaykh Murtada (son of Bamba), 36, 39, 54, 106, 229; and African heads of state, 73–74; and Balozi Harvey, 184–87, 230; in France, 61–62, 122, 125–32, 141; in Gabon, 72–75, 78; and *hijra* project, 189; photos of, 200 (plates 3.1, 3.2); as "Shaykh of the Diaspora," 73, 74, 218–19; US visits by, 164, 182, 191, 195, 198

Mbakke, Shaykh Murtada Abdul Ahad (son of Caliph Abdul Ahad), 61–62, 63

Mbakke, Shaykh Mustafa (great-grandson of Bamba), 130, 183, 184–85, 187, 260n39

Mbakke, Shaykh Mustafa (son of Bamba), 8, 47, 51, 54, 55

Mbakke, Xaadim, 36

Mbakke, Xaasim, 126, 186

Mbay, Alasaan, 115–16

Mbay, Elhaaj Jily, 252n100

Mbóoj, Mama, 107

Mbow, Amadu Makhtar, 119

Mbuub, Elhaaj Shaykh, 54, 58

McCord, Aisha, 209 (plate 3.15), 285n57

Mekouar, Aziz, 58

Memphis, TN, 206 (plate 3.10), 207 (plate 3.11)

Merle Des Isles, Paul, 1

Metcalf, Barbara, 178

migration: to Côte d'Ivoire, 51–52, 55–59, 64; as foundational to Muriddiya, 6–11; to France, 100–105, 216–17; and French colonialism, 9–10, 103, 216; and French immigration policy, 103–4, 134, 217, 265n20, 273n27; to Gabon, 66–68; internal within Senegal, 6, 8–9, 10, 27, 55, 56; rural-urban, 6, 9, 10, 159–60, 215–16; to United States, 155–58, 217, 274n11; and US immigration policy, 163–64; of women, 157, 171–72, 176, 279n68

Millman, Joel, 157

money transfer business, 165–66

Montagne Sainte, Libreville, 75, 76, 260n41

Montagne Sainte Mosque (Shaykh Ahmadu Bamba Mosque), 66, 76–78, 85, 97 (plate 1.18)

Muhammad, Elijah, 179

Muhammad, Warith Deen, 179, 180

Murid Islamic Community in America (MICA), 146, 186–87, 191, 196, 219, 288n90

Muridiyya: brief introduction to, 4–6; culture of mobility among, 13–15, 215; expansion within Senegal of, 8; and French colonial authorities, 5–6, 28–29, 215; hostility toward, 43–48, 79, 140–41, 161–63, 261n52; Tuubaa's significance for, 13, 30, 128, 182, 238n39; universalist vs. traditionalist conceptions of, 120–21, 123, 141–42, 190–92, 220; world population of, 6, 236n10

Muridiyya (diaspora): and African Americans, 178, 182–87, 189–92, 213; as agent of change, 2–3; antagonism toward, 79, 140–41, 161–63, 261n52; collective identity of, 1–2, 21, 64, 124–25, 158, 214, 217, 221; in Côte d'Ivoire, 50–64; degree of religiousness of, 110–11, 268n54; divisions within, 123, 130, 131, 141–42, 146, 189–92; in France, 99–123, 124–47; in Gabon, 65–85; generational divide within, 220–21; as majority of Senegalese abroad, 13, 52, 155, 275n12; in New York City, 155–76, 177–213; occupations in Côte d'Ivoire, 51, 58–59; occupations in France, 104–5, 106–9; occupations in Gabon, 69–70, 81–84; occupations in United States, 158–59, 162–63, 164–66, 171–72, 176;

in France, 125, 127–46, 147; in Gabon, 71, 75, 76–79, 84–85; and Murid collective identity, 1, 32, 64, 123, 124–25, 182, 196, 214; in New York, 169–70, 178, 185, 188, 192–96, 213, 284n48; and quest for personal space, 124–25; sacred and profane, 147; in Senegal, 26, 40–41, 44–46, 218, 243n9, 252n91; Sufi Islam on, 12–13; universalist message of, 118–20
Poroxaan, Senegal, 19, 91 (plate 1.7), 242n68
processions, 39–40, 196, 197–99, 250n69, 287n82
Putman, Lara, 158–59

Qasida Day, 194, 219, 220, 286n72
Quesnot, François, 54

race: Arab prejudices around, 16–17, 140, 240n53; Bamba on, 16–18; and consciousness, 15–16; White prejudice on, 280n81
Rahman, Muhammad Abdu al-, 188, 210
Ramadan, 78, 182
Ramadan, Tariq, 273n31
Rangel, Charles, 185
Representative Council of Islam in France (CORIF), 126–27
ritual cleanliness, 127–28
Roberts, Allen, 194
Roberts, Mary Nooter, 194
Rocheteau, Guy, 7, 108–9
Roots (Haley), 282n14, 282n20
Rufisque, Senegal, 10, 30, 243n6
rural-urban migration, 6, 9, 10, 159–60, 215–16

Sadji, Abdoulaye, 249n63
Saint-Louis, Senegal: Bamba in, 34, 36; as beacon of civilization, 249n63; Faidherbe statue in, 24, 45, 46, 49, 90 (plate 1.6), 242n3; under French colonialism, 25, 45, 243n7; history of Muridiyya in, 34–35; hostility toward Murids in, 43–46, 48; Màggal of two rakaas in, 34–37, 38, 248n58; middle-class neighborhoods of, 33, 247n47; Murid commemorations in, 26, 32, 33; Murid population in, 10, 248n55; renaming controversy in, 44–46, 252n91, 252n94
salafism, 140

Salem, Gerard, 105
Saliu, Shaykh, 39, 41, 131, 138–40, 143
Sall, Cerno Sulay, 51, 82
Sall, Shaykh, 117
Sandaga Market (Dakar), 40–41, 251n78
Schiffauer, Werner, 111
Schiller, Nina Glick, 2
Sekk, Daam, 54, 254n15
Sekk, Elhaaj Mayib, 53
Sekk, Gumaalo, 28, 29, 30
Senegal, 24–49; Catholic Church in, 29, 245n26; climate of, 236n13; droughts in, 57, 107, 266n39; educational system in, 10; and French colonialism, 5–6, 9–10, 25, 28–29, 45, 103, 215, 216, 243nn6–7; hostility to Muridiyya in, 43–48; industrial and transportation infrastructure of, 9, 55, 237n23; internal migration within, 6, 8–9, 10, 27, 55–56; neoliberal economic policies in, 33, 57–58; peanut production in, 8, 55–56, 215; transformation of dahira in, 31–34; urbanization of Muridiyya in, 10, 27–31. See also Dakar, Senegal; Saint-Louis, Senegal; Tuubaa, Senegal
Senghor, Leopold Sédar, 33, 67, 106, 122
September 11, 2001, events, 3, 138
Société de Construction et Batiment (SOCOBA), 67, 71
Société Immobilière du Cap Vert (SICAP), 33, 247n49
Soninke, 10; in France, 101, 104, 105, 157, 158
Sow, Cerno, 110
Sow, Elhaaj Amadi, 105–6
Sow, Ibrahima, 174
Stoller, Paul, 171
Strasbourg, France, 107
street vendors: in France, 134, 273n27; in Gabon, 80–81; in New York, 158–59, 161–63, 175
Stump, Robert, 193
Sufi Islam, 5, 140, 141–42, 182, 190, 193; and place making, 12–13; women's role in, 274n46
Sugu, Ahmed, 159
Sultana, Sister, 190–91
Sunni Islam, 178, 180, 213, 281n2
Suraŋ, Elhaaj Bamba, 252n100
Sy, Ababakar, 27, 244n17
Sy, Sëriñ Abdul Aziz, Senior, 180
Sylla, Yatu, 107, 108

Tariq, Imam, 180
Taverny Murid house, 135–46; activities at, 142–43; Aulnay comparison with, 143–45; complaints against, 141; photos from, *149* (plates 2.2, 2.3), *150* (plate 2.6), *152* (plates 2.7, 2.8); role of women at, 144
Thiès, Senegal, 10
Tijaniyya, 33–34, 41
Touré, Samory, 257n3
Treichville, Abidjan: *dahira* in, 62–63; Muridiyya in, 52–53
Triaud, J. L., 53
Trump, Donald, 161–62, 281n85
Turner, Victor, 43, 48
Tuubaa, Senegal: African Americans studying in, 189; Bamba on, 12, 61; Bamba's tomb in, 13, 221, 242n67; Great Màggal of, 1, 130, 139, 221, 248n58; Great Mosque of, 56, 88 (plate 1.4), 96 (plate 1.16); history of, 12; Murid bond with, 13, 30, 128, 182, 238n39; social conditions in, 238n42; Well of Mercy in, 89 (plate 1.5), 193
Tuubaa, Sëriñ. *See* Mbakke, Shaykh Ahmadu Bamba
Tuubaa Qassayit store, 174

Union Fraternelle des Musulmans de la Secte Mouride de la Côte d'Ivoire, 59–60

United States, 20, 155–76, 177–213; history of Senegalese immigration to, 155–56, 217, 274n1; immigration policy in, 163–64; Islamophobia and anti-immigrant sentiment in, 175, 281n85; occupations of Murid immigrants in, 158–59, 162–63, 164–66, 171–72, 176; race and racism in, 16, 280n81. *See also* African Americans; New York City
universalism: Dièye message of, 117–20; vs. traditionalist and parochial conceptions, 120–21, 123, 141–42, 189–92, 220
University of Dakar, 32, 34, 117, 139

Wade, Abdoulaye, 269n67
Wade, Madické, 35–36, 44
Wahhabism, 140, 143, 182
Washington, DC, 171, 233
Well of Mercy (Tuubaa), 89 (plate 1.5), 193
Werbner, Pnina, 198
Whitehouse, Bruce, 6
Wolof society, 109; and mobility, 7, 215
women: African American, 187, 283n38; and French Murids, 144; role of in Muridiyya, 18–19; and Senegalese migration to US, 157, 171–72, 176, 279n68; and Sufi Islam, 274n46
World Fair of Negro Arts, 106
Wright, Kathryn, 173